Singing the Living Tradition

SINGING the LIVING TRADITION

BEACON PRESS BOSTON
THE UNITARIAN UNIVERSALIST ASSOCIATION

Unitarian Universalist Association
25 Beacon Street
Boston, Massachusetts 02108-2892

PRINTED IN CANADA
First printing, May 1993

Printed on recycled paper

Music typeset by David Budmen, Abraham Borvinick Publishing
Readings typeset by Kevin Krugh, Technologies 'N Typography

Library of Congress Cataloging-in-Publication Data

Singing the living tradition.
p. cm.
Includes indexes.
ISBN 1-55896-260-3
1. Unitarian Universalist Association—Hymns. 2. Unitarian
Universalist churches—Hymns. 3. Hymns, English—United States.
I. Unitarian Universalist Association.
BV447.U2S56 1993
264'.0913202—dc20   92-13630

This is a corrected reprint.
Every effort has been made to ensure accuracy.
If you have any corrections, please send them to:
Editor, Unitarian Universalist Association,
25 Beacon St., Boston, MA 02108

10/00

Contents

Preface

THOUGH THE PAGES of this hymnbook are being bound in the twentieth century, they will open into the twenty-first. That realization permeated our work, for these will be simultaneously the last words of one era and the first words of the next. We remember the phrase of our predecessors: "Religion is a present reality; it is also an inheritance." Or to use a more current expression, a living faith must have both roots and wings. A hymnbook is one place where we find both.

Our living tradition began the twentieth century primarily as a liberal Christianity among Universalists and Unitarians, and ends that same century also embracing the riches of humanism, feminism, mysticism, natural theism, the Jewish tradition, many other world faith traditions, and the skepticism generated by this century's disillusioning woes and wars.

Within this thicket of diversity and doubt, the Hymnbook Resources Commission, with the help of many, sought to express the center and edges of our living tradition. We found a wealth of music and poetry, wisdom and beauty, from which we made a good and useful selection.

We knew very early that no single criterion could determine what materials should fill this book. Differing understandings of taste and relevance exist throughout the Unitarian Universalist Association and shall continue to do so. Governed by our charge to produce an inclusive hymnbook, we took the Principles and Purposes of our Association as the touchstones of our decision to proclaim our diversity. In structuring and indexing the book, we used as guides the five sources of our living tradition and seven principles. Inspired by various liberation philosophies, cross-cultural perspectives, and ecological awareness, we sought to express a full range of spiritual imagery. Most notable is our use of feminine imagery for the divine. We applied similar inclusive insights to carols and some familiar hymns so that our tradition is not merely received. Each selection has its place within the wide embrace of our heritage and vision.

Fully a third of the book is the work of Canadian and American Unitarian Universalists, present and past. But in this age of global awareness, we felt it imperative to reach out to other Unitarian Universalist traditions worldwide, and have included works from Nigeria, the Philippines, India, England, Transylvania, and Czechoslovakia. Music and texts from six continents are here, and words from the world's sacred writings. In selecting passages from the Bible we elected to use several versions to better engage the diversity of modern minds and hearts.

To help us in the difficult process of selection, we sang through each hymn and song many times and tested some of these in our congregations. Some hymns were obvious choices, some were elusive, and some we debated for years. We expect that some will require more thorough teaching than others. We encourage our congregations not to avoid the less familiar but richly rewarding works. A companion volume containing notes about the music and texts, suggestions on usage, and a pronunciation guide will be available. Tempo indications are merely suggestions. Adjust them as necessary to facilitate successful singing in your congregation and to accomodate the acoustics of your worship space.

During our five years we considered thousands of submissions. We engaged many to help research, evaluate, and edit. New works from a variety of authors and composers provided us with fresh expressions of faith not found in any other hymnbook. We extend our heartfelt gratitude to these gifted people.

The coming decades will undoubtedly bring new challenge and change and not a little surprise. We offer this book in the hope that its spirit, in word and song, will empower us to sing our Living Tradition in the twenty-first century.

THE HYMNBOOK RESOURCES
COMMISSION

T. J. Anderson
Mark L. Belletini, chair
Jacqui James, ex-officio
Ellen Johnson-Fay
Helen R. Pickett
Mark Slegers
Barbara L. Wagner
W. Frederick Wooden

Singing the Living Tradition

WE, THE MEMBER CONGREGATIONS OF THE UNITARIAN UNIVERSALIST ASSOCIATION, COVENANT TO AFFIRM AND PROMOTE:

The inherent worth and dignity of every person;
Justice, equity, and compassion in human relations;
Acceptance of one another and encouragement to spiritual growth
in our congregations;
A free and responsible search for truth and meaning;
The right of conscience and the use of the democratic process
within our congregations and in society at large;
The goal of world community with peace, liberty,
and justice for all;
Respect for the interdependent web of all existence
of which we are a part.

THE LIVING TRADITION WE SHARE DRAWS FROM MANY SOURCES:

Direct experience of that transcending mystery and wonder,
affirmed in all cultures, which moves us to a renewal of the spirit
and an openness to the forces that create and uphold life;
Words and deeds of prophetic women and men which challenge us
to confront powers and structures of evil with justice, compassion,
and the transforming power of love;
Wisdom from the world's religions which inspires us
in our ethical and spiritual life;
Jewish and Christian teachings which call us to respond to God's love
by loving our neighbors as ourselves;
Humanist teachings which counsel us to heed the guidance of reason
and the results of science, and warn us against
idolatries of the mind and spirit.
Spiritual teachings of Earth-centered traditions which celebrate
the sacred circle of life and instruct us to live in harmony
with the rhythms of nature.

Grateful for the religious pluralism which enriches and ennobles our faith,
we are inspired to deepen our understanding and expand our vision. As free
congregations we enter into this covenant, promising to one another our
mutual trust and support.

The Unitarian Universalist Association shall devote its resources to and exercise its corporate powers for religious, educational, and humanitarian purposes. The primary purpose of the Association is to serve the needs of its member congregations, organize new congregations, extend and strengthen Unitarian Universalist institutions, and implement its principles.

Adopted as a Bylaw by the 1984, 1985, and 1995 General Assemblies

May Nothing Evil Cross This Door

1

Words: Louis Untermeyer, 1885–1977, © 1923, renewed 1951 by
Louis Untermeyer, used by perm. of Harcourt Brace Jovanovich
Music: Robert N. Quaile, b. 1867

OLDBRIDGE
8.8.8.4.

THE CELEBRATION OF LIFE

Down the Ages We Have Trod

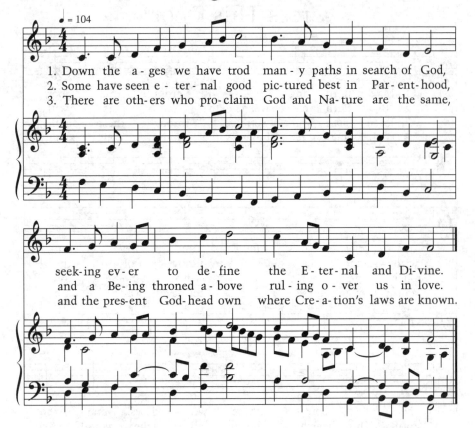

1. Down the a-ges we have trod man-y paths in search of God,
2. Some have seen e-ter-nal good pic-tured best in Par-ent-hood,
3. There are oth-ers who pro-claim God and Na-ture are the same,

seek-ing ev-er to de-fine the E-ter-nal and Di-vine.
and a Be-ing throned a-bove rul-ing o-ver us in love.
and the pres-ent God-head own where Cre-a-tion's laws are known.

4. There are eyes which best can see
   God within humanity,
   and God's countenance there trace
   written in the human face.

5. Where compassion is most found
   is for some the hallowed ground,
   and these paths they upward plod
   teaching us that love is God.

6. Though the truth we can't perceive
   this at least we must believe,
   what we take most earnestly
   is our living Deity.

7. Our true God we there shall find
   in what claims our heart and mind,
   and our hidden thoughts enshrine
   that which for us is Divine.

⊕ Words: John Andrew Storey, 1935–1997
⊕ Music: Thomas Benjamin, 1940– , © 1992 Unitarian Universalist Association

WOODLAND
7.7.7.7.

The World Stands Out on Either Side

1. The world stands out on ei-ther side no wi-der than the heart is wide; a-bove the world is stretched the sky no high-er than the soul is high.

2. The heart can push the sea and land so far a-way on ei-ther hand; the soul can split the sky in two and let the face of God shine through.

Words: Edna St. Vincent Millay, 1892–1950
Music: W. Frederick Wooden, 1953– ,
© 1992 Unitarian Universalist Association

RICKER
L.M.

4   I Brought My Spirit to the Sea

1. I brought my spir-it to the sea; I
2. And then there came a sense of peace, some
3. I brought my spir-it to the trees that
4. And then I felt an in-ner flame that

stood up-on the shore. I
whis-per calmed my soul. Some
loomed a-gainst the sky. I
fierce-ly burned my tears. Up-

gazed up-on in-fin-i-ty, I heard the wa-ters roar.
an-cient min-is-try of stars had made my spir-it whole.
touched each wan-d'ring care-less breeze to know if God was nigh.
right, I rose from bend-ed knee to meet the ask-ing years.

Words: Max Kapp, 1904–1979
Music: Alec Wyton, 1921– , © 1990 Alec Wyton

JACQUI
C.M.

THE CELEBRATION OF LIFE

It Is Something to Have Wept 5

1. It is some-thing to have wept as we have wept, and
2. It is some-thing to have smelt the mys-tic rose, al-
3. To have known the things that from the weak are furled, the
4. Lo, and bless-ed are our ears for they have heard: yea,

some-thing to have done as we have done; it is
though it break and leave the thorn-y rods; it is
fear-ful an-cient pas-sions, strange and high; it is
bless-ed are our eyes for they have seen: let the

some-thing to have watched when all have slept, and
some-thing to have hun - gered once as those must
some-thing to be wis - er than the world, and
thun-der break on hu - man, beast, and bird, and

seen the stars which nev - er see the sun.
hun - ger who have ate the bread of gods:
some - thing to be old - er than the sky.
light - ning. It is some - thing to have been.

Words: Gilbert Keith Chesterton, 1874–1936
Music: Robert L. Sanders, b. 1906, © 1964 Beacon Press

KEITH
11.10.11.10.

THE CELEBRATION OF LIFE

6 Just as Long as I Have Breath

♩ = 120

1. Just as long as I have breath, I must ans-wer,
2. Just as long as vi-sion lasts, I must ans-wer,
3. Just as long as my heart beats, I must ans-wer,

"Yes," to life; though with pain I made my way,
"Yes," to truth; in my dream and in my dark,
"Yes," to love; dis-ap-point-ment pierced me through,

still with hope I meet each day. If they ask what
al-ways: that e-lu-sive spark. If they ask what
still I kept on lov-ing you. If they ask what

I did well, tell them I said, "Yes," to life.
I did well, tell them I said, "Yes," to truth.
I did best, tell them I said, "Yes," to love.

Words: Alicia S. Carpenter, 1930– , © 1981 Alicia S. Carpenter
Music: Johann G. Ebeling, 1637–1676,
harmony rev. by John Edwin Giles, 1949–1996
© 1992 Unitarian Universalist Association

NICHT SO TRAURIG
7.7.7.7.7.7.

THE CELEBRATION OF LIFE

♩ = 108 *Unison*

1. The leaf un - furl - ing in the A - pril air, the
2. All life is one, a sin - gle branch - ing tree, all
3. The self - same bells for joy and sor - row ring. No

new - born child, the lov - ing par - ents' care; these
pain a part of hu - man mis - e - ry, all
one can know what the next hour will bring. We

con - stant, com - mon mir - a - cles we share:
hap - pi - ness a gift to you and me: Al - le -
cry, we laugh, we mourn, and still we sing:

lu - ia! Al - le - lu - ia! lu - ia!

⊕ Words: Don Cohen, 1946– , © 1982 Don Cohen
⊕ Music: John Corrado, 1940– , © 1982 John Corrado

ALL LIFE IS ONE
10.10.10.4.

THE CELEBRATION OF LIFE

Mother Spirit, Father Spirit

♩ = 72 *Unison*

1. Moth-er Spir-it, Fa-ther Spir-it, where are you?
2. Man-y drops are in the o-cean, deep and wide.
3. I am emp-ty, time flies from me; what is time?
4. Moth-er Spir-it, Fa-ther Spir-it, take our hearts.

In the sky song, in the for-est, sounds your cry.
Sun-light bounc-es off the rip-ples to the sky.
Dreams e-ter-nal, fears in-fer-nal haunt my heart.
Take our breath and let our voic-es sing our parts.

What to give you, what to call you, what am I?
What to give you, what to call you, who am I?
What to give you, what to call you, O, my God?
Take our hands and let us work to shape our art.

Words: Norbert F. Căpek, 1870–1942,
trans. by Paul and Anita Munk, © 1992 Unitarian Universalist Association,
English version by Richard Frederick Boeke, 1931–
Music: Norbert F. Căpek, 1870–1942,
harmony by David Dawson, 1939–

MĀTI SVETA
8.3.8.3.8.3.

Words: John Greenleaf Whittier, 1807–1892
Music: Van Dieman's Land (English folk),
⊕ arr. and ed. by Waldemar Hille, 1908–

VAN DIEMAN'S LAND
8.6.8.6.6.8.8.6.

Immortal Love

1. Im - mor - tal love, for - ev - er full, for - ev - er
2. Our out - ward lips con - fess the name all oth - er
3. Blow, winds of love, a - wake and blow the mists of
4. The let - ter fails, the sys - tems fall, and ev - ery

flow - ing free, for - ev - er shared, for -
names a - bove; but love a - lone knows
hate a - way; sing out, O Truth di -
sym - bol wanes; the Spir - it o - ver -

ev - er whole, a nev - er - end - ing sea!
whence it came and com - pre - hend - eth love.
vine, and tell how wide and far we stray.
see - ing all, E - ter - nal Love, re - mains.

Words: John Greenleaf Whittier, 1807–1892
Music: Irish melody

ST. COLUMBA
8.6.8.6.

THE CELEBRATION OF LIFE

O God of Stars and Sunlight   11

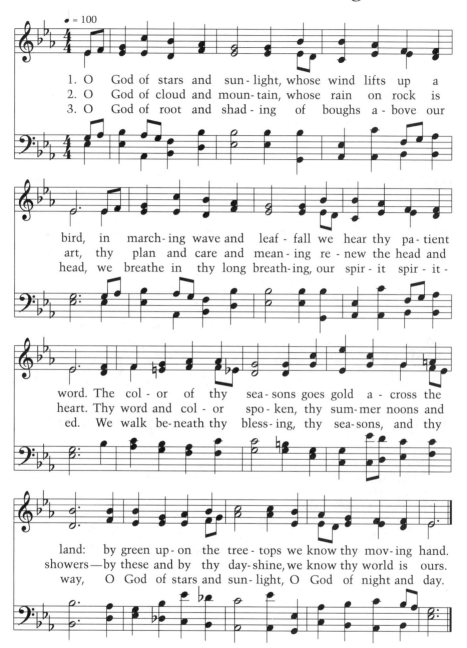

♩ = 100

1. O God of stars and sun-light, whose wind lifts up a
2. O God of cloud and moun-tain, whose rain on rock is
3. O God of root and shad-ing of boughs a-bove our

bird, in march-ing wave and leaf-fall we hear thy pa-tient
art, thy plan and care and mean-ing re-new the head and
head, we breathe in thy long breath-ing, our spir-it spir-it-

word. The col-or of thy sea-sons goes gold a-cross the
heart. Thy word and col-or spo-ken, thy sum-mer noons and
ed. We walk be-neath thy bless-ing, thy sea-sons, and thy

land: by green up-on the tree-tops we know thy mov-ing hand.
showers—by these and by thy day-shine, we know thy world is ours.
way, O God of stars and sun-light, O God of night and day.

Words: John Holmes, 1904–1962
Music: Felix Mendelssohn, 1809–1847

MUNICH
7.6.7.6.D.

12 O Life That Maketh All Things New

♩ = 108

1. O Life that mak - eth all things new, the bloom - ing
2. From hand to hand the greet - ing flows, from eye to
3. One in the free - dom of the truth, one in the
4. The fre - er step, the full - er breath, the wide ho -

earth, our thoughts with - in, our pil - grim feet, wet with thy
eye the sig - nals run, from heart to heart the bright hope
joy of paths un - trod, one in the soul's per - en - nial
ri - zon's grand - er view, the sense of life that knows no

dew, in glad - ness hith - er turn a - gain.
glows; the seek - ers of the light are one:
youth, one in the larg - er thought of God;
death, the Life that mak - eth all things new.

Words: Samuel Longfellow, 1819–1892
Music: Thomas Williams's *Psalmodia Evangelica*, 1789

TRURO
L.M.

THE CELEBRATION OF LIFE

1. Songs of spir-it, like a prayer breath-ing in the am-bient air;
2. In the bur-geon-ing of spring, in the sum-mer's scent-ed bloom,
3. Sing-ing, sing-ing ev-ery-where, at the heart of ev-ery-thing;

sing-ing in the morn-ing light, in the ra-diance of the day,
in the au-tumn's mel-low glow, in the win-ter's ice and snow;
in my soul I hear them sing; mys-tic mu-sic of the spheres;

in the twi-light shad-ows gray, in the brood-ing hush of night;
shade, or shine, or joy, or gloom, as the sea-sons come and go,
songs that, with my ut-most art, I can on-ly catch in part;

dark or light, or storm, or fair — sing-ing, sing-ing ev-ery-where.
bleak and bare, or blos-som-ing — still the songs that sing and sing!
bro-ken ech-oes, cold and bare, of the songs my spir-it hears.

Words: Marion Franklin Ham, 1867–1956
Music: Thomas Oboe Lee, 1945– ,
© 1992 Unitarian Universalist Association

SERVETUS
7.7.7.7.D.

THE CELEBRATION OF LIFE

14 The Sun at High Noon

♩ = 120

1. The sun at high noon, the stars in dark space, the
2. The green grass-y blade, the grass-hop-per's sound, the
3. The glad joys that heal the tears in our eyes, the

light of the moon on each up-turned face, the
crea-tures of shade that live in the ground, the
long-ings we feel, the light of sur - prise, our

high clouds, the rain clouds, the lark - song on
dark soil, the moist soil, where plants spring to
night dreams, our day dreams, our thoughts rang - ing

⊕ Words: Sydney Henry Knight, 1923–
⊕ Music: Thomas Benjamin, 1940– , © 1992 Unitarian Universalist Association

MACDOWELL
5.5.5.5.5.6.5.6.5.

THE CELEBRATION OF LIFE

high: we gaze up in won - der a - bove to the sky.
birth: we look down at won - der be - low in the earth.
wide: we live with a whole world of won - der in - side.

The Lone, Wild Bird 15

♩ = 108 *Unison*

1. The lone, wild bird in loft - y flight is still with
2. The ends of earth are in thy hand, the sea's dark

thee, nor leaves thy sight. And I am thine! I rest in
deep and far - off land. And I am thine! I rest in

thee. Great spir - it come and rest in me.
thee. Great spir - it come and rest in me.

Another accompaniment, 232
Words: H. R. MacFayden, 1877–1964
Music: William Walker's *Southern Harmony*, 1835

PROSPECT
L.M.

'Tis a Gift to Be Simple

Words: Joseph Bracket, 18th cent.
Music: American Shaker tune

SIMPLE GIFTS
Irregular with refrain

be our de-light, 'till by turn-ing, turn-ing we come 'round right.

Every Night and Every Morn   17

1. Ev - ery night and ev - ery morn some to
2. Joy and woe are wo - ven fine, cloth - ing
3. It is right it should be so: we were

mis - er - y are born; ev - ery morn and ev - ery
for the soul di - vine: un - der ev - ery grief and
made for joy and woe; and when this we right - ly

night some are born to sweet de - light.
pine runs a joy with silk - en twine.
know, safe - ly through the world we go.

Words: William Blake, 1757–1827
Music: Ralph Vaughan Williams, 1872–1958, adapt.

THE CALL
7.7.7.7.

18 What Wondrous Love

♩ = 72 *Unison*

1. What won-drous love is this, O my soul, O my soul, what
2. When I was sink-ing down, sink-ing down, sink-ing down, when
3. To love and to all friends I will sing, I will sing, to

won-drous love is this, O my soul? What won-drous love is
I was sink-ing down, sink-ing down, when I was sink-ing
love and to all friends I will sing. To love and to all

this that brings my heart such bliss, and takes a-way the
down be-neath my sor-rows ground, friends to me gath-er'd
friends who pain and sor-row mend, with thanks un-to the

pain of my soul, of my soul, and takes a-way the pain of my soul.
round, O my soul, O my soul, friends to me gath-er'd round, O my soul.
end I will sing, I will sing, with thanks un-to the end I will sing.

Words: American folk hymn
⊕ New words by Connie Campbell Hart, 1929– ,
© 1992 Unitarian Universalist Association
Music: Melody from *The Southern Harmony*, 1835

WONDROUS LOVE
12.9.12.12.9.

THE CELEBRATION OF LIFE

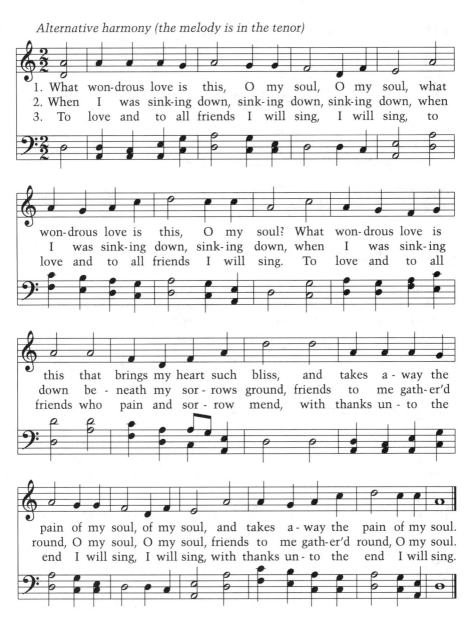

1. What won-drous love is this, O my soul, O my soul, what
2. When I was sink-ing down, sink-ing down, sink-ing down, when
3. To love and to all friends I will sing, I will sing, to

won-drous love is this, O my soul? What won-drous love is
I was sink-ing down, sink-ing down, when I was sink-ing
love and to all friends I will sing. To love and to all

this that brings my heart such bliss, and takes a-way the
down be-neath my sor-rows ground, friends to me gath-er'd
friends who pain and sor-row mend, with thanks un-to the

pain of my soul, of my soul, and takes a-way the pain of my soul.
round, O my soul, O my soul, friends to me gath-er'd round, O my soul.
end I will sing, I will sing, with thanks un-to the end I will sing.

Music: Melody from *The Southern Harmony*, 1835
Harm. by Carlton R. Young, 1926– , harmony © 1965 Abingdon Press

WONDROUS LOVE
12.9.12.12.9.

THE CELEBRATION OF LIFE

19 The Sun That Shines

♩ = 92 *Unison*

1. The sun that shines a - cross the sea, the wind that whis - pers in the tree, the lark that car - ols in the sky, the fleec - y clouds a - sail - ing by, O, I'm as rich as rich can be, for all these things be - long to me!

2. The rain - drops which re - fresh the earth, the spring - time man - tle of re - birth, the sum - mer days when all things grow, the au - tumn mist and win - ter snow, O, I'm as rich as rich can be, for all these things be - long to me!

3. The task well done, the fun of play, the wise who guide me on my way, the balm of sleep when each day ends, the joy of fam - i - ly and friends, O, I'm as rich as rich can be, for all these things be - long to me!

Words: Attrib. to Dimitri S. Bortniansky, 1751–1825, v. 1
⊕ John Andrew Storey, 1935–1997
⊕ Music: David Dawson, 1939–

BARNFIELD
8.8.8.8.8.8.

THE CELEBRATION OF LIFE

Be Thou My Vision

20

♩=108 *Unison*

1. Be thou my vi - sion, O God of my heart;
2. Be thou my wis - dom, and thou my true word;
3. Rich - es I heed not, nor world's emp - ty praise,

naught be all else to me, save that thou art.
I ev - er with thee and thou with me God;
thou my in - her - i - tance, now and al - ways;

Thou my best thought, by day or by night,
thou my soul's shel - ter, thou my high tower,
thou and thou on - ly, first in my heart,

wak - ing or sleep - ing, thy pres - ence my light.
raise thou me heaven - ward, O Power of my power.
Sov - 'reign of hea - ven, my trea - sure thou art.

Words: Ancient Irish, trans. by Mary E. Byrne, 1880–1931,
versed by Eleanor H. Hull, 1860–1935, alt.
Music: Traditional Irish melody, harm. by Carlton R. Young, 1926– ,
harmony renewal © 1992 Abingdon Press

SLANE
10.10.9.10.

21   For the Beauty of the Earth

♩ = 112

1. For the beau-ty of the earth, for the splen-dor
2. For the joy of ear and eye, for the heart and
3. For the won-der of each hour of the day and
4. For the joy of hu-man care, sis-ter, broth-er,

of the skies, for the love which from our birth
mind's de-light, for the mys-tic har-mo-ny
of the night, hill and vale and tree and flower,
par-ent, child, for the kin-ship we all share,

o-ver and a-round us lies:
link-ing sense to sound and sight:
sun and moon and stars of light: Source of all, to
for all gen-tle thoughts and mild:

thee we raise this, our hymn of grate-ful praise.

Words: Folliott Sandford Pierpoint, 1835–1917, adapt.
Music: Conrad Kocher, 1786–1872, abridged

DIX
7.7.7.7.7.7.

PRAISE AND TRANSCENDENCE

♩ = 100

1. Dear weav - er of our lives' de - sign whose
2. Take up the fab - ric of our lives with
3. Let eyes that in the plain - est cloth a

pat - terns all o - bey, with skill - ful fin - gers
hands that gen - tly hold; bind in the rag - ged
hid - den beau - ty see dis - cern in us our

gent - ly guide the stur - dy threads that
edge that care would sun - der and that
rich - est hues, show us the pat - terns

will sur - vive the tan - gle of our days.
pain would tear, and mend our rav - 'ling souls.
we may use to set our spir - its free.

⊕ Words: Nancy C. Dorian, 1936– ,
© 1992 Unitarian Universalist Association
Music: Nikolaus Herman, 1480–1561,
harmonized by J. S. Bach, 1685–1750

LOBT GOTT, IHR CHRISTEN
8.6.8.8.6.

PRAISE AND TRANSCENDENCE

23 Bring Many Names

1. Bring man-y names, beau-ti-ful and good;
cel-e-brate in par-a-ble and sto-ry, ho-li-ness in
glo-ry, liv-ing, lov-ing God: hail and ho-

2. Strong moth-er God, work-ing night and day,
plan-ning all the won-ders of cre-a-tion, set-ting each e-
qua-tion, ge-ni-us at play: hail and ho-

3. Warm fa-ther God, hug-ging ev-'ry child,
feel-ing all the strains of hu-man liv-ing, car-ing and for-
giv-ing till we're rec-on-ciled: hail and ho-

4. Old, ach-ing God, grey with end-less care,
calm-ly pierc-ing e-vil's new dis-guis-es, glad of new sur-
pris-es, wis-er than des-pair: hail and ho-

Words: Brian Wren, 1936– , © 1989 Hope Publishing Co.
Music: Carlton R. Young, 1926– , © 1989 Hope Publishing Co.

WESTCHASE
9.10.6.5.5.4.

PRAISE AND TRANSCENDENCE

- san - na, bring man - y names.
- san - na, strong moth- er God!
- san - na, warm fa - ther God!
- san - na, old, ach- ing God!

great, liv-ing God!

5. Young, growing God, eager still to know,
   willing to be changed by what you've started,
   quick to be delighted, singing as you go:
   hail and hosanna, young, growing God!

6. Great, living God, never fully known,
   joyful darkness far beyond our seeing,
   closer yet than breathing, everlasting home:
   hail and hosanna, great, living God!

Far Rolling Voices

♩ = 104

1. Far roll-ing voic-es of the sea chant loud up-on the
4. Your u-ni-ver-sal wa-ters sweep up-on the end-less

shore. They tell the an-cient mys-ter-y of
strands. Your love and mer-cy ev-er keep a-

God for-ev-er-more. 2. New-born, the sun in
surge in all thy lands. 5. Far roll-ing voic-es

glo-ry rides a-cross the heav-'nly fields. The
of the sea chant loud up-on the shore. They

star-ry host in si-lence bides and to the morn-ing yields.
tell the an-cient mys-ter-y, O God, for-ev-er-more.

⊕ Words: Max Kapp, 1904–1979
Music: I-to Loh, 1936– , © 1983 I-to Loh

OIKOUMENE
C.M.

PRAISE AND TRANSCENDENCE

3. White sea-birds wheel a - gainst the sky, com -
pan - ioned with the dawn. God,
lift our wing - ing souls on high, share
in cre - a - tion's morn.

25 God of the Earth, the Sky, the Sea

1. God of the earth, the sky, the sea,
maker of all above, below,
creation lives and moves in you;
your present life through all does flow.

2. Your love is in the sunshine's glow,
your life is in the quickening air;
when lightnings flash and storm-winds blow,
there is your power, your law is there.

3. We feel your calm at evening's hour,
your grandeur in the march of night;
and when the morning breaks in power,
we hear your word, "Let there be light."

4. But higher far, and far more clear,
you in our spirit we behold;
your image and yourself are there—
indwelling God, proclaimed of old.

Words: Samuel Longfellow, 1819–1892
Music: John Hatton, 1710–1793

DUKE STREET
L.M.

PRAISE AND TRANSCENDENCE

Holy, Holy, Holy

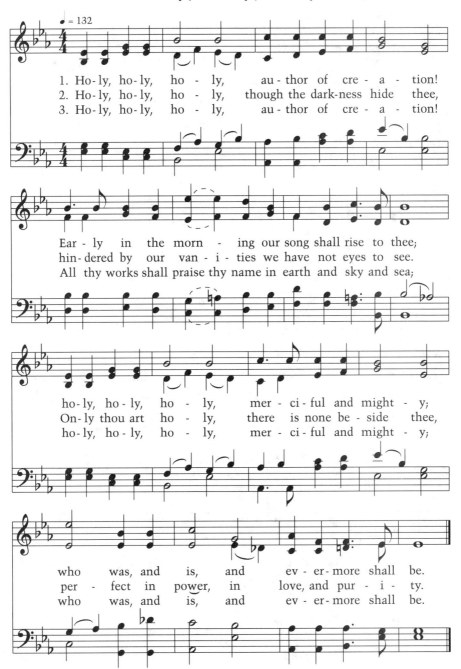

♩ = 132

1. Ho-ly, ho-ly, ho-ly, au-thor of cre-a-tion!
2. Ho-ly, ho-ly, ho-ly, though the dark-ness hide thee,
3. Ho-ly, ho-ly, ho-ly, au-thor of cre-a-tion!

Ear-ly in the morn-ing our song shall rise to thee;
hin-dered by our van-i-ties we have not eyes to see.
All thy works shall praise thy name in earth and sky and sea;

ho-ly, ho-ly, ho-ly, mer-ci-ful and might-y;
On-ly thou art ho-ly, there is none be-side thee,
ho-ly, ho-ly, ho-ly, mer-ci-ful and might-y;

who was, and is, and ev-er-more shall be.
per-fect in power, in love, and pur-i-ty.
who was, and is, and ev-er-more shall be.

This music in D, 39
Words: Reginald Heber, 1738–1826, arr.
Music: John Bacchus Dykes, 1823–1876

NICAEA
12.12.12.10. Irregular

PRAISE AND TRANSCENDENCE

26

27 I Am That Great and Fiery Force

1. I am that great and fie - ry force spar - kling in ev - ery - thing that lives; in shin - ing of the riv - er's course, in green - ing grass that glo - ry gives.

2. I shine in glit - ter on the seas, in burn - ing sun, in moon and stars. In un - seen wind, in ver - dant trees I breathe with - in, both near and far.

3. And where I breathe there is no death, and mea - dows glow with beau - ties rife. I am in all, the spir - it's breath, the thun - dered word, for I am Life.

Words: Hildegard of Bingen, 1098–1179
Music: Josquin Desprez, 1445–1521, adapt. by Anthony Petti, b. 1932

AVE VERA VIRGINITAS
L.M.

PRAISE AND TRANSCENDENCE

♩ = 92 *Unison*

1. View the star-ry realm of hea-ven, shin-ing
2. Great you are, be-yond con-cep-tion, God of
3. You, the One with-in all form-ing in my
4. Life is yours, in you I grow tall, seed will

dis-tant em-pires sing. Sky-song of ce-
gods and God of stars. My soul soars with
heart and mind and breath, you, my guide through
come to fruit I know. Trust that af-ter

les-tial chil-dren turns each win-ter in-to
your per-cep-tion, I es-cape from pris-on
hate's fierce storm-ing, cour-age in both life and
win-ter's snow-fall walls will melt and Truth will

spring, turns each win-ter in-to spring.
bars, I es-cape from pris-on bars.
death, cour-age in both life and death.
flow, walls will melt and Truth will flow.

Words: Norbert F. Čapek, 1870–1942,
trans. by Richard F. Boeke, 1931– , text © 1992 Unitarian Universalist Association
Music: Bodhana Haspel,
harmony by Betsy Jo Angebranndt, 1931– , © 1992 Unitarian Universalist Association

DACHAU
8.7.8.7.7.

PRAISE AND TRANSCENDENCE

29 Joyful, Joyful, We Adore Thee

1. Joy-ful, joy-ful, we a-dore thee, God of glo-ry,
2. All thy works with joy sur-round thee, earth and heav'n re-
3. Thou art giv-ing and for-giv-ing, ev-er bless-ing,

God of love; hearts un-fold like flowers be-fore thee,
flect thy rays, stars and plan-ets sing a-round thee,
ev-er blest; well-spring of the joy of liv-ing,

hail thee as the sun a-bove. Melt the clouds of
cen-ter of un-bro-ken praise; field and for-est,
o-cean-depth of hap-py rest. Ev-er sing-ing

sin and sad-ness; drive the pain of doubt a-way; giv-
vale and moun-tain, blos-soming mead-ow, flash-ing sea, chant-
march we on-ward, vic-tors in the midst of strife; joy-

Words: Henry Van Dyke, 1852–1933
Music: Ludwig van Beethoven, 1770–1827

HYMN TO JOY
8.7.8.7.D.

PRAISE AND TRANSCENDENCE

- er of im - mor - tal glad - ness, fill us with the joy of day.
- ing bird and flow-ing foun-tain call us to re - joice in thee.
- ful mu - sic lifts us sun - ward in the tri- umph song of life.

Over My Head 30

1. O - ver my head   I hear mu - sic in the air.
2. O - ver my head   I hear sing-ing in the air.
3. O - ver my head   I see trou-ble in the air.

O- ver my head   I hear mu - sic in the air.
O- ver my head   I hear sing-ing in the air.
O- ver my head   I see trou-ble in the air.

O- ver my head   I hear mu - sic in the air.
O- ver my head   I hear sing-ing in the air.
O- ver my head   I see trou-ble in the air.

There must   be a God some- where.

4. Over my head I feel gladness in the air... 5. Over my head I see angels in the air...

Words & music: African American spiritual, c. 1750–1875, arr. by Horace
Clarence Boyer, 1935– , © 1992 Unitarian Universalist Association

REEB
Irregular

31 Name Unnamed

Name un-named, hid-den and shown, know-ing and known.

Fine

Glo - ri - a!
1. Beau - ti-ful-ly mov-ing, cease - less - ly
2. Spin - ner of Cha- os, pull - ing and
3. Nudg - ing Dis - com-fort, prod - ding and

form-ing, grow-ing, e - merg-ing with awe-some de - light,
twist-ing, free-ing the fi - bers of pat - tern and form,
shak-ing, wak-ing our lives to cre - a - tive un - ease,

Words: Brian Wren, 1936– , © 1989 Hope Publishing Co.
Music: W. Frederick Wooden, 1953– , © 1992 Unitarian Universalist Association

SAMUEL
Irregular

D.C. al Fine

Mak - er of Rain - bows, glow - ing with col - or, arch - ing in
Weav - er of Sto - ries, famed or un - spo - ken, tan - gled or
Straight- talk - ing Lov - er, check - ing and hum - bling jar - gon and

won - der, en - er - gy flow - ing in dark - ness and light:
bro - ken, shap - ing a tap - es - try viv - id and warm:
grum - bling, speak - ing the truth that re - fresh - es and frees:

4. Midwife of Changes, skillfully guiding,
   drawing us out through the shock of the new,
   Woman of Wisdom, deeply perceiving,
   never deceiving,
   freeing and leading in all that we do:

5. Daredevil Gambler, risking and loving,
   giving us freedom to shatter your dreams,
   Lifegiving Loser, wounded and weeping,
   dancing and leaping,
   sharing the caring that heals and redeems.

Now Thank We All Our God

♩ = 108

1. Now thank we all our God with hearts and hands and
2. O may this boun-teous God through all our life be

voic - es, who won-drous things hath done, in
near - us, with ev - er joy - ful hearts and

whom this world re - joic - es; who from our par - ents'
bless - ed peace to cheer us; the one e - ter - nal

arms has blessed us on our way with
God, whom earth and heaven a - dore, for

count - less gifts of love, and still is ours to - day.
thus it was, is now, and shall be ev - er - more.

Words: Martin Rinkart, 1586–1649, trans. by Catherine Winkworth, 1827–1878
Music: Johann Crüger, 1598–1662

NUN DANKET ALLE GOTT
6.7.6.7.6.6.6.6.

PRAISE AND TRANSCENDENCE

Sovereign and Transforming Grace

1. Sovereign and transforming Grace,
   we invoke your quickening power;
   reign the spirit of this place,
   bless the purpose of this hour.

2. Holy and creative Light,
   we invoke your kindling ray;
   draw upon our spirit's night,
   as the darkness turns to day.

3. To the anxious soul impart
   hope, all other hopes above;
   stir the dull and hardened heart
   with a longing and a love.

Words: Frederick Henry Hedge, 1805–1890, rev.
Music: Jane M. Marshall, 1924– , © 1992 Unitarian Universalist Association

MANTON
7.7.7.7.

PRAISE AND TRANSCENDENCE

Though I May Speak
with Bravest Fire

1. Though I may speak with brav-est fire,
2. Though I may give all I pos-sess,
3. Come, Spir-it, come, our hearts con-trol,

and have the gift to all in-spire,
and striv-ing so my love pro-fess,
our spir-its long to be made whole.

and have not love, my words are vain,
but not be given by love with-in,
Let in-ward love guide ev-ery deed;

as sound-ing brass, and hope-less gain.
the prof-it soon turns strange-ly thin.
by this we wor - ship, and are freed.

Words: Hal Hopson, 1933– , (1 Cor. 13:1–3), © 1972 Hope Publishing Co.
Music: Trad. English melody, adapt. by Hal Hopson, 1933– ,
© 1972 Hope Publishing Co.

GIFT OF LOVE
L.M.

PRAISE AND TRANSCENDENCE

Unto Thy Temple, Lord, We Come

♩ = 92

1. Un - to thy tem - ple, Lord, we come
2. The com - mon home of rich and poor,
3. May thy whole truth be spo - ken here;

with thank - ful hearts to wor - ship thee;
of bond and free, and great and small;
thy gos - pel light for - ev - er shine;

and pray that this may be our home
large as thy love for - ev - er - more,
thy per - fect love cast out all fear,

un - til we touch e - ter - ni - ty:
and warm and bright and good to all.
and hu - man life be - come di - vine.

Words: Robert Collyer, 1823–1912
Music: John Hatton, c. 1710–1793

DUKE STREET
L.M.

When in Our Music

1. When in our mu - sic God is glo - ri - fied,
2. How of - ten, mak - ing mu - sic, we have found
3. So has the church, in lit - ur - gy and song,
4. Let ev - ery in - stru - ment be tuned for praise!

and ad - o - ra - tion leaves no room for pride,
a new di - men - sion in the world of sound,
in faith and love, through cen - tu - ries of wrong,
Let all re - joice who have a voice to raise!

it is as though the whole cre - a - tion cried
as wor - ship moved us to a more pro - found
borne wit - ness to the truth in ev - ery tongue,
And may God give us faith to sing al - ways

Words: Fred Pratt Green, 1903– , © 1972 Hope Publishing Co.
Music: Charles Villiers Stanford, 1852–1924

ENGELBERG
10.10.10. with Alleluia

PRAISE AND TRANSCENDENCE

God Who Fills the Universe 37

1. God who fills the u-ni-verse from the at-om
2. God who webs the u-ni-verse with a-maz-ing
3. God who keeps the u-ni-verse by the truths of

to the stars, make firm my change-ful heart
mys-ter-ies, make glad my frag-ile soul
liv-ing love, make strong that love in me

so I may do my part and bring joy to all the earth.
so I can see life whole and bring hope to all on earth.
so I can set it free and bring peace to all on earth.

Words: Carl G. Seaburg, 1922–1998, © 1992 Unitarian Universalist Association
Music: Transylvanian hymn, 1607,
harmony by Larry Phillips, 1948– , © 1992 Unitarian Universalist Association

FRANCIS DAVID
7.7.6.6.7.

38 Morning Has Broken

♩·= 56 *Unison*

1. Morn-ing has bro-ken like the first morn-ing, black-bird has
2. Sweet the rain's new fall sun-lit from heav-en, like the first
3. Mine is the sun-light! Mine is the morn-ing born of the

spo-ken like the first bird. Praise for the
dew-fall on the first grass. Praise for the
one light E-den saw play! Praise with e-

sing-ing! Praise for the morn-ing! Praise for them,
sweet-ness of the wet gar-den, sprung in com-
la-tion, praise ev-ery morn-ing, God's re-cre-

spring-ing fresh from the Word!
plete-ness where God's feet pass.
a-tion of the new day!

Words: Eleanor Farjeon, 1881–1965, used by perm. of David Higham Assoc., Ltd.
Music: Gaelic melody, © 1931 Oxford University Press, harmony by David
Evans, 1874–1948

BUNESSAN
5.5.5.4.D.

MORNING

Bring, O Morn, Thy Music 39

♩=132

1. Bring, O morn, thy mu - sic! Night, thy star - lit si - lence!
2. Life and death, thy crea - tures, praise thee, might-y Giv - er!
3. Life nor death can part us, O thou Love e - ter - nal,

O - ceans, laugh in rap - ture to the storm-winds cours - ing
Praise and prayer are ris - ing in thy beast and bird and
Shep - herd of the wan-dering star and souls that way-ward

free! Suns and plan - ets cho - rus, praise to Thee, Most
tree: Lo! they praise and van - ish, van - ish at thy
flee! Home-ward draws the spir - it to thy Spir - it

Ho - ly — Who was, and is, and ev - er-more shall be.
bid - ding — Who was, and is, and ev - er-more shall be.
yearn - ing — Who was, and is, and ev - er-more shall be.

This music in E-flat, 26
Words: William Channing Gannett, 1840–1923
Music: John Bacchus Dykes, 1823–1876

NICAEA
12.13.12.10.

MORNING

40 The Morning Hangs a Signal

1. The morn - ing hangs a sig - nal up-
2. A - bove the gen - er - a - tions the
3. The soul has lift - ed mo - ments, a-

on the moun - tain crest, while all the sleep - ing
lone - ly proph - ets rise, while truth flares as the
bove the drift of days, when life's great mean - ing

val - leys in si - lent dark - ness
day - star with - in their glow - ing
break - eth in sun - rise on our

rest. From peak to peak it flash - es, it
eyes; and oth - er eyes, be - hold - ing, are
ways. Be - hold the ra - diant to - ken of

Words: William Channing Gannett, 1840–1923, rev.
Music: William Lloyd, 1786–1852

MEIRIONYDD
7.6.7.6.D.

MORNING

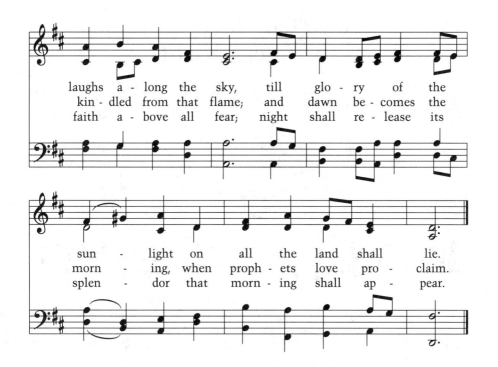

laughs a - long the sky, till glo - ry of the
kin - dled from that flame; and dawn be - comes the
faith a - bove all fear; night shall re - lease its

sun - light on all the land shall lie.
morn - ing, when proph - ets love pro - claim.
splen - dor that morn - ing shall ap - pear.

41 You That Have Spent the Silent Night

1. You that have spent the si - lent night in
2. Now lift your hearts, your voic - es raise, your

sleep and qui - et rest, and joy to see the
morn - ing trib - ute bring; all na - ture join in

cheer - ful light that ris - es in the
grate - ful praise — re - joice, give thanks, and

east, that ris - es in the east,
sing, re - joice, give thanks, and sing.

Words: George Gascoigne, 1540–1577, adapt.
Music: Nikolaus Herman, 1480–1561, harmony by J. S. Bach,
1685–1750

LOBT GOTT, IHR CHRISTEN
C.M. with repeat

Morning, So Fair to See 42

𝅗𝅥 = 66

1. Morn-ing, so fair to see, night, veiled in mys-ter-y—
2. Tall are the ver-dant trees; deep are the flash-ing seas;
3. Age af-ter age we rise, 'neath the e-ter-nal skies,

glo-rious the earth and re-splen-dent skies!
glo-rious each won-der the sea-sons bring.
in-to the light from the shad-owed past:

Pil-grims, we march a-long, sing-ing our
Bright-er is faith's sur-mise, shin-ing in
still shall our pil-grim song, buoy-ant and

joy-ous song, as through an earth-ly par-a-dise.
pil-grim eyes, from which our wak-ing spir-its spring.
brave and strong, re-sound while life and moun-tains last.

Words: Vincent B. Silliman, 1894–1979, recast 1991
Music: A. H. Hoffmann von Fallersleben's *Schlesische Volkslieder*, 1842,
harmony by T. Tertius Noble, 1867–1953

SCHÖNSTER HERR JESU
6.6.9.6.6.8.

MORNING

The Morning, Noiseless

♩ = 112 *Unison*

1. The morn-ing, noise-less, flings its gold, and still is
2. Night moves in si-lence round the pole, the stars sing
3. In qui-e-tude the spir-it grows, and deep-ens
4. At-tend, O soul; and hear at length the spir-it's

eve-ning's pace; and si-lent-ly the earth is
on un-heard; their mu-sic pierc-es to the
hour to hour; in calm e-ter-nal on-ward
si-lent voice; in still-ness la-bor; wait in

1.–3. 4.

rolled a-mid the vast of space.
soul, yet bor-rows not a word.
flows its all-re-deem-ing power.
strength; and, con-fi-dent, re-joice.

Music: Anon., recast 1960, 1990
Music: William Albright, 1944–1998, © 1992 Henmar Press, Inc. (C. F. Peters Corp.)
Tune commissioned by the First Unitarian Universalist Church of Ann Arbor, Michigan, for their 125th Anniversary

NATURE'S ADVENT
C.M.

Words: Ralph Waldo Emerson, 1803–1882, recast 1925, 1950, 1990,
© American Ethical Union
Music: William Walker's *Southern Harmony*, 1835

COMPLAINER
7.6.7.6.D.

45 Now While the Day in Trailing Splendor

♩ = 60 *Smoothly*

1. Now while the day in trail-ing splen-dor gives
2. Touch thou our eyes, their blind-ness heal-ing, till

way to glo-ries of the night, thanks-giv-ing to thy name we
all this com-mon earth and air to our il-lu-mined sight and

ren-der, O God of dark-ness and of light. Each
feel-ing thy glo-ry and thy-self de-clare; till

day from thee we have our be-ing, in all this won-drous
sto-ried mar-vel, sign, and to-ken, all pale be-fore the

⊕ Words: Frederick Lucian Hosmer, 1840–1929
Music: Thomas Oboe Lee, 1945– , © 1992 Unitarian Universalist Association

LEE
9.8.9.8.D.

EVENING

or - der set; thine om - ni - pres - ence blinds our
near - er thought of such vast mir - a - cles un -

see - ing, and in thy gifts we thee for - get.
bro - ken from hour to hour a - round us brought.

Now the Day Is Over 46

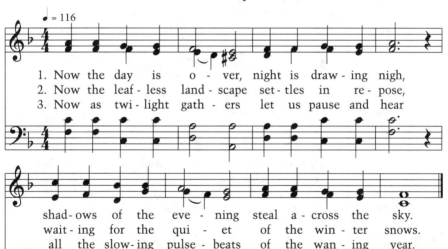

♩ = 116

1. Now the day is o - ver, night is draw - ing nigh,
2. Now the leaf - less land - scape set - tles in re - pose,
3. Now as twi - light gath - ers let us pause and hear

shad - ows of the eve - ning steal a - cross the sky.
wait - ing for the qui - et of the win - ter snows.
all the slow - ing pulse - beats of the wan - ing year.

4. May the season's rhythms,
   slow and strong and deep,
   soothe the mind and spirit,
   lulling us to sleep.

5. Sleep until the rising
   of another spring
   keeps the ancient promise
   fall and winter bring.

Words: v. 1, Sabine Baring-Gould, 1834–1924,
⊕ vs. 2–5, Marye B. Bonney, 1910–
Music: Friedrich Filitz, 1804–1860

WEM IN LEIDENSTAGEN
6.5.6.5.

E V E N I N G

47

Now on Land
and Sea Descending

♩ = 120

1. Now on land and sea de-scend-ing, brings the night its
2. Soon as dies the sun-set glo-ry, stars of heav'n shine
3. Now, our wants and bur-dens leav-ing, to the Care that
4. As the dark-ness deep-ens o'er us, lo, e-ter-nal

peace pro-found; let our ves-per hymn be blend-ing
out a-bove, tell-ing still the an-cient sto-ry—
cares for all, cease we fear-ing, cease we griev-ing;
stars a-rise; hope and faith and love rise glo-rious,

with the ho-ly calm a-round. Ju-bi-la-te!
their Cre-a-tor's change-less love. Ju-bi-la-te!
qui-et-ly our bur-dens fall. Ju-bi-la-te!
shin-ing in the spir-it's skies. Ju-bi-la-te!

Words: Samuel Longfellow, 1819–1892
Music: Russian melody, arr. by J. A. Stevenson, 1761–1833

VESPER HYMN
8.7.8.7. with refrain

48 Again, as Evening's Shadow Falls

1. A - gain, as eve - ning's shad - ow falls, we
2. May strug - gling hearts that seek re - lease here
3. Life's tu - mult we must meet a - gain; we

gath - er in these hal - lowed walls; and ves - per hymn and
find the rest of God's own peace: and, strength - ened here by
can - not at the shrine re - main; but in the spir - it's

ves - per prayer rise min - gling on the ho - ly air.
hymn and prayer, lay down the bur - den and the care.
se - cret cell may hymn and prayer for - ev - er dwell.

Words: Samuel Longfellow, 1819–1892
Music: Amzi Chapin, c. 1800

ROCKBRIDGE
L.M.

Stillness Reigns

1. Still - ness reigns, the winds are sleep - ing. All the world is bent on keep - ing tryst with night, whose wings are sweep - ing from the west each ray of light.

2. Dusk, a soft and silk - en cov - er, o - ver all is seen to hov - er in its read - i - ness to cov - er all the drow - sy world, good night.

3. Those who la - bored long, un - tir - ing, hail this time of rest de - sir - ing, strength re - newed through sweet re - tir - ing, wel - come thoughts of peace - ful night.

4. And through spa - ces real or seem - ing find the E - den of their dream - ing, soar to star - ry ways, re - deem - ing hours of toil and pain, good night.

Words: Guttormur J. Guttormsson
Music: German, 14th cent., harmony by Ralph Vaughan Williams, 1872–1958, QUEM PASTORES
used by perm. of Oxford University Press 8.8.8.7.

EVENING

50   When Darkness Nears

1. When dark-ness nears and em-bers die, the wind in trees a dis-tant sigh, the end of day like a lov-er's voice near-by.

2. The night draws close, a fond em-brace; the heart then slows its fran-tic pace, and fear drifts off as a calm breath takes its place.

3. The cra-dle of a vel-vet wing, it holds us in its gen-tle swing, and peace slips in with the songs our dreams will sing.

Words: Philip A. Porter, 1953– , © 1991 Philip A. Porter
Music: David Hurd, 1950– , © 1990 David Hurd

DOVER KNIGHT
8.8.11.

EVENING

4. The end of day, the pass-ing year, the rush of
time need cause no fear, we'll love the
night and its mys - t'ry now so near.

51 Lady of the Seasons' Laughter

1. La - dy
2. Sis - ter
3. Moth - er
4. God - dess

1. of the sea - sons' laugh - ter, in the sum - mer's warmth be
2. of the eve - ning star - light, in the fall - ing shad - ows
3. of the gen - er - a - tions, in whose love all life is
4. of all times' pro - gres - sion, stand with us when we en -

1. near; when the win - ter fol - lows af - ter, teach our
2. stay here a - mong us till the far light of to -
3. worth ev - er - last - ing cel - e - bra - tions, bring our
4. gage hands and hearts to end op - pres - sion, writ - ing

Words: Kendyl L. R. Gibbons, 1955– , © 1990 Unitarian Universalist Association
Music: David Hurd, 1950– , © 1983 G.I.A. Publications, Inc.

JULION
8.7.8.7.8.7.

THE SEASONS

spir - its not to fear. Hold us in your stead - y
- mor - row's dawn-ing ray. Hold us in your stead - y
la - bors safe to birth. Hold us in your stead - y
his - tory's fair - er page. Hold us in your stead - y

mer - cy, La - dy of the turn - ing year.
mer - cy, La - dy of the turn - ing day.
mer - cy, La - dy of the turn - ing earth.
mer - cy, La - dy of the turn - ing age.

Last time

52　　In Sweet Fields of Autumn

♩ = 104 *Unison*

1. In sweet fields of au - tumn the gold grain is
2. The snows of De - cem - ber shall fill wind - y
3. The still - ness of death shall stoop o - ver the

fall - ing, the white clouds drift lone - ly, the
hol - low; the bleak rain trails af - ter, and
wa - ter, the plov - er sweep low where the

wild swan is call - ing. A - las for the
March wind shall fol - low. The deer through the
pale stream - lets fal - ter; but deep in the

dai - sies, the tall fern and grass - es, when
val - leys leave print of their go - ing; and
earth clod the black seed is liv - ing; when

Words: Elizabeth Madison, b. 1883, used by perm. of Hodgin Press
Music: William James Kirkpatrick, 1838–1921, harmony by Ralph Vaughan
Williams, 1872–1958, © 1931 Oxford University Press

CRADLE SONG
12.12.12.12.

AUTUMN

wind - sweep and rain - fall fill low - lands and pass - es.
dia - monds of sleet mark the ridg - es of snow - ing.
spring sounds her bu - gles for rous - ing and giv - ing.

I Walk the Unfrequented Road 53

♩ = 120

1. I walk the un - fre - quent - ed road with
2. I filch the fruit of no one's toil — no
3. I gath - er where I did not sow, and

o - pen eye and ear; I watch a - field the
tres - pass - er am I — and yet I reap from
bind the mys - tic sheaf, the am - ber air, the

farm - er load the boun - ty of the year.
ev - ery soil and from the bound - less sky.
riv - er's flow, the rus - tle of the leaf.

4. A beauty springtime never knew
   haunts all the quiet ways,
   and sweeter shines the landscape through
   its veil of autumn haze.

5. I face the hills, the streams, the wood,
   and feel with all akin;
   my heart expands; their fortitude
   and peace and joy flow in.

Words: Frederick Lucian Hosmer, 1840–1929 in Stanton Coit's *Social Worship II*, 1913
Music: John Wyeth's *Repository of Sacred Music, Part II*, 1813

CONSOLATION
C.M.

AUTUMN

Now Light Is Less

1. Now light is less; noon skies are wide and deep; the rav - a - ges of wind and rain are healed. The haze of har - vest
2. The gar - den spi - der weaves a silk - en pear to keep in - clem - ent weath - er from its young. Straight from the oak, the
3. Lost hues of birds the trees take as their own. Long since, bronze wheat was gath - ered in - to sheaves. The walk - er trudg - es
4. The shoots of spring have mel - lowed with the year. Buds, long un - sealed, ob - scure the nar - row lane. The blood slows trance - like

Words: Theodore Roethke, 1908–1963, © 1939 Theodore Roethke
Music: Alfred Morton Smith, 1879–1971, © Church of the Ascension,
Atlantic City, New Jersey

SURSUM CORDA
10.10.10.10.

AUTUMN

drifts a - long the field un -
gos - sa - mer is hung. At
an - kle deep in leaves; the
in the al - tered vein; our

til clear eyes put on the look of sleep.
dusk our slow breath thick - ens on the air.
feath - er of the milk - weed flut - ters down.
ver - nal wis - dom moves through ripe to sere.

55 Dark of Winter

1. Dark of win-ter, soft and still, your qui-et calm sur-rounds me. Let my thoughts go where they will; ease my mind pro-found-ly. And then my soul will sing a song, a bless-ed song of love e-ter-nal. Gen-tle dark-ness, soft and still, bring your qui-et to me.

2. Dark-ness, soothe my wea-ry eyes, that I may see more clear-ly. When my heart with sor-row cries, com-fort and ca-ress me. And then my soul may hear a voice, a still, small voice of love e-ter-nal. Dark-ness, when my fears a-rise, let your peace flow through me.

Words & Music: Shelley Jackson Denham, 1950– ,
© 1988 Shelley Jackson Denham

WINTER MEDITATION
7.7.7.6.8.9.7.6.

WINTER

Bells in the High Tower

1. Bells in the high tower, ring - ing o'er the white hills,
2. Bells in the old tower, like the sum - mer chat - ter
3. Bells in the stone tower, ech - o - ing the soft sound
4. Bells in the cold tower, 'midst the snow of win - ter

mock - ing the win - ter, sing - ing like the spring rills;
from dart - ing bright birds, as the grapes turn red - der;
of au - tumn's mill wheel, as the wheat is spun round;
sound out the spring song that we may re - mem - ber;

bells in the high tower, in the cold fore - tell - ing
bells in the old tower, now the wine is brim - ming,
bells in the stone tower, see, the bread is yeast - ing
bells in the cold tower, af - ter the long snow - ing

the spring's up - well - ing.
new life be - gin - ning.
for time of feast - ing.
come months of grow - ing.

Words: Howard Box, 1926– , © 1992 Unitarian Universalist Association
Music: Hungarian carol, © 1992 Unitarian Universalist Association

KRISZTUS URUNKNAK
11.11.11.5.

WINTER

57 All Beautiful the March of Days

♩ = 120

1. All beau - ti - ful the march of days, as
2. O'er white ex - pans - es spar - kling clear the
3. O Thou from whose un - fath - omed law the

sea - sons come and go; the hand that shaped the
ra - diant morns un - fold; the sol - emn splen - dors
year in beau - ty flows, thy self the vi - sion

rose hath wrought the crys - tal of the snow; hath
of the night burn bright - er through the cold; life
pass - ing by in crys - tal and in rose. Day

sent the hoar - y frost of heaven, the
mounts in ev - ery throb - bing vein, love
un - to day doth ut - ter speech, and

⊕ Words: Frances Whitmarsh Wile, 1878–1939
Music: English melody, arr. by Ralph Vaughan Williams, 1872–1958,
used by perm. of Oxford University Press

FOREST GREEN
C.M.D.

WINTER

flow - ing wa - ters sealed, and laid a si - lent
deep - ens round the hearth, and clear - er sounds the
night to night pro - claim, in ev - er chang - ing

love - li - ness on hill and wood and field.
an - gel - hymn, "Good will to all on earth."
words of light, the won - der of thy name.

58 Ring Out, Wild Bells

1. Ring out, wild bells, to the wild, wild sky, the fly-ing cloud, the frost-y light: the year is dy-ing in the night; ring out, wild bells, and let it die.
2. Ring out the old, ring in the new, ring, hap-py bells, a-cross the snow: the year is go-ing, let it go; ring out the false, ring in the true.
3. Ring out the grief that saps the mind for those that here we see no more; ring out the feud of rich and poor; ring in re-dress to hu-man-kind.
4. Ring out false pride in place and blood, the civ-ic slan-der and the spite; ring in the love of truth and right; ring in the com-mon love of good.

Words: Alfred Lord Tennyson, 1809–1892
Music: Percy Carter Buck, 1871–1947, © Oxford University Press

GONFALON ROYAL
L.M.

WINTER

Almond Trees, Renewed in Bloom

♩ = 52 *Unison*

1. Al- mond trees, re- newed in bloom, do they not pro-
2. War des- troys a thou- sand- fold, ha- tred scars the

claim life re- turn- ing year by year, love that
earth, but the day when al- monds bloom is a

will re- main? Al- mond blos- som, sign of life
time of birth. Friends, give thanks for al- mond blooms

in the face of pain, rais- es hope in
sway- ing in the wind: to- ken that the

peo- ple's hearts: spring has come a- gain.
gift of life tri- umphs in the end.

Words: Fred Kaan, 1929–
Music: Nguyen-Duc Quang

CON X'OM LANG
7.5.7.5.D.

SPRING

In Time of Silver Rain

1. In time of sil - ver rain the
2. In time of sil - ver rain the

earth puts forth new life a - gain, green
but - ter - flies lift silk - en wings, and

grass - es grow and flow - ers lift their heads, and
trees put forth new leaves to sing in joy be -

Words: Langston Hughes, 1902–1967
Music: George Theophilus Walker, 1922– , © 1990 George Walker

LANGSTON
6.8.10.10.6.

SPRING

o - ver all the plain the won - der spreads of
- neath the sky in time of sil - ver rain, when

life, of life, of life!
spring and life are new.

61 Lo, the Earth Awakes Again

1. Lo, the earth a-wakes a-gain — from the win-ter's bond and pain. Al - le - lu - ia! Al - le - lu - ia! flower and spray —

2. Once a - gain the word comes true, Al - le - lu - ia! All the earth shall be made new. Now the dark, cold days are o'er, Al - le - lu - ia! Spring and glad - ness

3. Change, then, mourn-ing in - to praise, And, for dirg - es, an - thems raise. How our spir - its soar and sing, How our hearts leap

Bring we leaf and to a - dorn this

⊕ Words: Samuel Longfellow, 1819–1892, arr.
Music: Lyra Davidica, 1708, version of John Arnold's *Compleat
Psalmodist*, 1749

EASTER HYMN
7.7.7.7. with Alleluias

SPRING

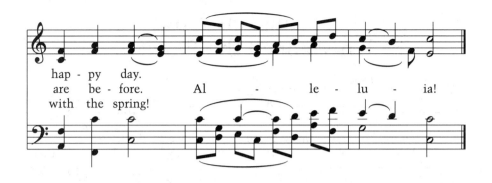

hap - py day.
are be - fore. Al - le - lu - ia!
with the spring!

When the Daffodils Arrive 62

$\circ = 66$

1. When the daf - fo - dils ar - rive
2. When the pus - sy wil - lows bloom
3. When the sweet rain show - ers come,

in the Eas - ter of the year, and the spir - it
in the spring - ing of the year, let the heart find
in the green - ing of the year, birds will sing and

starts to thrive, let the heart beat free and clear.
lov - ing room, spread their wel - come far and near.
bees will hum. Al - le - lu - ia time is here.

Words: Carl G. Seaburg, 1922–1998, © 1992 Unitarian Universalist Association
Music: From a Hasidic tune

HASIDIM
7.7.7.7.

SPRING

63

Spring Has Now
Unwrapped the Flowers

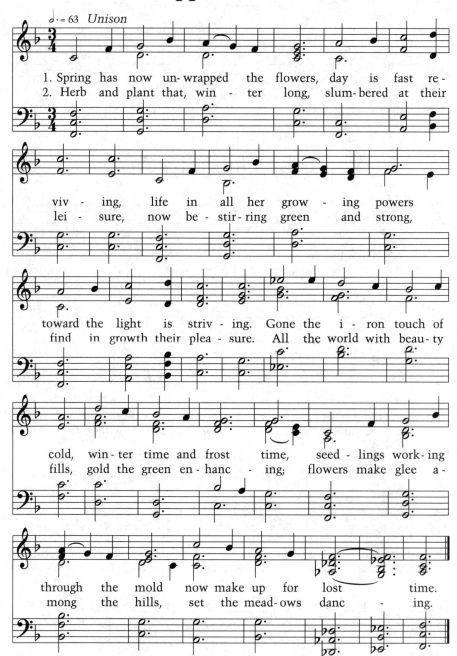

1. Spring has now un-wrapped the flowers, day is fast re-
viv - ing, life in all her grow - ing powers
toward the light is striv - ing. Gone the i - ron touch of
cold, win - ter time and frost time, seed - lings work-ing
through the mold now make up for lost time.

2. Herb and plant that, win - ter long, slum-bered at their
lei - sure, now be-stir-ring green and strong,
find in growth their plea - sure. All the world with beau-ty
fills, gold the green en-hanc - ing; flowers make glee a-
mong the hills, set the mead-ows danc - ing.

Words: Piae Cantiones, 1582
Music: Thomas Benjamin, 1940– , © 1992 Unitarian Universalist Association

BLACKBURN
7.6.7.6.D.

SPRING

Oh, Give Us Pleasure in the Flowers Today

64

1. Oh, give us pleasure in the flowers today; and give us not to think so far away as the uncertain harvest; keep us all simply in the springing of the year.

2. Oh, give us pleasure in the orchard white like nothing else by day, like ghosts by night; and make us happy in the happy bees, the swarm dilating round the perfect trees.

3. And make us happy in the darting bird that suddenly above the bees is heard, the meteor that thrusts in with needle bill, and off a blossom in mid air stands still.

4. For this is love and nothing else is love, the which it is reserved for God above to sanctify to what far ends he will, but which it only needs that we fulfill.

Words: Robert Frost, 1875–1963
Music: Cyril V. Taylor, b. 1907, © Hope Publishing Co.

COOLINGE
10.10.10.10.

SPRING

65 The Sweet June Days

1. The sweet June days are come a-gain; once more the glad earth yields its gold-en wealth of rip-'ning grain, and breath of clo-ver fields, and deep-'ning shade of sum-mer woods, and

2. The sweet June days are come a-gain; the birds are on the wing; bright an-thems, in their mer-ry strain, un-con-scious-ly they sing. Oh, how our cup o'er-brims with good these

Words: Samuel Longfellow, 1819–1892
Music: English melody, arr. by Ralph Vaughan Williams, 1872–1958,
used by perm. of Oxford University Press

FOREST GREEN
C.M.D.

SUMMER

glow of sum - mer air, and wing - ing thoughts and
hap - py sum - mer days; for all the joys of

hap - py moods of love and joy and prayer.
field and wood we lift our song of praise.

66
When the Summer Sun
Is Shining

1. When the sum-mer sun is shin-ing o-ver gold-en
2. When the sum-mer clouds of thun-der bring the long-a-
3. In the cool of sum-mer eve-ning, when the danc-ing

land and sea, and the flow-ers in the hedge-row
wait-ed rain, and the thirst-y soil is moist-ened
in-sects play, and in gar-den, street, and mead-ow

wel-come but-ter-fly and bee; then my o-pen
and the grass is green a-gain; then I long for
lin-ger ech-oes of the day; then my heart is

Words: Sydney Henry Knight, 1923–
Music: From *The Southern Harmony*, 1855, arr. by Margaret W. Mealy,
b. 1922, © 1984 Margaret W. Mealy

HOLY MANNA
8.7.8.7.D.

SUMMER

We Sing Now Together

♩ = 100

1. We sing now to-geth-er our song of thanks-giv-ing, re-
2. We sing of the free-doms which mar-tyrs and he-roes have
3. We sing of the proph-ets, the teach-ers, the dream-ers, de-
4. We sing of com-mu-ni-ty now in the mak-ing in

joic-ing in goods which the a-ges have wrought, for
won by their la-bor, their sor-row, their pain; the op-
sign-ers, cre-a-tors, and work-ers, and seers; our
ev-ery far con-ti-nent, re-gion, and land; with

Life that en-folds us, and helps and heals and holds us, and
press-ed be-friend-ing, our am-pler hopes de-fend-ing, their
own lives ex-pand-ing, our grat-i-tude com-mand-ing, their
those of all rac-es, all times and names and plac-es, we

leads be-yond the goals which our fore-bears once sought.
death be-comes a tri-umph, they died not in vain.
deeds have made im-mor-tal their days and their years.
pledge our-selves in cov-e-nant firm-ly to stand.

Words: Edwin T. Buehrer, 1894–1969, alt.
Music: Adrian Valerius's *Nederlandtsch Gedenckclanck*, 1626,
arr. by Edward Kremser, 1838–1914

KREMSER
12.11.13.12.

HARVEST AND THANKSGIVING

Come, Ye Thankful People 68

♩ = 126

1. Come, ye thank-ful peo-ple, come, raise a song of har-vest home:
2. All the world is but a field, giv-en for a fruit-ful yield;

fruit and crops are gath - ered in, safe be - fore the
wheat and tares to - geth - er sown, here for joy or

storms be - gin; God, our Mak - er, will pro - vide
sor - row grown: first the blade, and then the ear,

for our needs to be sup - plied; come to God's own
then the full corn shall ap - pear; God of har - vest,

tem - ple, come, raise a song of har - vest home.
grant that we whole - some grain and pure may be.

Words: Henry Alford, 1810–1871
Music: George Job Elvey, 1816–1893

ST. GEORGE'S WINDSOR
7.7.7.7.D.

HARVEST AND THANKSGIVING

Give Thanks

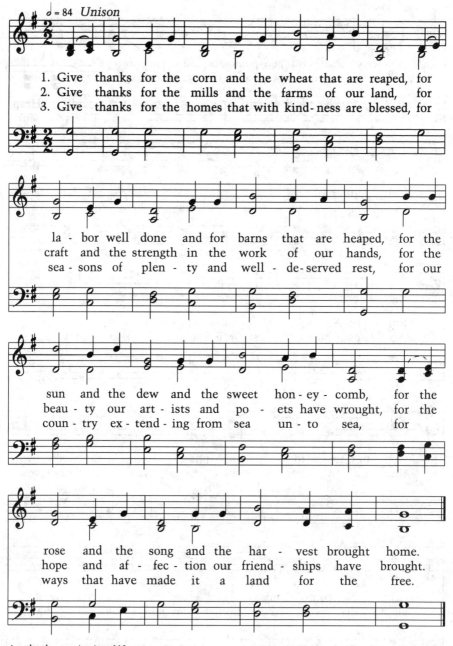

♩ = 84 *Unison*

1. Give thanks for the corn and the wheat that are reaped, for
2. Give thanks for the mills and the farms of our land, for
3. Give thanks for the homes that with kind-ness are blessed, for

la - bor well done and for barns that are heaped, for the
craft and the strength in the work of our hands, for the
sea - sons of plen - ty and well - de-served rest, for our

sun and the dew and the sweet hon - ey - comb, for the
beau - ty our art - ists and po - ets have wrought, for the
coun - try ex - tend - ing from sea un - to sea, for

rose and the song and the har - vest brought home.
hope and af - fec - tion our friend - ships have brought.
ways that have made it a land for the free.

Another harmonization, 112
Words: Anonymous, c. 1904, recast 1955, 1989
Music: William Caldwell's *Union Harmony*, 1837

FOUNDATION
11.11.12.12.

HARVEST AND THANKSGIVING

Heap High the Farmer's Wintry Hoard

♩· = 52

1. Heap high the farm - er's win - try hoard! Heap
2. Through vales of grass and meads of flowers our
3. We dropped the seed over hill and plain be -

high the gold - en corn! No rich - er gift has
plows their fur - rows made, while on the hills the
neath the sun of May, and fright - ened from our

au - tumn poured from out the lav - ish horn!
sun and showers of change - ful A - pril played.
sprout - ing grain the rob - ber crows a - way.

4. All through the long, bright days of June
   its leaves grew green and fair,
   and waved in hot mid-summer's noon
   its soft and yellow hair.

5. And now, with autumn's moonlit eyes,
   its harvest time has come,
   we pluck away the frosted leaves
   and bear the treasure home.

Words: John Greenleaf Whittier, 1807–1892
Music: American folk melody, arr. by Annabel Morris Buchanan, 1899–1983,
© 1938, renewed 1966 J. Fischer & Bros. Co.,
harm. by Charles H. Webb, 1933– , © 1989 J. Fischer & Bros. Co.

LAND OF REST
C.M.

HARVEST AND THANKSGIVING

71 In the Spring with Plow and Harrow

♩ = 116

1. In the spring, with plow and har - row,
2. Beau - ty adds to boun - ty's mea - sure
3. But earth's gar - den will not flou - rish

farm - ers worked in field and fur - row;
giv - ing free - ly for our plea - sure
if in greed we spoil and rav - ish

now we har - vest for to - mor - row.
sights and sounds and scents to trea - sure.
that which we should prize and cher - ish.

4. We must show a deeper caring,
   show compassion to the dying,
   cease from avarice and warring.

5. So may we at our thanksgiving
   give this pledge to all things living:
   that we will obey love's bidding.

Words: John Andrew Storey, 1935–1997
Music: David Dawson, 1939–

HEATON
8.8.8.

HARVEST AND THANKSGIVING

Has Summer Come Now, Dawning

1. Has sum-mer come now, dawn-ing a-midst the win-ter's
2. Al-read-y now the can-dles have blos-som'd on the
3. The old one now made youth-ful, just like a child at
4. In all our hearts is kin-dled a hearth-fire so sub-

snows? And shall we nest the ti - ny birds with-
tree to light the long-est win - ter night for
play, the bend-ing back now straight - en'd so
lime. Would that this yule-tide spir - it be

in the pine tree's boughs? And shall we nest the
all of us to see, to light the long - est
in our hearts we pray, the bend - ing back now
with us for all time. Would that this yule - tide

ti - ny birds with - in the pine tree's boughs?
win - ter night for all of us to see.
straight - en'd so in our hearts we pray.
spir - it be with us for all time.

Words: Finnish, English trans. by Jeanne Maki, 1943– , © 1984 Jeanne C. Maki
Music: German folk song, 1823

CHRISTMAS DAWN
7.6.8.6.8.6.

SOLSTICE AND EQUINOX

Chant for the Seasons

♩ = 80 *Unison*

Autumn: Sum - mer - time has turned the star - wheel,
Winter: Au - tumn cold has turned the star - wheel,
Spring: Win - ter rains have turned the star - wheel,
Summer: Ver - nal clouds have turned the star - wheel,

au - tumn is up - on us. Sweet the ang - ling
win - ter is up - on us. Grey the wind - y
spring-time is up - on us. Sharp the smell of
sum - mer is up - on us. Glid - ing are the

sun, sweet up-on the air the smell of blue mist ris - ing.
storms, cold up-on our cheeks the wet rain glist-ens, glist-ens.
loam, burst-ing in our eyes the tur - rets of the tu - lip.
hawks, hov - er-ing a - bove the hot and yel - low hill-side.

Sum - mer - time has turned the star-wheel, au - tumn is up -
Au - tumn cold has turned the star-wheel, win - ter is up -
Win - ter rains have turned the star-wheel, spring-time is up -
Ver - nal clouds have turned the star-wheel, sum - mer is up -

⊕ Words: Mark L. Belletini, 1949– , © 1992 Unitarian Universalist Association
  Music: Czech folk song, harmony © 1992 Unitarian Universalist Association   PRAHA
⊕ Arranged by Grace Lewis-McLaren, 1939–   Irregular

SOLSTICE AND EQUINOX

- on us. Glor - i - ous the trees, glor - i - ous the
- on us. Leap - ing is the fire, gold - en in the
- on us. Green - ing is the grass; soft up - on our
- on us. Crick - ets in the night, chirp - ing in our

sight of rust leaves fall - ing, fall - ing. Sum - mer - time has
glass the ci - der glows like am - ber. Au - tumn cold has
brows the sun - light warm car - ess - es. Win - ter rains have
ears the sound of moon - lit mu - sic. Ver - nal clouds have

turned the star - wheel, au - tumn is up - on us.
turned the star - wheel, win - ter is up - on us.
turned the star - wheel, spring - time is up - on us.
turned the star - wheel, sum - mer is up - on us.

SOLSTICE AND EQUINOX

74 On the Dusty Earth Drum

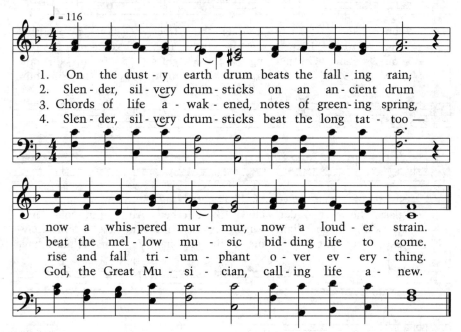

1. On the dust-y earth drum beats the fall-ing rain;
   now a whis-pered mur-mur, now a loud-er strain.
2. Slen-der, sil-very drum-sticks on an an-cient drum
   beat the mel-low mu-sic bid-ding life to come.
3. Chords of life a-wak-ened, notes of green-ing spring,
   rise and fall tri-um-phant o-ver ev-ery-thing.
4. Slen-der, sil-very drum-sticks beat the long tat-too —
   God, the Great Mu-si-cian, call-ing life a-new.

Words: Joseph S. Cotter, Jr., 1895–1919
Music: Friedrich Filitz, 1804–1860

WEM IN LEIDENSTAGEN
6.5.6.5.

75 The Harp at Nature's Advent

1. The harp at Na-ture's ad-vent strung has
2. The prayer is made, and praise is given, by
3. The green earth sends sweet in-cense up from

Words: John Greenleaf Whittier, 1807–1892
Music: Jane Manton Marshall, 1924– , © 1983 Jane Marshall

WALDEN
C.M.

THE WORLD OF NATURE

nev - er ceased to play; the song the stars of
all things near and far; the o - cean look - eth
man - y moun - tain shrines; from fold - ed leaf and

morn - ing sung has nev - er died a - way.
up to heaven and mir - rors ev - ery star.
dew - y cup now pours the sa - cred wine.

4. The blue sky is the temple's arch,
   its transept, earth and air;
   the music of its starry march,
   the chorus of a prayer.

5. So nature keeps the reverent frame
   with which all years begin;
   and nature's signs and voices shame
   the prayerless heart within.

76 For Flowers That Bloom about Our Feet

♩ = 108

1. For flowers that bloom a-bout our feet, for ten-der grass so
2. For blue of stream and blue of sky, for pleas-ant shade of
3. For this new morn-ing with its light, for rest and shel-ter

fresh and sweet, for song of bird and hum of bee, for
branch-es high, for fra-grant air and cool-ing breeze, for
of the night, for health and food, for love and friends, for

all things fair we hear or see:
beau-ty of the bloom-ing trees: Giv-er of all, we thank thee.
ev-ery-thing thy good-ness sends:

Words: Anonymous, c. 1904, alt.
Music: Severus Gastorius, c. 1675, adapt.

WAS GOTT THUT
8.8.8.8.8.7.

1. Seek not a - far for beau - ty; lo, it
2. Go not a - broad for hap - pi - ness; be -
3. In won - der - work - ings or some bush a -

glows in dew - wet grass - es all a - bout your
hold it is a flow - er bloom - ing at your
flame, we look for Truth and fan - cy it con -

feet, in birds, in sun - shine, child - ish fac - es
door. Bring love and laugh - ter home, and ev - er -
cealed; but in earth's com - mon things it stands re -

sweet, in stars and moun - tain sum - mits topped with snows.
more joy shall be yours as chang - ing years un - fold.
vealed, while grass and flowers and stars spell out the name.

Words: Minot Judson Savage, 1841–1918
Music: Cyril V. Taylor, b. 1907, © Hope Publishing Co.

COOLIDGE
10.10.10.10.

THE WORLD OF NATURE

78 Color and Fragrance

♩ = 76 *Unison*

1. Co - lor and fra - grance, ma - gi - cal rhy - thm,
2. O star - ry hea - vens, worlds of all splen - dor,
3. Hand full of peb - bles, high moun - tain pass - es,
4. Del - i - cate be - ings, lace - wing and spar - row

sweet chang - ing mu - sic will change us with them:
suns with - out num - ber, new life en - gen - der:
depths of the o - cean, dew on the grass - es:
in field and for - est, clo - ver and yar - row:

life with - in life, in - ner light gent - ly glow - ing,
wheel in a wheel with the light bright - ly glow - ing,
great things and small, with the light gent - ly glow - ing,
life greet - ing life with the light bright - ly glow - ing,

⊕ Words: Norbert F. Căpek, 1870–1942,
⊕ trans. by Paul and Anita Munk, © 1992 Unitarian Universalist Association,
⊕ English version by Grace Ulp, 1926–
⊕ Music: Norbert F. Căpek, 1870–1942

O BARVY VUNE
5.5.5.5.11.11.

THE WORLD OF NATURE

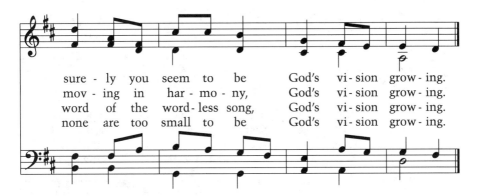

sure	-	ly	you	seem	to	be	God's	vi - sion grow - ing.
mov	-	ing	in	har - mo - ny,			God's	vi - sion grow - ing.
word	of	the	word - less song,				God's	vi - sion grow - ing.
none	are	too	small	to	be		God's	vi - sion grow - ing.

5. In human eyes burns the soul of living,
   illumines altars of loving giving:
   greeting, we meet, seeing light brightly glowing,
   share in a greater life, God's vision growing.

6. Shaper of all things, to us you've given
   our chance to keep here on earth, a heaven.
   Moving in harmony, light gently glowing,
   may we be, gratefully, God's vision growing.

79 No Number Tallies Nature Up

♩· = 40

1. No num - ber tal - lies na - ture up, no
2. It writes the past in char - ac - ters of
3. Must time and tide for - ev - er run, nor
4. Blend war and trade and creeds and song, let

tribe its house can fill; it is the shin - ing
rock and fire and scroll, the build - ing in the
winds sleep in the west? Will nev - er wheels which
rip - en race on race, the sun - burnt world that

fount of life and pours the del - uge still. And
cor - al sea, the plant - ing of the coal. And
whirl the sun and sat - el - lites have rest? Yet
we shall breed of all the count - less days. No

Words: Ralph Waldo Emerson, 1803–1882, rev.
Music: John W. Steffy's *The Valley Harmonist*, 1834, harmony by
Dale Grotenhuis, 1931– , © 1990 Dale Grotenhuis

RESIGNATION
C.M.D.

gath - ers   by   its frag - ile powers a - long the
thefts from   sat - el - lites and   rings and   bro - ken
whirl   the   glow - ing wheels once more, and mix   the
ray   is   dimmed, no   a - tom worn, the   old - est

cen - tu - ries from   race   on   race the   rar - est
stars   it   drew, and   out   of   spent and   ag - ed
bowl   a - gain; seethe, Fate,   the   an - cient el - e -
force   is   new,   and   fresh   the   rose   on   yon - der

flowers,   its   wreath shall noth - ing   miss.
things   it   formed the   world a - new.
ments, heat,   cold,   and peace, and   pain.
thorn   gives back   the heavens in   dew.

80   Wild Waves of Storm

1. Wild waves of storm, the won-der of the wind and crash-ing sea, na-ture in power and might and maj-es-ty, yet won-der more in deep tran-quil-li-ty, calm and still.

2. Mi-grat-ing birds, in flocks in-tent up-on far dis-tant shore great won-der hold; yet there is won-der more when lone-ly ea-gle, watch-ful on the tor, sits, calm and still.

3. All peo-ple one in ur-gent haste, on some great en-ter-prise, hearts beat-ing fast, great dreams to re-al-ize, yet in the soul a dream of rich-er prize, se-rene and still.

4. Then striv-ing cease: from trou-bled tur-moil seek an in-ward goal; tran-quil-li-ty shall make the spir-it whole. Be still, and know a Pres-ence in the soul, se-rene, a-live.

Words: Sydney Henry Knight, 1923–
Music: Libby Larsen, 1950– , © 1992 Unitarian Universalist Association

WILD WAVES
4.10.10.10.4.

THE WORLD OF NATURE

The Wordless Mountains Bravely Still

1. The word-less moun-tains brave-ly still, the ground be-low us firm and free, the gen-tle quilt of field and hill, shall grant us sol-id dig-ni-ty.

2. With breath-less wind through leaf-less trees, and gasp of cur-rents on the wing, our hearts soar high up-on the breeze of songs the spir-it longs to sing.

3. The crim-son flame of sum-mer sun, the glow of hearth on win-ter's eve, re-fin-ing fire shines through the One whose pas-sions lead us to be-lieve.

4. The slow and gracious ocean deep,
   and raindrops gathering one by one,
   feed well-springs in our souls to keep
   for times when tears like rivers run.

5. The earth and water, fire and air,
   the elements of wondrous grace,
   the glory of creation rare
   encircles us in its embrace.

Words: Philip A. Porter, 1953– , © 1991 Philip A. Porter
Music: Franz Joseph Haydn, 1732–1809

BROMLEY
L.M.

82 This Land of Bursting Sunrise

1. This land of burst-ing sun - rise, all lav - en - der and blue, its cloud-strewn, light-swept day skies flow, and ev - ery day re - new.

land of o - pen vis - tas, life root - ed deep and free, thy can - yoned plains, thy moun - tains vast, plumb earth's im - men - si - ty.

⊕ Words: John Haynes Holmes, 1879–1964,
⊕ adapt. by David Johnson, 1943–
   Music: David Hurd, 1950– , © 1984 G.I.A. Publications, Inc.

ANDUJAR
7.6.8.6.D.

THE WORLD OF NATURE

To east the glow of dawn - ing, to west the blaze of
Here in life's frag - ile bal - ance, the sun and stars a -

night, 'round all the long ho - ri - zon's rim, the
bove, find hand in hand, and heart to heart, the

1.
ev - er - last - ing light!
ev - er - last - ing

2.
2. This love.

83 Winds Be Still

1. Winds be still. Storm clouds pass and si-lence come.
2. Bird fly high. Lift our gaze toward dis-tant view.
3. Light shine in. Lu-mi-nate our in-ward view.

Peace grace this time with har-mo-ny.
Help us to sense life's mys-ter-y.
Help us to see with clar-i-ty.

Fly, bird of hope, and shine, light of love, and in
Fly high and far, and lead us each to see how we
Shine bright and true so we may join our songs in new

calm let all find tran - quil-li-ty.
move through the winds of e - ter-ni-ty.
sounds that be-come full sym-pho-ny.

Words: Richard S. Kimball, 1934– , © 1986 Tirik Productions
Music: Samuel Sebastian Wesley, 1810–1876

LEAD ME LORD
Irregular

MEDITATION AND MYSTICAL SONGS

♩ = 92 *Unison*

1. How far can reach a smile, how high
2. Is there a way to learn just how
3. For God pours out this love in all
4. If we then think our small a - mount

a help - ing hand can lift? How far is
a kind - ness speaks or where it goes? Should
that lives, through God we see that Life can
of help would not go far — and so don't

far e - nough to give?
love be caught to hold?
nev - er cease to give.
give, would we still live?

Words: Marjorie Jillson, © 1972 Carl Fischer, Inc.
Music: Heinz Werner Zimmermann, © 1972 Carl Fischer, Inc.

ZIMMERMANN
6.8.8.

MEDITATION AND MYSTICAL SONGS

85 Although This Life Is But a Wraith

♩ = 76

1. Al-though this life   is   but   a wraith,   al-though we
2. O - pen   my ears   to mu - sic, let   me thrill with
3. Ev - er   in - sur - gent let me be,   make me more
4. From com - pro - mise and things half - done, keep me, with

know   not what we   use,   al-though we grope with lit - tle
spring's first flutes and drums — but nev - er let   me dare for-
dar - ing than de - vout; from sleek con - tent - ment keep me
stern   and stub - born pride; and when, at last, the fight is

faith,   give   me the heart to fight and   lose.
get   the   bit - ter bal - lads of   the   slums.
free,   and   fill me with a buoy - ant doubt.
won,   O,   keep me still un - sat - is - fied.

Words: Louis Untermeyer, 1885–1977
Music: Vernon Griffiths, b. 1894, used by perm. of Faber Music, Ltd.

DUNEDIN
L.M.

Blessed Spirit of My Life

1. Bless-ed Spir-it of my life, give me strength through stress and strife; help me live with dig-ni-ty; let me know se-ren-i-ty. Fill me with a vis-ion, clear my mind of fear and con-fu-sion. When my thoughts flow rest-less-ly, let peace find a home in me.

2. Spir-it of great mys-ter-y, hear the still, small voice in me. Help me live my word-less creed as I com-fort those in need. Fill me with com-pas-sion, be the source of my in-tu-i-tion. Then, when life is done for me, let love be my leg-a-cy.

Words & music: Shelley Jackson Denham, 1950– ,
© 1987 Shelley Jackson Denham

PRAYER
7.7.7.7.6.9.7.7.

MEDITATION AND MYSTICAL SONGS

Nearer, My God, to Thee

♩ = 96

1. Near - er, my God, to thee, near - er to thee!
2. Though like the wan - der - er, the sun gone down,
3. There let the way ap - pear steps un - to heaven;

E'en though it be a cross that rais - eth me;
dark - ness be o - ver me, my rest a stone;
all that thou send - est me in mer - cy given;

still all my song shall be, near - er, my God, to thee,
yet in my dreams I'd be near - er, my God, to thee,
an - gels to beck - on me near - er, my God, to thee,

near - er, my God, to thee, near - er to thee!
near - er, my God, to thee, near - er to thee.
near - er, my God, to thee, near - er to thee.

⊕ Words: Sarah Flower Adams, 1805–1848
Music: Lowell Mason, 1792–1872

BETHANY
6.4.6.4.6.6.6.4.

MEDITATION AND MYSTICAL SONGS

4. Then, with my waking thoughts
bright with thy praise,
out of my stony griefs
Bethel I'll raise;
so by my woes to be
nearer, my God, to thee,
nearer, my God, to thee,
nearer to thee.

5. Or if on joyful wing
cleaving the sky,
sun, moon, and stars forgot,
upwards I fly,
still all my song shall be,
nearer, my God, to thee,
nearer, my God, to thee,
nearer to thee!

Calm Soul of All Things 88

1. Calm soul of all things, make it mine to feel, a-mid the cit-y's jar, that there a-bides a peace of thine I did not make, and can-not mar.

2. The will to nei-ther strive nor cry, the power to feel with oth-ers, give. Calm, calm me more; nor let me die be-fore I have be-gun to live.

Words: Matthew Arnold, 1822–1888
Music: Thomas Tallis, c. 1505–1585

TALLIS' CANON
L.M.

89 Come, My Way, My Truth, My Life

♩. = 56 *Unison*

1. Come, my way, my truth, my life: such a
2. Come, my light, my feast, my strength: such a
3. Come, my joy, my love, my heart: such a

way as gives us breath, such a truth as ends all
light as shows a feast, such a feast as mends in
joy as none can move, such a love as none can

strife, such a life as kill - eth death.
length, such a strength as makes a guest.
part, such a heart as joys in love.

Words: George Herbert, 1593–1633
Music: Ralph Vaughan Williams, 1872–1958, adapt.

THE CALL
7.7.7.7.

From All the Fret and Fever of the Day

♩ = 58

1. From all the fret and fe - ver of the
2. In qui - et - ness and sol - i - tude we

day, let there be mo - ments when we turn a -
find the sound - less wis - dom of the deep - er

way, and, deaf to all con - fus - ing out - er
mind; with clear har - mo - nious pur - pose let us

din, in - tent - ly lis - ten for the voice with - in.
then bring rich - er mean - ing to the world a - gain.

Words: Monroe Beardsley, b. 1915
Music: Cyril V. Taylor, b. 1907, © Hope Publishing Co.

COOLINGE
10.10.10.10.

MEDITATION AND MYSTICAL SONGS

91

Mother of All

1. Moth-er of all, in ev-ery age, in ev-ery
2. God-dess of nur-ture and of love, all na-ture
3. O spir-it of un-fold-ing grace and deep-est
4. Teach us to cher-ish this proud earth, its frag-ile

clime a - dored, by saint, by po - et,
sings your care. In life's ex - trav - a -
mys - ter - y, teach us com - pas - sion's
beau - ty praise, and for the dreams your

and by sage, your prais - es high have soared.
gance you prove the gift of giv - ing fair.
gen - tle face and wis - dom's mas - ter - y.
joy gives birth, a hope - ful fu - ture raise.

Words: v. 1, Alexander Pope, 1688–1744,
⊕ recast by Michael G. Young, vs. 2–4 by Michael G. Young, 1939– ,
© 1992 Unitarian Universalist Association
Music: Irish melody

ST. COLUMBA
8.7.8.7.

MEDITATION AND MYSTICAL SONGS

Mysterious Presence, Source of All

♩ = 126

1. Mys - te - rious Pres-ence, source of all — the world with-
2. Thou breath-est in the rush - ing wind, thy spir - it
3. Thy hand un - seen to ac - cents clear a - woke the
4. That touch di - vine a - gain im - part, still give the

out, the soul with - in — thou fount of life, O
stirs in leaf and flower; nor wilt thou from the
psalm - ist's trem - bling lyre, and touched the lips of
proph - et's burn - ing word; and vo - cal in each

hear our call, and pour thy liv - ing wa - ters in.
will - ing mind with - hold thy light and love and power.
ho - ly seer with flame from thine own al - tar fire.
wait - ing heart let liv - ing psalms of praise be heard.

Words: Seth Curtis Beach, 1837–1932
Music: William Knapp, 1698–1768

WAREHAM
L.M.

MEDITATION AND MYSTICAL SONGS

93   To Mercy, Pity, Peace, and Love

1. To Mercy, Pity, Peace, and Love all pray in their distress, and to those virtues of delight return their thankfulness, return their thankfulness.

2. For Mercy has a human heart, and Pity a human face; and Love, the human form divine, and Peace, the human dress, and Peace, the human dress.

3. Then every one, of every clime, that prays in deep distress, prays to the human form divine — Love, Mercy, Pity, Peace, Love, Mercy, Pity, Peace.

Words: William Blake, 1757–1827
Music: Nikolaus Herman, 1480–1561, harmony by J. S. Bach, 1685–1750

LOBT GOTT, IHR CHRISTEN
8.6.8.6.6.

MEDITATION AND MYSTICAL SONGS

What Is This Life

1. What is this life if, full of care, we have no time to stand and stare — no time to stand beneath the boughs and stare as long as sheep or cows;

2. No time to see, when woods we pass, where squir-rels hide their nuts in grass — no time to see, in broad day-light, streams full of stars, like stars at night;

3. No time to turn at Beau-ty's glance, and watch her feet, how they can dance. A poor life this if, full of care, we have no time to stand and stare.

Words: William Henry Davies, 1869–1941
Music: A. D. Carden's *Missouri Harmony*, 1820

DEVOTION
L.M.

95 There Is More Love Somewhere

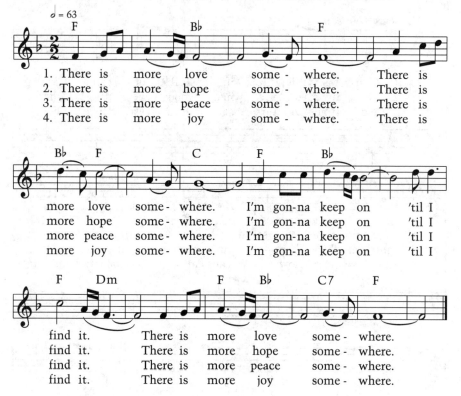

1. There is more love some - where. There is
2. There is more hope some - where. There is
3. There is more peace some - where. There is
4. There is more joy some - where. There is

more love some - where. I'm gon-na keep on 'til I
more hope some - where. I'm gon-na keep on 'til I
more peace some - where. I'm gon-na keep on 'til I
more joy some - where. I'm gon-na keep on 'til I

find it. There is more love some - where.
find it. There is more hope some - where.
find it. There is more peace some - where.
find it. There is more joy some - where.

Words & music: African American hymn

BIKO
6.6.9.6.

MEDITATION AND MYSTICAL SONGS

I Cannot Think
of Them as Dead

♩ = 100

1. I can-not think of them as dead who walk with me no
2. And still their si-lent min-is-try with-in my heart has
3. Their lives are made for-ev-er mine; what they to me have
4. Mine are they by an own-er-ship nor time nor death can

more; a-long the path of life I tread they
place as when on earth they walked with me and
been has left hence-forth its seal and sign en-
free; for God has given to love to keep its

are but gone be-fore, they are but gone be-fore.
met me face to face, and met me face to face.
grav-en deep with-in, en-grav-en deep with-in.
own e-ter-nal-ly, its own e-ter-nal-ly.

Words: Frederick Lucian Hosmer, 1840–1929
Music: W. Frederick Wooden, 1953– , © 1992 Unitarian Universalist Association

DISTANT BELOVED
8.6.8.6.6.

TRANSIENCE

97 Sometimes I Feel Like a Motherless Child

Words & music: African American spiritual, c. 1750–1875

WHEATLEY
10.10.10.5.5.

TRANSIENCE

long way from home, a long way from home.

Loveliest of Trees   98

♩. = 48 *Unison*

1. Love-liest of trees, the cher-ry now is hung with
2. Now of my three-score years and ten, twen-ty
3. And since to look at things in bloom fif-ty

bloom a - long the bough, and stands a - bout the
will not come a - gain, and take from sev'n - ty
springs are lit - tle room, a - bout the wood-lands

wood - land ride wear - ing white for Eas-ter-tide.
springs a score, leav - ing me just fif - ty more.
I will go, see-ing the cher-ry hung with snow.

Words: A. E. Housman, 1859–1936
Music: Medieval French melody, harmony by Carlton R. Young, 1926– ,
© 1989 United Methodist Publishing House

ORIENTIS PARTIBUS
8.7.8.7.

TRANSIENCE

Nobody Knows the Trouble I've Seen

♩ = 100

No-bod-y knows the trou-ble I've seen, no-bod-y knows my

sor-row. No-bod - y knows the trou - ble I've seen,

Fine

glo - ry, hal - le - lu - jah!

1. Some - times I'm up, some -
2. Al - though you see me
3. One day when I was

times I'm down, oh, yes, Lord! Some -
going 'long so, oh, yes, Lord! I
walk - ing 'long, oh, yes, Lord! The

D.C. al Fine

times I'm al - most to the ground, oh, yes, Lord!
have my trou - bles here be - low, oh, yes, Lord!
heav - ens broke and love came down, oh, yes, Lord!

Words & music: African American spiritual, c. 1750–1875

DUBOIS
Irregular with refrain

TRANSIENCE

1. I've got peace like a riv-er, I've got peace like a
2. I've got joy like a foun-tain, I've got joy like a
3. I've got love like an o-cean, I've got love like an
4. I've got pain like an ar-row, I've got pain like an

riv-er, I've got peace like a riv-er in my soul.
foun-tain, I've got joy like a foun-tain in my soul.
o-cean, I've got love like an o-cean in my soul.
ar-row, I've got pain like an ar-row in my soul.

I've got riv-er in my soul.
I've got foun-tain in my soul.
I've got o-cean in my soul.   (in my soul)
I've got ar-row in my soul.

5. I've got tears like the raindrops . . .   6. I've got strength like a mountain . . .

Words: vs. 1–3, Marvin V. Frey, 1918(?)–1992, © 1974 Marvin V. Frey,
vs. 4–6, Anonymous
Music: Marvin V. Frey, © 1974 Marvin V. Frey

WHITNEY
7.7.10.D.

TRANSIENCE

101 Abide with Me

1. A - bide with me, fast falls the e - ven - tide;
2. Swift to its close ebbs out life's lit - tle day;
3. I fear no foe, with thee at hand to bless;

the dark - ness deep - ens; still with me a - bide.
earth's joys grow dim, its glo - ries pass a - way;
ills have no weight, and tears no bit - ter - ness.

When oth - er help - ers fail, and com - forts flee,
change and de - cay in all a - round I see:
Where is death's sting? Where, grave, thy vic - to - ry?

help of the help - less, oh, a - bide with me.
O thou who chang - es not, a - bide with me.
I tri - umph still if thou a - bide with me.

Words: Henry Francis Lyte, 1793–1847
Music: William Henry Monk, 1823–1889

EVENTIDE
10.10.10.10.

TRANSIENCE

1. We the heirs of man-y a-ges, with the wise to
2. But the good we claim to cher-ish, all that Christ and
3. Cen-tu-ries of mor-al teach-ing, words of wis-dom,
4. Late in time, may we, for-sak-ing all our cru-el-

guide our ways, hon-or all earth's
Bud-dha taught, un-re-pen-tant
an-cient lore, all the proph-et
ty and scorn, see a new to-

seers and sag-es, build our tem-ples for their praise.
hearts let per-ish, spurn-ing truth most dear-ly bought.
souls' be-seech-ing leaves us heed-less as be-fore.
mor-row break-ing and a kind-er world be born.

Words: John Andrew Storey, 1935–1997
Music: I-to Loh, 1936– , © 1970 United Methodist Publishing House

BENG-LI
8.7.8.7.

EXEMPLARS AND PIONEERS

For All the Saints

♩ = 58

1. For all the saints who from their la-bors rest,
2. Thou wast their rock, their shel-ter, and their might;
4. And when the strife is fierce, the con-flict long,

who thee by faith be - fore the world con -
their strength and sol - ace in the well - fought
steals on the ear the dis - tant tri - umph -

fessed, thy name most ho - ly be for-ev - er
fight; thou, in the dark - ness deep their one true
song, and hearts are brave a - gain, and arms are

Words: William Walsham How, 1823–1897
Music: Ralph Vaughan Williams, 1872–1958, used by perm.
of Oxford University Press

SINE NOMINE
10.10.10. with Alleluias

EXEMPLARS AND PIONEERS

blest.
light. Al - le-lu - ia Al - le-lu - ia!
strong.

Harmony, Verse 3

3. O blest com - mu - nion of the saints di - vine! We live in

strug-gle, they in glo-ry shine; yet all are one in

Al - le-lu - ia!

thee, for all are thine. Al - le-lu - ia! Al - le-lu - ia!

When Israel Was
in Egypt's Land

♩ = 88

1. When Is - rael was in E - gypt's land,
2. The Lord told Mo - ses what to do, let my peo-ple
3. For you the cloud shall clear the way,
4. We need not al - ways weep and moan,

op - pressed so hard they could not stand,
go; to lead the tribe of Is - rael through,
a fire by night, a shade by day,
and wear these slav - 'ry chains for - lorn,

let my peo - ple go. Go down, Mo - ses,

Words & music: African American spiritual, c. 1750–1875
Music © 1947, 1974 Simon & Schuster, Inc. and Artist & Writers, Inc.,
renewed 1981 Simon & Schuster, Inc.

TUBMAN
8.5.8.5. with refrain

EXEMPLARS AND PIONEERS

way down in E - gypt land, tell old Pha - raoh, to let my peo - ple go.

105

From Age to Age

♩ = 92

1. From age to age how grand - ly rise the proph - et souls in line; a - bove the pass - ing
2. They wit - ness to one her - i - tage, one Spir - it's quick - 'ning breath, one wide - ning reign from
3. Their kin - dling power our souls con - fess; though dead they speak to - day: how great the cloud of
4. Through ev - ery race, in ev - ery clime, one song shall yet be heard: move on - ward in thy

⊕ Words: Frederick Lucian Hosmer, 1840–1929
⊕ Music: Thomas Benjamin, 1940– , © 1992 Unitarian Universalist Association

BENNINGTON
C.M. with repeat

EXEMPLARS AND PIONEERS

cen - tu - ries like bea - con lights they
age to age of free - dom and of
wit - ness - es en - com - pass - ing our
course sub - lime, O ev - er - last - ing

shine, like bea - con lights they shine.
faith, of free - dom and of faith.
way, en - com - pass - ing our way.
Word, O ev - er - last - ing Word.

106 Who Would True Valor See

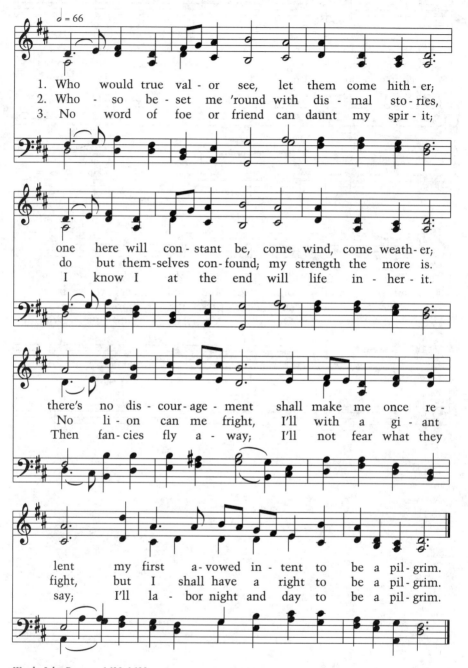

1. Who would true val-or see, let them come hith-er;
   one here will con-stant be, come wind, come weath-er;
   there's no dis-cour-age-ment shall make me once re-
   lent my first a-vowed in-tent to be a pil-grim.

2. Who-so be-set me 'round with dis-mal sto-ries,
   do but them-selves con-found; my strength the more is.
   No li-on can me fright, I'll with a gi-ant
   fight, but I shall have a right to be a pil-grim.

3. No word of foe or friend can daunt my spir-it;
   I know I at the end will life in-her-it.
   Then fan-cies fly a-way; I'll not fear what they
   say; I'll la-bor night and day to be a pil-grim.

Words: John Bunyan, 1628–1688
Music: English melody, arr. by Ralph Vaughan Williams, 1872–1958,
used by perm. of Oxford University Press

MONK'S GATE
6.5.6.5.6.6.6.5.

EXEMPLARS AND PIONEERS

Now Sing We of the Brave of Old

♩ = 116

1. Now sing we of the brave of old
2. Of those who fought a good - ly fight
3. Who, when no gleam did point the way,
4. Who long the world's old sor - rows bore

who would not sell them-selves for gold, yet left us
for lib - er - ty, for truth and right, their pa - tient
pressed ev - er on, by night, by day, and, spite of
and toiled and loved and suf - fered sore, and, be - ing

rich - es man - i - fold; Al - le - lu - ia!
love their chief - est might; Al - le - lu - ia!
pain, did ev - er say Al - le - lu - ia!
dead, live ev - er - more; Al - le - lu - ia!

Words: Albert M. P. Dawson, 1880–1963
Music: Giovanni Pierluigi da Palestrina, 1525–1594,
adapt. by W. H. Monk, 1823–1889

VICTORY
8.8.8. with Alleluia

EXEMPLARS AND PIONEERS

108　My Life Flows On in Endless Song

1. My life flows on in end-less song a-bove earth's la-men-ta-tion. I hear the real though far-off hymn that hails a new cre-a-tion. Through all the tu-mult and the strife I hear the mu-sic

2. What though the tem-pest 'round me roars, I know the truth, it liv-eth. What though the dark-ness 'round me close, songs in the night it giv-eth. No storm can shake my in-most calm while to that rock I'm

3. When ty-rants trem-ble as they hear the bells of free-dom ring-ing, when friends re-joice both far and near, how can I keep from sing-ing! To pris-on cell and dun-geon vile our thoughts to them are

Words: Traditional, Verse 3 by Doris Plenn
Music: Robert Lowry, 1826–1899

SINGING
8.7.8.7.D. Iambic

COMMITMENT AND ACTION

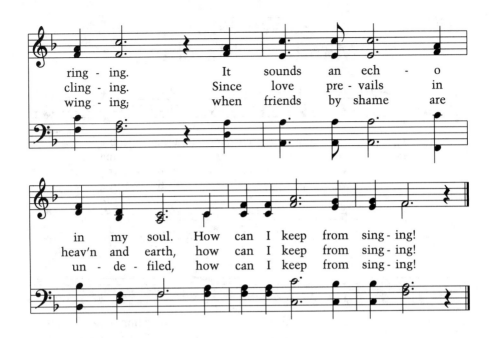

ring - ing.   It   sounds   an   ech - o
cling - ing.   Since   love   pre - vails   in
wing - ing;   when   friends   by   shame   are

in   my   soul. How   can   I   keep   from   sing - ing!
heav'n   and   earth, how   can   I   keep   from   sing - ing!
un - de - filed, how   can   I   keep   from   sing - ing!

109

As We Come
Marching, Marching

♩ = 108

1. As we come march-ing, march-ing, in the
2. As we come march-ing, march-ing, we
3. As we come march-ing, march-ing, un -
4. As we come march-ing, march-ing, we

beau - ty of the day, a mil - lion dark - ened
bat - tle too for men, for they are wom - en's
num - bered wom - en dead go cry - ing, through our
bring the great - er days: the ris - ing of the

kitch - ens, a thou - sand work - shops gray, are
chil - dren, and we moth - er them a - gain. Our
sing - ing, their an - cient song of bread! Small
wom - en means the ris - ing of the race. No

Words: James Oppenheim, 1882–1932, used by perm. of Hodgin Press
Music: Caroline Kohlsaat, used by perm. of Hodgin Press,
harmony by Betty A. Wylder, 1923–1994, © 1992 Unitarian Universalist
Association

BREAD AND ROSES
Irregular

COMMITMENT AND ACTION

touched with all the ra - diance that a
lives shall not be sweat - ed from
art and love and beau - ty their
more the drudge and i - dler, ten that

sud - den sun dis - clos - es: for the peo - ple hear us
birth un - til life clos - es: hearts starve as well as
drudg - ing spir - its knew: yes, it is bread we
toil where one re - pos - es, but a shar - ing of life's

sing - ing, "Bread and ro - ses, bread and ro - ses!"
bod - ies — give us bread, but give us ro - ses!
fight for, but we fight for ro - ses too!
glo - ries — bread and ro - ses, bread and ro - ses!

110 Come, Children of Tomorrow

1. Come, chil-dren of to-mor-row, come!
New glo-ry dawns up-on the world;
the war-ring ban-ners must be furled,
the earth be-come our com-mon home.

2. From plain and field and town there sound
the stir-ring ru-mors of the day;
old wrongs and bur-dens must make way
for all to tread the com-mon ground.

3. Di-vid-ed we have long with-stood
the love that is our com-mon speech.
The com-rade cry of each to each
is call-ing us to hu-man-hood.

Words: Zona Gale, 1874–1938
Music: Valentin Schumann's *Geistliche Lieder*, 1539,
harmony by Hans Leo Hassler, 1564–1612

VOM HIMMEL HOCH
L.M.

COMMITMENT AND ACTION

Life of Ages

♩ = 56

1. Life of a - ges, rich - ly poured, love of God,* un -
2. Nev - er was to cho - sen race that un - stint - ed
3. Breath - ing in the think - er's creed, puls - ing in the

spent and free, flow - ing in the
tide con - fined; yours is ev - ery
he - ro's blood, nerv - ing sim - plest

proph - et's word and the peo - ple's lib - er - ty —
time and place, foun - tain sweet of heart and mind.
thought and deed, fresh - en - ing time with truth and good,

4. Consecrating art and song,
   holy book and pilgrim way,
   quelling floods of tyrant wrong,
   widening freedom's sacred sway.

5. Life of ages, richly poured,
   love of God, unspent and free,
   flow still in the prophet's word
   and the people's liberty!

*or "love for all,"

Words: Samuel Johnson, 1822–1882
Music: Justin Heinrich Knecht, 1752–1817

VIENNA
7.7.7.7.

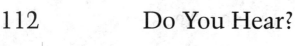
112   Do You Hear?

♩ = 84 *Unison*

1. Do you hear, oh my friend, in the
2. Through the roar, through the rush, through the
3. From the place where you stand to the

place where you stand, through the
throng, through the crush, do you
out - er - most strand, do you

sky, through the land, do you hear, do you hear? In the
hear in the hush of your soul, of your soul? Hear the
hear, oh my friend, do you hear, do you hear? All the

heights, on the plain, in the vale, on the main, in the
cry fear won't still, hear the heart's call to will, hear a
dreams, all the dares, all the sighs, all the prayers — they are

Another harmonization, 69

⊕ Words: Emily L. Thorn, 1915– , © 1992 Unitarian Universalist Association
Music: William Caldwell's *Union Harmony*, 1837,
harmony by Eugene Wilson Hancock, 1929– , © 1984 Eugene Hancock

FOUNDATION
6.6.6.6.D.

COMMITMENT AND ACTION

sun,   in the rain,   do you hear, do you hear?
sigh's star-tling trill   in your soul, in your soul?
yours, mine, and theirs— do you hear, do you hear?

Where Is Our Holy Church?   113

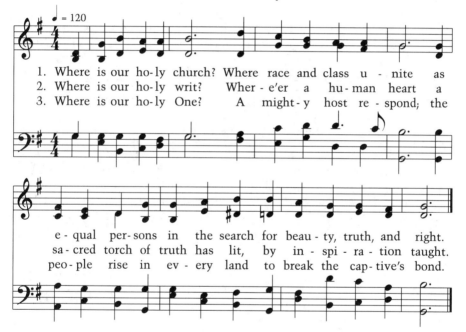

1. Where is our ho-ly church? Where race and class u - nite as
2. Where is our ho-ly writ?   Wher - e'er a   hu-man heart   a
3. Where is our ho-ly One?   A   might-y host re - spond; the

e - qual per-sons in   the search for beau - ty, truth, and   right.
sa - cred torch of truth has   lit,   by in - spi - ra - tion taught.
peo-ple rise in ev - ery land to break the cap-tive's bond.

4. Where is our holy land?
   Within the human soul,
   wherever free minds truly seek
   with character the goal.

5. Where is our paradise?
   In aspiration's sight,
   wherein we hope to see arise
   ten thousand years of right.

Words: Edwin Henry Wilson, 1898–1993, © 1992 Unitarian Univeralist Association
Music: Genevan psalter, 1551, adapt. by William Crotch, 1775–1847

ST. MICHAEL
S.M.

114 Forward through the Ages

1. For-ward through the a - ges, in un-bro-ken line,
   move the faith-ful spir - its at the call di - vine:
   gifts in dif-fering meas - ure, hearts of one ac - cord,
   man - i - fold the serv - ice, one the sure re - ward.

2. Wid - er grows the vi - sion, realm of love and light;
   for it we must la - bor, till our faith is sight.
   Proph - ets have pro-claimed it, mar - tyrs tes - ti - fied,
   po - ets sung its glo - ry, he - roes for it died.

3. Not a - lone we con - quer, not a - lone we fall;
   in each loss or tri - umph lose or tri - umph all.
   Bound by God's far pur - pose in one liv-ing whole,
   move we on to-geth - er to the shin-ing goal.

Words: Frederick Lucian Hosmer, 1840–1929
Music: Arthur Seymour Sullivan, 1842–1900

ST. GERTRUDE
6.5.6.5. Triple

COMMITMENT AND ACTION

For - ward through the a - ges, in un-bro-ken line,

move the faith - ful spir - its at the call di - vine.

115

God of Grace
and God of Glory

♩ = 112

1. God of grace and God of glo - ry, on thy peo - ple
2. Lo, the clouds of e - vil 'round us hide thy bright - ness
3. Cure thy chil- dren's war- ring mad- ness; bend our pride to
4. Fill us with a liv - ing vi - sion, heal our wounds that

pour thy power; crown thine an - cient church - 's sto - ry;
from our gaze; from the fears that long have bound us,
thy con - trol; shame our wan - ton, self - ish glad - ness,
we may be bound as one be - yond di - vi - sion

bring its bud to glo - rious flower. Grant us wis - dom,
free our hearts to faith and praise. Grant us wis - dom,
rich in things and poor in soul. Grant us wis - dom,
in the strug - gle to be free. Grant us wis - dom,

Words: Harry Emerson Fosdick, 1878–1969, alt.
Music: John Hughes, 1873–1932

CWM RHONDDA
8.7.8.7.4.4.7.7.

COMMITMENT AND ACTION

grant us cour - age, for the fac - ing of this hour,
grant us cour - age, for the liv - ing of these days,
grant us cour - age, make thy peace our dai - ly goal,
grant us cour - age, ears to hear and eyes to see,

for the fac - ing of this hour.
for the liv - ing of these days.
make thy peace our dai - ly goal.
ears to hear and eyes to see.

I'm On My Way

1. I'm on my way *I'm on my way* to the free-dom land.

to the free-dom land. I'm on my way *I'm on my way*

to the free-dom land. *to the free-dom land.*

Words & music: Traditional African American folk, c. 1750–1875,
arr. by Mary Allen Walden, 1946–1997, © 1992 Unitarian Universalist Association

ETHELRED
Irregular

I'm on my way
I'm on my way
to the free-dom land.
to the free-dom land.
I'm on my way,
I'm on my way
great
God, I'm on my way.
I'm on my way.

2. I asked my sister, come and go with me.
   I asked my sister, come and go with me.
   I asked my sister, come and go with me.
   I'm on my way, great God, I'm on my way.

3. I asked my brother, come and go with me.
   I asked my brother, come and go with me.
   I asked my brother, come and go with me.
   I'm on my way, great God, I'm on my way.

4. If they say no, I'll go anyhow.
   If they say no, I'll go anyhow.
   If they say no, I'll go anyhow.
   I'm on my way, great God, I'm on my way.

5. I'm on my way, and I won't turn back.
   I'm on my way, and I won't turn back.
   I'm on my way, and I won't turn back.
   I'm on my way, great God, I'm on my way.

117   O Light of Life

♩ = 92

1. O light of life that lives in us, help us to
2. O light of love, rain down on us, help us to
3. O love of life that lives in me, help me to
4. O light and life and love in us, help us to

turn a-way from war,   re-veal the hate that
heal our wound-ed world,   our dy-ing for-ests,
lift my head and sing,   let me know joy as
o-pen eyes and ears,   reach out and lis-ten,

lives in us, help us to live no more in
gut-ted plains, smol-der-ing cit-ies, wast-ed
well as pain, see beau-ty in the rain and
touch and love, that we may stand in strength and

fear.   Save us,   save our chil-dren.
fields.   Save us,   save our chil-dren.
wind.   Save me,   save my chil-dren.
peace.   Save us,   save our chil-dren.

Words: Emmon Bach, 1929– , © 1992 Unitarian Universalist Association
Music: Janet McLoud McGaughey, 1914–2000, © 1992 Unitarian Universalist Association

META
8.8.8.8.6.

COMMITMENT AND ACTION

This Little Light of Mine 118

1. This lit-tle light of mine, I'm gon-na let it shine.
2. Ev - 'ry - where I go, I'm gon-na let it shine.
3. Build - ing up a world, I'm gon-na let it shine.

Oh   Oh

This lit-tle light of mine, I'm gon-na let it shine.
Ev - 'ry - where I go, I'm gon-na let it shine.
Build - ing up a world, I'm gon-na let it shine.

Oh

This lit-tle light of mine, I'm gon-na let it shine. Let it
Ev - 'ry - where I go, I'm gon-na let it shine. Let it
Build - ing up a world, I'm gon-na let it shine. Let it

Oh

shine, let it shine, let it shine.
shine, let it shine, let it shine.
shine, let it shine, let it shine.

Words & music: African American spiritual, c. 1750–1875,
harmony by Horace Clarence Boyer, 1935–

LATTIMER
Irregular

Once to Every
Soul and Nation

♩ = 104

1. Once to ev-ery soul and na-tion comes the mo-ment
2. Though the cause of e-vil pros-per, yet 'tis truth a-

to de-cide, in the strife of truth with false-hood,
lone is strong; though its por-tion be the scaf-fold,

for the good or e-vil side: then to stand with
and up-on the throne be wrong. Then it is the

truth is no-ble, when we share its wretch-ed crust;
brave one choos-es, while the cow-ard stands a-side,

⊕ Words: James Russell Lowell, 1819–1891
Music: Thomas John Williams, 1869–1944

EBENEZER
8.7.8.7.D.

COMMITMENT AND ACTION

ere that cause bring fame and prof - it,
till the mul - ti - tude make vir - tue

and 'tis pros - perous to be just.
of the faith they have de - nied.

120 Turn Back

1. Turn back, turn back, for - swear thy fool - ish ways.
2. Earth might be fair, its peo - ple glad and wise.
3. Earth shall be fair, and all its peo - ple one;

Old now is earth, and none may count its days;
Age af - ter age our trag - ic em - pires rise,
nor till that hour shall God's whole will be done.

yet hu - man - kind, whose head is crowned with flame,
built while we dream, and in that dream - ing weep:
Now, e - ven now, once more from earth to sky,

still will not hear the in - ner God pro - claim —
would we but wake from out our haunt - ed sleep,
peals forth in joy that old un - daunt - ed cry —

Words: Clifford Bax, 1886–1962, used by perm. of The Peters Fraser &
Dunlop Group, Ltd.
Music: Genevan psalter, 1551

OLD 124TH
10.10.10.10.10.

COMMITMENT AND ACTION

"Turn back, turn back, for - swear thy fool - ish ways."
earth might be fair, and peo - ple glad and wise.
"Earth shall be fair, and all its peo - ple one."

121   We'll Build a Land

♩ = 120

1. We'll build a land where we bind up the bro - ken.
2. We'll build a land where we bring the good tid - ings to
3. We'll be a land build - ing up an - cient cit - ies,
4. Come, build a land where the man - tles of prais - es re -

We'll build a land where the cap - tives go free, where the
all the af - flict - ed and all those who mourn. And we'll
rais - ing up dev - as - ta - tions from old; re -
sound from spir - its once faint and once weak; where like

oil of glad - ness dis - solves all mourn - ing. Oh,
give them gar - lands in - stead of ash - es. Oh,
stor - ing ru - ins of gen - er - a - tions. Oh,
oaks of right - eous - ness stand her peo - ple. Oh,

Words: Barbara Zanotti (Isaiah/Amos), adapt.,
© 1979 Surtsey Publishing Co.
Music: Carolyn McDade, 1935– , © 1979 Surtsey Publishing Co.,
arr. by Betsy Jo Angebranndt, 1931– , © 1992 Unitarian
Universalist Association

CREATION OF PEACE
11.10.11.10. with refrain

COMMITMENT AND ACTION

we'll build a prom - ised land that can be.
we'll build a land where peace is born.
we'll build a land of peo - ple so bold.
come build the land, my peo - ple we seek.

Come build a land where sis - ters and broth - ers, a - noint - ed by

God, may then cre - ate peace: where jus - tice shall roll

down like wa - ters, and peace like an ev - er flow - ing stream.

122 Sound Over All Waters

♩ = 116

1. Sound o-ver all wa-ters, reach out from all lands the
2. Sing bri-dal of na-tions, with cho-rals of love! Sing
3. Sound trum-pets of tri-umph for march-es of peace, east,
4. Hark! Join-ing the cho-rus the heav-ens re-sound! The

cho-rus of voic-es, the clasp-ing of hands! Rise,
out the war vul-ture and sing in the dove! With
west, north, and south, let the long quar-rels cease! Sing
old day is end-ing, a new day is crowned! Rise,

hope of the a-ges, a-rise like the sun, all
glad ju-bi-la-tion sing hope for the world; the
songs of great joy that the an-gels be-gan, give
hope for the a-ges, a-rise like the sun, all

speech flow to mu-sic, all hearts beat as one!
great storm is end-ing, the clouds are all furled.
glo-ry to chil-dren, to wo-man and man!
speech flow to mu-sic, all hearts beat as one!

Words: John Greenleaf Whittier, 1807–1892, alt.
Music: Welsh melody from John Roberts's *Caniadau y Cyssegr*, 1839

ST. DENIO
11.11.11.11.

COMMITMENT AND ACTION

Spirit of Life

Spir - it of Life, come un - to me. Sing in my heart all the stir - rings of com - pas - sion. Blow in the wind, rise in the sea; move in the hand, giv - ing life the shape of jus - tice. Roots hold me close; wings set me free; Spir - it of Life, come to me, come to me.

Words & music: Carolyn McDade, 1935– , © 1981 Carolyn McDade, harmony by Grace Lewis-McLaren, 1939– , © 1992 Unitarian Universalist Association

SPIRIT OF LIFE
8.12.8.12.8.10.

LOVE AND COMPASSION

124 Be That Guide

♩ = 104

1. Be that guide whom love sus - tains. Rise a - bove the
2. Be that help - er noth - ing daunts — doubt of friend or
3. Be that build - er trust - ing good, bit - ter though the
4. Be that teach - er faith di - rects. Move be - yond the

dai - ly strife: lift on high the good you find.
taunt of foe. Ev - er strive for lib - er - ty.
test may be: through all a - ges they are right,
old fron - tier: though the fright - ened fear that faith,

Help to heal the hurts of life.
Show the path that life should go.
though they build in ag - o - ny.
be to - mor - row's pi - o - neer!

Words: Carl G. Seaburg, 1922–1998, © 1992 Unitarian Universalist Association
Music: Thomas Benjamin, 1940– , © 1992 Unitarian Universalist Association

WOODLAND
7.7.7.7.

LOVE AND COMPASSION

♩ = 80 *Unison*

1. From the crush of wealth and pow-er some-thing bro-ken in us all waits the spir-it's si-lent hour plead-ing with a poi-gnant call, bind all my wounds a - gain.

2. E - ven now our hearts are wa-ry of the friend we need so much. When I see the pain you car - ry, shall I, with a gen-tle touch, bind all your wounds a - gain?

3. When our love for one an-oth-er makes our bur-dens light to bear, find the sis-ter and the broth-er, hun-gry for the feast we share; bind all their wounds a - gain.

4. Ev - 'ry time our spir-its lan-guish ter-ri-fied to draw too near, may we know each oth-er's an-guish and, with love that casts out fear, bind all our wounds a - gain.

Words: Kendyl L. R. Gibbons, 1955– , © 1992 Unitarian Universalist Association
Music: Peter Cutts, 1937– , © 1969 Hope Publishing Co.

BRIDEGROOM
8.7.8.7.6.

LOVE AND COMPASSION

126   Come, Thou Fount of Every Blessing

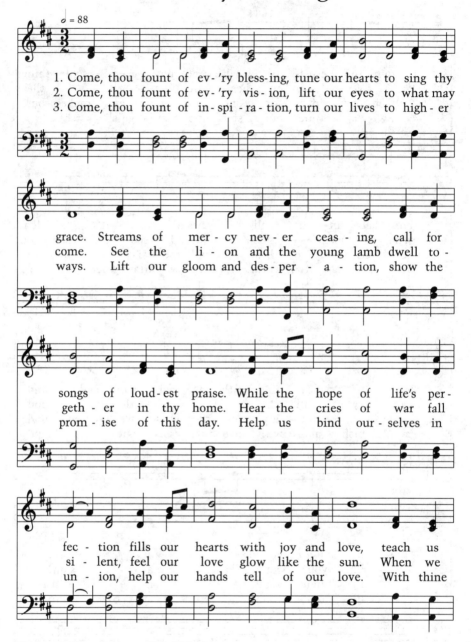

1. Come, thou fount of ev-'ry bless-ing, tune our hearts to sing thy
2. Come, thou fount of ev-'ry vis-ion, lift our eyes to what may
3. Come, thou fount of in-spi-ra-tion, turn our lives to high-er

grace. Streams of mer-cy nev-er ceas-ing, call for
come. See the li-on and the young lamb dwell to-
ways. Lift our gloom and des-per-a-tion, show the

songs of loud-est praise. While the hope of life's per-
geth-er in thy home. Hear the cries of war fall
prom-ise of this day. Help us bind our-selves in

fec-tion fills our hearts with joy and love, teach us
si-lent, feel our love glow like the sun. When we
un-ion, help our hands tell of our love. With thine

Words: v. 1, Robert Robinson, 1735–1790, adapt.,
⊕ vs. 2–3, Eugene B. Navias, 1928–
Music: John Wyeth, *Repository of Sacred Music, Part II*, 1813

NETTLETON
8.7.8.7.D.

LOVE AND COMPASSION

ev - er to be faith - ful, may we still thy good - ness prove.
all serve one an - oth - er, then our hea - ven is be - gun.
aid, O fount of jus - tice, earth be fair as heav'n a - bove.

Can I See Another's Woe?   127

♩ = 100

1. Can I see an - oth - er's woe, and not be in
2. Can I see a fall - ing tear, and not feel my
3. Can a moth - er sit and hear in - fant groan, an

sor - row too? Can I see an - oth - er's grief,
sor - row's share? Can a fa - ther see his child
in - fant fear? No, no, nev - er can it be!

and not seek for kind re - lief?
weep, nor be with sor - row filled?
Nev - er, nev - er can it be!

Words: William Blake, 1757–1827, arr.
Music: Melody based on "Veni Redemptor Gentium," *Enchiridion*,
Erfurt, 1524, harmony by Seth Calvisius, 1556–1615

NUN KOMM,
DER HEIDEN HEILAND
7.7.7.7.

LOVE AND COMPASSION

128   For All That Is Our Life

1. For all that is our life we sing our thanks and praise; for
2. For needs which oth-ers serve, for ser-vic-es we give, for
3. For sor-row we must bear, for fail-ures, pain, and loss, for
4. For all that is our life we sing our thanks and praise; for

all life is a gift which we are called to use to
work and its re-wards, for hours of rest and love; we
each new thing we learn, for fear-ful hours that pass: we
all life is a gift which we are called to use to

Words: Bruce Findlow, 1922–
Music: Patrick L. Rickey, 1964– , © 1992 Unitarian Universalist Association

SHERMAN ISLAND
6.6.6.6.6.6.

LOVE AND COMPASSION

build   the   com - mon good   and
come with praise and thanks for
come with praise and thanks for
build   the   com - mon good   and

make   our   own   days   glad.
all   that   is   our   life.
all   that   is   our   life.
make   our   own   days

glad.

129 Let Love Continue Long

1. Let love con-tin-ue long, and show to us the way, and if that love be strong, no hurt can have a say; and if that love re-main but strong, no hurt can ev-er have a say.

2. If love can-not be found, though com-mon faith pre-vails, when love does not a-bound, a com-mon faith will fail. When hu-man love does not a-bound, a com-mon faith will al-ways fail.

3. If we in love u-nite, de-bate can cause no strife: for with this love in sight, dis-putes en-rich our life. For with this bond of hu-man love, dis-putes can mean a rich-er life.

4. May love con-tin-ue long, and lead us on our way: for if that love be strong, no hurt can have a say. For if that love re-main but strong, no hurt can ev-er have a say.

Words: Berkley L. Moore
Music: John Ireland, 1879–1962, © 1924 John Ireland Trust

LOVE UNKNOWN
6.6.6.6.8.8.

LOVE AND COMPASSION

O Liberating Rose

1. O lib-er-at-ing Rose, that glows on rag-ged stem, your
beau-ty helps all hearts lose pow-er to con-demn. Your
buds are tight with proph-e-cy; your thorns, a tough-er
po-et-ry: you sign the whole and Gift of life.

2. O lib-er-at-ing Fire that calls for cleans-ing rage when-
ev-er hurt-ful lies dis-tort our pres-ent age. Your
danc-ing dreams our lib-er-ty to chal-lenge each in-
dig-ni-ty: you sign the whole and Faith of life.

3. O lib-er-at-ing Song whose ech-o now we sing, your
lyr-ic, swell-ing line re-kin-dles strength-en-ing. Your
har-mo-nies por-tray the time when seeds we sow shall
bloom sub-lime: you sign the whole and Hope of life.

4. O lib-er-at-ing Love, we hear you in a sigh; we
glimpse you when we see a wet or wea-ry eye; we
touch you when our hands ex-tend to soothe, or to embrace a friend: you sign the whole and Source of life.

⊕ Words: Mark L. Belletini, 1949– , © 1992 Unitarian Universalist Association
⊕ Music: Larry Phillips, 1948– , © 1984 Larry Phillips

INITIALS
6.6.6.6.8.8.8.8.

LOVE AND COMPASSION

131   Love Will Guide Us

Words: Sally Rogers, © 1985 Sally Rogers, used by perm. of
Thrushwood Press Publishing
Music: Traditional, arr. by Betty A. Wylder, 1923–1994
© 1992 Unitarian Universalist Association

OLYMPIA
L.M.

LOVE AND COMPASSION

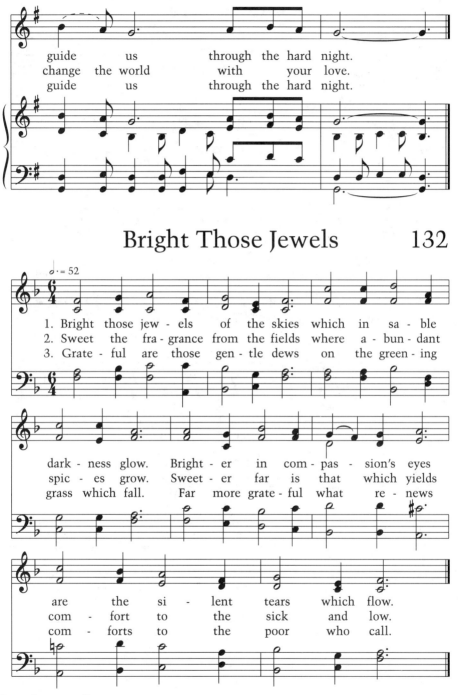

guide us through the hard night.
change the world with your love.
guide us through the hard night.

Bright Those Jewels   132

♩· = 52

1. Bright those jew - els of the skies which in sa - ble
2. Sweet the fra - grance from the fields where a - bun - dant
3. Grate - ful are those gen - tle dews on the green - ing

dark - ness glow. Bright - er in com - pas - sion's eyes
spic - es grow. Sweet - er far is that which yields
grass which fall. Far more grate - ful what re - news

are the si - lent tears which flow.
com - fort to the sick and low.
com - forts to the poor who call.

Words: Hosea Ballou II, 1796–1852
Music: Medieval French melody, harmony by Richard Redhead,
1820–1901

ORIENTIS PARTIBUS
7.7.7.7.

133 One World

♩ = 92 *Unison*

1. One world this, for all its sor-row; one world
2. World so ea-ger-ly ex-pect-ed, world so

shap-ing one to-mor-row; one hu-man-i-ty, though riv-en,
reck-less-ly re-ject-ed, one, as com-mon folk have willed it,

we, to whom a world is giv-en. From one
one, as cov-e-nants can build it: world of

world there is no turn-ing; for one
friend-ly ways and fac-es, cher-ished

Words: Vincent B. Silliman, 1894–1979, © 1955 American Ethical Union
Music: Dede Duson, 1938– , © 1992 Unitarian Universalist Association

SAVANNA
L.M.D.

LOVE AND COMPASSION

world the proph-et's yearn - ing.   One, the world of
arts and hon-ored rac - es,   one world, free in

po - ets, sag - es;   one world, goal   of all the a - ges.
word and sci - ence; peo - ple free,   its firm re - li - ance.

134   Our World Is One World

1. Our world is one world: what touches
2. Our world is one world: the thoughts we
3. Our world is one world: its ways of
4. Our world is one world, just like a

one affects us all: the seas that wash us
think affect us all: the way we build our
wealth affect us all: the way we spend, the
ship that bears us all: where fear and greed make

round about, the clouds that cover
at-ti-tudes, with love or hate, we
way we share, who are the rich or
man-y holes, but where our hearts can

us, the rains that fall.
make a bridge or wall.
poor, who stand or fall?
hear a dif-ferent call.

CHERNOBYL
5.8.8.6.4.

LOVE AND COMPASSION

How Happy Are They

1. How hap - py are they, born or taught, who do not
serve an - oth - er's will; whose ar - mor is their
hon - est thought, and sim - ple truth their high - est skill;

2. Whose pas - sions not their rul - ers are; whose souls are
still, and free from fear, not tied un - to the
world with care of pub - lic fame or pri - vate ear;

3. Who have their lives from ru - mors freed, whose con - science
is their strong re - treat, whose state no flat - ter -
y can feed, nor ru - in make op - pres - sors great.

4. All such are freed from ser - vile bands of hope to
rise, or fear to fall; they rule them - selves, but
rule not lands, and, hav - ing noth - ing, yet have all.

Words: Henry Wotton, 1568–1639, adapt.
Music: William Knapp, 1698–1768

WAREHAM
L.M.

LOVE AND COMPASSION

136 Where Gentle Tides Go Rolling By

1. Where gentle tides go rolling by along the salt sea strand, the colors blend and roll as one together in the sand. And often do the winds entwine to

2. Where road and wheat together rise among the common ground, the mare and stallion, light and dark, have thunder in their sound. The rainbow sign, the blended flood still

3. But we have come to plow the tides, the oat lies on the ground. I hear their fires in the field, they drive the stallion down. The roses bloom, both light and dark, the

Words: Richard Fariña, used by perm. of Hodgin Press
Music: Traditional Asian melody,
⊕ harmony by Betsy Jo Angebranndt, 1931– , © 1992 Unitarian Universalist Association

ASIA
C.M.D.

LOVE AND COMPASSION

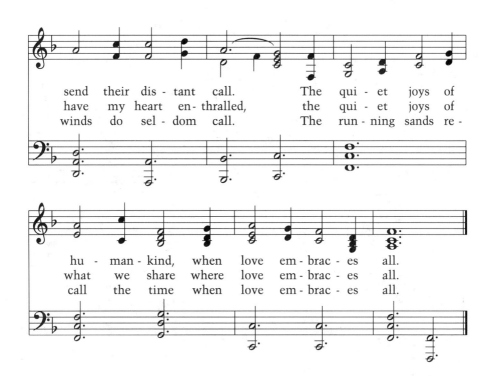

send their dis - tant call.   The qui - et   joys of
have my heart en- thralled,   the qui - et   joys of
winds do sel - dom call.   The run - ning sands re -

hu - man- kind, when love em - brac - es   all.
what we share where love em - brac - es   all.
call the time when love em - brac - es   all.

137   We Utter Our Cry

♩ = 40 *Unison*

1. We ut-ter our cry: that peace may pre-vail! That
2. We cry from the fright of our dai-ly scene for
3. We lift up our hearts for chil-dren un-born: give

earth will sur-vive and faith must not fail. We
strength to say "no" to all that is mean: de-
wis-dom, O God, that we may hand on, re-

pray with our life for the world in our care, for
signs bear-ing cha-os, ex-tinc-tion of life, all
plen-ished and tend-ed, this good plan-et earth, pre-

peo-ple di-min-ished by doubt and de-spair.
en-er-gy wast-ed on weap-ons of death.
serv-ing the fu-ture and won-der of birth.

Words: Fred Kaan, 1929– , © 1984 Hope Publishing Co.
Music: Peter Cutts, 1937– , © 1989 Hope Publishing Co.

UPPSALA
10.10.11.11.

These Things Shall Be 138

1. These things shall be: a loft - ier race than e'er the
2. Na - tion with na - tion, land with land, un - armed shall
3. High friend - ship, hith - er - to a sin, or by great
4. New arts shall bloom of loft - ier mold, and might - ier

world hath known shall rise, with flame of free - dom in their
live as com - rades free; in ev - ery mind and heart shall
po - ets half - di - vined, shall burn a stead - fast star with -
mu - sic thrill the skies, and ev - ery life a song shall

souls, and light of sci - ence in their eyes.
throb the pulse of one hu - man - i - ty.
in the calm, clear spir - it of the mind.
be when all the earth is par - a - dise.

Words: John Addington Symonds, 1840–1893
Music: Thomas Williams's *Psalmodia Evangelica*, 1789

TRURO
L.M.

139 Wonders Still the World Shall Witness

1. Won- ders still the world shall wit- ness nev- er known in
2. They shall rule with wing- ed free- dom worlds of health and
3. For a spir- it then shall move them we but vague- ly

days of old, nev- er dreamed by an- cient sag- es,
hu- man good, worlds of com- merce, worlds of sci- ence,
ap- pre- hend — aims mag- nif- i- cent and ho- ly,

how- so- ev- er free and bold. Sons and daugh- ters
all made one and un- der- stood. They shall know a
mak- ing joy and la- bor friend. Then shall bloom in

shall in- her- it won- drous arts to
world trans- fig- ured, which our eyes but
song and fra- grance har- mo- ny of

Words: Jacob Trapp, 1899–1992, © 1981 Jacob Trapp
Music: *Oude en nieuwe Hollantse Boerenlities en Contradanseu*, c. 1710

IN BABILONE
8.7.8.7.D.

IN TIME TO COME

us un - known,   when the dawn of
dim - ly see;   they shall make its
thought and deed,   fruits of peace and

peace its splen - dor o - ver all the world has thrown.
towns and wood- lands beau - ti - ful from sea to sea.
love and jus - tice — where to - day we plant the seed.

140 Hail the Glorious Golden City

1. Hail the glo - rious gold - en cit - y, pic - tured
2. We are build - ers of that cit - y. All our
3. And the work that we have build - ed, oft with

by the seers of old: ev - er - last - ing light shines
joys and all our groans help to rear its shin - ing
bleed - ing hands and tears, oft in er - ror, oft in

o'er it, won - drous things of it are told.
ram - parts; all our lives are build - ing - stones.
an - guish, will not per - ish with our years:

Wise and right - eous men and wom - en dwell with -
Wheth - er hum - ble or ex - alt - ed, all are
it will live and shine trans - fig - ured in the

Words: Felix Adler, 1851–1933
Music: Rowland Hugh Prichard, 1811–1887

HYFRYDOL
8.7.8.7.D.

IN TIME TO COME

- in its gleam - ing wall; wrong is ban - ished
called to task di - vine; all must aid a -
fi - nal reign of right: it will pass in -

from its bor - ders, jus - tice reigns su - preme o'er all.
like to car - ry for - ward one sub - lime de - sign.
to the splen - dors of the cit - y of the light.

141   I've Got a New Name

Words: Traditional
Music: African American spiritual, c. 1750–1875, arr. by Wendell Whalum, 1932–

NEW NAME
Irregular

IN TIME TO COME

mine,   it's mine,   it's mine, I de-clare, it's mine!
mine,   she's mine,   she's mine, I de-clare, she's mine!
mine,   he's mine,   he's mine, I de-clare, he's mine!
mine,   it's mine,   it's mine, I de-clare, it's mine!

mine, it's mine, it's mine, it's mine,

Let There Be Light   142

1. Let there be light,   let there be un-der-stand-ing,
2. O-pen our lips,   o-pen our minds to pon-der,
3. Per-ish the sword,   per-ish the an-gry judg-ment,
4. Let there be light,   o-pen our hearts to won-der,

let all the na-tions gath-er, let them be face to face.
o-pen the door of con-cord o-pen-ing in-to grace.
per-ish the bombs and hun-ger, per-ish the fight for gain.
per-ish the way of ter-ror, hal-low the world God made.

Words: Frances W. Davis, 1936–1976
Music: Robert J. B. Fleming, 1921–

CONCORD
4.7.7.6.

143 Not in Vain the Distance Beacons

1. Not in vain the dis-tance bea-cons. For-ward, for-ward let us range. Let the great world spin for-ev - er down the ring - ing grooves of change; through the shad - ow of the globe we

2. Oh, we see the cres-cent prom-ise of that spir - it has not set; an-cient founts of in-spi-ra - tion well through all our fan - cies yet; and we doubt not through the a - ges

3. Yea, we dip in - to the fut-ure, far as hu - man eye can see, see the vi - sion of the world, and all the won - der that shall be, hear the war - drum throb no long - er,

Words: Alfred Lord Tennyson, 1809–1892
Music: Ludwig van Beethoven, 1770–1827

HYMN TO JOY
8.7.8.7.D.

IN TIME TO COME

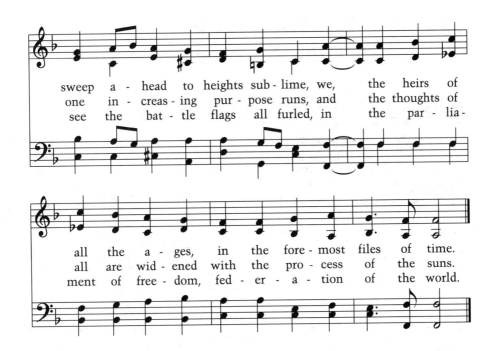

sweep a - head to heights sub - lime, we, the heirs of
one in - creas - ing pur - pose runs, and the thoughts of
see the bat - tle flags all furled, in the par - lia -

all the a - ges, in the fore - most files of time.
all are wid - ened with the pro - cess of the suns.
ment of free - dom, fed - er - a - tion of the world.

144

Now Is the
Time Approaching

♩ = 126

1. Now is the time ap-proach-ing, by proph-ets long fore-
2. Let all that now di-vides us re-move and pass a-
3. O long-ex-pect-ed dawn-ing, come with your cheer-ing

told, when all shall dwell to-geth-er, se-
way, like mists of ear-ly morn-ing be-
ray! Yet shall the prom-ise beck-on and

cure and man-i-fold. Let war be learned no
fore the blaze of day. Let all that now u-
lead us not a-stray. O sweet an-tic-i-

long-er, let strife and tu-mult cease, all
nites us more sweet and last-ing prove, a
pa-tion! It cheers the watch-ers on to

Words: Jane Laurie Borthwick, 1813–1897, recast
Music: George James Webb, 1803–1887

WEBB
7.6.7.6.D.

IN TIME TO COME

earth a bless-ed gar-den and God the god of peace.
clos-er bond of un-ion, in bless-ed lands of love.
pray, and hope, and la-bor, till all our work is done.

As Tranquil Streams 145

♩ = 108

1. As tran-quil streams that meet and merge and
2. Free from the bonds that bind the mind to
3. A free-dom that re-veres the past, but
4. Pro-phet-ic church, the fu-ture waits your

flow as one to seek the sea, our kin-dred hearts and
nar-row thought and life-less creed; free from a so-cial
trusts the dawn-ing fu-ture more; and bids the soul, in
lib-er-at-ing min-is-try; go for-ward in the

minds u-nite to build a church that shall be free —
code that fails to serve the cause of hu-man need:
search of truth, ad-ven-ture bold-ly and ex-plore.
power of love, pro-claim the truth that makes us free.

⊕ Words: Marion Franklin Ham, 1867–1956
Music: *Musicalisches Hand-buch*, Hamburg, 1690, adapt.

WINCHESTER NEW
L.M.

IN TIME TO COME

146   Soon the Day Will Arrive

♩ = 80 *Unison*

1. Soon the day will ar- rive when we will be to-
2. Some have dreamed, some have died to make a bright to-

geth- er, and no long- er will we live in fear.
mor- row, and our vi- sion re- mains in our hearts.

And the chil- dren will smile with- out won- der- ing
Now the torch must be passed with new hope, not in

wheth- er on that day thun- der- clouds will ap- pear.
sor- row, and a prom- ise to make a new start.

Words: Ehud Manor, 20th cent.
Music: Nurit Hirsch, 20th cent.

BASHANAH
6.7.9.D. with refrain

IN TIME TO COME

IN TIME TO COME

147 When All the Peoples on This Earth

♩ = 76

1. When all the peo - ples on this earth know deep in -
2. The choice to be the best we can be - gins the
3. The lights of Kwan - zaa now pro - claim that when we

side their pre-cious worth, when ev - ery sin - gle soul is
day we say, "I am." The u - ni - ty for which we
share our in - ner flame and nur- ture root and branch with

free, we'll earn the name Hu - man - i - ty.
sigh will nev - er come through hate or lie.
pride, we'll har - vest peace both far and wide.

Words: Anonymous

Music: Betsy Jo Angebranndt, 1931– , © 1992 Unitarian Universalist Association

CHRISTMAS HYMN
L.M.

KWANZAA

Let Freedom Span Both East and West

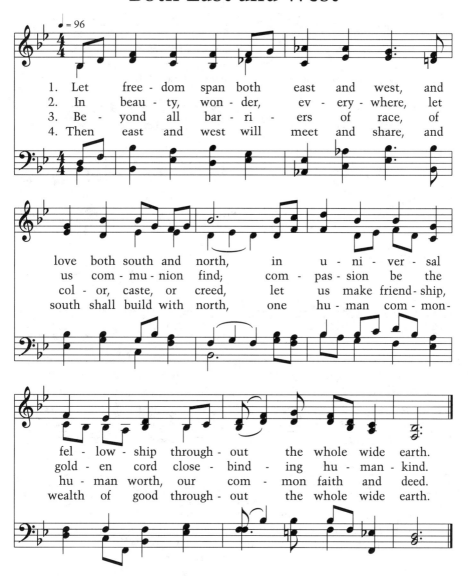

♩ = 96

1. Let free-dom span both east and west, and
2. In beau-ty, won-der, ev-ery-where, let
3. Be-yond all bar-ri-ers of race, of
4. Then east and west will meet and share, and

love both south and north, in u-ni-ver-sal
us com-mu-nion find; com-pas-sion be the
col-or, caste, or creed, let us make friend-ship,
south shall build with north, one hu-man com-mon-

fel-low-ship through-out the whole wide earth.
gold-en cord close-bind-ing hu-man-kind.
hu-man worth, our com-mon faith and deed.
wealth of good through-out the whole wide earth.

Words: Jacob Trapp, 1899–1992
Music: African American spiritual, c. 1750–1875, adapt. and harm.
by Harry T. Burleigh, 1866–1949

MCKEE
C.M.

FREEDOM

149   Lift Every Voice and Sing

1. Lift ev-ery voice and sing, till earth and heav-en
2. Ston-y the road we trod, bit-ter the chas-tening
3. God of our wea-ry years, God of our si-lent

ring, ring with the har-mo - nies of lib - er -
rod, felt in the days when hope un-born had
tears, thou who hast brought us thus far on the

ty; let our re-joic-ing rise high as the lis-tening
died; yet with a stead-y beat, have not our wea-ry
way; thou who hast by thy might led us in-to the

skies, let it re-sound loud as the roll - ing sea.
feet come to the place for which our fa - thers sighed?
light, keep us for-ev - er in the path, we pray.

Words: James Weldon Johnson, 1871–1938
Music: J. Rosamond Johnson, 1873–1954,
© 1921 Edward B. Marks Music Co., renewed

LIFT EVERY VOICE
Irregular

FREEDOM

Sing a song full of the faith that the dark past has
We have come o - ver a way that with tears has been
Lest our feet stray from the plac - es, our God, where we

taught us; sing a song full of the
wa - tered; we have come, tread - ing our
met thee; lest our hearts drunk with the

hope that the pres - ent has brought us; fac - ing the
path thru the blood of the slaugh - tered, out from the
wine of the world, we for - get thee; shad - owed be -

ris - ing sun of our new day be -
gloom - y past, till now we stand at
neath thy hand, may we for - ev - er

gun, let us march on till vic - to - ry is won.
last where the white gleam of our bright star is cast.
stand, true to our God, true to our na - tive land.

FREEDOM

150 All Whose Boast It Is

1. All whose boast it is that we come of fore-bears
brave and free, if there breathe on earth a slave,
are we tru - ly free and brave?
If we do not feel the chain

2. Is true free-dom but to break fet-ters for our
own dear sake, and with leath-ern hearts for - get
we owe hu - man - kind a debt?
No, true free - dom is to share

3. They are slaves who fear to speak for the fall - en
and the weak; they are slaves who will not choose
ha - tred, scoff - ing, and a - buse,
rath - er than in si - lence shrink

Words: James Russell Lowell, 1819–1891, alt.
Music: Jacob Hintze, 1622–1702, harmony by J. S. Bach, 1685–1750

SALZBURG
7.7.7.7.D.

FREEDOM

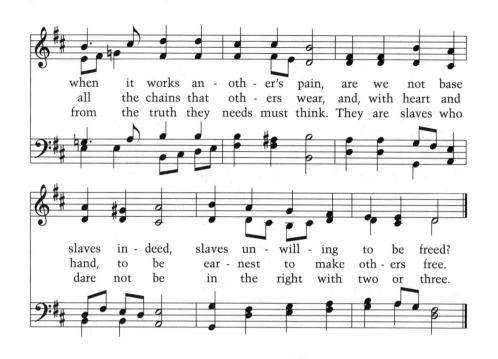

when   it   works an - oth - er's   pain,   are   we   not base
all   the chains that   oth - ers wear,   and, with heart and
from   the truth they needs must think. They are slaves who

slaves in - deed, slaves un - will - ing   to   be   freed?
hand,   to   be   ear - nest   to   make oth - ers   free.
dare   not be   in   the   right with two   or   three.

I Wish I Knew How   151

1. I   wish   I   knew   how   it   would   feel
2. I   wish   I   could share all the   love
3. I   wish   I   could give   all I'm   long -
4. I   wish   I   could be   like a   bird

Words & music: Billy Taylor and Dick Dallas,
arr. by Mary Allen Walden, 1946–1997, © 1992 Unitarian Universalist Association

MANDELA
11.11.11.6.6.6.6.

to be free.   I wish I could break
in my heart,   re - move all the bars
- ing to give.   I wish I could live
in the sky.   How sweet it would be

all these chains hold- ing me.   I
that still keep us a - part.   I
like I'm long - ing to live.   I
if I found I could fly.   I'd

wish I could say all the things I could say,
wish you could know what it means to be me,
wish I could do all the things I can do,
soar to the sun and look down at the sea,

FREEDOM

FREEDOM

152 Follow the Drinking Gourd

♩ = 112 *Unison*

Em A   Em   A

Fol-low   the drink-ing gourd,   fol-low   the

Em   G   D

drink-ing   gourd,   for the   old man is a-wait-ing for to

Fine

Em   Bm   Em   Bm   Em

car-ry you to free-dom,   fol-low the drink - ing   gourd.

Em7

1. When the sun comes back   and the first   quail calls,
2. Now the riv - er   bank makes a might-y good road,   the
3. Now the riv - er   ends   be - tween   two hills,

Many spirituals are code songs; this one is a map and timetable for the
Underground Railroad.
Words & music: African American traditional, c. 1750–1875

DRINKING GOURD
Irregular with refrain

153 Oh, I Woke Up This Morning

1. Oh, I woke up this morn-ing with my mind
2. I was walk-ing and talk-ing with my mind *and it was*
3. I was sing-ing and pray-ing with my mind
4. Oh, I woke up this morn-ing with my mind

stayed, stayed on free-dom. Woke up this morn-ing with my
stayed on free-dom. Walk-ing and talk-ing with my
stayed on free-dom. Sing-ing and pray-ing with my
stayed on free-dom. Woke up this morn-ing with my

mind   stayed on free-dom.
mind *and it was stayed,* stayed on free-dom.
mind   stayed on free-dom.
mind   stayed on free-dom.

Woke up this morn-ing with my mind   stayed on
Walk-ing and talk-ing with my mind *and it was stayed,* stayed on
Sing-ing and pray-ing with my mind   stayed on
Woke up this morn-ing with my mind   stayed on

Words & music: African American spiritual, c. 1750–1875

WATKINS HARPER
Irregular

FREEDOM

free-dom,
free-dom, Hal-le-lu, Hal-le-lu, Hal-le-lu - ia.
free-dom, *Hal-le-lu,* *Hal-le-lu,*
free-dom,

No More Auction Block for Me

154

♩ = 100

1. No more auc-tion block for me. No more, no more.
2. No more driv-er's lash for me. No more, no more.
3. No more peck of corn for me. No more, no more.
4. No more pint of salt for me. No more, no more.

No more auc-tion block for me, man-y thou-sand gone.
No more driv-er's lash for me, man-y thou-sand gone.
No more peck of corn for me, man-y thou-sand gone.
No more pint of salt for me, man-y thou-sand gone.

Words & music: African American spiritual, c. 1750–1875

AUCTION BLOCK
Irregular

FREEDOM

155 Circle 'Round for Freedom

Melody

Cir-cle 'round for free-dom, cir-cle 'round for peace, for
all of us im-pris-oned, cir-cle for re-lease,
cir-cle for the plan-et, cir-cle for each soul, for the

Melody line may be doubled by an instrument
Words & music: Linda Hirschhorn, 1947– , © 1985 Linda Hirschhorn

CIRCLE CHANT
Irregular

chil-dren of our chil-dren, keep the cir - cle whole.

chil-dren of our chil-dren, keep the cir - cle whole.

chil-dren of our chil-dren, keep the cir - cle whole.

156   Oh, Freedom

1. Oh, free-dom, oh, free-dom, oh, free-dom, o-ver me;
2. No more moan-ing, no more moan-ing, no more moan-ing, o-ver me;
3. There'll be sing-ing, there'll be sing-ing, there'll be sing-ing, o-ver me;

free-dom
moan-ing
sing-ing

and be-fore I'd be a slave, I'd be bur-ied in my grave, and go home to my God and be free.

Words & music: African American spiritual, c. 1750–1875,   ROSA
arr. by Horace Clarence Boyer, 1935– , © 1992 Unitarian Universalist Association   Irregular

FREEDOM

Step by Step
the Longest March

Step by step the long-est march can be won, can be won. Man-y stones can form an arch, sin-gly none, sin-gly none. And by un-ion, what we will can be ac-com-plished still; drops of wa-ter turn a mill, sin-gly none, sin-gly none.

Words: Anon.

Music: Irish folk song, adapt. and arr. by Waldemar Hille, 1908–1996,
© 1969 by Waldemar Hille

SOLIDARITY
7.6.7.6.D.

LABOR AND LEARNING

158   Praise the Source of Faith and Learning

♩ = 104

1. Praise the source of faith and learn-ing that has sparked and
2. Source of wis-dom, we ac-knowl-edge that our sci - ence
3. May our faith re-deem the blun - der of be - liev - ing
4. Praise for minds to probe the heav-ens, praise for strength to

stoked the mind   with   a   pas - sion   for   dis - cern - ing
and   our   art   and   the breadth of   hu - man knowl-edge
that   our thought has   dis - placed the grounds for   won - der
breathe the   air.   Praise   for   all   that   beau - ty   leav - ens,

how   the world has   been de - signed.   Let   the sense of
on - ly   par - tial   truth im - part.   Far   be - yond our
which   the   an - cient proph-ets   taught.   May   our learn - ing
praise   for   si - lence, mu - sic, prayer.   Praise   for   jus - tice

Words: Thomas H. Troeger, 1945– , © 1987 Thomas H. Troeger
Music: William Albright, 1944–1998, © 1992 Henmar Press, Inc. (C. F. Peters Corp.)
Tune commissioned by the First Unitarian Universalist Church of Ann Arbor,
Michigan, for their 125th Anniversary

PROCESSION
8.7.8.7.D.

won - der flow - ing   from   the won - ders   we   sur - vey
cal - cu - la - tion   lies   a   depth we   can - not   sound
curb the 'er - ror   which un - think - ing   faith can   breed
and com - pas - sion   and   for stran - gers, neigh-bors, friends.

keep our faith for - ev - er grow-ing and   re - new our need to pray.
where the pur - pose for cre - a - tion and the pulse of life are found.
lest we jus - ti - fy some ter - ror with   an an - ti - quat-ed creed.
Praise for hearts and lips to fash-ion praise for love that nev - er ends.

159 This Is My Song

1. This is my song, O God of all the na-tions,
2. My coun-try's skies are blu-er than the o-cean,

a song of peace for lands a-far and mine.
and sun-light beams on clo-ver-leaf and pine;

This is my home, the coun-try where my heart is;
but oth-er lands have sun-light too, and clo-ver,

here are my hopes, my dreams, my ho-ly shrine;
and skies are ev-ery-where as blue as mine.

but oth-er hearts in oth-er lands are beat-ing
O hear my song, thou God of all the na-tions,

Words: Lloyd Stone, 1912– , © 1934, 1962 Lorenz Publishing Co.
Music: Jean Sibelius, 1865–1957, arr. © 1933, renewed 1961 Presbyterian
Board of Christian Education

FINLANDIA
11.10.11.10.11.10.

PEACE

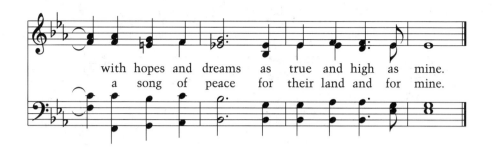

with hopes and dreams as true and high as mine.
a song of peace for their land and for mine.

Far Too Long, by Fear Divided 160

♩ = 108

1. Far too long, by fear di - vid - ed, we have set - tled
2. Now the na - tions are u - nit - ed, though as yet in
3. May, at last, we cease from war - ring, bar - ri - ers of

with the sword quar - rels which should be de - cid - ed
name a - lone, and the dis - tant goal is sight - ed
hate re - move, and, earth's rich - es free - ly shar - ing,

by the rec - on - cil - ing word.
which the proph - et souls have shown.
found the dy - nas - ty of love.

Words: John Andrew Storey, 1935–1997
Music: J. F. Naue's *Allgemeines Evangelisches Choralbuch*, 1829

LOBT DEN HERRN,
DIE MORGENSONNE
8.7.8.7.

PEACE

161   Peace! The Perfect Word

1. Peace! The per - fect word is sound-ing, like a
2. Toil - ing cen - tu - ries have strug- gled up - ward
3. All the old for - lorn lost caus - es, ev - ery
4. All the hopes of sub - ject peo - ples, all the

u - ni - ver - sal hymn un - der o - ceans,
on a ston - y way just to set the
fair for - bid - den dream, and the proph - et's
dreams of the op - pressed, must be ours, our

o - ver moun-tains, to the world's re - mot - est rim.
torch of free-dom where it flames a - loft to - day.
hope - less vi - sion, and the po - et's fit - ting gleam,
hopes, our vi - sions. We can nev - er stay or rest.

Another accompaniment, 213
Words: Odell Shepard, 1884–1967
Music: From *The Southern Harmony*, 1835, harmonized by Alastair
Cassels-Brown, 1927– , arr. © 1982 The Church Pension Fund

CHARLESTON
8.7.8.7.

PEACE

Gonna Lay Down My Sword and Shield 162

lay down my sword and shield, down by the riv-er-side,
lay down my bur - den, down by the riv-er-side,
shake hands a - round the world, ev - 'ry-where I roam,

down by the riv - er- side, down by the riv - er- side. Gon-na
down by the riv - er- side, down by the riv - er- side. Gon-na
ev - 'ry-where I roam, ev - 'ry-where I roam. Gon-na

Words and music: African American spiritual, c. 1750–1875,
arr. by Mary Allen Walden, 1946–1997
© 1992 Unitarian Universalist Association

DOWN BY THE
RIVERSIDE
Irregular

PEACE

PEACE

163 For the Earth Forever Turning

1. For the
2. For the
3. For the
4. For the

earth for - ev - er turn - ing; for the
moun - tains, hills, and pas - tures in their
sun, for rain and thun - der, for the
world we raise our voic - es, for the

skies, for ev - 'ry sea; for our
si - lent maj - es - ty; for the
sea - sons' har - mo - ny, for our
home that gives us birth; in our

Words: Kim Oler (et al. anon.), © 1990 Boosey & Hawkes, Inc.
Music: Kim Oler, © 1990 Boosey & Hawkes, Inc.
arr. by Nick Page, 1952– , and Jim Scott, 1946–

BLUE-GREEN HILLS OF EARTH
8.7.8.8.

PEACE

lives, for all we cher - ish, sing we our
stars, for all the heav - ens, sing we our
lives, for all cre - a - tion, sing we our
joy we sing re - turn - ing home to our

1.–3.   4.

joy - ful song of peace.
joy - ful song of peace.
joy - ful praise to Thee.
blue - green hills of earth.

PEACE

164 The Peace Not Past Our Understanding

♩ = 76 Unison

1. The peace not past our un-der-stand-ing falls like
2. Not schol-ar's calm, nor gift of church or state, nor
3. Days in-to years, the door-ways worn at sill, years

light up-on the soft white ta-ble-cloth at
ev-er-last-ing date of death's re-lease; but
in-to lives, the plans for long in-crease come

win-ter sup-per warm be-tween four walls, a
care-less noon, the hous-es light-ed late, har-
true at last for those of God's good will: these

thing too sim-ple to be tried as truth.
vest and hol-i-day: the peo-ple's peace.
are the things we mean by say-ing, Peace.

⊕ Words: John Holmes, 1904–1962
Music: Alfred Morton Smith, 1879–1971, © Church of the Ascension,
Atlantic City, New Jersey

SURSUM CORDA
10.10.10.10.

PEACE

When Windows That
Are Black and Cold

♩ = 69 *Unison*

1. When win-dows that are black and cold are lit a-
2. When wings pur-sue their prop-er flight and bring not
3. And when the sky is swept of wars and keeps but

new with fires of gold; when dusk in qui - et shall de-
ter - ror but de - light; when clouds are in - no-cent a-
gen - tle moon and stars, that peace-ful sky, that harm-less

scend and dark - ness come once more a friend;
gain and hide no storms of dead - ly rain;
air, how sweet, how sweet, the dark - ness there.

Words: Rachel Bates, used by perm. of Hutchinson, one of the publishers in the
Random Century Group
Music: English melody, © 1931 Oxford University Press, adapt. and harm.
by Ralph Vaughan Williams, 1872–1958

DANBY
L.M.

166 Years Are Coming

1. Years are com - ing, speed them on - ward when the
2. Years are com - ing when for - ev - er war's dread

sword shall gath - er rust, and the hel - met, lance, and
ban - ner shall be furled, and the an - gel Peace be

fal - chion sleep at last in si - lent dust.
wel - comed, re - gent of a hap - py world.

Earth has heard too long of bat - tle, heard the
Hail with song that glo - rious e - ra, when the

Words: Adin Ballou, 1803–1890
Music: Rowland Hugh Prichard, 1811–1887

HYFRYDOL
8.7.8.7.D.

PEACE

trum - pet's voice too long. But an - oth - er
sword shall gath - er rust, and the hel - met,

age ad - vanc - es, seers fore - told in an - cient song.
lance, and fal - chion sleep at last in si - lent dust.

Nothing but Peace Is Enough 167

Noth- ing but peace is e - nough for me.

Noth- ing but peace is e - nough, noth- ing but peace

is e - nough! Noth- ing but peace

is e - nough for me.

Words & music: Jim Scott, 1946– , © 1987 Jim Scott

NOTHING BUT PEACE
9.7.7.9.

PEACE

168 One More Step

♩·= 48 *Smoothly, Unison*

1. One more step, we will take one
2. One more word, we will say one
3. One more prayer, we will say one
4. One more song, we will sing one

more step, 'til there is peace for us and
more word, 'til ev-ery word is heard by
more prayer, 'til ev-ery prayer is shared by
more song, 'til ev-ery song is sung by

ev-ery-one, we'll take one more step.
ev-ery-one, we'll say one more word.
ev-ery-one, we'll say one more prayer.
ev-ery-one, we'll sing one more song.

⊕ Words & music: Joyce Poley, 1941– , © 1986 Joyce Poley,
⊕ harmony by Grace Lewis-McLaren, 1939– , © 1992 Unitarian Universalist
Association

ONE MORE STEP
Irregular

We Shall Overcome

1. We shall o - ver - come, we shall o - ver -
2. We'll walk hand in hand, we'll walk hand in
3. We shall all be free, we shall all be
4. We shall live in peace, we shall live in

come, we shall o - ver - come some - day!
hand, we'll walk hand in hand some - day!
free, we shall all be free some - day!
peace, we shall live in peace some - day!

Oh, deep in my heart I do be -
Oh, deep in my heart I do be -
Oh, deep in my heart I do be -
Oh, deep in my heart I do be -

lieve we shall o - ver - come some - day!
lieve we'll walk hand in hand some - day!
lieve we shall all be free some - day!
lieve we shall live in peace some - day!

Words & music: African American spiritual, c. 1750–1875,
adapt. by William Farley Smith, 1941–
Music adapt. © 1989 The United Methodist Publishing House

MARTIN
Irregular

JUSTICE

170

We Are a Gentle, Angry People

1. We are a gen - tle, an - gry peo - ple, and we are sing - ing, sing - ing for our lives.
2. We are a jus - tice - seek - ing peo - ple, and we are sing - ing, sing - ing for our lives.
3. We are young and old to - geth - er, and we are sing - ing, sing - ing for our lives.
4. We are a land of man - y col - ors, and we are sing - ing, sing - ing for our lives.

Words & music: Holly Near, 1944– , © 1979 Hereford Music,
arr. by Patrick L. Rickey, 1964– ,
arr. © 1992 Unitarian Universalist Association

SINGING FOR OUR LIVES
9.5.5.D.

We are a gen - tle, an - gry peo - ple, and we are
We are a jus - tice-seek-ing peo - ple, and we are
We are young and old to - geth - er, and we are
We are a land of man - y col - ors, and we are

sing - ing, sing - ing for our lives.
sing - ing, sing - ing for our lives.
sing - ing, sing - ing for our lives.
sing - ing, sing - ing for our lives.

5. We are gay and straight together,
   And we are singing, singing for our lives.
   We are gay and straight together,
   And we are singing, singing for our lives.

6. We are a gentle, loving people,
   And we are singing, singing for our lives.
   We are a gentle, loving people,
   And we are singing, singing for our lives.

N'kosi Sikelel' i Afrika

♩ = 88 Unison

(Zulu) N'ko-si, si-kel-el' i Af-ri-ka, mal-u-pha-ka-nyi-sw'u-
Bless, O God, our coun-try, Af-ri-ca, so that she may wak-en

phon-do lwa-yo. Yiz-wa i-mi-than-da-zo ye-thu.
from her sleep. Fill her horn with plen-ty, guide her feet.

N'ko-si si-kel-el-a. Thi-na lu-sa-pho lwa-yo.
Bless our moth-er Af-ri-ca. Bless our moth-er Af-ri-ca.

Wo-za mo-ya, (wo-za mo-ya,) wo-za mo-ya,
Spir-it de-scend, (spir-it, spir-it,) spir-it de-scend,

(wo-za mo-ya,) wo-za mo-ya o-wo-yi-ngcwe-le.
(spir-it, spir-it,) spir-it de-scend, spir-it de-scend.

Words & music: Enoch Sontongo, b. 1897

AFRIKA
Irregular

JUSTICE

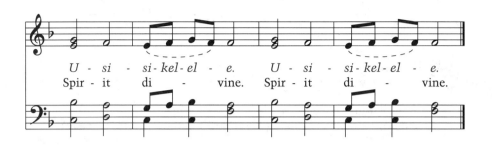

U - si - si - kel - el - e. U - si - si - kel - el - e.
Spir - it di - vine. Spir - it di - vine.

Siph' Amandla 172

♩ = 92

(Zulu) 1. Siph' a - man - dla N'ko - si. Wo - kung - e - sa - bi. Siph'
　　 1. O God, give us pow - er to rip down pris - ons. O
　　 2. O God, give us cour - age to with - stand ha - tred. O
　　 3. O God, give us pow - er and make us fear - less. O

a - man - dla N'ko - si. Si - ya - wa - ding - a.
God, give us pow - er to lift the peo - ple.
God, give us cour - age not to be bit - ter.
God, give us pow - er be - cause we need it.

Words & music: From South Africa, © 1984 Utryck, used by perm. of
Walton Music Corp.

TUTU
6.5.6.5.

173 In the Branches of the Forest

♩ = 88 *Unison*

1. In the branch-es of the for-est, in the
2. There's a blight up-on the moun-tain, there's a
3. In the thun-der new com-mand-ments sound a

pet-als of the mar-i-gold, on the shoul-der of the
sick-ness in the eve-ning sky, and we ask the age-old
warn-ing through the wil-der-ness, let the for-est be un-

moun-tain, in the vast-ness of the sea, you will
ques-tion: can we purge us of this sin? Can we
taint-ed, let the streams be un-de-filed, let the

find a brood-ing sad-ness o-ver all the an-cient
save the lit-tle nest-ling from the ven-om of the
wa-ters of the riv-er as they flow down to the

Words: David Arkin, used by perm. of Hodgin Press
Music: Waldemar Hille, 1908–1996

MOUNTAIN ALONE
8.9.8.7.D.

STEWARDSHIP OF THE EARTH

wa - ter - shed. You will see it writ-ten plain - ly on the
can- ker- worm? Can we clear the look of an - guish from the
o - cean be as sweet as in the old days when the

wind and in the sand.
soft eyes of the doe?
moun - tain stood a - lone.

174 O Earth, You Are Surpassing Fair

1. O earth, you are sur-pass-ing fair, from out your
store we're dai-ly fed, we breathe your life-sup-
port-ing air and drink the wa-ter that you
shed. Yet greed has made us mar your face,

2. Our grow-ing num-bers make de-mands that e'en your
boun-ty can-not meet; star-va-tion stalks through
hun-gry lands and some die hour-ly in the
street. The E-den-dream of long a-go

3. Has ev-o-lu-tion been in vain that life should
per-ish ere its prime? Or will we from our
greed re-frain and save our plan-et while there's
time? We must de-cide with-out de-lay

⊕ Words: John Andrew Storey, 1935–1997
Music: Joseph Parry, 1848–1918

MERTHYR TYDFIL
L.M.D.

STEWARDSHIP OF THE EARTH

pol-lute the air, make foul the sea: the fol-ly of the
is van-ish-ing be - fore our eyes; un - wise, un-heed-ing,
if we're to keep our race a - live: the choice is ours, and

hu - man race is bring - ing un - told mis-er - y.
still we go, de-stroy - ing hopes of par - a - dise.
we must say if we're to per - ish or sur- vive.

175 We Celebrate the Web of Life

1. We cel - e - brate the web of life, its
2. A frag - ment of the per - fect whole in
3. Of an - cient dreams we are the sum; our
4. Re - spect the wa - ter, land, and air which

mag - ni - tude we sing; for we can see di -
cac - tus and in quail, as much in ti - ny
bones link stone to star, and bind our fu - ture
gave all crea - tures birth; pro - tect the lives of

vin - i - ty in ev - ery liv - ing thing.
bar - na - cle as in the great blue whale.
worlds to come with worlds that were and are.
all that share the glo - ry of the earth.

Words: Alicia S. Carpenter, 1930– , © 1990 Alicia S. Carpenter
Music: Melchior Vulpius, c. 1560–1616

CHRISTUS DER IST MEIN LEBEN
C.M.

STEWARDSHIP OF THE EARTH

Daya Kar Daan Bhakti Ka   176

Da - ya ka - r daa - n bhak - ti ka, ha - me pa - ra -
ma - t - ma de - na. Da - ya ka - r na ha - na - ri
aa - t - ma me shu - ddh ta de - na.

Fine

1. Ha - na - re
2. Ba - ha - de
3. Ha - ma - ra

dhya - n me aa - o, pra - bhu aan khon me ba - s ja -
pre - m ki gan - ga, dil - o me pre - m ka sa
dhar - m ho se - va. Ha - ma - ra kar - m ho se -

o, an - dhe - re dil me aa ka - r ke, pa - ra - m jyo -
gar, ha - me aa - pas me mil - jul - kar, pra - bhu reh -
va, sa - da ee - ma - n ho se - va, va se - vak

D.S. al Fine

ti ja - ga de - na.
na si - kha de - na. Da - ya ka - r
char ba - na de - na.

Words: Hindu prayer
Music: Traditional Indian, arr. by Sanjeev Ramabhadran
This song, used by Indian Scouts and Guides, prays for a life of service,
harmony, and peace.

INDIAN PRAYER
8.8.8.8. with refrain

177 Sakura

♩ = 88

1. Sa - ku - ra,   sa - ku - ra,   ya - yo - i   no
1. Cher - ry blooms,   cher - ry blooms,   cher - ry blooms are
2. Cher - ry blooms,   cher - ry blooms,   all the world their

so - ra - wa.   Mi - wa - ta - su ka - gi - ri.
ev - 'ry - where,   like a cloud from out the sky!
beau - ty sees!   Yo - shin - o is cher - ry land;

Words: Japanese folk song, English words by Edwin Markham, 1852–1940
Music: Japanese folk song

SAKURA
6.7.7.7.7.6.6.

Ka - su - mi - ka ku - mo ka. Ni - o - i zo
Mists of blos - soms fill the air, cher - ries, cher - ries
tat - su - ta for ma - ple trees; ka - ra - sa - ki

i - zu - ru. I - za - ya, i - za - ya,
blos - som - ing! Come and see, come and see;
for the pine. Let us go, let us go —

Last time

mi - ni yu - ka - n.
let all now see and sing.
where pine trees green - ly shine.

⊕ Alternate text by William Wolff, b. 1909

1. Cherry blooms, cherry blooms,
pink profusion everywhere,
like a mist of gossamer rain
cherry blossoms fill the air,
covering Hiroshima's plain.
Come and see, spring is here,
it will not long remain.

2. Cherry blooms, cherry blooms,
when we die as we surely must,
why not under yonder tree?
And when we return to dust,
falling flowers our wreaths will be.
Come and see, come and see,
the fine Hiroshima tree.

178 Raghupati

♩ = 100 *Unison*

Ra-ghu-pa-ti, Ra-gha-va, Ra-ja Ram. Pa-ti-ta

Pa-ban, See-ta Ram.
1. See-ta Ram jai,
2. Ees-wa-ra Al-lah
3. See-ta Ram jai,

See-ta Ram. Pa-ti-ta Pa-ban, See-ta
te-re nam Sab-ko san-mo-ti de bhag
See-ta Ram. Pa-ti-ka Pa-ban See-ta

Refrain

Ram, See-ta Ram jai, See-ta Ram,
wan. Ees-wa-ra Al-lah te-re nam
Ram, See-ta Ram jai, See-ta Ram,

Words & music: Traditional Hindu hymn
This prayer song, which pleads for peace between Moslem and Hindu, was
used by Mahatma Gandhi at his daily prayer meetings.

RAM
Irregular

179 Words That We Hold Tight

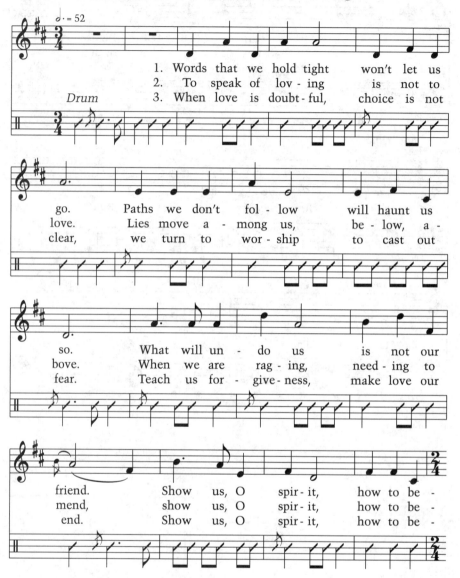

$\circ \cdot = 52$

Drum

1. Words that we hold tight won't let us
2. To speak of lov-ing is not to
3. When love is doubt-ful, choice is not

go. Paths we don't fol-low will haunt us
love. Lies move a-mong us, be-low, a-
clear, we turn to wor-ship to cast out

so. What will un-do us is not our
bove. When we are rag-ing, need-ing to
fear. Teach us for-give-ness, make love our

friend. Show us, O spir-it, how to be-
mend, show us, O spir-it, how to be-
end. Show us, O spir-it, how to be-

Words: Based on a text by Bishop Dr. Adedeji Ishola
Music: Traditional Yoruba tune

EKO A BA KO
9.9.9.9. with refrain

MUSIC OF THE CULTURES OF THE WORLD

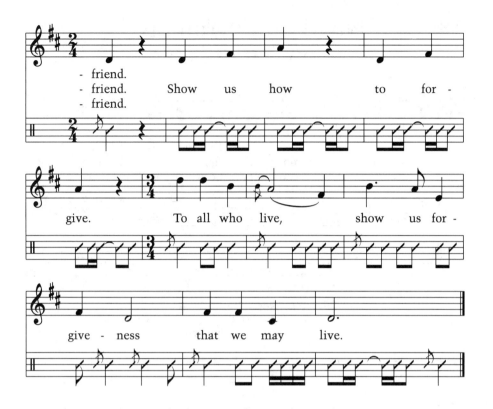

friend.
friend. Show us how to for -
friend.

give. To all who live, show us for -

give - ness that we may live.

Alhamdulillah 180

(Alleluia)

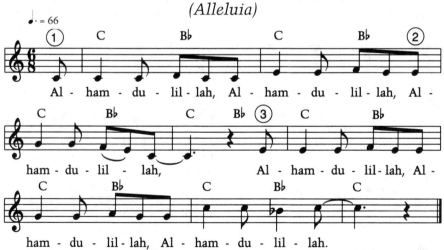

Al - ham - du - lil - lah, Al - ham - du - lil - lah, Al -

ham - du - lil - lah, Al - ham - du - lil - lah, Al -

ham - du - lil - lah, Al - ham - du - lil - lah.

Words & music: William Allaudin Mathieu, 1937– , © W. Allaudin Mathieu

MATHIEU
Irregular

MUSIC OF THE CULTURES OF THE WORLD

181 No Matter If You Live Now Far or Near

1. No mat-ter if you live now far or near, no matter what your weak-ness or your strength, there is not one a-live we count out-side. May deep-er joy for all now come at length, may deep-er joy for all now come at length.

2. Let none a-mong us lie or self-de-ceive; nor cul-ti-vate a ha-tred all or part, may nev-er one of us live by our rage nor wish an-oth-er in-ju-ry of heart, nor wish an-oth-er in-ju-ry of heart.

3. Just as the good-ly moth-er will pro-tect her child-ren, e'en at risk of her own life, so may we nur-ture an old mind-ful-ness, a bound-less heart be-yond all fear and strife, a bound-less heart be-yond all fear and strife.

Words: Sutta Nopata
Music: Old Indian song, harmony by Frédéric Mathil, 1950

INDIA
10.10.10.10.

WORDS FROM SACRED TRADITIONS

O, the Beauty in a Life

182

1. O, the beau-ty in a life that il - lu-mines hon - or a-
2. Let not ser - vice of the good be con -fined to great saints a-
3. O, the beau - ty of a life that il - lu-mines care of the

new, that mod - els wise and gra-cious ways to ev - ery
lone, but ev - ery hour be part of all our dai - ly
soul, that knows a love that is for self as well as

seek - er; that ev - ery day shall serve in
liv - ing. Set not the hope of wis - dom's
oth - ers, that ev - ery day em - bod - ies

joy and do the right. O, praise the
grace be - yond our ken; how wide the
praise for ev - ery good, this is the

life whose beau - ty shows a jus - tice true.
path, how close the goal, which love has shown.
faith to which we turn, our God and goal.

⊕ Words: Based on a text by Bishop Toribio Quimada
Music: Traditional Visayan (Filipino) folk tune

QUIMADA
Irregular

183 The Wind of Change Forever Blown

♩ = 96

1. The wind of change for - ev - er blown a - cross the tu - mult
2. For us the la - bor and the heat, the bro - ken se - crets
3. With fu - tile hands we seek to gain our in - ac - ces - si -
4. The end, e - lu - sive and a - far, still lures us with its

of our way, to - mor - row's un - born griefs de - pose the
of our pride, the stren - uous les - sons of de - feat, the
ble de - sire, di - vin - er sum - mits to at - tain, with
beck - 'ning flight, and our im - mor - tal mo - ments are a

sor - rows of our yes - ter - day. Dream yields to dream, strife
flower de - ferred, the fruit de - nied; but not the peace, su -
faith that sinks and feet that tire; but nought shall con - quer
ses - sion of the in - fi - nite. How shall we reach the

Words: Sarojini Naidu, 1879–1949
Music: Johann Hermann Schein, 1586–1630, harmony by
J. S. Bach, 1685–1750

MACH'S MIT MIR, GOTT
8.8.8.8.8.8.

WORDS FROM SACRED TRADITIONS

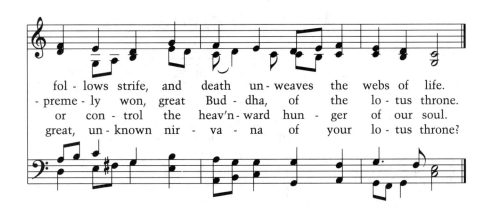

fol - lows strife, and death un - weaves the webs of life.
- preme - ly won, great Bud - dha, of the lo - tus throne.
or con - trol the heav'n - ward hun - ger of our soul.
great, un - known nir - va - na of your lo - tus throne?

Be Ye Lamps unto Yourselves   184

♩ = 66 *Unison*

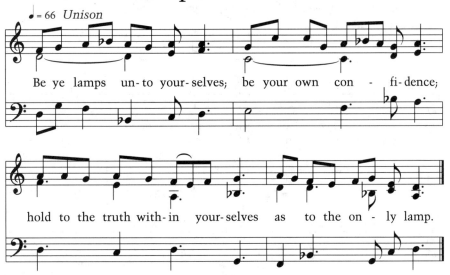

Be ye lamps un-to your-selves; be your own con - fi-dence;

hold to the truth with-in your-selves as to the on - ly lamp.

Words: Attributed to Gautama Buddha, 5th cent. B.C.E., tr. anon.
Music: From a melody in the *Sarum Antiphonal*

LUMINA
Irregular

185 Your Mercy, Oh Eternal One

1. Your mer-cy, Oh E-ter-nal one
2. I give the whole and not the part
3. And when in si-lent awe we wait,

by no heart mea-sured yet;
of all you gave to me;
and word and sign fore-bear,

in joy, or grief, or shade, or sun
my goods, my life, my soul, my heart
the hing-es of the gold-en gate

I nev-er will for-get.
I yield them all as free.
move sound-less at our prayer.

Words: Rabindranath Tagore, 1861–1941
Music: Scottish psalter, 1615, harmony by Thomas Ravenscroft, 1592–1635

DUNDEE
C.M.

Grieve Not Your Heart 186

♩ = 76 *Unison*

1. Grieve not your heart for want of place, nor
   yearn for ea-sy praise; but fit your-self some
   task to do, and well em-ploy your days.

2. From wise and fool-ish both a-like we
   should all try to learn, for one can show us
   how to live, the oth-er what to spurn.

3. Be fair to peo-ple when they err, when
   good, your plea-sure show; their faults be quick to
   un-der-stand, in judg-ing them be slow.

4. But this a-bove all else o-bey, it
   is the best of goals, what you would wish not
   done to you, do not to oth-er souls.

Words: Confucius, 551–479 B.C.E.,
recast by John Andrew Storey, 1935–1997
Music: From *Kentucky Harmony*, 1816

PRIMROSE
C.M.

187   It Sounds Along the Ages

1. It sounds a - long the a - ges, soul an - swer - ing to
2. From Si - nai's cliffs it ech - oed, it breathed from Bud - dha's
3. It calls — and lo, new jus - tice! It speaks — and lo, new

soul; it kin - dles on the pag - es of
tree, it charmed in Ath - ens' mar - ket, it
truth! In ev - er no - bler stat - ure and

ev - ery Bi - ble scroll; the psalm - ist heard and
hal - lowed Gal - i - lee; the ham - mer stroke of
un - ex - haust - ed youth. For - ev - er on re -

sang it, from mar - tyr lips it broke, and
Lu - ther, the Pil - grims' sea - side prayer, the
sound - ing, and know - ing nought of time, our

⊕ Words: William Channing Gannett, 1840–1923
Music: Melody of the Bohemian Brethren, *Hemlandssånger*, Rock Island,
Illinois, 1892, arr.

FAR OFF LANDS
7.6.7.6.D.

OUR COMMON GROUND

proph- et tongues out - rang it till sleep-ing na - tions woke.
or - a - cles of Con-cord one ho - ly word de - clare.
laws but catch the mu - sic of its e - ter - nal chime.

Come, Come, Whoever You Are   188

Come, come, who - ev - er you are, wan - der - er,
wor - ship- er, lov- er of leav - ing. Ours is no car - a - van
of de - spair. Come, yet a - gain come.

Words: Adapt. from Rumi, 1207–1273
✠ Music: Lynn Adair Ungar, 1963–

PILGRIMAGE
Irregular

189 Light of Ages and of Nations

$\circ = 56$

1. Light of a - ges and of na - tions, ev - ery race and
2. Rea - son's no - ble as - pi - ra - tion truth in grow - ing
3. Lo, that word a - bid - eth ev - er; rev - e - la - tion

ev - ery time has re - ceived thine in - spi - ra - tions,
clear - ness saw; con - science spoke its con - dem - na - tion,
is not sealed; an - swering now to our en - deav - or,

glimps - es of thy truth sub - lime. Al - ways spir - its
or pro - claimed e - ter - nal law. While thine in - ward
truth and right are still re - vealed. That which came to

in rapt vi - sion passed the heaven - ly
rev - e - la - tions told thy saints their
an - cient sag - es, Greek, Bar - bar - ian,

Another tune, 190

⊕ Words: Samuel Longfellow, 1819–1892

Music: *Oude en nieuwe Hollantse Boerenlities en Contradanseu*, c. 1710

IN BABILONE
8.7.8.7.D.

OUR COMMON GROUND

veil with - in,   al - ways hearts bowed
prayers were heard,   proph - ets   to   the
Ro - man,   Jew,   writ - ten   in   the

in con - tri - tion found sal - va - tion from their sin.
guilt - y na - tions spoke thine ev - er - last - ing word.
soul's deep pag - es, shines to - day, for - ev - er new.

190 Light of Ages and of Nations

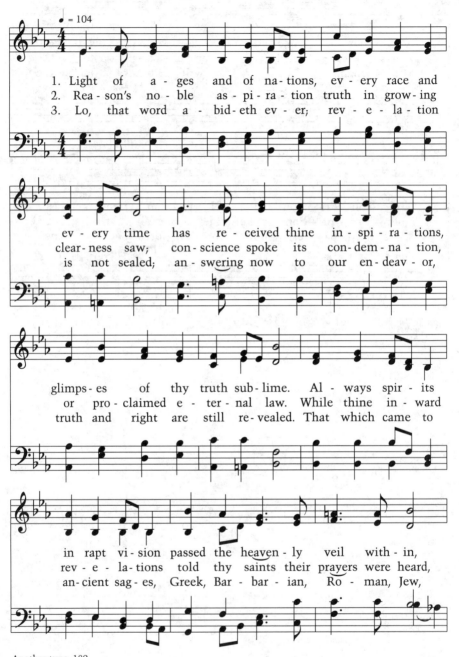

♩ = 104

1. Light of a - ges and of na - tions, ev - ery race and
2. Rea - son's no - ble as - pi - ra - tion truth in grow - ing
3. Lo, that word a - bid - eth ev - er; rev - e - la - tion

ev - ery time has re - ceived thine in - spi - ra - tions,
clear - ness saw; con - science spoke its con - dem - na - tion,
is not sealed; an - swering now to our en - deav - or,

glimps - es of thy truth sub - lime. Al - ways spir - its
or pro - claimed e - ter - nal law. While thine in - ward
truth and right are still re - vealed. That which came to

in rapt vi - sion passed the heaven - ly veil with - in,
rev - e - la - tions told thy saints their prayers were heard,
an - cient sag - es, Greek, Bar - bar - ian, Ro - man, Jew,

Another tune, 189
⊕ Words: Samuel Longfellow, 1819–1892
Music: Franz Joseph Haydn, 1732–1809

AUSTRIA
8.7.8.7.D.

OUR COMMON GROUND

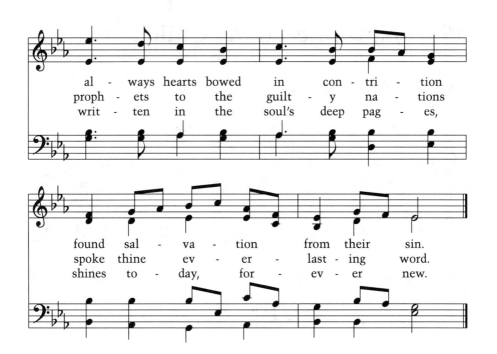

al - ways hearts bowed in con - tri - tion
proph - ets to the guilt - y na - tions
writ - ten in the soul's deep pag - es,

found sal - va - tion from their sin.
spoke thine ev - er - last - ing word.
shines to - day, for - ev - er new.

191   Now I Recall My Childhood

1. Now I re-call my child-hood when the sun burst
2. Then look-ing on the world with sim-ple joy, on
3. Now when I turn to think of com-ing death, I

to my bed-side with the day's sur-prise; faith
in-sects, birds, and beasts, and com-mon weeds, the
find life's song in star-songs of the night, in

in the mar-velous bloomed a-new each dawn, flowers
grass and clouds had full-est wealth of awe; my
rise of cur-tains and new morn-ing light, in

Words: Rabindranath Tagore, 1861–1941, recast, based on poem LXXI
in Tagore's *Crossing*
Music: Alfred Morton Smith, 1879–1971, © Church of the Ascension,
Atlantic City, New Jersey

SURSUM CORDA
10.10.10.10.

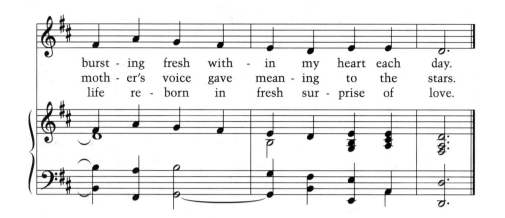

burst - ing fresh with - in my heart each day.
moth - er's voice gave mean - ing to the stars.
life re - born in fresh sur - prise of love.

192　Nay, Do Not Grieve

♩ = 72

1. Nay, do not grieve though life be full of sad-ness,
2. Nay, do not pine though life be marred with trou-ble,
3. Nay, do not weep; new hopes, new dreams, new fac-es,

dawn will not veil its splen-dor for your grief, nor
time will not pause or tar-ry on its way; to-
joy yet un-spent of all the un-born years, will

spring de - ny their bright ap-point-ed beau-ty
day that seems so long, so strange, so bit-ter,
prove your heart a trai - tor to its sor-row

to lo - tus blos-som and a - sho-ka leaf.
will soon be some for-got-ten yes-ter-day.
and make your eyes un-faith-ful to their tears.

Words: Sarojini Naidu, 1879–1949
Music: Libby Larsen, 1950– , © 1992 Unitarian Universalist Association

NAIDU
11.10.11.10.

Our Faith Is but a Single Gem 193

1. Our faith is but a single gem up-
2. Con - fu - cian wis - dom, Chris - tian care, the
3. From man - y lips, in ev - ery age, the
4. Be - side the no - blest of our race our

on a ro - sa - ry of beads; the thread of truth which
Bud - dhist way of self - con - trol, the Mus - lim's dai - ly
truth e - ter - nal is pro - claimed by West - ern saint, and
lives as yet can - not com - pare: may we at length their

runs through them sup - ports our var - ied hu - man needs.
call to prayer are prov - en path - ways to the goal.
East - ern sage, and all the good, how - ev - er named.
truth em - brace and in their sa - cred mis - sion share.

Words: John Andrew Storey, 1935–1997
Music: *The Southern Harmony*, 1835

DISTRESS
L.M.

194 Faith Is a Forest

♩ = 76 *Unison*

1. Faith is a for-est in which doubts play and hide;
2. Seeds of both meek and strong are scat-tered in air;
3. For-tune and fam-ine ride the swift winds of chance;

in-sight can hear the still small voice deep in-side.
dig-ni-ty shines un-dimmed by big-ot-ry's glare.
sor-row and plea-sure seem u-nit-ed in dance.

Web of Life, may this thread I weave
Web of Life, may this thread I weave
Web of Life, may this thread I weave

strength-en com-mit-ment to all I be-lieve.
help me bear wit-ness to all I be-lieve.
min-gle com-pas-sion with all I be-lieve.

✚ Words: Shelley Jackson Denham, 1950– , © 1992 Unitarian Universalist Association
Music: Chinese folk song, adapt. by I-to Loh, 1936– , © 1980 I-to Loh

MO-LI-HUA
Irregular

THE INTERDEPENDENT WEB

Vi - sion be my guide as I seek my way,
Jus - tice be my guide as I seek my way,
Mer - cy be my guide as I seek my way,

lead me in - to this ten - der day;
lead me in - to this ten - der day;
lead me in - to this ten - der day;

speak through me in all I do and say.
speak through me in all I do and say.
speak through me in all I do and say.

195 Let Us Wander Where We Will

1. Let us wan-der where we will, some-thing kin-dred
2. Dew and rain fall ev-ery-where, har-vests ri-pen,
3. And the live air, fanned with wings, bright with breeze and

greets us still: some-thing seen on
flow'rs are fair, and the whole round
sun - shine, brings in - to con - tact

vale or hill falls fa-mil-iar on the heart.
earth is bare to the sun-shine and the sun.
dis-tant things, and makes all the coun - tries one.

Words: Robert Louis Stevenson, 1850–1894
Music: Traditional Taiwanese melody, harmony by I-to Loh, 1936– ,
© 1983 The United Methodist Publishing House

TOA-SIA
7.7.7.7.

THE INTERDEPENDENT WEB

Singer of Life

1. Sing- er of Life, all flow-ers are songs, with pet- als do you write. Sing- er of Life, you col - or the earth, daz-zling the eye with birds red and bright. Joy is for us! The flow - ers are spread! Sing - ing is our de - light!

2. Mor- tal are we, with all liv-ing things, with ea-gles in the sky. E - ven all gold and jade will not last; sing-ing a-lone, I know, can-not die. Here in this house of spring-time be - stow songs that like birds can fly.

Words: From a Texcoco Nahuatl poem
Music: Native American melody, harmony by Richard Proulx, 1937– ,
© 1986 G.I.A. Publications, Inc.

LACQUIPARLE
Irregular

197 There Are Numerous Strings

Words & music: Rabindranath Tagore, 1861–1941
Harmony by Betsy Jo Angebranndt, 1931– ,
© 1992 Unitarian Universalist Association

TAGORE
Irregular

D.S.

heart will be one with your song. There are

2. A - midst your num - ber-less stars, let me

D.S.

place my own lit - tle lamp. There are 3. In the

dance of your fes - ti-val of lights my heart will

D.S.

throb and my life will be one with your smile. There are

God of Many Names

1. God of man - y names, gath - ered in - to One,
2. God of Jew - ish faith, Ex - o - dus and Law,
3. God of wound - ed hands, web and loom of love,

in your glo - ry come and meet us,

moving, end - less - ly be - com - ing: God of hov - ering wings,
joy of Mir - i - am and Mo - ses: God of Je - sus Christ,
Car - pen - ter of new cre - a - tion: God of man - y names

Words: Brian Wren, 1936– , © 1986 Hope Publishing Co.
Music: William P. Rowan, 1951– , © 1986 Hope Publishing Co.

MANY NAMES
5.5.8.8.D. with refrain

womb and birth of time, joy - ful - ly we sing your prais - es,
rab - bi of the poor, joy - ful - ly we sing your prais - es,
gath - ered in - to One, joy - ful - ly we sing your prais - es,

breath of life in ev - ery peo - ple,
cru - ci - fied, a - live for - ev - er, hush, hush, hal - le -
mov - ing, end - less - ly be - com - ing,

lu - ia, hal - le - lu - ia! Shout, shout, hal - le - lu - ia, hal - le - lu - ia!

Sing, sing, hal - le - lu - ia, hal - le - lu - ia! Sing God is love, God is love!

199 Precious Lord, Take My Hand

♩ = 72 *Unison*

Pre - cious Lord, take my hand, lead me on, let me stand, I am tired, I am weak, I am worn; through the storm, through the night, lead me on to the light, take my hand, pre - cious Lord, lead me home.

Words: Thomas A. Dorsey, 1899–1993
Music: Thomas A. Dorsey, 1899–1993, © copyright 1938 by Hill & Range
Songs, Inc., copyright renewed, all rights controlled by Unichappell Music,
Inc. (Rightsong Music, Publisher), international copyright secured, all rights
reserved, used by permission

PRECIOUS LORD
Irregular

1. When my way grows drear, pre-cious Lord, lin-ger
2. When the dark-ness ap-pears and the night draws

near, when my life is al-most gone, hear my
near, and the day is past and gone, at the

cry, hear my call, hold my hand lest I fall; take my
riv-er I stand, guide my feet, hold my hand; take my

hand, pre-cious Lord, lead me home.
hand, pre-cious Lord, lead me home.

200　　A Mighty Fortress

♩ = 92

1. A might-y for-tress is our God, a bul-wark nev-er fail - ing; our
2. God's word a-bove all earth - ly powers, no thanks to them, a - bid - eth; the

help-er sure a - mid the flood of mor - tal ills pre - vail - ing. For
spir- it and the gifts are ours, through God who with us sid - eth. Let

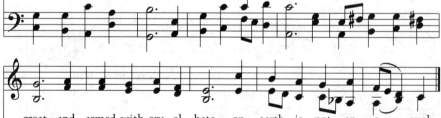

still our an - cient foe doth seek to work us woe; with craft and pow- er
goods and kin- dred go, this mor-tal life al - so; the bod - y they may

great; and, armed with cru - el hate, on earth is not an e - qual.
kill, God's truth a - bid-eth still; whose king-dom is for - ev - er.

Words: Martin Luther, 1483–1546,
⊕ trans. by Frederick Henry Hedge, 1805–1890
Music: Martin Luther, 1483–1546, harmony by J. S. Bach, 1685–1750

EIN' FESTE BURG
8.7.8.7.6.6.6.6.7.

Glory, Glory, Hallelujah! 201

1. Glo - ry, glo - ry, hal - le - lu - jah!
Since I laid my bur - den down.
Glo - ry, glo - ry, hal - le - lu - jah!
Since I laid my bur - den down.

2. Feel like shouting, "Hallelujah!" . . .

3. Life is sweeter, so much sweeter. . . .

4. Feel like dancing, hallelujah! . . .

5. Love is shining all around me, . . .

Words: Traditional

Music: Traditional, arr. by Mary Allen Walden, 1946–1997,
harmony © 1992 Unitarian Universalist Association

SOJOURNER
Irregular

202   Come Sunday

Oo   Oo   Come Sun-day, oh, come Sun-day, that's the day.   Lord, dear Lord a-bove, God Al-might-y, God of love,   please look down and see my peo-ple

Words & music: Duke Ellington, 1899–1974, © 1966, renewed G. Schirmer, Inc.

ELLINGTON
Irregular

203

All Creatures of
the Earth and Sky

1. All crea-tures of the earth and sky, come,
2. Swift rush-ing wind so wild and strong, white
3. Cool flow-ing wa-ter, pure and clear, make

kin-dred, lift your voic-es high, Al-le-lu-ia, Al-le-
clouds that sail in heav'n a-long, Al-le-lu-ia, Al-le-
mu-sic for all life to hear, Al-le-lu-ia, Al-le-

lu-ia! Bright burn-ing sun with gold-en beam, soft
lu-ia! Fair ris-ing morn in praise re-joice, high
lu-ia! Dance, flame of fire, so strong and bright, and

Words: Attributed to St. Francis of Assisi, 1182–1226, alt.
Music: From *Ausserlesene Catholische Kirchengesang*, 1623, adapt. and
harm. by Ralph Vaughan Williams, 1872–1958, music used by perm. of
Oxford University Press

LASST UNS ERFREUEN
8.8.4.4.8.8.
with Alleluias

WORSHIP

shin - ing moon with sil - ver gleam: Al - le -
stars of eve - ning find a voice: Al - le -
bless us with your warmth and light: Al - le -

lu - ia, Al - le - lu - ia, Al - le - lu - ia, Al - le -
lu - ia, Al - le - lu - ia, Al - le - lu - ia, Al - le -
lu - ia, Al - le - lu - ia, Al - le - lu - ia, Al - le -

lu - ia, Al - le - lu - ia!
lu - ia, Al - le - lu - ia!
lu - ia, Al - le - lu - ia!

4. Embracing earth, you, day by day,
   bring forth your blessings on our way,
   Alleluia, Alleluia!
   All herbs and fruits that richly grow,
   let them the glory also show:
   Alleluia, Alleluia, Alleluia, Alleluia,
   Alleluia!

5. All you of understanding heart,
   forgiving others, take your part,
   Alleluia, Alleluia!
   Let all things now the Holy bless,
   and worship God in humbleness:
   Alleluia, Alleluia, Alleluia, Alleluia,
   Alleluia!

WORSHIP

204   Come, O Sabbath Day

*or "rising"

Words: After Gustav Gottheil, 1827–1903
Music: A. W. Binder, 1895–1966

SABBATH
7.7.7.7. with refrain

Amazing Grace! 205

1. A - maz - ing grace! How sweet the sound that saved a wretch* like me! I once was lost but now am found, was blind but now I see.
2. 'Twas grace that taught my heart to fear, and grace my fears re - lieved; how pre - cious did that grace ap - pear the hour I first be - lieved!
3. Through man - y dan - gers, toils, and snares, I have al - read - y come; 'tis grace that brought me safe thus far, and grace will lead me home.
4. When we've been there ten thou - sand years, bright shin - ing as the sun, we've no less days to sing God's praise than when we'd first be - gun.

*or "soul"

Alternative accompaniment, 206
Words: John Newton, 1725–1807
Music: Columbian Harmony, 1829, harmony by Austin Cole Lovelace, 1919–,
© renewed 1992 Abingdon Press

AMAZING GRACE
C.M.

206 Amazing Grace!

Alternative accompaniment, ♩ = 80

A-maz - ing grace! How sweet the sound that saved a wretch* like

*or "soul"

Words: John Newton, 1725–1807
Music: Columbian Harmony, 1829, arr. and acc. by J. Jefferson Cleveland, 1937–1986,
© 1981 J. Jefferson Cleveland

AMAZING GRACE
C.M.

me! I once was lost but now am found, was blind but now I see.

(Verse 2, etc.)

207 Earth Was Given as a Garden

1. Earth was giv - en as a gar - den, cra - dle
2. Show to us a - gain the gar - den where all
3. Bless the earth and all your chil - dren, one cre -

for hu - man - i - ty; tree of life and tree of
life flows fresh and free. Gent - ly guide your sons and
a - tion: make us whole, in - ter - wo - ven, all con -

knowl - edge placed for our dis - cov - er - y.
daugh - ters in - to full ma - tu - ri - ty.
nect - ed, plan - et wide and in - most soul.

Here was home for all your crea - tures born of
Teach us how to trust each oth - er, how to
Ho - ly moth - er, life be - stow - ing, bid our

Words: Roberta Bard, 1940– , © 1992 Roberta Bard Ruby
Music: Rowland Hugh Prichard, 1811–1887

HYFRYDOL
8.7.8.7.D.

WORSHIP

land and sky and sea; all cre - at - ed
use for good our power, how to touch the
waste and war - fare cease. Fill us all with

in your im - age, all to live in har - mo - ny.
earth with rev - 'rence. Then once more will E - den flower.
grace o'er-flow - ing. Teach us how to live in peace.

208 Every Time I Feel the Spirit

♩ = 116

Ev - 'ry time I feel the Spir - it mov - ing

in my heart, I will pray. Yes, ev - 'ry time I feel the

Fine

Spir - it mov - ing in my heart, I will pray.

1. Up - on the moun - tain, my God spoke, o'er the
2. The Riv - er Jor - dan runs right cold, chills the

Words: African American spiritual, c. 1750–1875
Music: African American spiritual, adapt. and arr. by William Farley Smith,
1941– , © 1989 The United Methodist Publishing House

PENTECOST
Irregular

mount came fire and smoke. All a - round me looks so
bod - y, not the soul. Ain't but one train on this

D.C. al Fine

shine, ask my God if all was mine.
track, runs to heav - en and right back.

O Come, You
Longing Thirsty Souls

♩ = 120

1. O come, you long-ing thirst-y souls, drink
2. For as the rain and snow a-bove fall
3. For we shall go in peace se-cure and

free-ly from the spring. And come, you wea-ry,
not in van-i-ty, but for this pur-pose
leave in joy sub-lime! The hills out-side will

fam-ished folk, and end your hun-ger-ing. Why
wa-ter earth: to feed hu-man-i-ty. So
burst with song, the trees will clap in time! No

Words: Isaiah 55, metrical version
Music: English melody, harmony by Ralph Vaughan Williams, 1872–1958,
used by perm. of Oxford University Press

FOREST GREEN
C.M.D.

spend your - self on emp - ty air? Why
shall the word of spir - it serve as
more shall thorns and net - tles grow! The

not be sat - is - fied? For ev - ery - where a
seed with - in our loam, that we may bear so
bay tree and the pine shall sign for us th'e -

feast is spread that's al - ways at our side.
rich a yield as brings the har - vest home.
ter - nal Name that makes the world a shrine.

210 Wade in the Water

♩ = 63 Unison

Wade in the wa-ter, wade in the
wa-ter, chil-dren, wade in the wa-ter,

Fine

God's gon-na trou-ble the wa-ter.

1. See that band all dressed in white.
2. See that band all dressed in red.

Words & music: African American spiritual, c. 1750–1875,
arr. by Mary Allen Walden, 1946– , © 1992 Unitarian Universalist Association

MCCREE
Irregular

God's gon-na trou-ble the wa-ter. The lead - er looks like an
It looks like the band that

D.C. al Fine

Is - rael- ite.
Mo- ses led.
God's gon-na trou-ble the wa-ter.

211

We Are Climbing
Jacob's Ladder

♩ = 92

1. We are climb - ing Ja - cob's lad - der, we are
2. Ev - 'ry round goes high - er, high - er, ev - 'ry
3. If I stum - ble, will you help me? If I
4. Though the road is steep and rug - ged, though the

climb - ing Ja - cob's lad - der, we are climb - ing
round goes high - er, high - er, ev - 'ry round goes
stum - ble, will you help me? If I stum - ble,
road is steep and rug - ged, though the road is

Ja - cob's lad - der, we are climb - ing on.
high - er, high - er, we are climb - ing on.
will you help me? We are climb - ing on.
steep and rug - ged, we are climb - ing on.

This music in C, 212
Words & music: African American spiritual, c. 1750–1875

JACOB'S LADDER
8.8.8.5.

We Are Dancing Sarah's Circle

212

♩ = 92

1. We are danc-ing Sa-rah's cir-cle, we are danc-ing Sa-rah's cir-cle, we are danc-ing Sa-rah's cir-cle, sis-ters, broth-ers, all.
2. Here we seek and find our his-to-ry, here we seek and find our his-to-ry, find our his-to-ry, sis-ters, broth-ers, all.
3. We will all do our own nam-ing, we will all do our own nam-ing, our own nam-ing, sis-ters, broth-ers, all.

4. Every round a generation,
   every round a generation,
   every round a generation,
   sisters, brothers, all.

5. On and on the circle's moving,
   on and on the circle's moving,
   on and on the circle's moving,
   sisters, brothers, all.

This music in D♭, 211

⊕ Words: Carole A. Etzler, 1944– , © 1975 Carole A. Etzler
Music: African American spiritual, c. 1750–1875

JACOB'S LADDER
8.8.8.5.

213 There's a Wideness in Your Mercy

♩· = 56 *Unison*

1. There's a wide-ness in your mer-cy like the wide-ness
2. But we make your love too nar-row by false lim-its
3. For the love of God is broad-er than the mea-sures

of the sea; there's a kind-ness in your jus-tice
of our own, and we mag-ni-fy your strict-ness
of our minds and the heart of the E-ter-nal

which is more than lib-er-ty.
with a zeal you will not own.
is most won-der-ful-ly kind.

Another accompaniment, 161
Words: Frederick William Faber, 1814–1863, alt.
Music: Amos Pilsbury's *United States' Sacred Harmony*, 1799

CHARLESTON
8.7.8.7.

Shabbat Shalom

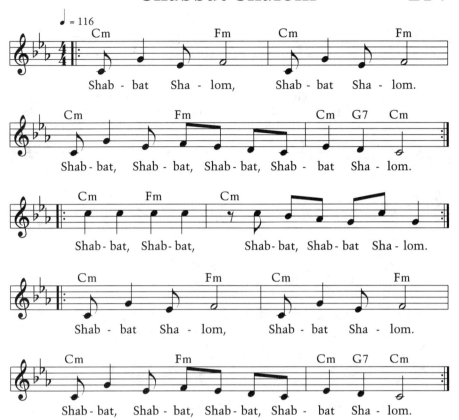

Words: Traditional Hebrew
Music: Traditional Hebrew, arr. by S. Secunda, 1894–1974, © 1964
Mills Music, Inc., used by perm. of Belwyn-Mills

SHABBAT SHALOM
Irregular

215 Praise to the Living God

♩ = 138

1. Praise to the liv-ing God! All prais-ed be The
2. Un-formed all love-ly forms de-clare God's love-li-
3. The spir-it flow-eth free, high surg-ing where it
4. E-ter-nal life hath God im-plant-ed in the

Name, which was, and is, and is to be, for
ness; no ho-li-ness on earth can e'er The
will; in proph-et's word did speak of old, and
soul; such love shall be our strength and stay while

aye the same. The one e-ter-nal
Name ex-press whose love en-folds us
speak-eth still. The To-rah rests se-
a-ges roll. Praise to the liv-ing

God ere aught that now ap-pears: the
all; whose laud the earth dis-plays. Yea,
cure, and change-less it shall stand, deep
God! All prais-ed be The Name which

Words: Daniel Ben Judah, 14th cent.
Music: Synagogue melody, adapt. by Meyer Lyon, 1751–1797

LEONI
6.6.8.4.D.

THE JEWISH SPIRIT

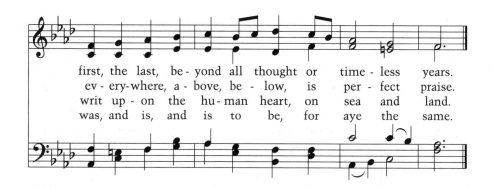

first, the last, be - yond all thought or time - less years.
ev - ery-where, a - bove, be - low, is per - fect praise.
writ up - on the hu - man heart, on sea and land.
was, and is, and is to be, for aye the same.

Hashiveinu 216

Ha - shi - vei - nu, ha - shi - vei - nu, A - do - nai ei -

le - cha ve - na - shu - va. Ve - na - shu - va.

Cha - deish, cha - deish ya - mei - nu ke - ke - dem.

Words: Traditional Hebrew
Music: Traditional Hebrew

HASHIVEINU
Irregular

O Sing Hallelujah

Words: Adapt. from Psalm 150 and Avinu Malkeinu
Music: A. W. Binder, 1895–1966

AVINU MALKEINU
Irregular with refrain

Who Can Say

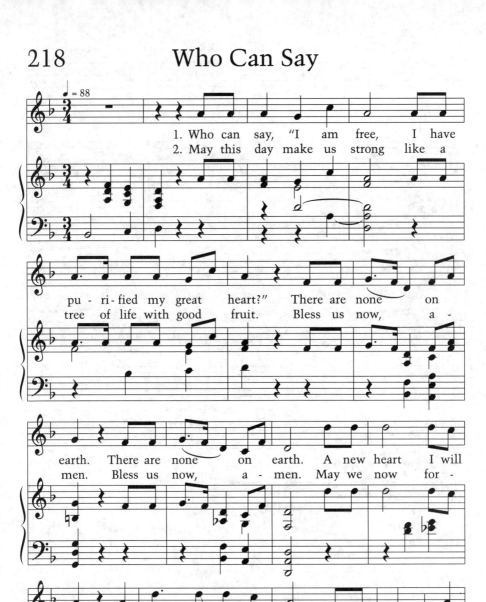

♩ = 88

1. Who can say, "I am free, I have
2. May this day make us strong like a

pu-ri-fied my great heart?" There are none on
tree of life with good fruit. Bless us now, a-

earth. There are none on earth. A new heart I will
men. Bless us now, a-men. May we now for-

give, not stone, but one that frees. A new heart I will
give, a-tone, that we may live, may we now for-

Words: Adapt. from *Gates of Repentance*
Music: Max Janowski, 1912–1991, © Friends of Jewish Music, Inc.

YIH'YU L'RATZON
Irregular

DAYS OF AWE

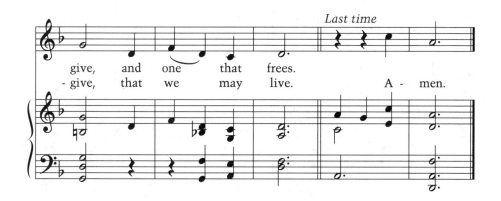

give, and one that frees.
-give, that we may live. A - men.

Last time

O Hear, My People 219

1. O hear, my peo - ple, hear me well: "I have no
2. Then source of peace, lead us to peace, a place pro-
3. May deeds we do in - scribe our names as bless - ings

need for sac - ri - fice; but mer - cy, lov - ing
found, and whol - ly true. And lead us to a
in the Book of Life. O source of peace, lead

kind - ness shall a - lone for life and good suf - fice."
mas - te - ry o'er drives in us that war pur - sue.
us to heal. O source of peace, lead us from strife.

Words: From Rabbi Nachman of Bratzlav, 1770–1811
Music: L. Lewandowski, 1821–1894

L'CHA DODI
L.M.

DAYS OF AWE

220 Bring Out the Festal Bread

♩ = 116

Bring out the fes-tal bread, and sing songs of free-dom.

Fine

Shout with the slaves who fled, and sing songs of free-dom.

1. What mod-ern phar-aohs live in ar-ro-gance crown-éd?
2. Chains still there are to break; their days are not fin-ished.
3. Still does re-sent-ment bind each broth-er and sis-ter.

⊕ Words: Mark L. Belletini, 1949– , © 1992 Unitarian Universalist Association
Music: Hebrew folk song

GILU HAGALILIM
6.6.6.6. with refrain

PESACH/PASSOVER

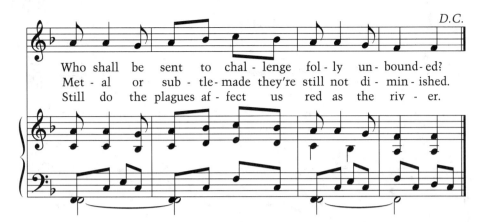

Who shall be sent to chal - lenge fol - ly un - bound-ed?
Met - al or sub - tle-made they're still not di - min - ished.
Still do the plagues af - fect us red as the riv - er.

4. Long be our journeying,
   yet justice is worth it;
   dance, sister Miriam,
   and help us to birth it.

5. O people, lift your heads
   and look to the mountains;
   bushes aflame still call us,
   rocks still gush fountains!

221   Light One Candle

1. Light one can-dle for the Mac - ca-bee chil - dren with
2. Light one can-dle for the strength that we need to
3. What is the mem-'ry that's val - ued so high - ly we

thanks that their light did - n't die.
nev - er be - come our own foe.
keep it a - live in that flame?

Light one can - dle for the pain they en - dured when their
Light one can - dle for those who are suf - f'ring the
What's the com - mit-ment to those who have died when we

Words & music: Peter Yarrow, 1938– , © Silver Dawn Music
⊕ arr. by Betty A. Wylder, 1923–

MACCABEE
Irregular

HANNUKAH

right to ex - ist was de - nied.
pain we learned so long a - go.
cry out they've not died in vain?

Light one can - dle for the ter - ri - ble sac - ri - fice
Light one can - dle for all we be - lieve in, that
Have we come this far al - ways be - liev - ing that

jus - tice and free - dom de - mand. But
an - ger won't tear us a - part. And
jus - tice would some - how pre - vail?

HANNUKAH

light one can-dle for the wis-dom to know when the
light one can-dle to bring us to-geth - er with
This is the bur-den and this is the prom - ise and

peace- mak- er's time is at hand.
peace as the song in our heart.
this is why we will not fail.

Chorus

Don't let the light go out, it's last-ed for so man-y

HANNUKAH

years.   Don't let   the   light   go   out,   let it

shine   through   our   love   and   our   tears.

Mi Y'Malel

Words & music: Hebrew folk song

MI Y'MALEL
Irregular

D.C. al Fine

- deh,   U v'ya men - u kol am Yis - ra -
- store,   and to - day our peo - ple, as we

el,   Yi - ta - ched, ya - kum v' yi - ga - el.
dreamed,   will a - rise, u - nite, and be re - deemed.

8va

223 Rock of Ages, Let Our Song

♩ = 116

1. Rock of A - ges, let our song praise your sav - ing
2. Kin - dling new the ho - ly lamps, priests, un - bowed by
3. Chil - dren of the proph - et's word wheth - er free or

pow - er; you a - midst the rag - ing foes
suf - fering, pu - ri - fied the na - tion's shrine,
fet - tered, wake the ech - oes of the songs

were our shel - tering tow - er. Rag - ing they as -
brought to God their of - fering. And in lands sur -
where you may be scat - tered. Yours the mes - sage

sailed us, but your arm a - vailed us, and your word
round - ing hear the joy a - bound - ing, hap - py throngs
cheer - ing that the time is near - ing which shall see

Words: Leopold Stein, 1810–1882, adapt. from the German by
Marcus M. Jastrow, 1829–1903, Gustav Gottheil, 1827–1903, alt.
Music: German synagogue melody

MOOZ TSUR
7.6.7.6.6.6.3.3.6.

HANNUKAH

broke their sword   when   our   own strength   failed   us.
sing - ing songs   with   a   might - y   sound - ing.
na - tions free,   ty - rants dis - ap - pear - ing.

Let Christmas Come   224

♩ = 69 *Unison*

1. Let Christ-mas come,   its sto - ry   told,   when days are
2. Let Christ-mas come,   its great star glow,   on   qui - et

short   and winds are cold;   let Christ-mas come,   its love-ly
cit - y,   parks of snow;   let Christ-mas come,   its ta - ble

song,   when eve - ning's soon   and night is   long.
gleam,   love born a - gain: the truth of   dream.

Words: John Hanly Morgan, 1918– , © 1984 John Hanly Morgan
Music: English melody, adapt. and harm. by Ralph Vaughan Williams,
1872–1958, © 1931 Oxford University Press

DANBY
L.M.

225
O Come, O Come, Emmanuel

1. O come, O come, Emmanuel, and with your captive children dwell. Give
2. O come, you Splendor very bright, as joy that never yields to might. O
3. O come, you Day-spring, come and cheer our spirits by your presence here. And
4. O come, you Wisdom from on high, from depths that hide within a sigh, to

Words: Latin c. 9th cent., trans. composite based on John Mason Neale, 1818–1866, recast
Music: Adapt. by Thomas Helmore, 1811–1890, harmony by John Weaver, 1937– , harm. © 1990 John Weaver, all rights reserved

VENI EMMANUEL
8.8.8.8.8.8.

ADVENT

com - fort to all ex - iles here, and
come, and turn all hearts to peace, that
dawn in ev - ery bro - ken soul as
tem - per knowl-edge with our care, to

to the ach - ing heart bid cheer. Re-joice! Re-joice! Em-
greed and war at last shall cease. Re-joice! Re-joice! Em-
vi - sion that can see the whole. Re-joice! Re-joice! Em-
ren - der ev - ery act a prayer. Re-joice! Re-joice! Em-

man - u - el shall come with - in as Love to dwell.
man - u - el shall come with - in as Truth to dwell.
man - u - el shall come with - in as Light to dwell.
man - u - el shall come with - in as Hope to dwell.

People, Look East

♩. = 54

1. Peo - ple, look east. The time is near of the
2. Fur - rows, be glad. Though earth is bare, one more
3. Stars, keep the watch. When night is dim, one more

crown - ing of the year. Make your house fair as you are
seed is plant - ed there. Give up your strength the seed to
light the bowl shall brim, shin - ing be - yond the frost - y

Peo - ple, look

a - ble, trim the hearth and set the ta - ble.
nour - ish, that in course the flower may flour - ish.
weath - er, bright as sun and moon to - geth - er.

east and sing to - day:

Peo - ple, look east: Love, the Guest, is on the way.
                                         Love, the Rose, is on the way.
        Peo - ple, look east: Love, the Star, is on the way.

Words: Eleanor Farjeon, 1881–1965, used by perm. of David Higham Assoc. Ltd.
Music: Traditional French carol, harmony by Martin Shaw, 1875–1958, used by
perm. of Oxford University Press

BESANÇON
8.7.9.8.8.7.

ADVENT

♩ = 80 *Unison*

1. Crèche flick-ers bright here, sing by the light here
2. Fa - ther's be - side them, sheep near-ly hide them.
3. Crèche flick-ers bright here, sing by the light here

at night fall, at night fall.
An - gels call, an - gels call.
at night fall, at night fall.

Moth - er's here keep - ing a child who's sleep-ing
Shep - herds and sag - es bow through the a - ges,
This is our to - ken, by sign un - spok - en:

in the stall, in the stall.
kin - dred all, kin - dred all.
peace to all, peace to all.

⊕ Words: Howard Box, 1926– , © 1992 Unitarian Universalist Association
Music: Traditional Hungarian folk song, arr. by Thomas Legrady, © 1992
Unitarian Universalist Association

MENNYBOL
5.5.6.D.

CHRISTMAS

228   Once in Royal David's City

♩ = 92

1. Once in roy - al Da - vid's cit - y stood a low - ly cat - tle shed, where a moth - er laid her ba - by in a man - ger for his bed; so may
2. Shep - herds came to see this won - der, and to kneel in ho - ly awe at that low - ly sta - ble man - ger where the in - fant lay on straw; so may
3. From a - far three ma - gi jour - neyed to that sta - ble rude and bare, to pay hom - age to the in - fant, of - fering gifts both rich and rare; so may
4. In that hap - py Christ - mas spir - it, hear the an - gels from on high sing their an - cient sal - u - ta - tions: joy's a gift you can - not buy. So may

⊕ Words: Carl G. Seaburg, 1922–1998, based on a text of Mrs. C. F. Alexander
Music: Henry John Gauntlett, 1805–1876, harmony by Arthur Henry Mann,
1850–1929, © 1957, renewed 1985 Novello & Co., Ltd.

IRBY
8.7.8.7.7.7.

CHRISTMAS

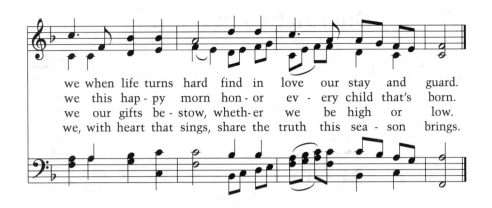

we when life turns hard find in love our stay and guard.
we this hap-py morn hon-or ev-ery child that's born.
we our gifts be-stow, wheth-er we be high or low.
we, with heart that sings, share the truth this sea-son brings.

Gather 'Round the Manger 229

♩ = 112

1. Gath-er 'round the man-ger, soft-ly, soft-ly.
2. Sim-ple shep-herds greet you, Je-su, Je-su.
3. Ma-ry gent-ly holds you, soft-ly, soft-ly.
4. Through the e-ons reach-ing, Je-su, Je-su.

See the pre-cious stran-ger.
State-ly ma-gi seek you.
Jo-seph's love en-folds you. Sing Al-le-lu.
Love's great les-son teach-ing.

LOVE'S GIFT
6.4.6.4.

230 Duermete, Niño Lindo

Words: Hispanic folk song, trans. by John Donald Robb, 1892–1989, alt.
Music: Hispanic folk song, arr. by John Donald Robb

A LA RU
Irregular with refrain

pe — na de mi do — lor.
na — die te ha de o — fen — der.
soothed and put to rest.
sings you a la ru.

A la ru, a la
mè, a la ru, a la mè, a la ru, a la
mè, a la ru, a la ru, a la mè.

231 Angels We Have Heard on High

1. Angels we have heard on high sweetly singing o'er the plains and the mountains in reply ech-o-ing their joy-ous strains. Glo - - - ri - a
2. Shepherds, why this jubilee? Why these songs of happy cheer? What great bright-ness did you see? What glad tid-ings did you hear?
3. See him in a manger laid whom the angels praise above; Mary, Joseph, lend your aid, while we raise our hearts in love.

Words: Earl Bowman Marlatt, 1892–1940
Music: French carol, 1855

GLORIA
7.7.7.7. with refrain

CHRISTMAS

in ex - cel - sis De - o. De - o.

The Hills Are Bare at Bethlehem 232

1. The hills are bare at Beth-le-hem, no fu-ture for the world they show; yet here new life be-gins to grow, from earth's old dust a green-wood stem.
2. The stars are cold at Beth-le-hem, no warmth for those be-neath the sky; yet here the ra-diant an-gels fly, and joy burns new, a fi-'ry gem.
3. The heart is tired at Beth-le-hem, no hu-man dream un-bro-ken stands; yet here God comes to mor-tal hands, and hope re-newed cries out: "A-men!"

Another accompaniment, 15
Words: Royce J. Scherf, 1929– , © 1978 Augsburg Fortress
Music: From *The Southern Harmony*, 1835, harmony by Thomas Somerville, 1969

PROSPECT
L.M.

CHRISTMAS

Bring a Torch,
Jeannette, Isabella

1. Un flam-beau, Jean-nette, Is-a-bel-le, un flam-beau, cour-ons au ber-ceau! C'est Jé-sus, bonnes gens du ha-meau, le Christ est né, Ma-rie ap-pel-le, Ah! Ah! Ah! Que la mère est

1. Bring a torch, Jean-nette, Is-a-bel-la, bring a torch and quick-ly run. Christ is born, good folk of the vil-lage, Christ is born and Ma-ry's call-ing, Ah! Ah! Beau-ti-ful is the

2. Come and see with-in the sta-ble, come and see the Ho-ly one, come and see the love-ly Je-sus, brown his brow, his cheeks are ros-y. Hush! Hush! Qui-et-ly now he

Words: Traditional Provençal, 17th cent.
Music: French carol

BRING A TORCH
Irregular

CHRISTMAS

bel - le, Ah! Ah! Ah! que l'En - fant est beau!
moth - er, Ah! Ah! Beau - ti - ful is her child.
slum - bers, Hush! Hush! Qui - et - ly now he sleeps.

In the Gentle of the Moon 234

1. In the gen - tle of the moon, in the gar - net
2. Soon the ap - ple tree will bud, and the crim - son
3. Touch the treas - ure of a faith that the myth - ic

of a star, feel the pres - ence of a hope
fruit will fall; but with - in the sta - ble shed
East - erns hear. See the meas - ure of a love

where the crowd - ing shep - herds are.
there's no thought of that at all.
come can - des - cent down the air.

Words: Carl G. Seaburg, 1922–1998, © 1992 Unitarian Universalist Association
Music: Hasidic tune

HASIDIM
7.7.7.7.

CHRISTMAS

235

Deck the Hall
with Boughs of Holly

♩ = 76

Verses:

1. Deck the hall with boughs of hol - ly,
2. See the blaz - ing Yule be - fore us, fa la la la la, la
3. Fast a - way the old year pass - es,

la la la. 'Tis the sea - son to be jol - ly,
Strike the harp and join the cho - rus,
Hail the new, ye lads and lass - es,

fa la la la la, la la la la. Don we now our
Fol - low me in
Sing we joy - ous

gay ap - par - el, Troll the an - cient
mer - ry meas - ure, fa la la la la la, la la la. While I tell of
all to - geth - er, Heed - less of the

Words: Traditional Welsh
Music: Old Welsh carol

YULE
Irregular

CHRISTMAS

Yule - tide car - ol,
Yule - tide treas - ure, fa la la la la, la la la la.
wind and weath - er,

O Thou Joyful Day 236

♩ = 96 *Unison*

1. O thou joy - ful day, O thou bless - ed day,
2. O *sanc - tis - si - ma,* O *sanc - tis - si - ma,*

glad - some, peace - ful Christ - mas - tide. Earth's hope a - wak - en,
glad - some, peace - ful Christ - mas - tide. Light now is beam - ing,

Love life has tak - en. Joy, O, joy to all at Christ - mas - tide.
our souls re - deem - ing. Joy, O, joy to all at Christ - mas - tide.

Words: Traditional
Music: Sicilian melody, first pub. *The European Magazine & London Review*, 1792, alt.

SICILIAN MARINERS
5.5.7.5.5.9.

CHRISTMAS

The First Nowell

1. The first No-well the an-gel did say was to
2. They look-ed up and saw a star, shin-ing
3. And by the light of that same star, three

cer-tain poor shep-herds, in fields as they lay, in
in the east be-yond them far, and
ma - gi came from coun - try far; to

fields where they lay keep-ing their sheep, on a
to the earth it gave great light, and
seek a king was their in - tent, and to

cold win-ter's night that was so deep.
so it con-tin-ued both day and night. No - well, No -
fol-low the star wher - ev - er it went.

Words: English carol
Music: William Sandys's *Christmas Carols Ancient and Modern*, 1833,
harmony by John Stainer, 1840–1901

THE FIRST NOWELL
Irregular with refrain

CHRISTMAS

- well, No - well, No - well, born is the king of Is - ra - el.

Within the Shining of a Star 238

1. With - in the shin - ing of a star we catch a
2. The mir - a - cle of each new birth can shake and

glimpse of who we are; in ev - ery in - fant born we
save the ston - y earth; tri - um - phant - ly the new-born's

see the hope of our na - tiv - i - ty.
cry strikes ech - oes from the wait - ing sky.

Words: Robert S. Lehman, 1913–
Music: Betsy Jo Angebranndt, 1931– , © 1992 Unitarian Universalist Association

CHRISTMAS HYMN
L.M.

CHRISTMAS

239 Go Tell It on the Mountain

Go tell it on the moun-tain, o-ver the hills and ev-'ry-where;

go tell it on the moun-tain that Je-sus Christ is born!

1. While shep-herds kept their watch-ing o'er
2. The shep-herds feared and trem-bled when
3. Down in a low-ly man-ger the

Words & music: African American spiritual, c. 1750–1875
Music arr. by Paul Sjolund, 1935– , harmony © 1971 Walton Music Corp.

GO TELL IT
ON THE MOUNTAIN
7.6.7.6. with refrain

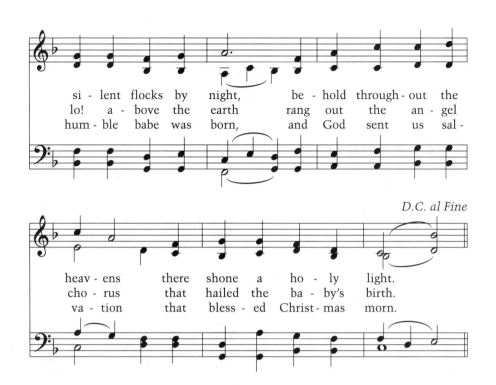

D.C. al Fine

si - lent flocks by night, be - hold through - out the
lo! a - bove the earth rang out the an - gel
hum - ble babe was born, and God sent us sal -

heav - ens there shone a ho - ly light.
cho - rus that hailed the ba - by's birth.
va - tion that bless - ed Christ - mas morn.

240

I Heard the Bells
on Christmas Day

♩. = 56

1. I heard the bells on Christ - mas Day their old fa-
2. I thought how, as the day had come, the bel - fries
3. And in de - spair I bowed my head: "There is no

mil - iar car - ols play, and wild and sweet the
of all Chris - ten - dom had rolled a - long th'un-
peace on earth," I said, "for hate is strong and

words re - peat of peace on earth, to all good - will.
bro - ken song of peace on earth, to all good - will.
mocks the song of peace on earth, to all good - will."

4. Then pealed the bells more loud and deep:
   "God is not dead, nor doth God sleep;
   the wrong shall fail, the right prevail,
   with peace on earth, to all goodwill."

5. Till, ringing, singing on its way,
   the world revolved from day to day,
   a voice, a chime, a chant sublime
   of peace on earth, to all goodwill.

⊕ Words: Henry Wadsworth Longfellow, 1807–1882
Music: English traditional melody, coll., arr., and harmonized by Ralph
Vaughan Williams, 1872–1958, used by perm. of Oxford University Press

HERONGATE
L.M.

In the Bleak Midwinter 241

1. In the bleak mid-win-ter frost-y wind made moan,
2. Christ a home-less strang-er, so the gos-pels say,
3. Once more child and moth-er weave their mag-ic spell,

earth stood hard as i-ron, wa-ter like a stone;
cra-dled in a man-ger and a bed of hay;
touch-ing hearts with won-der words can nev-er tell;

snow had fall-en, snow on snow, snow on snow,
in the bleak mid-win-ter sta-ble-place suf-ficed
in the bleak mid-win-ter, in this world of pain,

in the bleak mid-win-ter long a-go.
Ma-ry and her ba-by, Je-sus Christ.
where our hearts are o-pen love is born a-gain.

Words: Christina Georgina Rossetti, 1830–1894
⊕ New words by John Andrew Storey, 1935–1997
Music: Gustav Theodore Holst, 1874–1934

CRANHAM
6.5.6.5.D.

242 In the Lonely Midnight

♩ = 76 *Unison*

1. In the lone-ly mid - night, on the win-try hill,
2. Though in Da-vid's cit - y an - gels sing no more,
3. Though the child of Ma - ry, her - ald - ed on high,

shep-herds heard the an - gels sing-ing, "Peace, good will."
love makes an - gel mu - sic on earth's far - thest shore.
in his man - ger cra - dle may no long - er lie,

Lis - ten, O ye wea - ry, to the an - gels' song,
Though no heaven - ly glo - ry meet your won - dering eyes,
love will reign for - ev - er, though the proud world scorn;

un - to you the tid - ings of great joy be - long.
love can make your dwell - ing bright as par - a - dise.
if you tru - ly seek peace, Christ for you is born.

Words: From Theodore Chickering Williams, 1855–1915
Music: Solesmes version of the plainsong melody, adapt.

ADORO TE DEVOTE
6.5.6.5.D.

CHRISTMAS

Jesus, Our Brother

1. Je-sus, our broth-er, kind and good, was hum-bly
2. "I," said the don-key, shag-gy and brown, "I car-ried his
3. "I," said the cow, all white and red, "I gave him my
4. "I," said the sheep with curl-y horn, "I gave him my

born in a sta-ble rude, and the friend-ly beasts a-
moth-er up-hill and down, I car-ried her safe-ly to
man-ger for his bed, I gave him hay to
wool for his blan-ket warm, he wore my coat on

round him stood, Je-sus, our broth-er, kind and good.
Beth-le-hem town; I," said the don-key, shag-gy and brown.
pil-low his head; I," said the cow, all white and red.
Christ-mas morn; I," said the sheep with curl-y horn.

5. "I," said the dove, from the rafters high,
"I cooed him to sleep that he should not cry,
we cooed him to sleep, my mate and I;
I," said the dove, from the rafters high.

6. And all the beasts, by some good spell,
in the stable dark were glad to tell
of the gifts they gave Emmanuel,
the gifts they gave Emmanuel.

Words: 12th cent. French carol, trans. anon., based on Luke 2:7
Music: Medieval French melody, harmony by Carlton R. Young, 1926– ,
© 1989 The United Methodist Publishing House

ORIENTIS PARTIBUS
Irregular

CHRISTMAS

It Came upon
the Midnight Clear

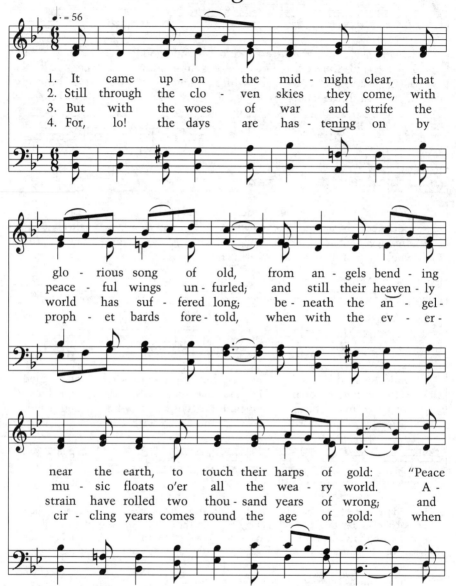

1. It came up-on the mid-night clear, that
2. Still through the clo-ven skies they come, with
3. But with the woes of war and strife the
4. For, lo! the days are has-ten-ing on by

glo-rious song of old, from an-gels bend-ing
peace-ful wings un-furled; and still their heaven-ly
world has suf-fered long; be-neath the an-gel-
proph-et bards fore-told, when with the ev-er-

near the earth, to touch their harps of gold: "Peace
mu-sic floats o'er all the wea-ry world. A-
strain have rolled two thou-sand years of wrong; and
cir-cling years comes round the age of gold: when

Words: Edmund Hamilton Sears, 1810–1876
Music: Richard Storrs Willis, 1819–1900

CAROL
C.M.D.

CHRISTMAS

on   the earth,   to   all   good   will,   from
\- bove   its   sad   and   low - ly   plains   they
we   who   fight   the   wars   hear   not   the
peace   shall   o - ver   all   the   earth   its

heaven   the   news   we   bring." The   world   in   sol - emn
bend   on   hov - ering wing;   and   ev - er   o'er   its
love   song which   they   bring.   O   hush   the   noise   of
an - cient splen - dors fling,   and   the whole world give

still - ness   lay   to   hear   the   an - gels   sing.
Ba - bel   sounds   the   bless - ed   an - gels   sing.
bat - tle   strife,   and   hear   the   an - gels   sing.
back   the   song   which   now   the   an - gels   sing.

245   Joy to the World!

♩ = 100

1. Joy to the world! The Word is come: let earth with
2. Joy to the earth! Now glad-ness reigns: let hearts their
3. No more let sins and sor-rows grow, nor thorns in-

prais - es ring. Let ev - ery heart pre -
songs em - ploy, while fields and floods, rocks,
fest the ground. Let right - eous - ness its

pare a room, and heaven and na - ture
hills, and plains re - peat the sound - ing
glor - ies show as far as love is

1. and
2. re -
3. as

Words: Isaac Watts, 1674–1748, alt.
Music: *Methodist Collection of Tunes*, 1833

COMFORT
C.M.

CHRISTMAS

sing,   and heaven and na - ture sing,   and
joy,   re - peat the sound-ing joy,   re -
found,   as far as love is found,   as

heaven and na - ture sing, and heaven and na - ture
- peat the sound-ing joy, re - peat the sound-ing
far as love is found, as far as love is

heaven, and heaven and na - ture sing.
peat, re - peat the sound - ing joy.
far, as far, as love is found.

sing,
joy,
found,

246 O Little Town of Bethlehem

♩ = 116

1. O lit - tle town of Beth - le - hem, how still we see thee lie! A - bove thy deep and dream - less sleep the si - lent stars go by; yet in thy dark streets shin - eth the

2. For Christ is born of Ma - ry, and gath - ered all a - bove, while mor - tals sleep, the an - gels keep their watch of won - dering love. O morn - ing stars, to - geth - er pro -

3. How si - lent - ly, how si - lent - ly the won - der is made known, when God im - parts to hu - man hearts the gift that is our own. No ear may hear that com - ing, but

Another tune, 247
Words: Phillips Brooks, 1835–1893, alt.
Music: Lewis H. Redner, 1831–1908

ST. LOUIS
C.M.D.

CHRISTMAS

ev - er - last - ing light; the hopes and fears of
- claim the ho - ly birth. Let prais - es ring: from
in this world - ly din, when souls are tru - ly

all the years are met in thee to - night.
God they bring good - will to all on earth.
hum - ble, then the dear babe rests with - in.

247 O Little Town of Bethlehem

Another tune, 246
Words: Words: Phillips Brooks, 1835–1893, alt.
Music: English melody, harmony by Ralph Vaughan Williams,
1872–1958, used by perm. of Oxford University Press

FOREST GREEN
8.6.8.6.7.6.8.6.

ev - er - last - ing light; the hopes and fears of
- claim the ho - ly birth. Let prais - es ring: from
in this world - ly din, when souls are tru - ly

all the years are met in thee to - night.
God they bring good - will to all on earth.
hum - ble, then the dear babe rests with - in.

248 O We Believe in Christmas

1. O we be-lieve in Christ - mas, and we keep Christ-mas
2. And we will join at Christ - mas the song of hope and
3. Then sing we all at Christ - mas the song of that new
4. Shine out ye lights of Christ - mas from hearth and tree and

day; and we will hon - or Christ - mas the
joy that finds its theme at Christ - mas in
birth which holds the hope of Christ - mas and
star! And let the warmth of Christ - mas shed

an - cient world - wide way: the Christ-mas of all
ev - ery girl and boy. The flame of life will
brings its joy to earth; which knits the gen - er -
kind - ness near and far! And clang, ye bells of

Words: Percival Chubb, 1860–1960, © 1955 American Ethical Union
Music: American folk hymn melody in *The Revivalist*, 1868

ADLER
7.6.7.6.D.

peo - ples, the sun's re - turn - ing cheer rung
dwin - dle as fades the sun - set sky un -
- a - tions, each daugh - ter and each son, be -
Christ - mas, up - on the frost - y air! And

out from towers and stee - ples at mid-night of the year.
til a child shall kin - dle new light and raise it high.
yond all tribes and na - tions, and makes the man - y one.
may the joy of Christ-mas spread glad-ness ev - ery-where!

249   On This Day Everywhere

1. On this day ev - ery - where chil - dren's songs fill the air, greet the child, new and fair, Christ - mas gift so ho - ly, born in sta - ble low - ly.
2. Sweet the babe, strange his bed, man - ger hay round his head, cat - tle there in the shed; Ma - ry, Jo - seph by him, shep - herds draw - ing nigh him.
3. Ma - gi three find their way by a star's shin - ing ray to the child in the hay; give their won - drous pres - ents, gold and myrrh and in - cense.

Words: Composite, 1958, based on Theodoric Petri's *Piae Cantiones*, 1582
Music: Theodoric Petri's *Piae Cantiones*, 1582,
arr. by Gustav Theodore Holst, 1874–1934

PERSONENT HODIE
6.6.6.6.6. with refrain

CHRISTMAS

I - de - o - o - o. I - de - o - o - o.

I - de - o glo - ri - a in ex - cel - sis De - o!

250   purer than purest

1. pur - er than pur-est pure whis-per of whis-per
2. child-ful-ly se-ri-ous flow-er of ho-li-
3. flam-ing a cool-ly bell touch-es most mere un-

so, so (big with in - no - cence) for-
ness a pil - grim from be - yond, be-
til (e - ter-nal-ly) with (now) with (now) with

giv-ing-ly a once of ea - ger glo - ry,
yond, be-yond, the fu - ture, im - me-di-ate like new, like some
lu - mi-nous the shad - ow of love him-self: who's

Words: e. e. cummings, 1894–1962, from XAIPE, © 1950 by e. e. cummings,
© 1979, 1978, 1973 Nancy T. Andrews, © 1979, 1973 George James Firmage,
used by perm. of Liveright Publishing Corp.
Music: Vincent Persichetti, 1915–1988, © 1956 Elkan-Vogel, Inc.

STAR
Irregular

CHRISTMAS

Last time

no more mir - a - cle may grow
new - ly re-mem - bered dream   4. and ev-ery world, be-fore
we — nor   can you die   or   i

si - lence be - gins   a   star   A - men.

251   Silent Night, Holy Night

1. Si - lent night, ho - ly night, all is calm,
2. Si - lent night, ho - ly night, shep - herds quake
3. Si - lent night, ho - ly night, child of God,

all is bright round yon vir - gin moth - er and child.
at the sight, glo - ries stream from heav - en a - far,
love's pure light ra - diant beams from thy ho - ly face,

Ho - ly in - fant so ten - der and mild, sleep in heav - en - ly
heaven - ly hosts sing "Al - le - lu - ia," sleep in heav - en - ly
with the dawn of re - deem - ing grace, sleep in heav - en - ly

peace,   sleep in heav - en - ly peace.
peace,   sleep in heav - en - ly peace.
peace,   sleep in heav - en - ly peace.

Words: Joseph Mohr, 1792–1848
Music: Franz Xaver Gruber, 1787–1863

STILLE NACHT
Irregular

CHRISTMAS

Stille Nacht

Words: Joseph Mohr, 1792–1848
Music: Franz Xaver Gruber, 1787–1863

STILLE NACHT
Irregular

CHRISTMAS

253   O Come, All Ye Faithful

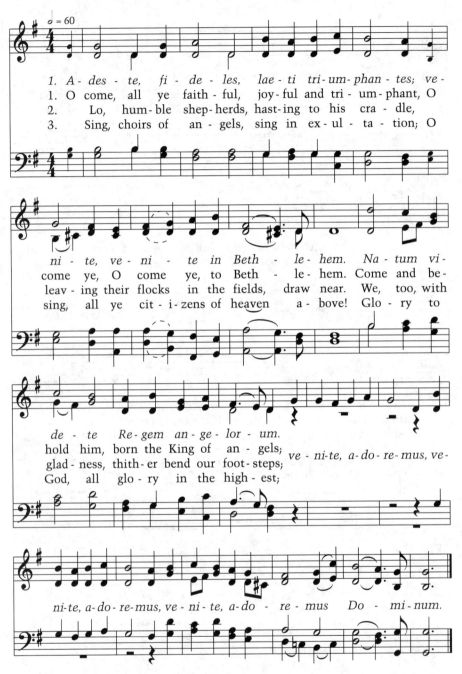

1. A - des - te, fi - de - les, lae - ti tri - um - phan - tes; ve -
1. O come, all ye faith - ful, joy - ful and tri - um - phant, O
2. Lo, hum - ble shep - herds, hast - ing to his cra - dle,
3. Sing, choirs of an - gels, sing in ex - ul - ta - tion; O

ni - te, ve - ni - te in Beth - le - hem. Na - tum vi -
come ye, O come ye, to Beth - le - hem. Come and be -
leav - ing their flocks in the fields, draw near. We, too, with
sing, all ye cit - i - zens of heaven a - bove! Glo - ry to

de - te Re - gem an - ge - lor - um.
hold him, born the King of an - gels;
glad - ness, thith - er bend our foot - steps;   ve - ni - te, a - do - re - mus, ve -
God, all glo - ry in the high - est;

ni - te, a - do - re - mus, ve - ni - te, a - do - re - mus Do - mi - num.

Words: John Francis Wade, 1711–1786, tr. by Frederick Oakeley, 1802–1880, et al.   ADESTE FIDELES
Music: John Francis Wade's manuscript, c. 1740–1743   Irregular

CHRISTMAS

Sing We Now of Christmas 254

♩ = 84 *Unison*

1. Sing we now of Christ-mas, No - el, sing we here!
2. An-gels called to shep-herds, "Leave your flocks at rest,
3. In the town they found him, Jo - seph, and Ma - ry mild,

Hear our grate-ful prais - es to the babe so dear.
jour - ney forth to Beth - l'hem, find the child so blest."
seat - ed by the man - ger, watch-ing the ho - ly child.

Refrain

Sing we No - el, the child is born, No - el!

Sing we now of Christ - mas, sing we now No - el!

4. From the eastern country
came the kings afar,
bearing gifts to Bethl'hem,
guided by a star.

Refrain

5. Gold and myrrh they took there,
gifts of greatest price.
There was ne'er a stable
so like paradise.

Refrain

Words: Traditional French carol
Music: Medieval French carol, harmony by Marcel Dupré, 1886–1971,
© Alphonse Leduc, Paris

NOEL NOUVELET
11.11.10.11.

CHRISTMAS

255   There's a Star in the East

1. There's a star in the East on Christ-mas morn,
2. If you hark to the an-gel's ho-ly word,

rise up, shep-herd, and fol-low. It will lead to the place where the
rise up, shep-herd, and fol-low. You'll for-get your flock, you'll for-

babe is born; rise up, shep-herd, and fol-low.
get your herd; rise up, shep-herd, and fol-low.

Leave your ewes and leave your lambs, rise up, shep-herd, and

Words: Traditional
Music: African American spiritual, c. 1750–1865

DOUGLASS
Irregular

CHRISTMAS

Winter Night

♩ = 138

1. Win - ter night,
2. Drops of pain
3. Ho - ly Child,

clear and bright: a wea - ry world is sleep - ing. And
flow like rain: tell why your tears are fall - ing: for
Ev - ery Child, your life will have its sea - son. And

then a cry fills earth and sky: a new - born child is
hu - man - kind, so frail, un - kind, or for your own life's
each new day your heart may pray for grace, for peace, for

Words & music: Shelley Jackson Denham, 1950– ,
© 1988 Shelley Jackson Denham

WINTER LULLABY
6.7.8.7. with refrain

CHRISTMAS

weep-ing.
call-ing?   Hush-a - bye,   lul-la - by,
rea - son.

bless - ed   lit - tle   ba - by.

ba- by.

257 'Twas in the Moon of Wintertime

♩ = 76 *Unison*

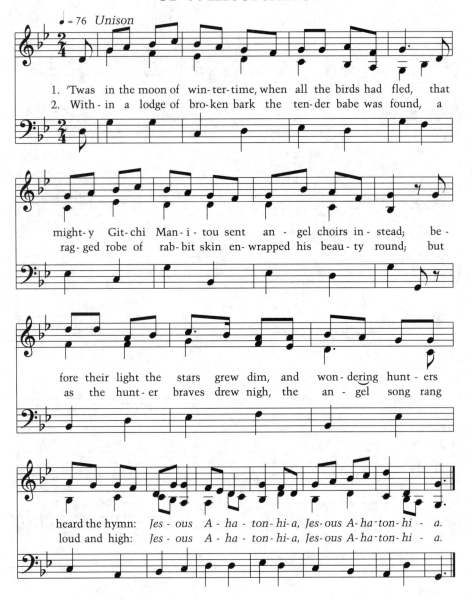

1. 'Twas in the moon of win-ter-time, when all the birds had fled, that
2. With-in a lodge of bro-ken bark the ten-der babe was found, a

might-y Git-chi Man-i-tou sent an - gel choirs in - stead; be -
rag-ged robe of rab-bit skin en-wrapped his beau-ty round; but

fore their light the stars grew dim, and won-dering hunt - ers
as the hunt - er braves drew nigh, the an - gel song rang

heard the hymn: Jes - ous A - ha - ton-hi-a, Jes-ous A-ha-ton-hi - a.
loud and high: Jes - ous A - ha - ton-hi-a, Jes-ous A-ha-ton-hi - a.

Words: Jean de Brébeuf, 1593–1649, tr. by Jesse Edgar Middleton, 1872–1960,
English text © The Frederick Harris Music Co., Ltd., all rights reserved
Music: Canadian carol, arr. by H. Barrie Cabena, 1933– , © H. Barrie Cabena

JESOUS AHATONHIA
8.6.8.6.8.8.
with refrain

CHRISTMAS

Whence, O Shepherd Maiden? 258

♩ = 108 *Unison*

1. Whence, O shep-herd maid-en, whence came you?
2. What saw you there, maid-en, what saw you?
3. Noth-ing more then, maid-en, noth-ing more?

Whence, O shep-herd maid-en, whence came you?
What saw you there, maid-en, what saw you?
Noth-ing more then, maid-en, noth-ing more?

I come from the man-ger, walk-ing on my way,
I saw ly-ing cra-dled there a ti-ny child,
Ma-ry, ho-ly moth-er, nurs-ing babe at breast,

noth-ing ev-er strang-er seen with-in my day.
in the new straw hud-dled, soft-ly it was piled.
Jo-seph, ho-ly fa-ther, with the cold op-pressed.

Words & music: 17th cent. French Canadian carol

D'OÙ VIENS TU, BERGÈRE
9.9.6.5.6.5.

CHRISTMAS

259 We Three Kings of Orient Are

1. We three kings of O - ri - ent are; bear - ing gifts we tra - verse a - far, field and foun - tain, moor and moun - tain, fol - low - ing yon - der star.
2. Frank - in - cense to of - fer have I, in - cense owns a De - i - ty nigh. Prayer and prais - ing, all are rais - ing, wor - ship God most high.
3. Myrrh is mine, its bit - ter per - fume breathes a life of gath - er - ing gloom; sor - rowing, sigh - ing, bleed - ing, dy - ing, sealed in the stone - cold tomb.
4. Born a babe on Beth - le - hem's plain, gold I bring to crown him a - gain, love for - ev - er, ceas - ing nev - er, in our hearts to reign.

Words & music: John Henry Hopkins, Jr., 1820–1891

KINGS OF ORIENT
Irregular

EPIPHANY

O star of won - der, star of light,

star, with roy - al beau - ty bright, west - ward lead - ing,

still pro - ceed - ing, guide us through this per - fect night.

Oshana, Shira Oshana 260

O - sha-na, shi - ra o - sha - na! O - sha- na,

shi - ra o - sha - na! O - sha - na, shi - ra o -

sha - na! O - sha - na ha na - vi ha - va vshem A - do - nai.

Words: From Mark 11:9
Music: Traditional Hebrew

HEVENU
Irregular

PALM SUNDAY

261   When Jesus Wept

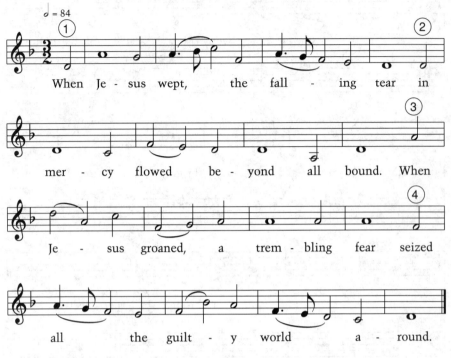

♩ = 84

When Je - sus wept, the fall - ing tear in
mer - cy flowed be - yond all bound. When
Je - sus groaned, a trem - bling fear seized
all the guilt - y world a - round.

Words & music: William Billings, 1746–1800

WHEN JESUS WEPT
L.M.

262   Hosanna in the Highest

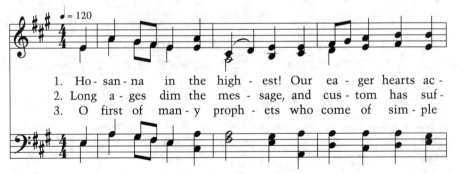

♩ = 120

1. Ho - san - na in the high - est! Our ea - ger hearts ac -
2. Long a - ges dim the mes - sage, and cus - tom has suf -
3. O first of man - y proph - ets who come of sim - ple

Words: John Howland Lathrop, 1880–1967
Music: X. L. Hartig's *Vollständige Sammlung*, c. 1833

ELLACOMBE
7.6.7.6.D.

PALM SUNDAY

-claim   the   proph - et   of   the   king - dom,   who
-ficed   for   mer - chants   and   for   princ - es   to
folk   to   free   us   from   our   bond - age,   to

bears   Mes - si - ah's   name.   O   bold,   O   fool - ish
bow,   and   own   him   Christ.   But   when   an - oth - er
break   op - pres - sion's   yoke: re - store   our   minds   to

peas - ants,   to   deem   that   he   should   reign!   The
spir - it   a - ris - es   from   the   plain,   the
wis - dom,   make   known   the   life,   the   way   that

tem - ple   and   the   pal - ace   look   down   in   high   dis - dain.
courts   of   pow - er   trem - ble,   and   cru - ci - fy   a - gain.
leads   through   love   and   jus - tice   un - to   the   peace - crowned   day.

263 When Jesus Looked from Olivet

♩ = 96 Unison

1. When Je - sus looked from Ol - i - vet on
2. He found the dream of proph - ets past, of
3. They cried "Ho - san - na" on that day while

cit - y gold with tow - ers white, with
jus - tice crown - ing ev - ery head, now
strew - ing palms up - on the path, but

sud - den grief his eyes grew wet, and
shat - tered: by the truth of caste, by
who was sigh - ing all the way? And

soon his weep - ing drowned his sight.
chil - dren lost, by lack of bread.
what the na - ture of his wrath?

⊕ Words: Mark L. Belletini, 1949– , © 1992 Unitarian Universalist Association
Music: William Billings, 1746–1800, harmony by Richard D. Wetzel, 1972,
© 1972 Westminster Press

WHEN JESUS WEPT
L.M.

PALM SUNDAY

Now in the Tomb Is Laid   264

1. Now in the tomb is laid, who in the wide world walked, and talked with one and all. Now in the tomb is laid.
2. Now in the tomb is laid, who told the spar-row's worth, the lil-y's prais-es said. Now in the tomb is laid.
3. Per-fect, no wound nor mark! By thine own hard-est hour, do live with-in my heart. Per-fect, no wound nor mark!

Words: Padraic Colum, 1881–1972, © Devin-Adair Publishers, Inc.
Music: Gerald Kechley, © 1992 Unitarian Universalist Association

COLUM
6.6.6.6.

GOOD FRIDAY

265 O Sacred Head, Now Wounded

1. O sacred head, now wounded, with grief and shame bowed down, now scornfully surrounded with thorns, thy only crown: how art thou pale with anguish, with

2. What language shall I borrow to thank thee, dearest friend, for this thy dying sorrow, thy pity without end? Let me be thine forever. And,

Words: Based on Latin attr. to Bernard of Clairvaux, 1091–1153,
German version by Paulus Gerhardt, 1607–1676, from trans. by
James Waddell Alexander, 1804–1859
Music: Hans Leo Hassler, 1564–1612, harmony by J. S. Bach, 1685–1750

PASSION CHORALE
7.6.7.6.D.

GOOD FRIDAY

sore a - buse and scorn! How does that vis - age
should I faint - ing be, oh, let me nev - er,

lan - guish which once was bright as morn!
nev - er, out - live my love to thee.

266 Now the Green Blade Riseth

♩ = 84 *Unison*

1. Now the green blade ris-eth from the bur-ied grain,
2. In the grave they laid him, Love by ha-tred slain,
3. When our hearts are win-try, griev-ing, or in pain,

wheat that in dark earth man-y days has lain;
think-ing that nev-er he would wake a-gain,
Love's touch can call us back to life a-gain,

Love lives a-gain, that with the dead has been:
laid in the earth, like grain that sleeps un-seen:
fields of our hearts that dead and bare have been:

Refrain

Love is come a-gain like wheat that spring-eth green.

Words: John MacLeod Campbell Crum, 1872–1958, alt.,
© 1964 Oxford University Press
Music: Medieval French carol, harmony by Marcel Dupré, 1886–1971,
© Alphonse Leduc, Paris

NOEL NOUVELET
11.10.10.11.

EASTER

When Mary through the Garden Went
267

1. When Ma - ry through the gar - den went, there
2. When Ma - ry through the gar - den went, the
3. When Ma - ry through the gar - den went, her

was no sound of an - y bird, and yet, be - cause the
dew lay still on flower and grass, the wav - ing palms a -
eyes, for weep - ing long, were dim. The grass be - neath her

night was spent, the lit - tle grass - es light - ly stirred, the
bove her sent their fra - grance out as she did pass. No
foot - step bent, the sol - emn lil - ies, white and slim, these

flowers a - woke, the lil - ies heard.
light up - on the branch - es was.
al - so stood and wept for him.

Words: Mary Coleridge, 1861–1907
Music: Severus Gastorius, b. c. 1675, adapt.

WAS GOTT THUT
8.8.8.8.8.8.

EASTER

268 Jesus Christ Is Risen Today

♩ = 112

1. Je - sus Christ is risen to-day,
2. Love's re - deem - ing work is done,
3. Hearts are strong, and voic - es sing,
4. Soar we now where Christ has led,

Al - le -

lu - ia!

Earth and heaven in cho - rus say,
Fought the fight, the bat - tle won,
Where, O death, is now thy sting?
Liv - ing out the words he said,

Al - le - lu - ia!

Raise your joys and
Death in vain for -
As he died his
Made like him, like

Words: Charles Wesley, 1707–1788, alt.
Music: Lyra Davidica, 1708

EASTER HYMN
7.7.7.7. with Alleluias

tri - umphs high,
- bids him rise,
truth to save, Al - le - lu - ia!
him we rise,

Sing, ye heavens, and earth re - ply,
Christ has o - pened par - a - dise,
Where thy vic - to - ry, O grave?
Ours the cross, the grave, the skies,

Al - le - lu - ia!

269 Lo, the Day of Days Is Here

1. Lo, the day of days is here,
   Fes-ti-val of hope and cheer!
   At the south-wind's gen-ial breath—
   Na-ture wakes from seem-ing death,

2. Fields are smil-ing in the sun, Al - le-lu - ia!
   Loos-ened stream-lets sea-ward run, Al - le-lu - ia!
   Ten-der blade and leaf ap - pear; Al - le-lu - ia!
   'Tis the spring-tide of the year, Al - le-lu - ia!

3. Lo, the Eas-ter-tide is here,
   Mu-sic thrills the at-mo-sphere.
   Join, you peo-ple all, and sing—
   Love and praise and thanks-giv-ing,

Words: From Frederick Lucian Hosmer, 1840–1929
Music: Robert Williams, c. 1781–1821, harmony by John Roberts, 1822–1877

LLANFAIR
7.7.7.7. with Alleluias
EASTER

O Day of Light and Gladness   270

♩ = 66

1. O day of light and glad-ness, of proph-e-cy and
2. Earth feels the sea-son's joy-ance; from moun-tain range to
3. O Dawn of life e-ter-nal, to thee our hearts up-

song, what thoughts with-in us wak-en, what hal-lowed mem-'ries
sea the tides of life are flow-ing, fresh, man-i-fold, and
raise the Eas-ter song of glad-ness, the Pass-o-ver of

throng! The soul's ho-ri-zon wid-ens, past, pres-ent, fu-ture
free. In val-ley and on up-land, by for-est path-ways
praise. Thine are the man-y man-sions, the dead die not to

blend; and ris-es on our vi-sion the life that has no end.
dim, all na-ture lifts in cho-rus the res-ur-rec-tion hymn.
thee, who fill-est from thy full-ness time and e-ter-ni-ty.

⊕ Words: Frederick Lucian Hosmer, 1840–1929
Music: Henry Smart, 1813–1879

LANCASHIRE
7.6.7.6.D.

E A S T E R

271 Come Down, O Love Divine

1. Come down, O Love divine, seek thou this soul of
2. O let it freely burn, till earthly passions
3. And so the glory strong, for which the soul will

mine, and visit it with thine own ardor glowing;
turn to dust and ashes in its heat consuming;
long, shall far outpass the power of human telling;

O Comforter, draw near, within my heart ap-
and let its glorious light shine ever on my
for none can guess its grace, till we become the

pear, and kindle it, thy holy flame bestowing.
sight, and clothe me round, the while my path illuming.
place wherein the holy Spirit makes a dwelling.

Words: Bianco da Siena, d. c. 1434, tr. Richard Frederick Littledale, 1833–1890, alt.
Music: Ralph Vaughan Williams, 1872–1958

DOWN AMPNEY
6.6.11.D.

O Prophet Souls
of All the Years

♩ = 108

1. O proph-et souls of all the years, speak
2. From trop-ic clime and zones of frost they
3. One Life to-geth-er we con-fess, one

yet to us in love; your far-off vi-sion,
come of ev-ery name; this, this our day of
all-in-dwell-ing Word, one ho-ly Call to

toil, and tears to their ful-fill-ment move.
Pen-te-cost, on us the tongues of flame.
right-eous-ness with-in the si-lence heard:

4. One Law that guides the shining spheres
   as on through space they roll,
   and speaks in flaming characters
   on Sinais of the soul:

5. One Love, unfathomed, measureless,
   an ever-flowing sea,
   that holds within its vast embrace
   time and eternity.

⊕ Words: Frederick Lucian Hosmer, 1840–1929
Music: W. Tans'ur's *Compleat Melody*, 1735, harmony by John Wilson, b. 1905

BANGOR
C.M.

PENTECOST

273 Immortal, Invisible

1. Im - mor - tal, in - vis - i - ble, God on - ly wise. In
light in - ac - ces - si - ble hid from our eyes, most
bless - ed, most glo - rious, the An - cient of Days, al -
might - y, vic - to - rious, thy great name we praise.

2. Un - rest - ing, un - hast - ing, and si - lent as light, nor
want - ing, nor wast - ing, thou rul - est in might; thy
jus - tice like moun - tains high soar - ing a - bove thy
clouds which are foun - tains of good - ness and love.

3. To all, life thou giv - est, to great and to small; in
all life thou liv - est, the true life of all; all
laud we would ren - der; oh, help us to see, 'tis
on - ly the splen - dor of light hid - eth thee.

Another accompaniment, 122
Words: From Walter Chalmers Smith, 1824–1908, based on 1 Timothy 1:17
Music: John Roberts's *Caniadau y Cyssegr*, 1839

ST. DENIO
11.11.11.11.

THE CHRISTIAN SPIRIT

Dear Mother-Father of Us All 274

1. Dear Moth-er - Fa - ther of us all, for - give our fool-ish
2. In sim - ple trust like theirs who heard, be - side the Syr-ian
3. O Sab-bath rest by Gal - i - lee, O calm of hills a -

ways. Re - clothe us in our right - ful mind, in
sea, the gra - cious call - ing of the Word, let
bove, where Je - sus knelt to share with thee the

pur - er lives thy serv-ice find, in deep - er rev-erence, praise.
us, like them, our faith re-stored, rise up and fol - low thee.
si - lence of e - ter - ni - ty, in - ter - pret-ed by love.

4. With that deep hush subduing all
   our words and works that drown
   the tender whisper of thy call,
   as noiseless let thy blessing fall
   as fell thy manna down.

5. Drop thy still dews of quietness,
   till all our strivings cease;
   take from our souls the strain and stress,
   and let our ordered lives confess
   the beauty of thy peace.

Words: John Greenleaf Whittier, 1807–1892, alt.
Music: Frederick Charles Maker, 1844–1927

REST
8.6.8.8.6.

THE CHRISTIAN SPIRIT

Joyful Is the Dark

♩ = 66

1. Joy - ful is the dark, ho - ly, hid - den God,
2. Joy - ful is the dark, Spir - it of the deep,
3. Joy - ful is the dark, shad - owed sta - ble floor;

roll - ing cloud of night be - yond all nam - ing:
wing - ing wild - ly o'er the world's cre - a - tion,
an - gels flick - er, God on earth con - fess - ing,

maj - es - ty in dark - ness, en - er - gy of love,
silk - en sheen of mid-night, plum - age black and bright,
as with ex - ul - ta - tion, Ma - ry, giv - ing birth,

Words: Brian Wren, 1936– , © 1989 Hope Publishing Co.
Music: Carlton R. Young, 1926– , © 1990 Carlton R. Young

LINDNER
10.10.11.10.

THE CHRISTIAN SPIRIT

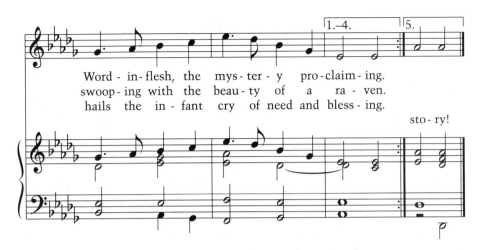

Word - in - flesh, the mys - ter - y pro - claim - ing.
swoop - ing with the beau - ty of a ra - ven.
hails the in - fant cry of need and bless - ing.

sto - ry!

4. Joyful is the dark
   coolness of the tomb,
   waiting for the wonder of the morning;
   never was that midnight
   touched by dread and gloom:
   darkness was the cradle of the dawning.

5. Joyful is the dark
   depth of love divine,
   roaring, looming thundercloud of glory,
   holy, haunting beauty,
   living, loving God.
   Hallelujah! Sing and tell the story!

276 O Young and Fearless Prophet

1. O young and fear-less Proph-et of an - cient Gal - i-
2. O help us stand un-swerv-ing a-gainst war's blood - y
3. Cre - ate in us the splen-dor that dawns when hearts are
4. Stir up in us a pro - test a-gainst un - need - ed

lee: your life is still a sum - mons to
way, where hate and lust and false - hood hold
kind, that knows not race nor sta - tion as
wealth; for some go starved and hun - gry who

serve hu - man - i - ty, to make our thoughts and
back your ho - ly sway; for - bid false love of
bound - 'ries of the mind; that learns to val - ue
plead for work and health. Once more give us your

ac - tions less prone to please the crowd, to
coun - try, that turns us from your call who
beau - ty, in heart, or mind, or soul, and
chal - lenge a - bove our nois - y day, and

Words: S. Ralph Harlow, alt., 1885–1972
Music: William Lloyd, 1786–1852

MEIRIONYDD
7.6.7.6.D.

THE CHRISTIAN SPIRIT

stand with hum - ble cour - age for truth with hearts un - bowed.
lifts a - bove the na - tion the neigh - bor - hood of all.
longs to see God's chil - dren as sa - cred, per - fect, whole.
come to lead us for - ward a - long your ho - ly way.

When We Wend Homeward 277

♩· = 48

1. When we wend home - ward to our land, like
2. For though our sow - ing work is hard, and

dream - ers we shall be; like leap - ing riv - ers
tears do free - ly flow, on har - vest day we'll

in the spring we'll joy - ful be and free!
shoul - der sheaves, our hearts will o - ver - flow!

Words: Psalm 126
Music: American folk melody, arr. by Annabel Morris Buchanan, 1889–1983,
© 1938, renewed 1966 J. Fischer & Bros. Co., harmony by Charles H. Webb,
1933– , © 1989 J. Fischer & Bros. Co.

LAND OF REST
C.M.

PSALMS

278 Praise Be to God, the Almighty

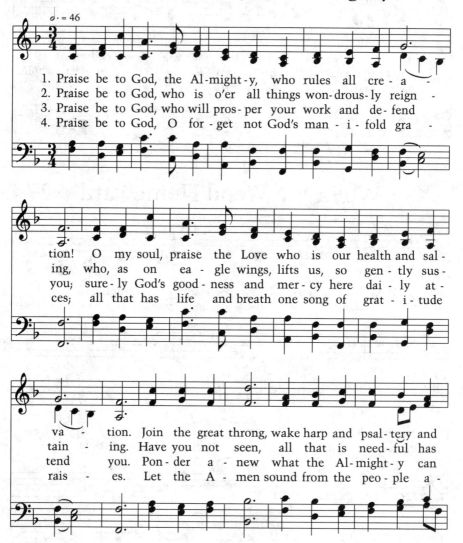

♩· = 46

1. Praise be to God, the Al-might-y, who rules all cre - a -
2. Praise be to God, who is o'er all things won-drous-ly reign -
3. Praise be to God, who will pros-per your work and de-fend
4. Praise be to God, O for-get not God's man - i-fold gra -

tion! O my soul, praise the Love who is our health and sal -
ing, who, as on ea - gle wings, lifts us, so gen - tly sus -
you; sure-ly God's good-ness and mer - cy here dai - ly at -
ces; all that has life and breath one song of grat - i - tude

va - tion. Join the great throng, wake harp and psal - ter-y and
tain - ing. Have you not seen, all that is need-ful has
tend you. Pon - der a - new what the Al-might-y can
rais - es. Let the A - men sound from the peo - ple a -

Words: Joachim Neander, 1650–1680, trans. based on Catherine Winkworth, 1827–1878, alt.
Music: *Erneuertes Gesangbuch II*, Stralsund, 1665, from Catherine Winkworth's *Chorale Book for England*, 1863

LOBE DEN HERREN
14.14.4.7.8.

PSALMS

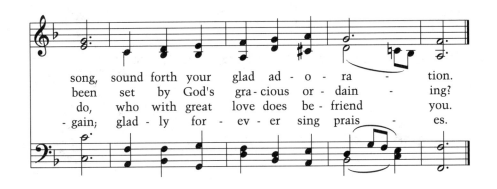

song, sound forth your glad ad - o - ra - tion.
been set by God's gra - cious or - dain - ing?
do, who with great love does be - friend you.
- gain; glad - ly for - ev - er sing prais - es.

By the Waters of Babylon   279

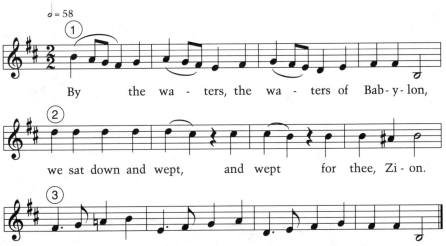

♩ = 58

① By the wa - ters, the wa - ters of Bab - y - lon,

② we sat down and wept, and wept for thee, Zi - on.

③ We re - mem - ber, we re - mem - ber, we re - mem - ber thee, Zi - on.

Words: Psalm 137
Music: Anon.

UNKNOWN
Irregular

280 Haleluhu

Ha - le - lu - hu, ha - le - lu - hu, be - tsil - tse - lei sha - ma.

Ha - le - lu - hu, ha - le - lu - hu, be - tsil - tse - lei te -

ru - a. Kol ha - n'sha - ma te - ha - leil yah,

1.
Ha - le - lu - yah, ha - le - lu - yah!
2.
ha - le - lu - yah!

Words & music: Traditional Hebrew
⊕ Music arr. by Mark Slegers, 1948–

HALELUHU
Irregular

PSALMS

O God, Our Help in Ages Past   281

1. O God, our help in ages past,
   our hope for years to come,
   our shelter from the storm-y blast,
   and our e-ter-nal home:

2. Be-fore the hills in or-der stood,
   or earth re-ceived its frame,
   from ev-er-last-ing thou art God,
   to end-less years the same.

3. A thou-sand a-ges in thy sight
   are like an eve-ning gone,
   short as the watch that ends the night
   be-fore the ris-ing sun.

4. Time, like an ever-rolling stream,
   soon bears us all away:
   we fly forgotten, as a dream
   dies at the opening day.

5. O God, our help in ages past,
   our hope for years to come,
   be thou our guard while troubles last,
   and our eternal home.

Words: Isaac Watts, 1674–1748, paraphrase of Psalm 90
Music: William Croft, 1678–1727

ST. ANNE
C.M.

282 Let the Whole Creation Cry

♩ = 126

1. Let the whole cre - a - tion cry, "Glo - ry be to
2. Chant in hon - or, o - cean fair; earth, soft rush - ing
3. You to whom the arts be - long, add your voic - es

God on high!" Heaven and earth, a - wake and sing,
through the air; birds, with morn and dew e - late,
to the song; bards of knowl - edge and of law,

to your God your prais - es bring.
sing with joy at heav - en's gate.
to the glo - rious cir - cle draw.

Sun and moon, up - lift your voice,
Let the blos - soms of the earth
From the north to south - ern pole

Words: From Stopford Augustus Brooke, 1832–1916, based on Psalm 148
Music: George Job Elvey, 1816–1893

ST. GEORGE'S WINDSOR
7.7.7.7.D.

night and stars, in God re - joice; sun - shine, dark - ness,
join the u - ni - ver - sal mirth; men and wom - en,
let the might - y cho - rus roll: "Ho - ly, ho - ly,

cloud, and storm, rain and snow in praise per - form.
young and old, raise the an - them man - i - fold.
ho - ly," cry; "Glo - ry be to God on high!"

283 The Spacious Firmament on High

1. The spa - cious fir - ma - ment on high, with
all the blue e - the - real sky, and span - gled
heavens, a shin - ing frame, their great O - rig - i -

2. Soon as the eve - ning shades pre - vail, the
moon takes up the won - drous tale, and night - ly
to the lis - tening earth re - peats the sto - ry

3. What though in sol - emn si - lence all move
round the dark ter - res - trial ball? What though no
re - al voice nor sound a - mid their ra - diant

Words: Joseph Addison, 1672–1719, paraphrase of Psalm 19:1–6
Music: Franz Joseph Haydn, 1732–1809, adapt. *Dulcimer, or New York Collection of Sacred Music*, 1850, alt.

CREATION
L.M.D.

- nal pro - claim. The un-wea - ried sun from
of its birth; whilst all the stars that
orbs be found? In rea - son's ear they

day to day does its Cre - a - tor's
round it burn, and all the plan - ets
all re - joice, and ut - ter forth a

power dis - play; and pub - lish - es to ev - ery
in their turn, con - firm the ti - dings, as they
glo - rious voice; for - ev - er sing - ing as they

land the work of an al - might - y hand.
roll and spread the truth from pole to pole.
shine, "The hand that made us is di - vine."

284 Praise, O My Heart, to You

1. Praise, O my heart, to you, O Source of
2. Your glo - ry is for - ev - er, and with
3. They wait for you a - lone, all liv - ing
4. They go a - gain to be the dust they

Life, you are my tide of joy, my sea, my
dance you move a - mong your works and they to
things, to have their food from you, and they are
tread. You breathe up - on the dust, they rise and

shore, my field of sky with stars that nev - er
you. You look up - on the earth, and at your
fed. When your hand o - pens they are sat - is -
are. I will sing prais - es to you while life

set; now I will learn your won - ders all my
glance it sways with trem - bling, and a - bove the
fied; you give; they gath - er. When they think you
fills my flesh with breath; as long as life shall

Words: Ridgely Torrence, 1875–1950, based on Psalm 104
Music: Robert L. Sanders, b. 1906, © 1963 Beacon Press

ADAM'S SONG
10.10.10.10.10.

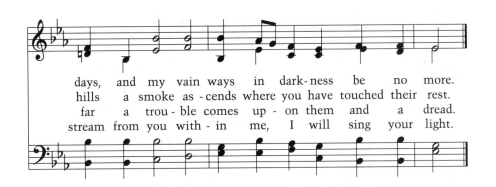

days,   and my vain ways   in dark-ness   be   no   more.
hills   a smoke as-cends where you have touched their rest.
far   a trou-ble comes   up-on them   and   a   dread.
stream from you with-in   me,   I will   sing   your   light.

285 We Worship Thee, God

1. We wor-ship thee, God, be-low and a-bove, and
2. We tell of thy might and sing of thy grace, en-
3. The earth with its store of won-ders un-told, thy
4. Though chil-dren of dust, as fee-ble as frail, by

grate-ful-ly sing thy power and thy love. Our
robed by the light and crown-ed by space. Thy
pow-er and care has found-ed from old, es-
thy end-less trust we fear not to fail. Thy

shield and de-fend-er, the An-cient of Days pa-
zeal for the just the deep thun-der-cloud forms, and
tab-lish-ed na-ture's un-chang-ing de-cree, and
wing with its shel-ter-ing touch does us mend, for

vil-ioned in splen-dor, and gird-ed with praise.
dark is thy path on the wings of the storm.
round it has cast, like a man-tle, the sea.
thou art our mak-er, re-deem-er, and friend.

Words: Robert Grant, 1779–1834, recast
Music: William Gardner's *Sacred Melodies*, 1815

LYONS
10.10.11.11.

PSALMS

A Core of Silence

♩ = 72 *Unison*

1. A core of si - lence breathes be - yond all words,
2. And half the mu - sic lies with - in the pause
3. The "True Re - li - gion" gath - ers up its text:

or else the words have lit - tle worth;
be - tween the arch - es of the heart;
"In the be - gin - ning was the Word."

to "Heart" or "Soul" or "Spir - it" it comes forth
the print up - on the page means less than ink
But I seek qui - et - ness be - hind that start

(the words we name them mat - ter not).
un - less the white and black both speak.
and name it noth - ing, much less "God."

Words & music: Jim Reilly, 1943– , © 1986 Jim Reilly

TRUE RELIGION
10.8.10.8.

287   Faith of the Larger Liberty

1. Faith of the larg-er lib-er-ty, source of the light ex-pand-ing, law of the church that is to be, old bond-age not-with-stand-ing: faith of the free! By

2. He-roes of faith in ev-ery age, far see-ing, self-de-ny-ing, wrought an in-creas-ing her-i-tage, mon-arch and creed de-fy-ing. Faith of the free! In

3. Faith for the peo-ple ev-ery-where, what ev-er their op-pres-sion, of all who make the world more fair, liv-ing their faith's con-fes-sion: faith of the free! What-

Words: Vincent B. Silliman, 1894–1979
Music: Bohemian Brethren, *Kirchengesang*, 1566

MIT FREUDEN ZART
8.7.8.7.8.8.7.

THE LIFE OF INTEGRITY

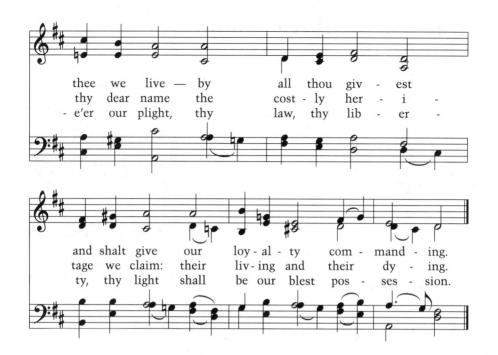

thee we live — by   all thou giv - est
thy dear name the   cost - ly her - i -
- e'er our plight, thy   law, thy lib - er -

and shalt give our   loy - al - ty com - mand - ing.
tage we claim: their   liv - ing and their dy - ing.
ty, thy light shall   be our blest pos - ses - sion.

All Are Architects

♩ = 104

1. All are ar-chi-tects of fate, work-ing in these walls of time; some with mas-sive deeds and great, some with or-na-ments of rhyme.

2. For the struc-ture that we raise time is with ma-te-rials filled; our to-days and yes-ter-days are the blocks with which we build.

3. Build to-day, then, strong and sure, with a firm and am-ple base; and as-cend-ing and se-cure shall to-mor-row find its place.

⊕ Words: Henry Wadsworth Longfellow, 1807–1882
⊕ Music: Thomas Benjamin, 1940– , © 1992 Unitarian Universalist Association

WOODLAND
7.7.7.7.

T H E   L I F E   O F   I N T E G R I T Y

Creative Love, Our Thanks We Give

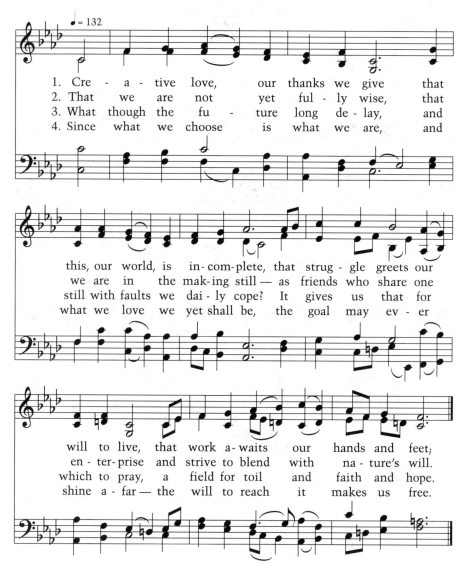

♩ = 132

1. Cre - a - tive love, our thanks we give that
2. That we are not yet ful - ly wise, that
3. What though the fu - ture long de - lay, and
4. Since what we choose is what we are, and

this, our world, is in - com - plete, that strug - gle greets our
we are in the mak - ing still — as friends who share one
still with faults we dai - ly cope? It gives us that for
what we love we yet shall be, the goal may ev - er

will to live, that work a - waits our hands and feet;
en - ter - prise and strive to blend with na - ture's will.
which to pray, a field for toil and faith and hope.
shine a - far — the will to reach it makes us free.

Words: William DeWitt Hyde, 1858–1917,
⊕ adapt. by Beth Ide, 1921–
Music: English melody, harmony by Ralph Vaughan Williams, 1872–1958,
used by perm. of Oxford University Press

TRUTH FROM ABOVE
L.M.

THE LIFE OF INTEGRITY

290 Bring, O Past, Your Honor

♩ =132

1. Bring, O Past, your hon - or; bring, O Time, your
2. Ring, in glad thanks - giv - ing, bell of grief and
3. Shrine of fron - tier cour - age, Si - nai of its
4. Church of pure re - form - ers, pi - o - neers un -

har - vest, gold - en sheaves of hal - lowed lives and
glad - ness, forth to town and prai - rie let our
vi - sion, home and hearth of com - mon quest for
daunt - ed, com - pa - ny of com - rades sworn to

minds by Truth made free; come, you faith - ful
fes - tal greet - ing go. Voic - es long de -
life's im - mor - tal good, stand, in years on -
keep the spir - it free; long o'er life's swift

Words: Charles H. Lyttle, 1884–1980
Music: John Bacchus Dykes, 1823–1876

NICAEA
12.13.12.10.

THE LIFE OF INTEGRITY

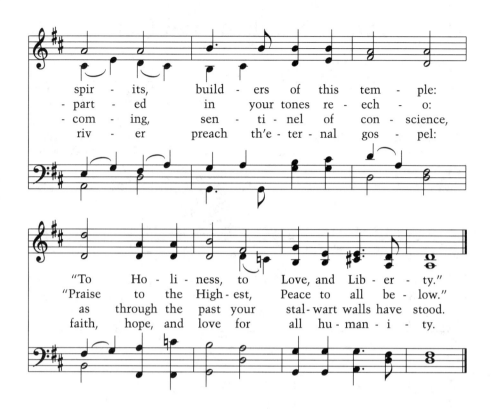

spir - its, build - ers of this tem - ple:
- part - ed in your tones re - ech - o:
- com - ing, sen - ti - nel of con - science,
riv - er preach th'e - ter - nal gos - pel:

"To Ho - li - ness, to Love, and Lib - er - ty."
"Praise to the High - est, Peace to all be - low."
as through the past your stal - wart walls have stood.
faith, hope, and love for all hu - man - i - ty.

291   Die Gedanken Sind Frei

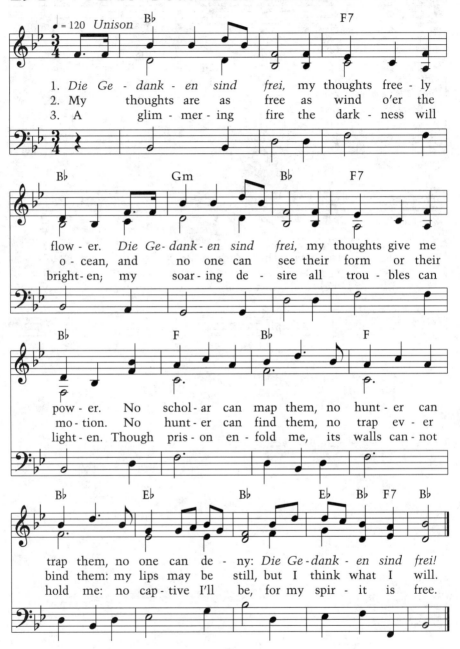

1. Die Ge-dank-en sind frei, my thoughts free-ly flow-er. Die Ge-dank-en sind frei, my thoughts give me pow-er. No schol-ar can map them, no hunt-er can trap them, no one can de-ny: Die Ge-dank-en sind frei!

2. My thoughts are as free as wind o'er the o-cean, and no one can see their form or their mo-tion. No hunt-er can find them, no trap ev-er bind them: my lips may be still, but I think what I will.

3. A glim-mer-ing fire the dark-ness will bright-en; my soar-ing de-sire all trou-bles can light-en. Though pris-on en-fold me, its walls can-not hold me: no cap-tive I'll be, for my spir-it is free.

Words: German folk song, English version, v. 1 by Arthur Kevess,
vs. 2–3 by Elizabeth Bennett, © 1955 American Ethical Union
Music: Alsatian folk tune

DIE GEDANKEN SIND FREI
6.6.6.6.6.6.6.5.6.

If I Can Stop
One Heart from Breaking

If I can stop one heart from break-ing, I shall not live in vain. If I can ease one life the ach-ing or cool one pain, or help one faint-ing rob-in un-to his nest a-gain, I shall not live in vain.

Words: Emily Dickinson, 1830–1886
Music: Leo Smit, 1921– , © 1990 Leo Smit

SMIT
Irregular

THE LIFE OF INTEGRITY

293　O Star of Truth

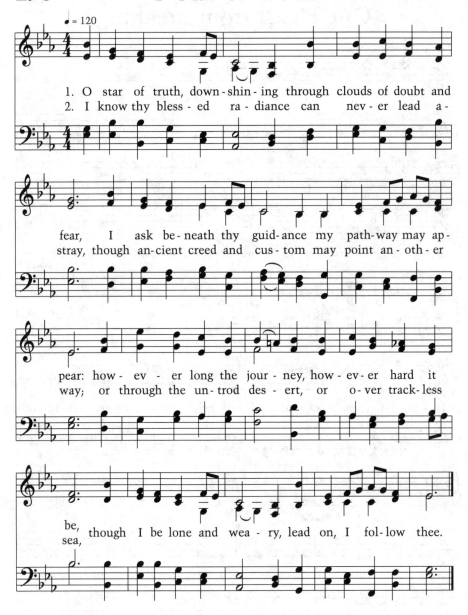

1. O star of truth, down-shin-ing through clouds of doubt and
2. I know thy bless-ed ra-diance can nev-er lead a-

fear, I ask be-neath thy guid-ance my path-way may ap-
stray, though an-cient creed and cus-tom may point an-oth-er

pear: how-ev-er long the jour-ney, how-ev-er hard it
way; or through the un-trod des-ert, or o-ver track-less

be, though I be lone and wea-ry, lead on, I fol-low thee.
sea,

Words: Minot Judson Savage, 1841–1918
Music: Finnish melody, adapt. by David Evans, 1874–1948, arr.

NYLAND
7.6.7.6.D.

THE LIFE OF INTEGRITY

Our Praise We Give

294

1. Our praise we give for har-vests earned, the fruits of
2. Our praise we give for har-bor's lee, for moor-ings
3. Our praise we give for jour-ney's end, the inn, all

la - bor gar - nered in; but praise we more the
safe in wa - ters still; but more the leagues of
warmth and light and cheer; but more for length-'ning

soil un-turned from which the yield is yet to win.
o - pen sea, where fa - voring gales our can-vas fill.
roads that wend through dust and heat and hill-tops clear.

Words: John Coleman Adams, 1849–1922
Music: Percy Carter Buck, 1871–1947, © Oxford University Press

GONFALON ROYAL
L.M.

THE LIFE OF INTEGRITY

295 Sing Out Praises for the Journey

♩ = 108

1. Sing out prais- es for the jour- ney, pil- grims, we, who
2. Look in - side, your soul's the kin - dling of the hearth fire
3. Stand we now up - on the thresh- old, fac- ing fu - tures

car - ry on, search- ers in the soul's deep yearn- ings,
pil- grims knew. Find the spir - it, al - ways rest - less,
yet un - known. Hearth be - hind us, way - side hos - tel

like our fore - bears in their time. We seek out the
find it in each mind and heart. Touch and hold that
built by those who knew wild roads. Guard we e'er their

spir - it's whole- ness in the end- less hu - man quest.
an - cient yearn - ing, kin- dling for a new- found truth.
sa - cred em - bers car - ried in our minds and hearts.

⊕ Words: Mark M. DeWolfe, 1953–1988,
⊕ rev. by Joyce Painter Rice, © 1991 Unitarian Universalist Association
Music: Henry Purcell, 1659–1695

WESTMINSTER ABBEY
8.7.8.7.8.7.

THE LIFE OF INTEGRITY

O Ye Who Taste That Love Is Sweet

O filii et filiæ, Alleluia.

1. O ye who taste that love is sweet, set way-marks for the doubt-ful feet that stum-ble on in search of it.

2. Sing hymns of love; that some who hear far off, in pain, may lend an ear. Rise up and won-der and draw near. Alleluia.

3. Lead lives of love; that oth-ers who be-hold your lives may kin-dle too with love, and cast their lot with you.

Words: Christina Georgina Rossetti, 1830–1894
Music: 15th cent. French melody

O FILII ET FILIAE
8.8.8. with Alleluias

297　The Star of Truth

1. The star of truth but dim - ly shines be-
2. The cer - tain - ty for which we crave no
3. Though for safe har - bor we may long, we
4. From hon - est doubt we shall not flee, nor

hind the veil - ing clouds of night, but
mor - tal ones can ev - er know; un -
must not let our cour - age fail, and,
fet - ter the in - quir - ing mind, for

ev - 'ry search - ing eye di - vines some
chart - ed wa - ters we must brave, and
though the winds of doubt blow strong, up -
where the hearts of all are free, a

Words: John Andrew Storey, 1935–1997
Music: Dede Duson, 1938– , © 1992 Unitarian Universalist Association

MCNAUGHTON
L.M.

THE LIFE OF INTEGRITY

par - tial glim - mer of its light.
face what - ev - er winds may blow.
- on the track - less o - cean sail.
tru - er faith we there shall find.

298 Wake, Now, My Senses

♩=108 *Unison*

1. Wake, now, my sens - es, and hear the earth call;
2. Wake, now, my rea - son, reach out to the new;
3. Wake, now, com - pas - sion, give heed to the cry;

feel the deep pow - er of be - ing in all;
join with each pil - grim who quests for the true;
voic - es of suf - fer - ing fill the wide sky;

keep, with the web of cre - a - tion your vow,
hon - or the beau - ty and wis - dom of time;
take as your neigh - bor both strang - er and friend,

giv - ing, re - ceiv - ing as love shows us how.
suf - fer thy lim - it, and praise the sub - lime.
pray - ing and striv - ing their hard - ship to end.

⊕ Words: Thomas J. S. Mikelson, 1936–
Music: Traditional Irish melody, harmony by Carlton R. Young, 1926– ,
renewal © 1992 Abingdon Press

SLANE
10.10.10.10.

THE LIFE OF INTEGRITY

4. Wake, now, my conscience,
   with justice thy guide;
   join with all people
   whose rights are denied;
   take not for granted
   a privileged place;
   God's love embraces
   the whole human race.

5. Wake, now, my vision
   of ministry clear;
   brighten my pathway
   with radiance here;
   mingle my calling
   with all who will share;
   work toward a planet
   transformed by our care.

Make Channels for the Streams of Love

299

1. Make chan-nels for the streams of love where
   they may broad-ly run; and love has o-ver-
   flow-ing streams to fill them ev-ery one.

2. But if at an-y time we cease such
   chan-nels to pro-vide, the ver-y founts of
   love for us will soon be parched and dried.

3. For we must share, if we would keep this
   gift all else a-bove; we cease to give, we
   cease to have — such is the law of love.

Words: From Richard Chenevix Trench, 1807–1886
Music: American folk melody, arr. by Annabel Morris Buchanan, 1889–1983,
© 1938, renewed 1966 J. Fischer & Bros. Co., harmony by Charles H. Webb,
1933– , © 1989 J. Fischer & Bros. Co.

LAND OF REST
C.M.

THE LIFE OF INTEGRITY

300 With Heart and Mind

1. With heart and mind and voice and hand may
   we this time and place tran - scend to
   make our pur - pose un - der - stood: a
   mor - tal search for mor - tal good, a

2. A mind that's free to seek the truth; a
   mind that's free in age and youth to
   choose a path no threat im - pedes, wher -
   ev - er light of con - science leads. Our

3. A heart that's kind, a heart whose search makes
   Love the spir - it of our church, where
   we can grow, and each one's gift is
   sanc - ti - fied, and spir - its lift, where

Words: Alicia S. Carpenter, 1930– , © 1990 Alicia S. Carpenter
Music: Johann Hermann Schein, 1586–1630, harmony by
J. S. Bach, 1685–1750

MACH'S MIT MIR, GOTT
8.8.8.8.8.8.

THE LIFE OF INTEGRITY

firm com - mit - ment to the goal of
mar - tyrs died so we could be a
ev - ery door is o - pen wide for

jus - tice, free - dom, peace for all.
church where ev - ery mind is free.
all who choose to step in - side.

301 Touch the Earth, Reach the Sky!

♩·= 52 *Unison*

1. Touch the earth, reach the sky! Walk on shores while
2. Touch the earth, reach the sky! Chil - dren ask the
3. Touch the earth, reach the sky! All are born and

spir - its fly o- ver the o - cean, o- ver the land, our
rea - sons why. In our lives the an - swers show, and
all shall die; life's the time left in be - tween, to

faith a quest to un - der - stand.
by our love they learn and grow.
fol - low a star, to build a dream.

4. Touch the earth, reach the sky!
   Hug the laughter, feel the cry.
   May we see where we can give,
   for this is what it means to live.

5. Touch the earth, reach the sky!
   Soar with courage ever high;
   spirits joining as we fly,
   to touch the earth, to reach the sky.

Words & music: Grace Lewis-McLaren, 1939– ,
© 1988 Grace Lewis-McLaren

TOUCH THE EARTH
6.7.9.8.

THE LIFE OF INTEGRITY

Children of the Human Race 302

♩ = 56 *Smoothly*

1. Chil - dren of the hu - man race, off - spring of our Moth - er Earth,
2. Should some sign of oth - ers reach this, our lone - ly plan - et Earth,

not a - lone in end - less space has our plan - et giv - en birth.
dif - ferenc - es of form and speech must not hide our com - mon worth.

Far a - cross the cos - mic skies count - less suns in glo - ry blaze,
When at length our minds are free, and the clouds of fear dis - perse,

and from un - told plan - ets rise end - less can - ti - cles of praise.
then at last we'll learn to be Chil - dren of the U - ni - verse.

Words: John Andrew Storey, 1935–1997
Music: Thomas Oboe Lee, 1945– , © 1992 Unitarian Universalist Association

SERVETUS
7.7.7.7.D.

We Are the Earth
Upright and Proud

1. We are the earth up-right and proud; in us the earth is
2. We lift our voic-es, fill the skies with our ex-ul-tant

know - ing. Its winds are mu - sic in our mouths, in
sing - ing. We ded - i - cate our minds and hearts, to

us its riv - ers flow - ing. The sun is our hearth-
or - der, beau - ty bring - ing. Our la - bor is our

fire; warm with the earth's de - sire, and
strength; our love will win at length; our

Words: Kenneth L. Patton, 1911–1994, © 1980 Kenneth L. Patton
Music: Martin Luther, 1483–1546, harmony by J. S. Bach, 1685–1750

EIN' FESTE BURG
8.7.8.7.6.6.6.6.7.

HUMANITY: WOMEN AND MEN

with its pur - pose strong, we sing earth's pil - grim
minds will find the ways to live in peace and

song; in us the earth is grow - ing.
praise. Our day is just be - gin - ning.

304 · A Fierce Unrest

𝅘𝅥 = 58 *Unison*

1. A fierce un-rest seethes at the core of all ex-ist-ing
2. But for the urge of this un-rest these joy-ous spheres are
3. From deed to dream, from dream to deed, from dar-ing hope to

things: it was the ea-ger wish to soar that
mute; but for the reb-el in our breast had
hope, the rest-less wish, the in-stant need, still

gave the gods their wings. There throbs through all the
we re-mained as brutes. When baf-fled lips de-
drove us up the slope. Sing we no gov-erned

worlds that are this heart-beat hot and strong, and
mand-ed speech, speech trem-bled in-to birth; one
fir-ma-ment, cold, or-dered, reg-u-lar; we

Words: Don Marquis, 1878–1937
Music: Ananias Davisson's *Kentucky Harmony*, c. 1815

SALVATION
C.M.D.

HUMANITY: WOMEN AND MEN

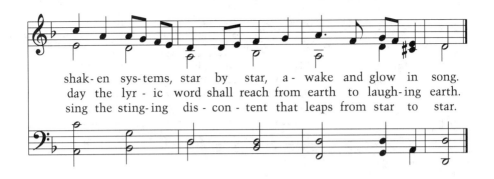

shak-en sys-tems, star by star, a-wake and glow in song.
day the lyr-ic word shall reach from earth to laugh-ing earth.
sing the sting-ing dis-con-tent that leaps from star to star.

De Colores 305

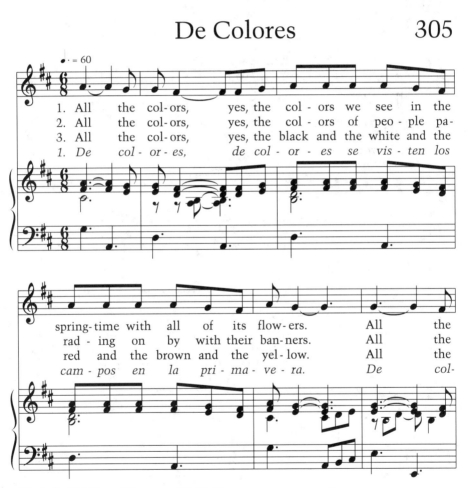

♩. = 60

1. All the col-ors, yes, the col-ors we see in the
2. All the col-ors, yes, the col-ors of peo-ple pa-
3. All the col-ors, yes, the black and the white and the
1. *De col-or-es, de col-o-res se vis-ten los*

spring-time with all of its flow-ers. All the
rad-ing on by with their ban-ners. All the
red and the brown and the yel-low. All the
cam-pos en la pri-ma-ve-ra. De col-

Words: David Arkin, used by perm. of Hodgin Press
Music: Traditional Spanish folk,
⊕ arr. by Betty A. Wylder, 1923–1994, © 1992 Unitarian Universalist Association

DE COLORES
Irregular with refrain

col - ors, when the sun - light shines out through a
col - ors, yes, the col - ors of pen - nants and
col - ors, all the col - ors of peo - ple who
- or - es, de col - or - es son los pa - ja -

rift in the cloud and it show - ers. All the
stream - ers and plumes and ban - dan - nas. All the
smile and shake hands and say "Hel - lo!" All the
ri - tos que vien - en de a fue - ra. De col -

col - ors, as a rain - bow ap - pears when a
col - ors, yes, the col - ors of peo - ple now
col - ors, yes, the col - ors of peo - ple who
or - es, de col - or - es es al ar - co

storm cloud is touched by the sun.
tak - ing their place in the sun. All the
know that their free - dom is won. Y por
ir - is que ve - mos lu - cir.

col - ors a - bound for the whole world a - round and for
e - so los gran - des a - mo - res de much - os col-

ev - 'ry - one un - der the sun.
or - es me gus - tan a mi.

Interlude

306 Sing of Living, Sing of Dying

1. Sing of liv-ing, sing of dy - ing, let them both be joined in one,
2. O - pen to a deep-er lov - ing, o - pen to the gift of care,

parts of an e - ter-nal pro - cess like the ev - er-cir-cling
search-ing for a high-er jus - tice, help-ing oth - ers in des -

sun. From the fresh-ness of each in - fant giv-ing
pair. Through the ten - der bonds of liv - ing in a

hope in what is new, to the wis-dom of the
more in-clu - sive way we are o-pened more to

Words: Thomas J. S. Mikelson, 1936–
Music: W. Frederick Wooden, 1953– , © 1992 Unitarian Universalist Association

ENOCH
8.7.8.7.D.

a - ged deep - ened by a long - er view.
suf - fering from the loss - es of each day.

The Human Touch
Can Light the Flame
307

1. The hu-man touch can light the flame which gives a
2. The lov-er's kiss, the friend's em - brace, the clasp of
3. May all who come with - in our reach be kin-dled

bright - ness to the day, the spir - it us - es mor - tal
hands to show we care, the light of wel - come on the
by our in - ner glow, not just in spir - it's words we

flame, life's ve - hi - cle for work and play.
face are treas - ured mo - ments all can share.
preach, in hu - man touch love's faith we show.

Words: John Andrew Storey, 1935–1997
Music: Lee Hastings Bristol, Jr., 1923–1979, © 1962 Theodore Presser Co.

DICKINSON COLLEGE
L.M.

308   The Blessings of the Earth and Sky

♩ = 92

1. The bless-ings of the earth and sky up-
2. The wind up-on the lakes and hills per-
3. Here we re-store an-ces-tral dreams en-

on our friend-ly house do lie. The
forms its na-tive rit-u-als. The
shrined in floor and wall and beam, a

right-ness of a mas-ter's art has
wor-ship of our hu-man toil brings
mon-u-ment where-in we build that

⊕ Words: Kenneth L. Patton, 1911–1994, © 1980 Kenneth L. Patton
Music: Johann Hermann Schein, 1586–1630, harmony by
J. S. Bach, 1685–1750

MACH'S MIT MIR, GOTT
8.8.8.8.8.8.

blessed with grace its ev - ery part. The warmth of man - y
sac - ra - ment from sun and soil. With words and mu - sic,
their high pur - pose be ful - filled, a tool to help our

hands is strewn in hu - man bless - ing on this stone.
we, the earth, in na - ture's won - der seek our worth.
chil - dren prove an earth of prom - ise and of love.

309 Earth Is Our Homeland

♩ = 112 *Unison*

1. Earth is our home-land: a song of stars, a grace
2. Word is our glo-ry, our breath of air, our cry!
3. Mu-sic is won-der, an al-che-my of art,
4. Hope is our high star, the cer-ti-tude love brings;

wrought of the a-ges, an o-pal spun in
Par-a-bles, let-ters, or star-names in the
love's pure en-chant-ment, com-mu-nion for the
si-lence our cen-ter, our liv-ing wa-ter's

space! Dawn's far blue hill, soft night-time still, dark
sky, or myths that play as po-ets pray bring
heart! From chants to Psalms, from jazz to Brahms, no
spring. Though ach-ing heart know self a-part from

⊕ Words: Mark L. Belletini, 1949– , and
⊕ Helen R. Pickett, 1929– , © 1992 Unitarian Universalist Association
Music: Johannes Brahms, 1833–1897, arr. by Fred Bock, 1939– ,
adapt. © 1976 Fred Bock Music Co.

SYMPHONY
11.11.8.6.8.9.

HUMANITY: WOMEN AND MEN

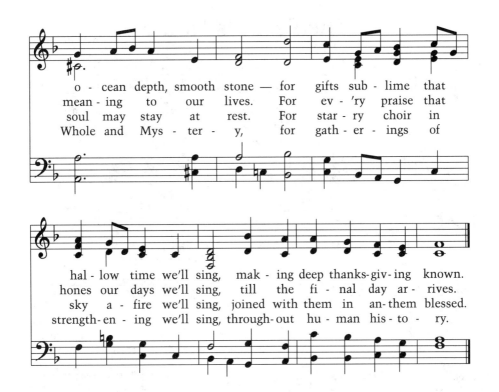

o - cean depth, smooth stone — for gifts sub - lime that
mean - ing to our lives. For ev - 'ry praise that
soul may stay at rest. For star - ry choir in
Whole and Mys - ter - y, for gath - er - ings of

hal - low time we'll sing, mak - ing deep thanks-giv-ing known.
hones our days we'll sing, till the fi - nal day ar - rives.
sky a - fire we'll sing, joined with them in an-them blessed.
strength-en - ing we'll sing, through-out hu - man his - to - ry.

310 The Earth Is Home

1. The earth is home and all a-
2. She is our friend, our an-cient
3. We suck-le from the fount un-

bun- dant, source of what was be - fore
moth- er; her fate and all her ways
tir - ing, we chil- dren born of earth's

we were, and will be, till all
are ours; each at - om proves our
de - sir - ing; for we and all our

⊕ Words: Kenneth L. Patton, 1911–1994, © 1980 Kenneth L. Patton
⊕ Music: William Albright, 1944–1998, © 1973 Elkan-Vogel, Inc.

ALBRIGHT
9.8.9.8.

HUMANITY: WOMEN AND MEN

life in end - ing, the fi - nal
com - mon jour - ney, bred as we
for - ward yearn - ing are yet a

seed shakes in its burr.
were of dust and stars.
spark in na - ture's burn - ing.

8va

Optional instrumental ostinato

pp

Instructions:

1. Play the 9 pitches in the order given and in any register (except low); let vibrate.

2. Play steadily in any tempo (MM 52–120); each player should choose a different tempo.

3. Starting with the first note only, add one series note to each repetition (1; 1+2; 1+2+3; etc.). When the series is completed, reverse the process.

4. When the entire cycle is completed, begin again without interruption.

5. The instruments begin shortly before the organ (or piano) and at the end they continue briefly after the accompaniment stops.

6. Instruments should blend with one another as much as possible to create an overall "celestial" effect, or spaced out at a distance.

311 Let It Be a Dance

Let it be a dance we do. May I have this dance with you? Through the good times and the bad times, too, let it be a dance.

May be sung unaccompanied

⊕ Words & music: Ric Masten, 1929– , © 1977 Mastenville Music (BMI),
⊕ arr. by Betty A. Wylder, 1923–1994, © 1992 Unitarian Universalist Association

MASTEN
Irregular

1. Let a danc-ing song be heard.
2. Ev-ery-bod-y turn and spin,
3. Morn-ing star comes out at night,

Play the mu-sic, say the words,
let your bod-y learn to bend,
with-out the dark there is no light.

and fill the sky with sail-ing birds.
and, like a wil-low with the wind,
If noth-ing's wrong, then noth-ing's right.

Let it be a dance. Let it be a dance. Let it be a
let it be a dance. Let it be a dance. Let it be a
Let it be a dance. Let it be a dance. Let it be a

dance. Learn to fol-low, learn to lead,
dance. A child is born, the old must die;
dance. Let the sun shine, let it rain;

feel the rhy-thm, fill the need
a time for joy, a time to cry.
share the laugh-ter, bear the pain,

to reap the har - vest, plant the seed.
Take it as it pass - es by.
and round and round we go a - gain.

Let it be a dance.
Let it be a dance.
Let it be a dance.

312 Here on the Paths of Every Day

1. Here on the paths of every day—here on the
   common human way—is all the stuff the gods would
   take to build a heaven, to mold and make New E - dens.
   Ours the task sub - lime to build e - ter - ni - ty in time.

2. We need no oth - er stones to build the tem - ple
   of the un - ful - filled—no oth - er i - vory for the
   doors—no oth - er mar - ble for the floors—no oth - er
   ce - dar for the beam and dome of our im - mor - tal dream.

Words: From Edwin Markham, 1852–1940
Music: William Walker's *Southern Harmony*, 1835

FILLMORE
8.8.8.8.8.8.

O What a Piece of Work Are We 313

♪. = 58 *Unison*

1. O what a piece of work are we, how
2. Why need to look for mir - a - cles out -
3. But give us room to move and grow, but

mar - vel - ous - ly wrought; the quick con - triv - ance
side of na - ture's law? Hu - man - i - ty we
give our spir - it play, and we can make a

of the hand, the won - der of our
won - der at with ev - ery breath we
world of light out of the com - mon

thought, the won - der of our thought.
draw, with ev - ery breath we draw!
clay, out of the com - mon clay.

⊕ Words: Malvina Reynolds, 1900–1978, © 1958 Schroder Music;
renewed 1986 N. Schimmel
Music: *The Southern Harmony*, 1835, harmony by Charles H. Webb, 1933– ,
© 1989 The United Methodist Publishing House

DOVE OF PEACE
8.6.8.6.6.

HUMANITY: WOMEN AND MEN

314 We Are Children of the Earth

1. We are chil-dren of the earth, chil-dren of the earth, and we love our moth - er earth, love our moth - er earth. From the moun-tain and the streams, from the flow - ing streams, comes the foun-tain here be - side us

2. We dream of a vil - lage fair, of a vil - lage fair. Laugh-ing chil-dren play - ing there, chil-dren play - ing there, and our el - ders can be found, el - ders can be found, here be - side us

3. There is noth-ing to de - sire, noth-ing to de - sire, more than home and hearth and fire, home and hearth and fire, in a vil - lage that we love, vil - lage that we love, liv - ing side by

Words: Alicia S. Carpenter, 1930– , © 1990 Alicia S. Carpenter
Music: Nguyen-Duc Quang

CON X'OM LANG
7.5.7.5.D.

HUMANITY: WOMEN AND MEN

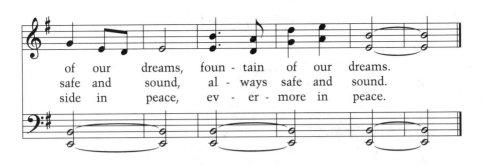

of our dreams, foun-tain of our dreams.
safe and sound, al-ways safe and sound.
side in peace, ev-er-more in peace.

This Old World 315

1. This old world is full of sor-row,
2. We're all chil-dren of one fam-ily;
3. This old world can be a gar-den,
4. It is said now, "Love thy neigh-bor,"

full of sick-ness, weak and sore; if you love your
we're all broth-ers, sis-ters, too; if you cher-ish
full of fra-grance, full of grace; if we love our
and we know well that is true; this, the sum of

neigh-bor tru-ly, love will come to you the more.
one an-oth-er, love and friend-ship come to you.
neigh-bors tru-ly, we must meet them face to face.
hu-man la-bor, true for me as well as you.

Words: American folk tune, adapt.
Music: Melody from *The Southern Harmony*, 1835

RESTORATION
8.7.8.7.

Tradition Held Fast

♩ = 112

1. Tra-

di - tion held fast through var - ied time and
2. Freed from the world - ly bur - dens that we
3. Now though we turn to sep - arate lives, re -

place, the rais - ing of voic - es, the
bear, re - leased in this time of for -
newed, our cir - cle of peace will not

Words & music: Jim Scott, 1946– , © 1990 Jim Scott

CIRCLE OF SPIRIT
11.11.9.10.

touch - ing of hands. Cir - cle of spir - it,
- giv-ing, heal-ing, shar - ing. Lift - ed by the power of
break as we part. Though form is gone as

coun - cil of grace, all faith finds ex - pres - sion 'cross
our com - mu - nion, held in the warmth of a
we con - clude, through us will it o - pen to

Last time

count - less lands.
com - mon car - ing.
ev - ery fate of life and ev-ery o - pen heart.

317   We Are Not Our Own

1. We are not our own. Earth forms us,
2. We are not a - lone. Earth names us:
3. There - fore let us make thanks - giv - ing,
4. Let us be a house of wel - come,

hu - man leaves on na - ture's grow - ing vine,
past and pres - ent, peo - ples near and far,
and with jus - tice, will - ing and a - ware,
liv - ing stone up - hold - ing liv - ing stone,

fruit of man - y gen - er - a - tions,
fam - i - ly and friends and strang - ers
give to earth, and all things liv - ing,
glad - ly show - ing all our neigh - bors

Words: Brian Wren, 1936– , © 1988 Hope Publishing Co.
Music: David Hurd, 1950– , © 1990 David Hurd

NEXUS
8.9.8.5.

HUMANITY: WOMEN AND MEN

seeds   of   life   di - vine.
show   us who   we   are.
lit - ur - gies   of   care.
we   are not   our own!

318 We Would Be One

1. We would be one as now we join in sing-ing
2. We would be one in build-ing for to-mor-row

our hymn of love, to pledge our-selves a - new
a no - bler world than we have known to - day.

to that high cause of great-er un - der - stand-ing
We would be one in search-ing for that mean-ing

of who we are, and what in us is true.
which binds our hearts and points us on our way.

Words: Samuel Anthony Wright, 1919–
Music: Jean Sibelius, 1865–1957, arr. from *The Hymnal*, 1933,
© 1933, renewed 1961 Presbyterian Board of Christian Education

FINLANDIA
11.10.11.10.11.10.

We would be one in living for each other
As one, we pledge ourselves to greater service,

to show to all a new community.
with love and justice, strive to make us free.

319 Ye Earthborn Children of a Star

♩ = 108

1. Ye earth-born chil-dren of a star a - mid the
2. Look out, with awe, up - on the art of count-less
3. Be - yond the won-der you have wrought with - in your

depths of space, the cos - mic won-der from a -
liv - ing things; the coun-ter-point of part with
lit - tle time; the knowl-edge won, the wis - dom

far with - in your minds em - brace.
part, as na-ture's cho - rus sings.
sought, the or - na - ments of rhyme.

⊕ Words: John G. MacKinnon, 1903–1983
Music: Dede Duson, 1938– , © 1992 Unitarian Universalist Association

GREENVILLE
C.M.

4. Seek deeper still within your souls
   and sense the wonder there;
   the ceaseless thrust to noble goals
   of life, more free and fair.

5. Ye earthborn children of a star
   who seek and long and strive,
   take humble pride in what you are:
   be glad to be alive.

The Pen Is Greater 320

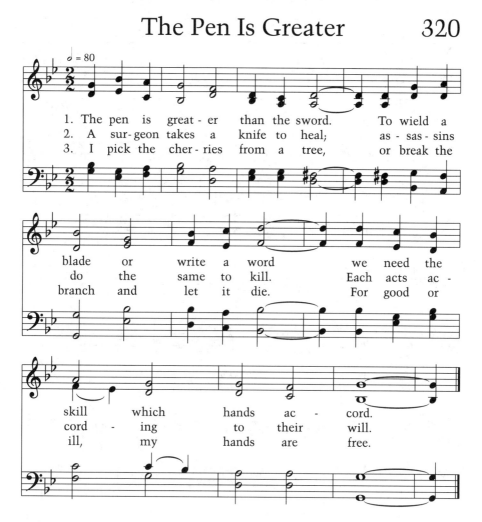

1. The pen is great-er than the sword. To wield a
   blade or write a word we need the
   skill which hands ac - cord.

2. A sur-geon takes a knife to heal;
   as - sas-sins do the same to kill. Each acts ac -
   cord - ing to their will.

3. I pick the cher-ries from a tree,
   or break the branch and let it die. For good or
   ill, my hands are free.

4. With fingers I can soothe a brow,
   or make a fist and strike a blow,
   kindness or cruelty bestow.

5. Then let us now this lesson see:
   like life itself our hands can be
   for evil used, or charity.

Words: John Andrew Storey, 1935–1997
Music: David Dawson, 1939–

GRAGARETH
8.8.8.

HUMANITY: WOMEN AND MEN

Here in the Flesh

1. Here in the flesh is all that we can know,
2. Here in the flesh is all that we will find,

all beau-ty, all won-der, all the pow-er,
swift in the blood and throb-bing in the bone,

all the un-earth-ly col-ors, all the glow,
Beau-ty her-self, the u-ni-ver-sal mind,

Words: John Masefield, 1878–1967
Music: T. J. Anderson, 1928– , © 1992 Unitarian Universalist Association

SONG SPRINGS
Irregular

HUMANITY: WOMEN AND MEN

here in the self which with-ers like a flow-er.
e - ter-nal A - pril wan-der-ing a-

lone.

322   Thanks Be for These

1. Thanks be for these, life's ho - ly times,
   mo - ments of grief, days of de - light;
   tri - umph and fail - ure in - ter - twine,
   shap - ing our vi - sion of the right.

2. Thanks be for these, for birth and death;
   life in be - tween with mean - ing full;
   ho - ly be - comes the quick - ened breath;
   we cel - e - brate life's in - ter - val.

3. Thanks be for these, en - no - bling art,
   im - ag - es wel - come to our sight;
   mu - sic ca - ress - ing ear and heart,
   in - vit - ing us to loft - ier height.

4. Thanks be for these, who question why;
who noble motives do obey;
those who know how to live and die;
comrades who share this holy way.

5. Thanks be for these, we celebrate;
sing and rejoice, our trust declare;
press all our faith into our fate;
bless now the destiny we share.

Words: Richard Seward Gilbert, 1936– , and
Joyce Timmerman Gilbert, 1936– , © 1992 Unitarian Universalist Association
Music: Hungarian melody, 16th cent.,
arr. by Robert L. Sanders, 1906–

TRANSYLVANIA
L.M.

HUMANITY: WOMEN AND MEN

Break Not the Circle 323

♩ = 60

1. Break not the cir - cle of en - a - bling
2. Come, won - der at this love that comes to
3. Join then the move-ment of the love that

love where peo - ple grow, for - giv - en and for -
life, where words of free-dom are with hu - mor
frees, till peo - ple of what - ev - er race or

giv - ing; break not that cir - cle, make it wid - er
spo - ken, and peo - ple keep no score of wrong and
na - tion will tru - ly be them-selves, stand on their

still, till it in - cludes, em - brac - es all the liv - ing.
guilt, but will that hu - man bonds re-main un - bro - ken.
feet, see eye to eye with laugh-ter and e - la - tion.

Words: Fred Kaan, 1929– , © 1975 Hope Publishing Co.
Music: Thomas Benjamin, 1940– , © 1992 Unitarian Universalist Association

YADDO
10.11.10.11.

HUMANITY: WOMEN AND MEN

324 Where My Free Spirit Onward Leads

♩ = 116

1. Where my free spir-it on-ward leads, well, there shall be my way; by my own light il-lu - mined I've jour-neyed night and day; my age, a time-worn cloak I wear as

2. My fam-i - ly is not con-fined to moth - er, mate, and child; but it in-cludes all crea - tures be they tame or be they wild; my fam-i - ly up - on this earth in -

3. The ev - er spin-ning u - ni-verse, well, there shall be my home; I sing and spin with-in it as through this life I roam; e - ter-ni - ty is hard to ken and

Words: Alicia S. Carpenter, 1930– , © 1989 Alicia S. Carpenter
Music: English traditional melody, harmony and arr. by Ralph Vaughan
Williams, 1872–1958, used by perm. of Oxford University Press

KINGSFOLD
C.M.D.

HUMANITY: WOMEN AND MEN

once I wore my youth; I cel - e - brate life's
- cludes all liv - ing things on land, or in the
hard - er still is this: a hu - man life when

mys - ter - y; I cel - e - brate death's truth.
o - cean deep, or borne a - loft on wings.
tru - ly seen is brief - er than a kiss.

325 Love Makes a Bridge

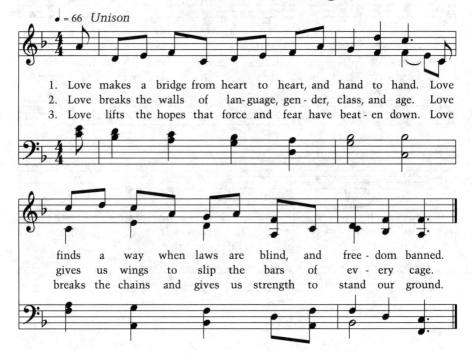

♩ = 66 *Unison*

1. Love makes a bridge from heart to heart, and hand to hand. Love
2. Love breaks the walls of lan-guage, gen - der, class, and age. Love
3. Love lifts the hopes that force and fear have beat - en down. Love

finds a way when laws are blind, and free - dom banned.
gives us wings to slip the bars of ev - ery cage.
breaks the chains and gives us strength to stand our ground.

4. Love rings the bells of wanted birth
and wedding day.
Love guides the hands that promise more
than words can say.

5. Love makes a bridge that winds may shake,
yet not destroy.
Love carries faith through life and death,
to endless joy.

Words: Brian Wren, 1936– , © 1983 Hope Publishing Co.
Music: Gerald Wheeler, b. 1929, © Gerald Wheeler

EMERY
8.4.8.4.

Let All the Beauty
We Have Known

326

♩ = 69 *Unison*

1. Let all the beau-ty we have known il-lu-mi-
2. We cel-e-brate with sing-ing hearts the love-li-
3. Life's mu-sic and its po-et-ry sur-round and

nate our hearts and minds. Re-joice in won-ders dai-ly
ness of sky and earth, the in-spi-ra-tion of the
bless us through our days. For these we sing in har-mo-

shown, in faith and joy, and love that binds.
arts, the mir-a-cle of ev-'ry birth.
ny, to-geth-er giv - ing thanks and praise.

⊕ Words: Dana McLean Greeley, 1908–1986
Music: English melody, adapt. and harmony by Ralph Vaughan Williams, 1872–1958, © 1931 Oxford University Press

DANBY
L.M.

BEAUTY, TRUTH, AND GOODNESS

Joy, Thou Goddess

Words: Friedrich Schiller, 1759–1805
Music: Ludwig van Beethoven, 1770-1827

HYMN TO JOY
8.7.8.7.D.

BEAUTY, TRUTH, AND GOODNESS

joins	a	-	gain;	hu	-		man	-	kind	is
orbs	of		light;	dis	-		tant	spheres	o	-
streng	*ge*	-	*teilt,*	*al*	-		*le*	*Men*	-	*schen*
Fir	-	*ma*	-	*ment,*	*Sphä*	-	*ren*	*rollt*	*sie*

one	for	-	ev	-	er	'neath	thy	mild	and	gen	-	tle	reign.
bey	her		pow	-	er,	far	be -	yond	all	mor	-	tal	sight.
wer	-	*den*	*Brü*	-	*der,*	*wo*	*dein*	*sanf* -	*ter*	*Flü*	-	*gel*	*weilt.*
in	*den*	*Räu*	-	*men,*	*die*	*des*	*Se* -	*hers*	*Rohr*	*nicht*	*kennt.*

328 I Sought the Wood in Summer

♩ = 126 *Unison*

1. I sought the wood in sum-mer when ev-ery twig was
2. "How frail a thing is Beau-ty," I said, "when ev-ery
3. I sought the wood in win-ter when ev-ery leaf was
4. "How sure a thing is Beau-ty," I cried. "No bolt can

green; the rud-est boughs were ten - der, and
breath she gives the va-grant sum - mer but
dead; be - hind the wind-whipped branch - es the
slay, nor wave nor shock de - spoil her, nor

buds were pink be - tween. Light - fin-gered as - pens
swift - er woos her death. For this the star dust
win - ter sun was red. The birch - es, white and
rav - ish - ers dis - may. The gran - ite hills are

Words: Willa Cather, 1893–1947
Music: Hal Hopson, 1933– , © 1983 Hope Publishing Co.

MERLE'S TUNE
7.6.7.6.D.

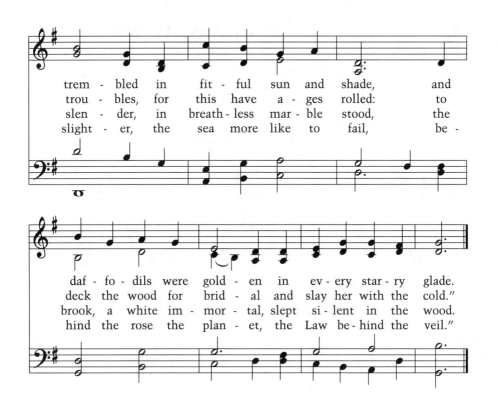

trem - bled in fit - ful sun and shade, and
trou - bles, for this have a - ges rolled: to
slen - der, in breath - less mar - ble stood, the
slight - er, the sea more like to fail, be -

daf - fo - dils were gold - en in ev - ery star - ry glade.
deck the wood for brid - al and slay her with the cold."
brook, a white im - mor - tal, slept si - lent in the wood.
hind the rose the plan - et, the Law be - hind the veil."

329 Life Has Loveliness to Sell

♩ = 100 *Unison*

1. Life has love-li-ness to sell, all beau-ti-ful and splen-did things, blue waves whit-ened on a cliff, soar-ing fire that sways and sings, and
2. Life has love-li-ness to sell, as mu-sic, like a curve of gold, scent of pine trees in the rain, eyes that love you, arms that hold, and
3. Spend all you have for love-li-ness, to buy and nev-er count the cost: for one sing-ing hour of peace count a year of strife well lost, and

Words: Sara Teasdale, 1884–1933   BLISS
Music: Leo W. Collins, 1925– , © 1985 Leo W. Collins   7.8.7.7.8.7.

BEAUTY, TRUTH, AND GOODNESS

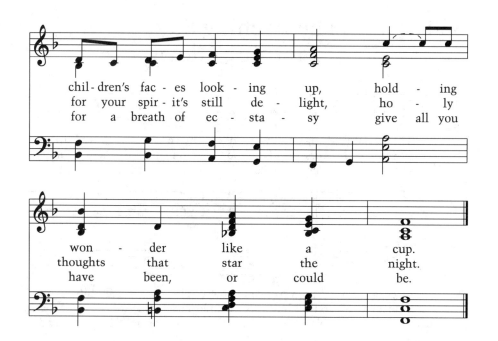

chil - dren's fac - es look - ing up, hold - ing
for your spir - it's still de - light, ho - ly
for a breath of ec - sta - sy give all you

won - der like a cup.
thoughts that star the night.
have been, or could be.

330

The Arching Sky of Morning Glows

1. The arch - ing sky of morn - ing glows like
2. The col - ors of our con - toured land no
3. When - ev - er sounds the sa - cred sigh be -

fres - coes high in vault - ed rows. The rag - ged hills of
art - ist born could hue as grand, but con - tours of the
neath this ga - ble of the sky, the forms of art and

green - ing spring like cho - rus mas - ters bid us sing.
hu - man heart sole ground-ings are for ev - ery art!
spir - it blend; by craft and morn our hearts tran - scend.

Words: Mark L. Belletini, 1949– , © 1992 Unitarian Universalist Association
Music: Thomas Tallis, c. 1505–1585

TALLIS' CANON
L.M.

♩ = 96 *Unison*

1. Life is the great-est gift of all the rich-es on this
2. Mind is the bright-est gift of all, its thought no bar-rier
3. We are of life, its shin-ing gift, the meas-ure of all

earth; life and its crea-tures, great and small, of
mars; it seeks cre-a-tion's hid-den plan, its
things; up from the dust our tem-ples lift, our

high and low-ly birth: so trea-sure it and
quest sur-mounts all bars; it reins the wind, it
vi-sion soars on wings; for seed and root, for

mea-sure it with deeds of shin-ing worth.
chains the storm, it weighs the out-most stars.
flower and fruit, our grate-ful spir-it sings.

Words: From William E. Oliver,
⊕ adapt. by Waldemar Hille, 1908–1996, used by perm. of Hodgin Press
Music: James Leith McBeth Bain, c. 1840–1925,
⊕ arr. by David Dawson, 1939–

BROTHER JAMES' AIR
8.6.8.6.8.6.

BEAUTY, TRUTH, AND GOODNESS

332 Perfect Singer

1. Per-fect Sing-er, songs of earth rise on ev-ery field and hearth; let our voic-es sound a-gain an-cient songs of joy and pain.
2. All your crea-tures strive for life, suf-fer hurt in an-gry strife, seek com-pas-sion, find re-lease in the cov-e-nant of peace.
3. Sing a sa-cred mel-o-dy for the jus-tice that shall be; let our har-mo-nies re-solve dis-so-nance in stead-fast love.
4. Stead-fast Seek-er, find our song wo-ven in-to lives made strong; let the pat-terns of sur-prise kin-dle hope with each sun-rise.

⊕ Words: George Kimmich Beach, 1935–
⊕ Music: Béla Bartók, 1881–1945, © 1946 by Hawkes & Son (London) Ltd., renewed 1973

CHORALE
7.7.7.7.

BEAUTY, TRUTH, AND GOODNESS

Alone She Cuts and Binds the Grain

1. A - lone she cuts and binds the grain, and sings a mel - an - chol - y strain: O lis - ten! for the vale pro - found is o - ver - flow - ing with the sound.

2. Will no one tell me what she sings? Per - haps the plain - tive num - bers flow for old, un - hap - py far - off things, and for the bat - tles long a - go.

3. Or is it some more hum - ble lay, fa - mil - iar mat - ter of to - day? Some nat - u - ral sor - row, loss, or pain, that once has been, may be a - gain?

4. I lis - tened, mo - tion - less and still, and, as I mount - ed up the hill, the mu - sic in my heart I bore long af - ter it was heard no more.

Words: William Wordsworth, 1770–1850
Music: A.D. Carden's *Missouri Harmony*, 1820

DEVOTION
L.M.

334   When Shall We Learn

1. When shall we learn, what should be clear as day,
2. For through our live-ly traf-fic all the day,
3. Or else we make a scare-crow of the day,

we can-not choose what we are free to love?
in my own per-son I am forced to know
loose ends and jum-ble of our com-mon world;

We are cre-a-ted with and from the world
how much must be for-got-ten out of love,
or else our chang-ing flesh can nev-er know

Words: W. H. Auden, 1907–1973, © 1943, renewed 1971 by W. H. Auden,
used by perm. of Random House, Inc.
Music: Carl Flentge Schalk, b. 1929, © 1979 Carl Flentge Schalk

FLENTGE
10.10.10.10.

INSIGHT AND WISDOM

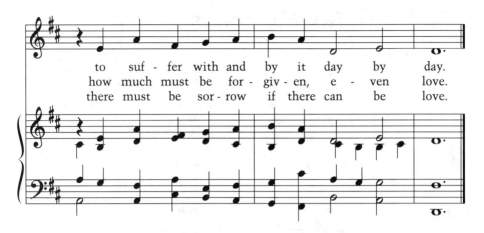

to suf - fer with and by it day by day.
how much must be for - giv - en, e - ven love.
there must be sor - row if there can be love.

Once When My Heart
Was Passion Free

335

♩ = 84 *Unison*

1. Once when my heart was pas - sion free to
2. I held the se - crets of the deep and
3. And for a mo - ment's in - ter - val the

learn of things di - vine, the soul of na - ture
of the heavens a - bove; I knew the har - mo -
earth, the sky, the sea — my soul en - com - passed

sud - den - ly out - poured it - self in mine.
nies of sleep, the mys - ter - ies of love.
each and all, as they en - com - pass me.

Words: John B. Tabb, 1845–1909
Music: From *Kentucky Harmony*, 1816

PRIMROSE
C.M.

INSIGHT AND WISDOM

336   All My Memories of Love

1. All my memories of love hang upon high stars.
2. Willows in September touch the water clear,
3. Many are the graceful hearts hung upon this tree.

All the souls I've lost to tears now the autumn jars;
set among the rushes tall of the flowing year.
And it seems there's room for mine on these branches free;

and the air around me here thickens with their song;
Rising up from sunlit past comes the shadowed sigh
and the sky above the tree, whether wet or bright,

Words: Anna Akhmatova, c. 1888–1966,
⊕ trans. by Mark L. Belletini, 1949–
Music: Solesmes version of plainsong melody, adapt.

ADORO TE DEVOTE
7.5.7.5.D.

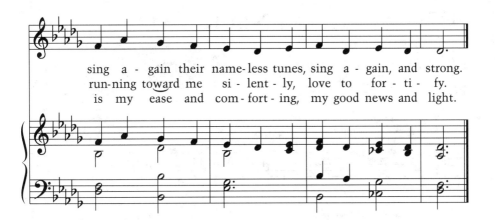

sing a - gain their name-less tunes, sing a - gain, and strong.
run-ning toward me si - lent - ly, love to for - ti - fy.
is my ease and com - fort - ing, my good news and light.

337 Have I Not Known

Unison

♩ = 76

1. Have I not known the sky and sea put on a look as hushed and stilled as if some an-cient proph-e-cy drew close up-on to be ful-filled? Like mist the hous-es shrink and

2. And life and death but one thing are — and I have seen this wing-less world cursed with im-per-ma-nence and whirled like dust a-cross the sum-mer swirled, and I have dealt with Pres-enc-

Words: Don Marquis, 1878–1937, © 1946 Doubleday & Company
Music: Charles Hubert Hastings Parry, 1848–1918, arr. by Janet Wyatt, b. 1934

JERUSALEM
L.M.D.

INSIGHT AND WISDOM

swell, like blood the high - ways throb and beat, the sap-less
- es be - hind the veils of Time and Place, and I have

stones be - neath my feet turn fo - li - ate with mir - a -
seen this world a star — bright, shin-ing, won - der - ful in

1.
cle.

2.
space.

Alternative arrangement, next page

INSIGHT AND WISDOM

I Seek the Spirit of a Child   338

♩·= 60 *Unison*

1. I seek the spir-it of a child, the child who meets life nat-ural-ly, the child who sings the world a-live, and greets the morn-ing sun with glee. Chil-dren are real be-yond all art.   May I see: Joy's a gift to our heart.

2. I seek the free-dom of a child, a child who loves in-stinc-tive-ly, who lights our day with just a smile, and shines that light on all we see. Chil-dren are real be-yond all fears.   May I see: Hope's a gift to our tears.

3. I seek the won-der of a child, a child who sees de-light-ful-ly, now clowns in cloud, now gold in sun — im-ag-i-na-tions true and free. Chil-dren are real be-yond all lies.   May I see: Faith's a gift to our eyes.

⊕ Words: Carl G. Seaburg, 1922–1998, © 1992 Unitarian Universalist Association
Music: Traditional English melody, arr. and harmony by Ralph Vaughan Williams, 1872–1958, used by perm. of Oxford University Press

SUSSEX CAROL
8.8.8.8.8.9.

INSIGHT AND WISDOM

339 Knowledge, They Say

1. Knowl - edge, they say, drives won - der from the world; they say it still, though all the dust's a - blaze with mar - vels at their feet, while New - ton's laws fore - tell that knowl-edge one day shall be song.

2. We seem like chil - dren wan - dering by the shore, gath - er - ing peb - bles col - ored by the wave; while the great sea of truth, from sky to sky stretch - es be - fore us, bound-less, un - ex - plored.

Words: Arthur Noyes, 1880–1958, recast
Music: Cyril V. Taylor, b. 1907, © 1985 Hope Publishing Co.

SHELDONIAN
10.10.10.10.

INSIGHT AND WISDOM

Though Gathered Here to Celebrate

340

♩ = 100

1. Though gath-ered here to cel-e-brate, my spir-it's burn-ing
2. There have been loss-es on the way; a par-ent, part-ner,
3. The still-ness strips the masks a-way, ex-pos-es lone-ly

low; in-stead of serv-ing, now I wait, the
friend. At times I need to grieve and say, "I
hearts; self-pit-y must not have its way; I'll

breath of wor-ship's not too late, breathe, let the em-bers glow.
have e-nough to bear to-day, be near and help me mend."
live my life from day to day, and now the heal-ing starts.

Words: Christine Doreian Michaels, 1942–
Music: W. Frederick Wooden, 1953– ,
© 1992 Unitarian Universalist Association

DISTANT BELOVED
8.6.8.8.6.

INSIGHT AND WISDOM

341   O World, Thou Choosest Not the Better Part

1. O world, thou choos-est not the bet-ter part!
2. Our knowl-edge is a torch of smok-y pine

It is not wis-dom to be on-ly wise,
that lights the path-way but one step a - head

and on the in - ward vi - sion close the eyes,
a - cross a void of mys-ter - y and dread.

but it is wis-dom to be-lieve the heart.
Bid, then, the ten-der light of faith to shine

Words: George Santayana, 1863–1952
Music: Orlando Gibbons, 1583–1625, harmony by Ralph Vaughan Williams,
1872–1958, used by perm. of Oxford University Press

SONG I
10.10.10.10.10.10.

INSIGHT AND WISDOM

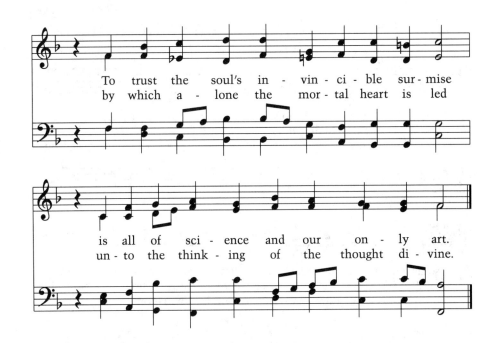

To trust the soul's in - vin - ci - ble sur - mise
by which a - lone the mor - tal heart is led

is all of sci - ence and our on - ly art.
un - to the think - ing of the thought di - vine.

342 O Slowly, Slowly, They Return

♩ = 66 *Unison*

1. O slow - ly, slow - ly, they re - turn to
2. As pa - tient stars they build in air tier
3. They stand in wait - ing all a - round, up -

some small wood - land let a - lone: great trees, out - spread - ing
af - ter tier a tim - bered choir, stout beams up - hold - ing
ris - ings of their na - tive ground, down - com - ings of the

and up - right, a - pos - tles of the liv - ing light.
weight - less grace of song, a bless - ing on this place.
dis - tant light; they are the ad - vent they a - wait.

4. Receiving sun and giving shade,
their life's a benefaction made,
and is a benediction said
o'er all the living and the dead.

5. In fall their brightened leaves, released,
fly down the wind, and we are pleased
to walk in radiance, amazed.
O light come down to earth, be praised.

Words: Wendell Berry, 1934– , excerpted from *Sabbaths*, © 1987 Wendell Berry,
used by perm. of North Point Press
Music: Swiss melody, 1826

SOLOTHURN
L.M.

A Firemist and a Planet 343

♩ = 76 Unison

1. A fire-mist and a plan-et, a crys-tal and a
2. Haze on the far ho-ri-zon, the in-finite ten-der
3. Like tides on cres-cent sea-beach, when moon's so new and
4. A sen-try lone and fro-zen, a moth-er starved for her

cell, a star-fish and a sau-rian, and caves where an-cients
sky, the ripe, rich tints of corn-fields, and wild geese sail-ing
thin, in-to our hearts high yearn-ings come well-ing, surg-ing
brood, and Soc-ra-tes' dread hem-lock, and Je-sus on the

dwelt; the sense of law and beau-ty, a face turned from the
high; and o-ver high and low-land, the charm of gold-en-
in, come from the mys-tic o-cean whose rim no foot has
rood; and mil-lions, who, though name-less, the straight, hard path-way

sod — some call it ev-o-lu-tion, and oth-ers call it God.
rod — some peo-ple call it au-tumn, and oth-ers call it God.
trod — some peo-ple call it long-ing, and oth-ers call it God.
trod — some call it con-se-cra-tion, and oth-ers call it God.

Words: From William Herbert Carruth, 1859–1924
Music: New England folk melody

NEW ENGLAND
7.6.7.6.D.

A Promise
through the Ages Rings

1. A prom - ise through the a - ges rings, that
2. A life is made of man - y things: bright
3. En - tombed with - in our deep de - spair, our
4. For some - thing al - ways, al - ways sings. This

al - ways, al - ways, some-thing sings. Not just in May, in
stars, bleak years, and bro - ken rings. Can it be true that
pain seems more than we can bear; but days shall pass, and
is the mes - sage Eas - ter brings: from deep de - spair and

finch-filled bower, but in De - cem-ber's cold - est hour, a
through all things, there al - ways, al - ways some-thing sings? The
na - ture knows that deep be - neath the win - ter snow a
per - ished things a green shoot al - ways, al - ways springs, and

Words: Alicia S. Carpenter, 1930– , rev., © 1983 Alicia S. Carpenter
Music: Severus Gastorius, c. 1675, ed. by A. Waggoner

WAS GOTT THUT
8.8.8.8.8.

HOPE

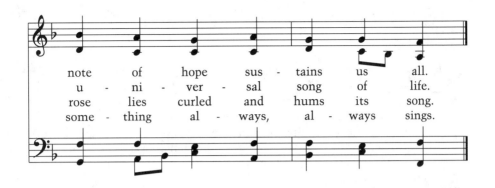

note of hope sus - tains us all.
u - ni - ver - sal song of life.
rose lies curled and hums its song.
some - thing al - ways, al - ways sings.

With Joy We Claim the Growing Light

345

♩ = 108

1. With joy we claim the grow - ing light, ad -
2. With wid - er view, come loft - ier goal; with

vanc - ing thought, and wid - ening view, the larg - er free - dom,
full - er light, more good to see; with free - dom, tru - er

clear - er sight, which from the old un - fold the new.
self - con - trol; with knowl - edge, deep - er rev - erence be.

Words: Samuel Longfellow, 1819–1892
Music: *Musicalisches Handbuch*, Hamburg, 1690, adapt.

WINCHESTER NEW
L.M.

HOPE

346 Come, Sing a Song with Me

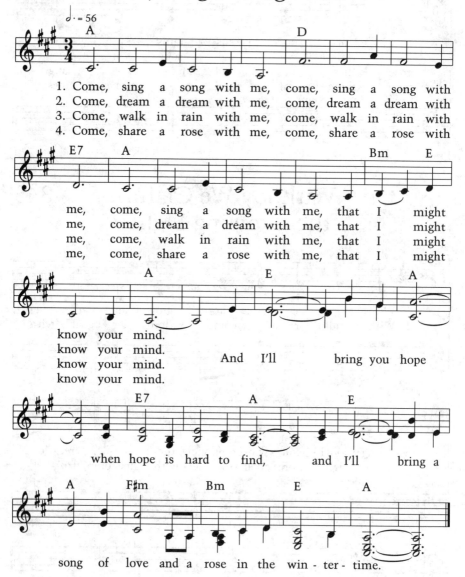

♩· = 56

1. Come, sing a song with me, come, sing a song with me, come, sing a song with me, that I might know your mind.
2. Come, dream a dream with me, come, dream a dream with me, come, dream a dream with me, that I might know your mind.
3. Come, walk in rain with me, come, walk in rain with me, come, walk in rain with me, that I might know your mind.
4. Come, share a rose with me, come, share a rose with me, come, share a rose with me, that I might know your mind.

And I'll bring you hope when hope is hard to find, and I'll bring a song of love and a rose in the win - ter - time.

Words & music: Carolyn McDade, 1935– , © 1976 Surtsey Publishing Co.

A ROSE IN WINTER
Irregular

HOPE

Gather the Spirit

1. Gath-er the spir-it, har-vest the power.
2. Gath-er the spir-it of heart and mind.
3. Gath-er the spir-it grow-ing in all,

Our sep-'rate fires will kin-dle one flame.
Seeds for the sow-ing are laid in store.
drawn by the moon and fed by the sun.

Wit-ness the mys-ter-y of this hour. Our
Nur-tured in love, and con-science re-fined, with
Win-ter to spring, and sum-mer to fall, the

GATHER THE SPIRIT
9.9.9.10. with refrain

HOPE

Gath-er in hope, com-pas-sion and strength.

Gath-er to cel-e-brate once a-gain.

348 Guide My Feet

♩ = 72

1. Guide my feet
2. Hold my hand
3. Stand by me
4. Search my heart

while I run this race.

Guide my feet
Hold my hand
Stand by me
Search my heart

while I run this race.

Guide my feet
Hold my hand
Stand by me
Search my heart

while I run this race, for I

don't want to run this race in vain! *(race in vain!)*

Words: Traditional
Music: Spiritual from the collection of Willis Laurence James, 1900–1966
harmony by Wendell Whalum, 1932–

GUIDE MY FEET
Irregular

HOPE

We Gather Together

1. We gath-er to-geth-er in joy-ful thanks-giv-ing, ac-
2. We gath-er to-geth-er to join in the jour-ney, con-

claim-ing cre-a-tion, whose boun-ty we share; both
firm-ing, com-mit-ting our pas-sage to be a

sor-row and glad-ness we find now in our liv-ing, we
true af-fir-ma-tion, in joy and trib-u-la-tion, when

sing a hymn of praise to the life that we bear.
bound to hu-man care and hope — then we are free.

⊕ Words: Dorothy Caiger Senghas, 1930– , and
⊕ Robert E. Senghas, 1928– , ⊕ © 1992 Unitarian Universalist Association
Music: Adrian Valerius's *Nederlandtsch Gedenckclanck*, 1626,
arr. by Edward Kremser, 1838–1914

KREMSER
12.11.13.12.

HOPE

350

The Ceaseless Flow
of Endless Time

1. The cease-less flow of end-less time no
2. The pres-ent slips in-to the past, and
3. The past and fu-ture ev-er meet in

one can check or stay; we'll view the past with
dream-like melts a-way; the break-ing of to-
the e-ter-nal now: to make each day a

no re-gret, nor fu-ture with dis-may.
mor-row's dawn be-gins a new to-day.
thing com-plete shall be our New Year vow.

Words: John Andrew Storey, 1935–1997
Music: African American spiritual, c. 1750–1875, adapt. and harmony by
Harry T. Burleigh, 1866–1949

MCKEE
C.M.

A Long, Long Way the Sea-Winds Blow

♩ = 76

1. A long, long way the sea-winds blow a-
2. And work we must, and love we must, and
3. A long, long way the sea-winds blow — but

cross the sea-plains blue, but long-er far my
do the best we may, and take the hope of
some-where lies a shore — thus down the tide of

heart must go be - fore its dreams come true.
dreams in trust to keep us day by day.
time shall flow my dreams for - ev - er - more.

Words: William Stanley Braithwaite, 1878–1962
Music: M. C. H. Davis in *Southern Harmony*, 1835

LIVERPOOL
C.M.

HERE AND NOW

352   Find a Stillness

1. Find a still-ness, hold a still-ness, let the still-ness car-ry me.
2. Seek the es-sence, hold the es-sence, let the es-sence car-ry me.

Find the si-lence, hold the si-lence, let the si-lence car-ry me.
Let me flow-er, help me flow-er, watch me flow-er, car-ry me.

In the spir-it, by the spir-it, with the spir-it giv-ing pow-er,
In the spir-it, by the spir-it, with the spir-it giv-ing pow-er,

I will find true har - mo - ny.
I will find true har - mo - ny.

Words: Carl G. Seaburg, 1922–1998, based on a Unitarian Transylvanian text,
© 1992 Unitarian Universalist Association
Music: Transylvanian hymn tune,
harmony by Larry Phillips, 1948– , © 1992 Unitarian Universalist Association

SIGISMUND
8.7.8.7.8.7.7.

HERE AND NOW

Golden Breaks the Dawn   353

♩ = 108

1. Gold-en breaks the dawn; comes the east-ern sun
2. As the spin-ning globe rolls a-way the night,

o - ver lake and lawn, sets its course to run.
na-ture wears a robe spun of morn-ing light.

Birds a - bove us fly, flow - ers bloom be - low,
Dawn break in me too, as in skies a - bove;

through the earth and sky life's great mer - cies flow.
teach me to be true, fill my heart with love.

Words: v. 1 from the Chinese of T. C. Chao, b. 1888,
trans. by Frank W. Price and Daniel Niles,
⊕ v. 2 by John Andrew Storey, 1935–1997
Music: Hu Te-Ai, b.c. 1900,
⊕ harmony by David Dawson, 1939–

LE P'ING
5.5.5.5.D.

354 We Laugh, We Cry

♩. = 58 *Unison*

1. We laugh, we cry, we live, we die; we dance, we sing our
2. A child is born a-mong us and we feel a spe-cial
3. Our lives are full of won-der and our time is ver-y
4. We seek e-lu-sive an-swers to the ques-tions of this

song. We need to feel there's some-thing here to
glow. We see time's end-less jour-ney as we
brief. The death of one a-mong us fills us
life. We seek to put an end to all the

which we can be-long. We need to feel the
watch the ba-by grow. We thrill to hear im-
all with pain and grief. But as we live, so
waste of hu-man strife. We search for truth, e-

⊕ Words & music: Shelley Jackson Denham, 1950– , © 1980 Shelley Jackson Denham,
⊕ harmony by Betsy Jo Angebranndt, 1931– , © 1992 Unitarian Universalist Association

CREDO
Irregular

free-dom just to have some time a - lone. But
- ag - i - na - tion free - ly run - ning wild. We
shall we die, and when our lives are done the
- qual - i - ty, and bless - ed peace of mind. And

most of all we need close friends we can call our ver - y
ded - i - cate our minds and hearts to the spir - it of this
mem - o - ries we shared with friends, they will lin - ger on and
then, we come to - geth - er here, to make sense of what we

own. And we be - lieve in life, and in the
child. And we be - lieve in life, and in the
on. And we be - lieve in life, and in the
find. And we be - lieve in life, and in the

strength of love; and we have found a need to be to-
strength of love; and we have found a time to be to-
strength of love; and we have found a place to be to-
strength of love; and we have found a joy be-ing to-

HERE AND NOW

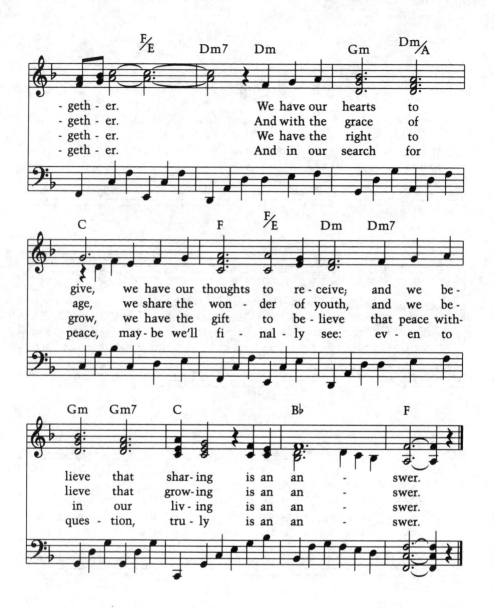

We Lift Our Hearts in Thanks 355

♩ = 120

1. We lift our hearts in thanks to-day for
2. And, next, the beau - ty of the earth, its
3. Then, har - vests of its teem - ing soil in
4. And, most, the gifts of hope and love, of

all the gifts of life; and, first, for peace that
flowers and love - ly things, the spring's great mir - a -
or - chard, croft, and field; but, more, the ser - vice
wis - dom, truth, and right, the gifts that shine like

turns a - way the en - mi - ties of strife.
cle of birth, with sound of songs and wings.
and the toil of those who helped them yield.
stars a - bove to chart the world by night.

Words: Percival Chubb, 1860–1960, © 1955 American Ethical Union
Music: *Harmoniae Hymnorum Scholae Gorlicensis*, 1599

PRAETORIUS
C.M.

356 Will You Seek in Far-Off Places?

♩ = 108 *Unison*

1. Will you seek in far-off plac-es? Sure-ly you come
2. Joy and peace are in this hour, here, not in an-

home at last; in fa-mil-iar forms and fac-es,
oth-er place. Here in this be-lov-ed flow-er;

things best known, you find the best.
now, in this be-lov-ed face.

Optional ostinato

⊕ Words: Alicia S. Carpenter, 1930– , based on a text by Walt Whitman,
© 1976 Walton Music Corp.
Music: From J. A. Freylinghausen's *Geistreiches Gesangbuch*, 1705,
arr. by Norman Luboff, 1917–1987, © 1976 Walton Music Corp.

GUTER HIRTE
8.7.8.7.

HERE AND NOW

Bright Morning Stars

1. Bright morn-ing stars are ris-ing. Bright
2. Oh, where are our dear moth-ers? Oh,
3. They are sow-ing seeds of glad-ness. They are

morn-ing stars are ris-ing. Bright
where are our dear moth-ers? Oh,
sow-ing seeds of glad-ness. They are

morn-ing stars are ris-ing.
where are our dear moth-ers?
sow-ing seeds of glad-ness.

Day is a-break-ing in my soul.

4. Oh, where are our dear fathers?
Oh, where are our dear fathers?
Oh, where are our dear fathers?
Day is a-breaking in my soul.

5. They are in the fields a-plowing.
They are in the fields a-plowing.
They are in the fields a-plowing.
Day is a-breaking in my soul.

Words: Anonymous
Music: American folk song, arr. by James A. Lucas,
© 1983 Plymouth Music, used by perm. of Walton Music Corp.

BRIGHT MORNING STARS
7.7.7.8.

ENTRANCE SONGS

358 Rank by Rank Again We Stand

1. Rank by rank again we stand,
from the four winds gath-ered hith-er. Loud the hal-lowed
walls de-mand whence we come and how, and whith-er.

2. Ours the years' me-mo-rial store,
hon-ored days and names we reck-on, days of com-rades
gone be-fore, lives that speak and deeds that beck-on.

3. Though the path be hard and long,
still we strive in ex-pec-ta-tion; join we now their
age-less song one with them in as-pi-ra-tion.

Words: From John Huntley Skrine, 1848–1923
⊕ New words by Carl G. Seaburg, 1922–1998
Music: Henry Walford Davies, 1869–1941, © Oxford University Press

REUNION
7.8.7.8.7.7.7.7.

ENTRANCE SONGS

From their still - ness / break - ing clear,
From the dream - ing / of the night
One in name, in / hon - or one,

ech - oes wake to / warn or cheer; high - er truth from
to the la - bors / of the day, shines their ev - er -
guard we well the / crown they won; what they dreamed be

saint and seer / call to us as - sem - bled here.
last - ing light, / guid - ing us up - on our way.
ours to do, / hope their hopes, and seal them true.

359   When We Are Gathered

1. When we are gath-ered for a time of
2. For youth shall pass and time is wise, and

wor-ship and of song, let none for-get the
count-less sea-sons turn, so day by day our

joys and griefs that mark each path of life, and thus we
years in-crease un-til at last by life re-leased our

⊕ Words: Grace Lewis-McLaren, 1939– , © 1992 Unitarian Universalist Association
Music: Charles Hubert Hastings Parry, 1848–1918

REPTON
8.6.8.6.8.6.

reach for those who love, we reach for those who love.
spir - its shine like stars, our spir - its shine like stars.

360 Here We Have Gathered

♩ = 76

1. Here we have gath - ered, gath - ered side by side;
2. Here we have gath - ered, called to cel - e - brate
3. Life has its bat - tles, sor - rows, and re - gret:

cir - cle of kin - ship, come and step in - side!
days of our life - time, mat - ters small and great:
but in the shad - ows, let us not for - get:

May all who seek here find a kind - ly
we of all a - ges, wom - en, chil - dren,
we who now gath - er know each oth - er's

word; may all who speak here
men, in - fants and sa - ges,
pain; kind - ness can heal us:

Words: Alicia S. Carpenter, 1930– , © 1979 Alicia S. Carpenter
Music: Genevan psalter, 1543

OLD 124TH
10.10.10.10.10.

ENTRANCE SONGS

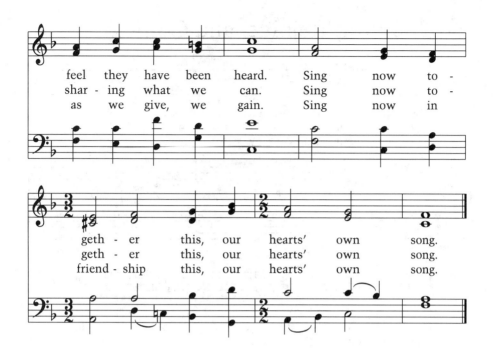

feel they have been heard. Sing now to-
shar - ing what we can. Sing now to-
as we give, we gain. Sing now in

geth - er this, our hearts' own song.
geth - er this, our hearts' own song.
friend - ship this, our hearts' own song.

361   Enter, Rejoice, and Come In

♩ = 112

1. En - ter, re - joice, and come in.
2. O - pen your ears to the song.
3. O - pen your hearts ev - 'ry - one.

En - ter, re - joice, and come in.
O - pen your ears to the song.
O - pen your hearts ev - 'ry - one.

To - day will be a

joy - ful day; en - ter, re - joice, and come in.

4. Don't be afraid of some change.
   Don't be afraid of some change.
   Today will be a joyful day;
   enter, rejoice, and come in.

5. Enter, rejoice, and come in.
   Enter, rejoice, and come in.
   Today will be a joyful day;
   enter, rejoice, and come in.

Words & music: Louise Ruspini,
⊕ arr. by Betty A. Wylder, 1923–1994, © 1992 Unitarian Universalist Association

REJOICE
7.7.8.7.

ENTRANCE SONGS

Rise Up, O Flame

Rise up, O flame, by thy light glow - ing,

show to us beau - ty, vi - sion, and joy.

Words: Anonymous
Music: Christoph Praetorius

CHALICE
4.5.5.4.

363 Alleluia! Sang Stars

Al - le - lu - ia! sang stars that gave us birth! Al - le - lu - ia! re-sounds our home, the earth! Al - le - lu - ia! shall

Words: Mark L. Belletini, 1949– , © 1992 Unitarian Universalist Association
Music: Patrick L. Rickey, 1964– , © 1992 Unitarian Universalist Association

DOXOLOGY
10.10.10.10.

PRAISE SONGS AND DOXOLOGIES

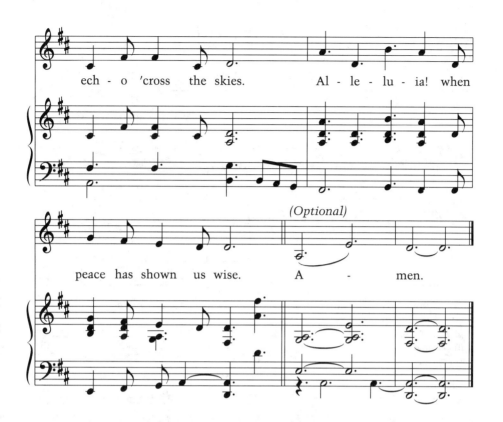

ech - o 'cross the skies. Al - le - lu - ia! when

peace has shown us wise. A - men.

(Optional)

Alleluia, Alleluia 364

♩ = 88

Al - le - lu - ia. Al - le - lu - ia. Al - le - lu -

ia. Al - le - lu - ia. Al - le - lu - ia!

BERTHIER
Irregular

Music: Jacques Berthier, 1923– , © 1978 G.I.A. Publications, Inc.

PRAISE SONGS AND DOXOLOGIES

365 Praise God

Praise God, praise God, the love we all may share. Praise God, praise God, the beauty ev-ery-where. Praise God, the

⊕ Words: Charles H. Lyttle, 1884–1980
Music: Patrick L. Rickey, 1964– , © 1992 Unitarian Universalist Association

DOXOLOGY
10.10.8.8.

hope of good to be. Praise God, the

(Optional)

truth that makes us free. A - men.

Heleluyan　366

(Alleluia)

♩ = 112

He - le - lu-yan, he - le - lu-yan; he - le, he - le - lu - yan;

he - le - lu-yan, he - le - lu-yan; he - le, he - le - lu - yan.

Optional ostinato

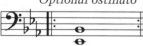

Words & music: Traditional Muskogee (Creek) Indian,
music transcription © 1989 The United Methodist Publishing House

HELELUYAN
Irregular

367
Allelu, Allelu

Words and music: Anonymous

ALLELU
Irregular

Now Let Us Sing

♩ = 116

1. Sing to the power of the
Now let us sing, sing,

faith with-in. Sing to the power of the
sing, sing. Now let us sing, sing,

faith with-in. Lift up your voice,
sing, sing. Lift up your voice, be not a-

be not a-fraid; sing to the power of the faith with-in.
fraid; now let us

2. Sing to the power of the hope within. . . .

3. Sing to the power of the love within. . . .

4. Sing to the power of the joy within. . . .

ROBESON
Irregular

Words & music: Anonymous

This Is the Truth
That Passes Understanding

This is the truth that pass-es un-der-stand - ing,

this is the joy to all for-ev - er free:

life springs from death and shat-ters ev-ery fet - ter,

and win-ter turns to spring e-ter - nal-ly.

⊕ Words: Robert Terry Weston, 1898–1988
Music: Genevan psalter, 1551

DONNE SECOURS
11.10.11.10.

All People That on Earth Do Dwell

1. All people that on earth do dwell,
2. O welcome in this day with praise;
3. For we believe that life is good,

sing ye aloud with cheerful voice;
approach with joy your God unto;
love doth abide forevermore;

let hearts in exultation swell;
give thanks, and faith proclaim always,
truth, firmer than a rock hath stood,

come now together and rejoice.
for it is seemly so to do.
and shall from age to age endure.

Words: William Kethe, d. c. 1608,
recast by Alicia S. Carpenter, 1930– , © 1990 Alicia S. Carpenter
Music: Genevan psalter, 1551

OLD HUNDREDTH
L.M.

PRAISE SONGS AND DOXOLOGIES

These three long meter tunes can be used interchangeably with texts 374 to 382.

371

Music: Genevan Psalter, 1551

OLD HUNDREDTH
L.M. modern form

372

Music: Thomas Tallis, c. 1561

TALLIS' CANON
L.M.

373

Music: Valentin Schumann's *Geistliche Lieder*, 1539

VOM HIMMEL HOCH
L.M.

374

Since what we choose is what we are,
and what we love we yet shall be,
the goal may ever shine afar —
the will to win it makes us free.

WILLIAM DE WITT HYDE, 1858–1917

375

As saffron trees now capture fire
and memories our hopes inspire;
we'll praise imagination's grace —
the human heart's best resting place.

ANONYMOUS

376

Sing loudly till the stars have heard.
In joy, feast on this bounteous word!
Our praises call us to explore
till suns shall rise and set no more.

ANONYMOUS

377

In greening lands begins the song
which deep in human hearts is strong.
In cheerful strains your voices raise,
to fill the whole spring world with praise!

ANONYMOUS

378

Let those who live in every land
declare that fear and war are done —
joined by the labor of their hands,
in love and understanding, one.

⊕ Kenneth L. Patton, 1911–1994
© 1980 Kenneth L. Patton

379

Ours be the poems of all tongues,
all things of loveliness and worth.
All arts, all ages, and all songs,
one life, one beauty on the earth.

⊕ Kenneth L. Patton, 1911–1994
© 1980 Kenneth L. Patton

PRAISE SONGS AND DOXOLOGIES

380

Rejoice in love we know and share,
in love and beauty everywhere;
rejoice in truth that makes us free,
and in the good that yet shall be.

CHARLES H. LYTTLE, 1884–1980
© 1955 American Ethical Union

381

From all that dwell below the skies
let songs of hope and faith arise;
let peace, good will on earth be sung
through every land, by every tongue.

COMPOSITE BASED ON ISAAC WATTS, 1674–1748

382

De todos bajo el gran sol
surja esperanza, fe, amor
verdad, y belleza cantando,
de cada tierra, cada voz.

BASED ON ISAAC WATTS, 1674–1748

383 Alleluia Amen

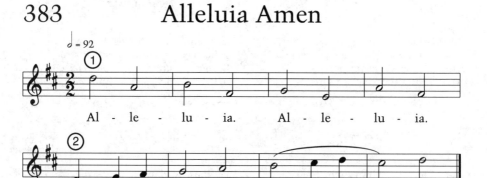

Music: Anonymous

ALLELUIA AMEN
Irregular

Alleluia 384

Al - le - lu - ia, al - le - lu - ia; al - le -
lu - ia, al - le - lu - ia. Al - le - lu - ia, al -
le - lu - ia; al - le - lu - ia, al - le - lu - ia.
Al - le - lu - ia, al - le - lu - ia.

Music: Wolfgang Amadeus Mozart, 1756–1791

AMADEUS
Irregular

Gloria 385

Glo - ri - a, glo - ri - a, in ex - cel - sis De - o!
Glo - ri - a, glo - ri - a, Al - le - lu - ia, Al - le - lu - ia!

Music: Jacques Berthier, 1923– , © 1978 G.I.A. Publications, Inc.

JACQUES
Irregular

RESPONSES, ROUNDS, AND CHANTS

386   Alleluia Chaconne

① G   D   Em   Bm   C   G   Am   D

Al - le - lu - ia,   al - le - lu - ia.

② *2 and 3 ad libitum*

Al - le - lu - ia,   al - le - lu - ia,   al - le - lu - ia,   al - le - lu - ia,

al - le - lu - ia,   al - le - lu - ia,   al - le - lu - ia,   al - le - lu - ia.

③

Al - le - lu - ia,   al - le - lu - ia,   al - le - lu - ia,   al - le - lu - ia.

Music: Johann Pachelbel, 1653–1706

PACHELBEL'S CANON
Irregular

387   The Earth, Water, Fire, Air

The earth, the wa - ter, the fire, the air, re -

turn, re - turn, re - turn, re - turn.

Words & music: Anonymous

ELEMENTS
Irregular

RESPONSES, ROUNDS, AND CHANTS

Dona Nobis Pacem 388

Do - na no - bis pa - cem, pa-cem; do - na no - bis pa - cem. Do - na no - bis pa - cem; do - na no - bis pa - cem. Do - na no - bis pa-cem; do - na no - bis pa - cem.

Words: Traditional Latin
Music: Traditional canon

DONA NOBIS PACEM
Irregular

Gathered Here 389

Gath - ered here in the mys-ter-y of the hour. Gath-ered here in one strong bod - y. Gath - ered here in the strug - gle and the power. Spir - it, draw near.

Words & music: Philip A. Porter, 1953– , © 1991 Philip A. Porter

GATHERING CHANT
Irregular

RESPONSES, ROUNDS, AND CHANTS

390   Gaudeamus Hodie

Words: Traditional
Music: Natalie Sleeth, 1930– , © 1972 Carl Fischer, Inc.

GAUDEAMUS HODIE
Irregular

RESPONSES, ROUNDS, AND CHANTS

Voice Still and Small

Voice still and small, deep in-side all, I hear you call,
sing-ing. In dark and rain, sor-row and pain,
still you re-main sing-ing. Calm-ing my fears,
quench-ing my tears, through all the years, sing-ing.

VOICE STILL AND SMALL
Irregular

392   Hineh Mah Tov

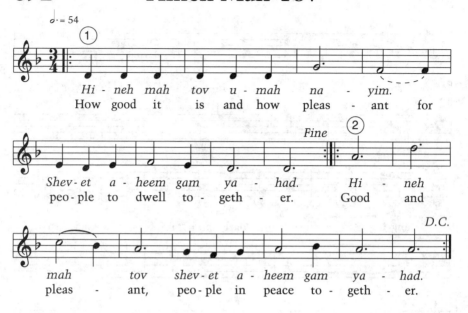

Hi - neh mah tov u - mah na - yim.
How good it is and how pleas - ant for

Shev - et a - heem gam ya - had. Hi - neh
peo - ple to dwell to - geth - er. Good and

Fine

D.C.

mah tov shev - et a - heem gam ya - had.
pleas - ant, peo - ple in peace to - geth - er.

Words: Psalm 133:1
Music: Hebrew round

PSALM 133
Irregular

393   Jubilate Deo

Ju - bi - la - te De - o. Ju - bi - la - te

De - o. Al - le - lu - ia!

Words: Traditional
Music: Michael Praetorius

JUBILATE DEO
Irregular

Hava Nashirah

Ha - va na - shir - ah. Shir - ah al - le - lu - ia!
Come, let's be sing - ing. Sing al - le - lu - ia!

Ha - va na - shir - ah. Shir - ah al - le - lu - ia!
Come, let's be sing - ing. Sing al - le - lu - ia!

Ha - va na - shir - ah. Shir - ah al - le - lu - ia!
Come, let's be sing - ing. Sing al - le - lu - ia!

Words & music: Hebrew round

HAVA NASHIRAH
Irregular

Sing and Rejoice

Sing and re - joice. Sing and re - joice.

Let all things liv - ing now sing and re - joice.

Words & music: Traditional round

MOORE
Irregular

396   I Know This Rose Will Open

♩ = 112

(1) (2) (3) (4)

I know this rose will o - pen. I
know my fear will burn a - way. I know my soul will un-
furl its wings. I know this rose will o - pen.

⊕ Words & music: Mary E. Grigolia, 1947– , © 1989 Mary E. Grigolia

GRIGOLIA
7.8.9.7.

397   Morning Has Come

𝅗𝅥 · = 48

(1) (2)

Morn - ing has come. Night is a - way.

(3) (4)

Rise with the sun and wel - come the day.

Words & music: Traditional round

MOORE
4.4.4.5.

RESPONSES, ROUNDS, AND CHANTS

To See the World

To see the world in a grain of sand, and a hea-ven in a wild-flower, hold in-fin - i-ty in the palm of your hand, and e-ter-ni-ty in an hour.

Words: William Blake, 1757–1827
Music: Norway, c. 1600,
⊕ arr. by Edvard Grieg, 1843–1907

DEN STORE HVIDE FLOK
9.8.11.8.

399   Vine and Fig Tree

And ev-'ry one 'neath a vine and fig tree shall live in peace and un-a-fraid. And ev-'ry fraid. And in-to plow-shares turn their swords, na-tions shall learn war no more. war no more.

Words: From Micah 4:3–4
Music: Traditional Hebrew

VINE AND FIG TREE
Irregular

400   Shalom Havayreem

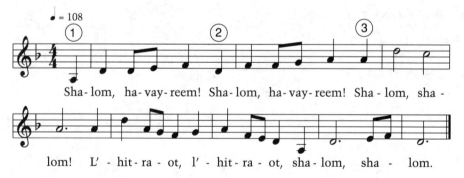

Sha-lom, ha-vay-reem! Sha-lom, ha-vay-reem! Sha-lom, sha-lom! L'-hit-ra-ot, l'-hit-ra-ot, sha-lom, sha-lom.

Words & music: Traditional Hebrew round

SHALOM
Irregular

Kum ba Yah

(Come by Here)

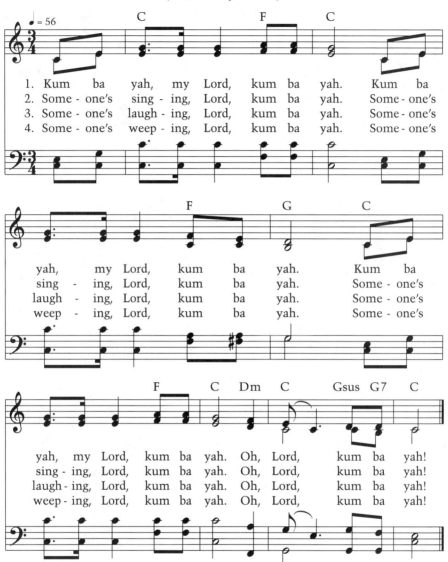

5. Someone's praying, Lord . . .   6. Kum ba yah, my Lord . . .

Words: African American spiritual, c. 1750–1875
Music: African American spiritual, harmony by Carlton R. Young, 1926– ,
© 1989 The United Methodist Publishing House

DESMOND
Irregular

RESPONSES, ROUNDS, AND CHANTS

402 From You I Receive

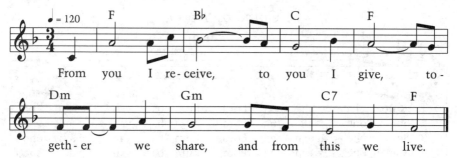

From you I re-ceive, to you I give, to-
geth-er we share, and from this we live.

Words & music: Joseph and Nathan Segal, © 1969 Nathan Segal

RABBI
Irregular

403 Spirit of Truth, of Life, of Power

Spir-it of truth, of life, of power, we bring ourselves as gifts to thee: oh, bind our hearts this
sa-cred hour in faith and hope and char-i-ty.

⊕ Words: Horace Westwood, 1884–1956
Music: Lowell Mason, 1792–1872

HAMBURG
L.M.

OFFERTORIES AND ASCRIPTIONS

What Gift Can We Bring 404

1. What gift can we bring, what pres-ent, what
2. Give thanks for the past, for those who had
3. This gift we now bring, this pres-ent, this

to-ken? What words can con-vey it, the joy of this
vi-sion, who plant-ed and wa-tered so dreams could come
to-ken, these words can con-vey it, the joy of this

day? When grate-ful we come, re-mem-ber-ing, re-
true. Give thanks for the now, for stud-y, for
day! When grate-ful we come, re-mem-ber-ing, re-

joic-ing, what song can we of-fer in hon-or and praise?
wor-ship, for mis-sion that bids us turn prayer in-to deed.
joic-ing, this song we now of-fer in hon-or and praise!

Words & music: Jane Marshall, 1924– , © 1982 Hope Publishing Co.

ANNIVERSARY SONG
11.11.11.11.

405 This Do in Memory of Me

1. This do in mem-o-ry of me; eat now this bro-ken bread. This is my life from death set free, here on my ta-ble spread.

2. This do in mem-o-ry of me; drink now this cup, I said. This shows my love for all to see, here on my ta-ble spread.

3. We praise your liv-ing mem-o-ry, re-mem-bering all you said. Your words and life have set us free, here through your ta-ble spread.

Words: Wayne Bradley Robinson
Music: Gordon Slater, 1896–1979, © 1930 Oxford University Press, used by perm.

ST. BOTOLPH
C.M.

Let Us Break Bread Together   406

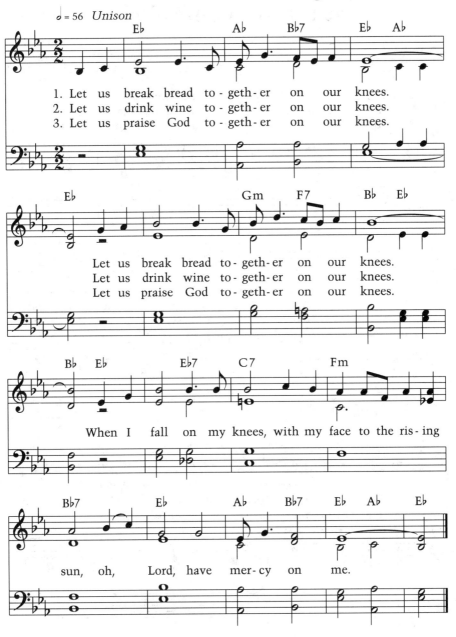

1. Let us break bread to-geth-er on our knees.
2. Let us drink wine to-geth-er on our knees.
3. Let us praise God to-geth-er on our knees.

Let us break bread to-geth-er on our knees.
Let us drink wine to-geth-er on our knees.
Let us praise God to-geth-er on our knees.

When I fall on my knees, with my face to the ris-ing

sun, oh, Lord, have mer-cy on me.

Words & music: Traditional

LET US BREAK BREAD
10.10. with refrain

COMMUNION

407

We're Gonna Sit
at the Welcome Table

1. We're gon-na sit at the wel-come ta-ble.
2. All kinds of peo-ple a-round that ta-ble.
3. No fan-cy style at the wel-come ta-ble.

We're gon-na sit at the wel-come
All kinds of peo-ple a-round that
No fan-cy style at the wel-come

ta-ble one of these days, hal-le-lu-jah! We're gon-na
ta-ble one of these days, hal-le-lu-jah! All kinds of
ta-ble one of these days, hal-le-lu-jah! No fan-cy

Words & music: Traditional,
arr. by Mary Allen Walden, 1946–1997, © 1992 Unitarian Universalist Association

WELCOME TABLE
Irregular

sit at the wel - come ta - ble, gon - na
peo - ple a - round that ta - ble, gon - na
style at the wel - come ta - ble, gon - na

sit at the wel-come ta-ble one of these days.
sit at the wel-come ta-ble one of these days.
sit at the wel-come ta-ble one of these days.

1.-2.   3.

408 Wonder of Wonders

Wonder of wonders, life is beginning, fragile as blossom, strong as the earth. Shaped in a person, love has new meaning, parents and people sing at their birth.

Words: Brian Wren, 1936– , © 1974 Hope Publishing Co.
Music: Alan Hovhaness, 1911– , © 1992 Unitarian Universalist Association

WONDER OF WONDERS
5.5.5.4.5.5.5.4.D.

NAMINGS, DEDICATIONS, AND CHRISTENINGS

Now with re-joic-ing, make cel-e-bra-tion;
joy full of prom-ise, laugh-ter through tears, nam-ing and bless-ing,
bring ded-i-ca-tion, hum-ble in pur-pose o-ver the years.

409 Sleep, My Child

♩ = 96

1. Sleep, my child, and peace at-tend you, all through the
2. Moth-er, I can feel you near me, all through the
3. While the moon her watch is keep-ing, all through the

night. I who love you shall be near you,
night. Fa-ther, I know you can hear me,
night; while one-half the world is sleep-ing,

all through the night. Soft the drows-y
all through the night. And when I am
all through the night. E-ven while the

⊕ Words: Adapt. by Alicia S. Carpenter, 1930– , © 1990 Alicia S. Carpenter
Music: Welsh melody, c. 1784

AR HYD Y NOS
8.4.8.4.8.8.8.4.

NAMINGS, DEDICATIONS, AND CHRISTENINGS

hours are creep-ing, hill and vale in slum-ber sleep-ing,
your age near-ly, still I will re-mem-ber clear-ly,
sun comes steal-ing, vi-sions of the day re-veal-ing,

I my lov-ing vig-il keep-ing, all through the night.
how you sang and held me dear-ly, all through the night.
breathes a pure and ho-ly feel-ing, all through the night.

410   Surprised by Joy

1. Sur-prised by joy no song can tell, no thought can
2. Be-yond all oth - er gifts is this, best gift, a-
3. Faith, hope, and love here come a - live; life's deep - est

com - pass, here we stand to cel - e - brate e - ter - nal
lone to mor - tals given; the love of par - ent, lov - er,
treas - ure is made known when in for - giv - ing, giv - ing

love, to reach for one an - oth - er's hand.
friend at - tunes our hearts to bliss of heaven.
all, in - sep - 'ra - bly, two are as one.

Words: Eric Routley, 1917–1982, © 1985 Hope Publishing Co.
⊕ adapt. by Joan Goodwin, 1926–
Music: English folk melody, harmony by John Weaver, 1937– ,
© 1990 John Weaver, all rights reserved

O WALY, WALY
L.M.

Part in Peace

411

1. Part in peace! The day before us. Praises sing for life and light. Are the shadows length-'ning o'er us? Bless thy care who guards the night.

2. Part in peace! With deep thanksgiving, rend-'ring as we homeward tread, love and service to the living, gentle mem-'ry to the dead.

3. Part in peace! Our voices raising, in thy presence always be. This the worship and the praising, bring-ing peace to you and me.

⊕ Words: Sarah Flower Adams, 1805–1848
Music: From *The Southern Harmony*, 1835, harmony by Alastair Cassels-Brown, b. 1927, © 1982 The Church Pension Fund

CHARLESTON
8.7.8.7.

412   Let Hope and Sorrow Now Unite

1. Let hope and sor - row now u - nite to con - se - crate life's end - ing. And praise good friends now gone from sight, though grief and loss are rend - ing. The sto - ry in a well - loved face, the years and days our

2. With faith, or doubt, or o - pen mind we whis - per life's great ques - tion. The ebb and flow of space and time sur - pass our small per - cep - tion; yet knowl - edge grows with joy - ful gains and finds out won - ders

Words: Brian Wren, 1936– , © 1979 Hope Publishing Co.
Music: Nikolaus Decius, c. 1490–1541, harmony by Hieronymus Praetorius,
c. 1560–1629

ALLEIN GOTT
IN DER HÖH
8.7.8.7.8.8.7.

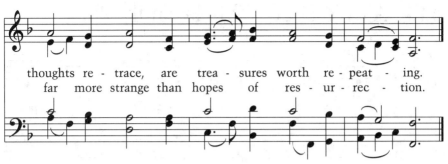

thoughts re - trace, are trea - sures worth re - peat - ing.
far more strange than hopes of res - ur - rec - tion.

Go Now in Peace   413

Go now in peace. Go now in peace.

May the love of God sur - round you ev - ery - where,

ev - ery - where you may go.

Optional ostinati

Words & music: Natalie Sleeth, 1930– , based on Luke 2:29,
© 1976 Hinshaw Music, Inc.

GO IN PEACE
Irregular

RECESSIONALS

414 As We Leave This Friendly Place

As we leave this friend-ly place, love give light to ev-'ry face;

may the kind-ness which we learn light our hearts till we re-turn.

Words: Vincent B. Silliman, 1894–1979
Music: J. S. Bach, 1685–1750, adapt. from *Chorale 38*

SEGNE UNS
7.7.7.7.

415 Hevenu Shalom Aleychem

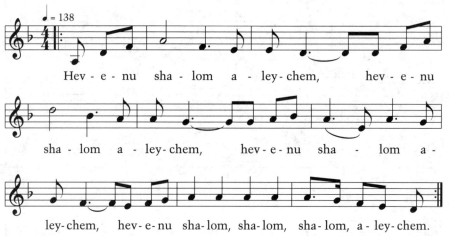

Hev-e-nu sha-lom a-ley-chem, hev-e-nu

sha-lom a-ley-chem, hev-e-nu sha-lom a-

ley-chem, hev-e-nu sha-lom, sha-lom, sha-lom, a-ley-chem.

Words & music: Traditional Hebrew

HEVENU
Irregular

Readings

Opening Words

416

Holy and beautiful the custom
  which brings us together,
In the presence of the Most High:

To face our ideals,
To remember our loved ones in
  absence,
To give thanks, to make
  confession,
To offer forgiveness,
To be enlightened, and to be
  strengthened.

Through this quiet hour breathes
The worship of ages,
The cathedral music of history.

Three unseen guests attend,
Faith, hope, and love:
Let all our hearts prepare them
  place.

⊕ Robert French Leavens

417

For the beauty of the earth,
this spinning blue green ball, yes!
Gaia, mother of everything
we walk gently across your back
to come together again
in this place
to remember how we can live
to remember who we are
to create how we will be.
Gaia, our home,
the lap in which we live—
welcome us.

⊕ Barbara J. Pescan

418

Come into the circle of love and
  justice.
Come into the community of
  mercy, holiness, and health.
Come and you shall know peace
  and joy.

adapted from Israel Zangwill

419

Look to this day!
For it is life, the very life of life.
In its brief course lie all the
  verities
and realities of your existence:
  The bliss of growth,
  The glory of action,
  The splendor of beauty;
For yesterday is but a dream,
And tomorrow is only a vision;
But today, well lived, makes every
  yesterday
A dream of happiness
And every tomorrow a vision of
  hope.
Look well, therefore, to this day.

attributed to Kalidasa

420

We are here to abet creation and
  to witness to it,
to notice each other's beautiful
  face and complex nature
so that creation need not play to
  an empty house.

Annie Dillard

421

O sing a new song to the Eternal.
Shout praise, all earth, break into
   music and song!
Praise the Eternal with the lyre,
   with lyre and song.
Let the sea and all within it
   thunder praise,
the world and its inhabitants,
let rivers clap their hands,
let mountains sing in chorus.
O sing a new song to the Eternal!

PSALM 98

422

Surely the Lord is in this
   place—and I did not know it.
How awesome is this place!
This is none other than the house
   of God,
and this is the gate of heaven.

GENESIS 28

423

It is a joy to give thanks to the
   Eternal,
to sing thy praise, O thou Most
   High,
to proclaim thy goodness in the
   morning
to the sweet music of the lyre.
I sing for joy at all that thou hast
   done.

PSALM 92

424

Have you entered the storehouses
   of the snow?
Or have you seen the treasuries of
   the hail?
From whose womb did the ice
   come forth,
and who has given birth to the
   hoarfrost of heaven?
The waters become hard like
   stone,
and the face of the deep is frozen.

JOB 38

425

Thus have you prepared the land,
drenching its furrows,
breaking up its clods, softening it
   with showers,
blessing its yield.
You have crowned the year with
   your bounty
and with abundant harvest.
The fallow meadows overflow,
the valleys are blanketed with
   flocks.
They shout and sing for joy!

PSALM 65

426

The wilderness and dry land shall
   be glad,
the desert shall rejoice and
   blossom;
like the crocus it shall blossom
   abundantly
and rejoice with joy and singing.

ISAIAH 35

427

Who has cut a channel for the
  torrents of rain
and a way for the thunderbolt
to bring rain on a land where no
  one lives,
on the desert, which is empty of
  human life,
to make the ground put forth
  grass?

JOB 38

428

Come out of the dark earth
Here where the minerals
Glow in their stone cells
Deeper than seed or birth.

Come into the pure air
Above all heaviness
Of storm and cloud to this
Light-possessed atmosphere.

Come into, out of, under
The earth, the wave, the air.

Love, touch us everywhere
With primeval candor.

⊕ MAY SARTON

429

Come into this place of peace
and let its silence heal your spirit;
Come into this place of memory
and let its history warm your soul;
Come into this place of prophecy
  and power
 and let its vision change your
  heart.

⊕ WILLIAM F. SCHULZ

430

For now the winter is past,
the rain is over and gone.
The flowers appear on the earth;
the time of singing has come.
The fig tree puts forth its figs,
and the vines are in blossom;
they give forth fragrance.

SONG OF SOLOMON 2

431

O Spinner, Weaver, of our lives,
Your loom is love.
May we who are gathered here
be empowered by that love
to weave new patterns of Truth
and Justice into a web of life that
  is strong,
beautiful, and everlasting.

⊕ BARBARA WELLS

432

If someone would scatter seed on
  the ground
And would sleep and rise night
  and day,
The seed would sprout and grow.
The earth produces of itself
First the blade, then the ear, then
  the full corn in the ear.
When the grain is ripe, the
  harvest has come.

MARK 4

433

How rare it is, how lovely, this fellowship of those who meet together.

FROM PSALM 133

434

May we be reminded here of our
  highest aspirations,
and inspired to bring our gifts of
  love and service to the altar of
  humanity.

May we know once again that we
  are not isolated beings
but connected, in mystery and
  miracle, to the universe,
to this community and to each
  other.

ANONYMOUS

435

We come together this morning to
  remind one another
To rest for a moment on the
  forming edge of our lives,
To resist the headlong tumble
  into the next moment,
Until we claim for ourselves
Awareness and gratitude,
Taking the time to look into one
  another's faces
And see there communion: the
  reflection of our own eyes.

This house of laughter and
  silence, memory and hope,
is hallowed by our presence
  together.

⊕ KATHLEEN MCTIGUE

436

We come to this time and this
  place:

*To rediscover the wondrous gift
  of free religious community;*

To renew our faith in the
  holiness, goodness, and beauty
  of life;

*To reaffirm the way of the open
  mind and full heart;*

To rekindle the flame of memory
  and hope; and

*To reclaim the vision of an
  earth made fair, with all her
  people one.*

⊕ DAVID C. POHL

437

LET US WORSHIP

Let us worship with our eyes and ears and fingertips;

Let us love the world through heart and mind and body.

We feed our eyes upon the mystery and revelation in the faces of our brothers and sisters.

We seek to know the wistfulness of the very young and the very old, the wistfulness of people in all times of life.

We seek to understand the shyness behind arrogance, the fear behind pride, the tenderness behind clumsy strength, the anguish behind cruelty.

All life flows into a great common life, if we will only open our eyes to our companions.

Let us worship, not in bowing down, not with closed eyes and stopped ears.

Let us worship with the opening of all the windows of our beings, with the full outstretching of our spirits.

Life comes with singing and laughter, with tears and confiding, with a rising wave too great to be held in the mind and heart and body, to those who have fallen in love with life.

Let us worship, and let us learn to love.
⊕ Kenneth L. Patton

438

Morning

From the east comes the sun, bringing a new and unspoiled day.

It has already circled the earth and looked upon distant lands and far-away peoples.

It has passed over mountain ranges and the waters of the seven seas.

It has shone upon laborers in the fields, into the windows of homes, and shops, and factories.

It has beheld proud cities with gleaming towers,

And also the hovels of the poor.

It has been witness to both good and evil, the works of honest men and women and the conspiracy of knaves.

It has seen marching armies, bomb-blasted villages and "the destruction that wasteth at noonday."

Now, unsullied from its tireless journey, it comes to us, messenger of the morning,

Harbinger of a new day.
⊕ Clinton Lee Scott

439

We Gather in Reverence

We gather in reverence before the wonder of life—

The wonder of this moment

The wonder of being together, so close yet so apart—

Each hidden in our own secret chamber,

Each listening, each trying to speak—

Yet none fully understanding, none fully understood.

We gather in reverence before all intangible things—
That eyes see not, nor ears can detect—

That hands can never touch, that space cannot hold, and time cannot measure.
⊕ Sophia Lyon Fahs

440

FROM THE FRAGMENTED WORLD

From the fragmented world of our everyday lives we gather together in search of wholeness.

By many cares and preoccupations, by diverse and selfish aims are we separated from one another and divided within ourselves.

Yet we know that no branch is utterly severed from the Tree of Life that sustains us all.

We cherish our oneness with those around us and the countless generations that have gone before us.

We would hold fast to all of good we inherit even as we would leave behind us the outworn and the false.

We would escape from bondage to the ideas of our own day and from the delusions of our own fancy.

Let us labor in hope for the dawning of a new day without hatred, violence, and injustice.

Let us nurture the growth in our own lives of the love that has shone in the lives of the greatest of men and women, the rays of whose lamps still illumine our way.

In this spirit we gather.
In this spirit we pray.

⊕ PHILLIP HEWETT

441

To WORSHIP

To worship is to stand in awe
  under a heaven of stars,
before a flower, a leaf in sunlight,
  or a grain of sand.

*To worship is to be silent,
  receptive,
before a tree astir with the
  wind,
  or the passing shadow of a
  cloud.*

To worship is to work with
  dedication and with skill;
it is to pause from work and
  listen to a strain of music.

*To worship is to sing with the
  singing beauty of the earth;
it is to listen through a storm
  to the still small voice within.*

Worship is a loneliness seeking
  communion;
it is a thirsty land crying out for
  rain.

*Worship is kindred fire within
  our hearts;
it moves through deeds of
  kindness and through acts of
  love.*

Worship is the mystery within us
reaching out to the mystery
beyond.

*It is an inarticulate silence
  yearning to speak;
it is the window of the moment
  open to the sky of the eternal.*

⊕ JACOB TRAPP

442

We Bid You Welcome

We bid you welcome, who come
with weary spirit seeking rest.

*Who come with troubles that
are too much with you,
Who come hurt and afraid.*

We bid you welcome, who come
with hope in your heart.

*Who come with anticipation in
your step,
Who come proud and joyous.*

We bid you welcome, who are
seekers of a new faith.

*Who come to probe and explore.
Who come to learn.*

We bid you welcome, who enter
this hall as a homecoming,

*Who have found here room for
your spirit.
Who find in this people a family.*

Whoever you are, whatever you
are,
Wherever you are on your journey,

We bid you welcome.
⊕ Richard S. Gilbert

443

We Arrive Out of Many Singular Rooms

We arrive out of many singular
rooms, walking over the branching
streets.

*We come to be assured that
brothers and sisters surround us,
to restore their images on our
eyes.*

We enlarge our voices in common
speaking and singing.

*We try again that solitude found
in the midst of those who with us
seek their hidden reckonings.*

Our eyes reclaim the remembered
faces; their voices stir the surround-
ing air.

*The warmth of their hands as-
sures us, and the gladness of our
spoken names.*

This is the reason of cities, of
homes, of assemblies in the houses
of worship.

It is good to be with one another.
⊕ Kenneth L. Patton

444

This House

This house is for the ingathering of
nature and human nature.

*It is a house of friendships, a
haven in trouble, an open room
for the encouragement of our
struggle.*

It is a house of freedom, guarding
the dignity and worth of every person.

(continued)

It offers a platform for the free voice, for declaring, both in times of security and danger, the full and undivided conflict of opinion.

It is a house of truth-seeking, where scientists can encourage devotion to their quest, where mystics can abide in a community of searchers.

It is a house of art, adorning its celebrations with melodies and handiworks.

It is a house of prophecy, outrunning times past and times present in visions of growth and progress.

This house is a cradle for our dreams, the workshop of our common endeavor.

⊕ Kenneth L. Patton

445

The Womb of Stars

The womb of stars embraces us; remnants of their fiery furnaces pulse through our veins.

We are of the stars, the dust of the explosions cast across space.

We are of the earth: we breathe and live in the breath of ancient plants and beasts.

Their cells nourish the soil; we build our communities on their harvest of gifts.

Our fingers trace the curves carved in clay and stone by forebears unknown to us.

We are a part of the great circle of humanity gathered around the fire, the hearth, the altar.

We gather anew this day to celebrate our common heritage.

May we recall in gratitude all that has given us birth.

⊕ Joy Atkinson

446

To the Four Directions
(A reading for Individual Voices)

Spirit of the East, spirit of air, of morning and springtime: Be with us as the sun rises, in times of beginning, times of planting. Inspire us with the fresh breath of courage as we go forth into new adventures.

Spirit of the South, spirit of fire, of noontime and summer: Be with us through the heat of the day and help us to be ever growing. Warm us with strength and energy for the work that awaits us.

Spirit of the West, spirit of water, of evening and autumn: Be with us as the sun sets and help us to enjoy a rich harvest. Flow through us with a cooling, healing quietness and bring us peace.

Spirit of the North, spirit of earth,
of nighttime and winter:
Be with us in the darkness,
in the time of gestation.

Ground us in the wisdom of the
  changing seasons
as we celebrate the spiraling
  journey of our lives.

⊕ JOAN GOODWIN

Chalice Lightings

447

At times our own light goes out and
is rekindled by a spark from another
person. Each of us has cause to
think with deep gratitude of those
who have lighted the flame within
us.

⊕ ALBERT SCHWEITZER

448

We gather this hour as people of
  faith
With joys and sorrows, gifts and
  needs.

We light this beacon of hope,
sign of our quest
for truth and meaning,
in celebration of the life we share
  together.

⊕ CHRISTINE ROBINSON

449

We hallow this time together by
kindling the lamp of our heritage.

⊕ ALBERT THELANDER

450

Blessed is the match consumed in
  kindling flame.
Blessed is the flame that burns in
  the heart's secret places.
Blessed is the heart with strength
  to stop its beating for honor's
  sake.
Blessed is the match consumed in
  kindling flame.

HANNAH SENESH

451

Flame of fire, spark of the universe
that warmed our ancestral
  hearth—
agent of life and death,
symbol of truth and freedom.
We strive to understand ourselves
and our earthly home.

⊕ LESLIE POHL-KOSBAU

452

Life is a gift for which we are
  grateful.
We gather in community to
  celebrate the glories and the
  mysteries of this great gift.

⊕ MARJORIE MONTGOMERY

453

May the light we now kindle
inspire us to use our powers
to heal and not to harm,
to help and not to hinder,
to bless and not to curse,
to serve you, Spirit of freedom.

PASSOVER HAGGADAH

454

In our time of grief, we light a flame
of sharing, the flame of ongoing life.
In this time when we search for understanding and serenity in the face
of loss, we light this sign of our
quest for truth, meaning, and community.

⊕ CHRISTINE ROBINSON

455

Each morning we must hold out the
chalice of our being to receive, to
carry, and give back.

DAG HAMMARSKJÖLD

456

EXTINGUISHING THE CHALICE

We extinguish this flame but not
  the light of truth,
the warmth of community,
  or the fire of commitment.
These we carry in our hearts until
  we are together again.

⊕ ELIZABETH SELLE JONES

Affirmations, Covenants, and Confessions

Affirmations

457

I am only one
But still I am one.
I cannot do everything,
But still I can do something.
And because I cannot do
  everything
I will not refuse to do the
  something that I can do.

⊕ EDWARD EVERETT HALE

458

Mindful of truth ever exceeding
  our knowledge
and community ever exceeding
  our practice,
reverently we covenant together,
beginning with ourselves as
  we are,
to share the strength of integrity
and the heritage of the spirit
in the unending quest for wisdom
  and love.

⊕ WALTER ROYAL JONES, JR.

459

This is the mission of our faith:
To teach the fragile art of
   hospitality;
To revere both the critical mind
   and the generous heart;
To prove that diversity need not
   mean divisiveness;
And to witness to all that we
   must hold the whole world in
   our hands.

⊕ William F. Schulz

460

The line in life, nature, science, philosophy, religion constantly returns into itself. The opposite poles become one when the circle is completed. All truth revolves about one center. All is a manifestation of one law.

⊕ Sarah Alden Ripley

461

We Must Be Saved

Nothing worth doing is completed in our lifetime;

Therefore, we are saved by hope.

Nothing true or beautiful or good makes complete sense in any immediate context of history;

Therefore, we are saved by faith.

Nothing we do, however virtuous, can be accomplished alone;

Therefore, we are saved by love.

No virtuous act is quite as virtuous from the standpoint of our friend or foe as from our own;

Therefore, we are saved by the final form of love which is forgiveness.

Reinhold Niebuhr

462

I shall take my voice wherever there are those who want to hear the melody of freedom or the words that might inspire hope and courage in the face of despair and fear. My weapons are peaceful, for it is only by peace that peace can be attained. The song of freedom must prevail.

Paul Robeson

463

My heart is moved by all I cannot
   save:
So much has been destroyed
I have to cast my lot with those
   who, age after age,
perversely, with no extraordinary
   power, reconstitute the world.

Adrienne Rich

464

And Then

And then all that has divided us will merge

And then compassion will be wedded to power

And then softness will come to a
world that is harsh and unkind

   And then both men and women
   will be gentle

And then both women and men
will be strong

   And then no person will be sub-
   ject to another's will

And then all will be rich and free
and varied

   And then the greed of some will
   give way to the needs of many

And then all will share equally in
the Earth's abundance

   And then all will care for the sick
   and the weak and the old

And then all will nourish the young

   And then all will cherish life's
   creatures

And then all will live in harmony
with each other and the Earth

   And then everywhere will be
   called Eden once again
                  JUDY CHICAGO

465

THE WISDOM TO SURVIVE

If we will have the wisdom to
  survive,
to stand like slow-growing trees
on a ruined place,

   Renewing, enriching it,

If we will make our seasons
  welcome here,

asking not too much of earth or
  heaven,

   Then a long time after we are
   dead
   the lives our lives prepare will
   live here,

Their houses strongly placed upon
the valley sides,

   Fields and gardens
   rich in the windows. The river
   will run clear,
   as we will never know it,

And over it, birdsong like a
canopy.

   On the levels of the hills will
   be green meadows,
   stock bells in noon shade.

On the steeps where greed and
  ignorance cut down the old
  forest,

   An old forest will stand,
   its rich leaf-fall drifting on its
   roots.

The veins of forgotten springs will
  have opened.
Families will be singing in the
  fields.

   In their voices they will hear a
   music
   risen out of the ground.

They will take nothing from the
  ground they will not return,
whatever the grief at parting.

   Memory, native to this valley,
   will spread over it
   like a grove, and memory will
   grow into legend,

*legend into song, song into
sacrament.*

The abundance of this place,
the songs of its people and its
birds,
will be health and wisdom and
indwelling light.

*This is no paradisal dream.
Its hardship is its possibility.*
                        WENDELL BERRY

466

RELIGION

Let religion be to us life and joy.

*Let it be a voice of renewing chal-
lenge to the best we have and
may be; let it be a call to generous action.*

Let religion be to us a dissatisfac-
tion with things that are, which
bids us serve more eagerly the true
and right.

*Let it be the sorrow that opens for
us the way of sympathy, understanding, and service to suffering
humanity.*

Let religion be to us the wonder and
lure of that which is only partly
known and understood:

*An eye that glories in nature's
majesty and beauty, and a heart
that rejoices in deeds of kindness
and of courage.*

Let religion be to us security and
serenity because of its truth and
beauty, and because of the enduring

worth and power of the loyalties
which it engenders;

*Let it be to us hope and purpose,
and a discovering of opportunities to express our best through
daily tasks:*

Religion, uniting us with all that is
admirable in human beings everywhere;

*Holding before our eyes a pros-
pect of the better life for humankind, which each may help to
make actual.*
            ⊕ VINCENT B. SILLIMAN

467

LISTEN, ISRAEL

Listen, Israel: the Eternal, the Eternal alone, is our God.

*And you must love the Eternal
your God with all your mind, and
all your soul, and all your
strength.*

These words you must learn by
heart, you must impress them on
your children.

*You must talk about them when
you are sitting at home and when
you are on the road, when you lie
down and when you rise up.*
                        DEUTERONOMY 6

468

We Need One Another

We need one another when we mourn and would be comforted.

We need one another when we are in trouble and afraid.

We need one another when we are in despair, in temptation, and need to be recalled to our best selves again.

We need one another when we would accomplish some great purpose, and cannot do it alone.

We need one another in the hour of success, when we look for someone to share our triumphs.

We need one another in the hour of defeat, when with encouragement we might endure, and stand again.

We need one another when we come to die, and would have gentle hands prepare us for the journey.

All our lives we are in need, and others are in need of us.

GEORGE E. ODELL

469

The Spirit Of Wisdom

I am mortal, like everyone else, a descendant of the first formed child of earth, and in the womb of a mother was I moulded into flesh within a period of ten months.

When I was born I began to breathe the common air, and fell upon the kindred earth. My first sound was a cry, as is true of all.

I was nursed with care in swaddling cloths; no king has had a different beginning of existence.

There is for all one entrance and one way out. Therefore I prayed, and the spirit of wisdom came to me.

WISDOM OF SOLOMON 7

470

Affirmation

We affirm the unfailing renewal of life.

Rising from the earth, and reaching for the sun, all living creatures shall fulfill themselves.

We affirm the steady growth of human companionship.

Rising from ancient cradles and reaching for the stars, people the world over shall seek the ways of understanding.

We affirm a continuing hope

That out of every tragedy the spirits of individuals shall rise to build a better world.

⊕ LEONARD MASON

Unto the Church Universal

Unto the church universal, which is the depository of all ancient wisdom and the school of all modern thought;

Which recognizes in all prophets a harmony, in all scriptures a unity, and through all dispensations a continuity;

Which abjures all that separates and divides, and always magnifies all that unifies and brings peace;

Which seeks truth in freedom, justice in love, and individual discipline in social duty;

And which shall make of all sects, classes, nations, and races, one global community;

Unto this church and unto all its members, known and unknown throughout the world,

We pledge the allegiance of our hands and hearts.

KESHAB CHANDRA SEN
ARRANGED BY
⊕ JOHN HAYNES HOLMES

471

Love is the doctrine of this church,
The quest of truth is its
    sacrament,
And service is its prayer.

To dwell together in peace,
To seek knowledge in freedom,
To serve human need,
To the end that all souls shall
grow into harmony with
    the Divine—

Thus do we covenant with each
other and with God.

ARRANGED BY
⊕ L. GRISWOLD WILLIAMS

472

In the freedom of the truth,
And the spirit of Jesus,
We unite for the worship of God
And the service of all.

⊕ CHARLES GORDON AMES

473

Love is the spirit of this church,
    and service its law.
This is our great covenant:
To dwell together in peace,
To seek the truth in love,
And to help one another.

⊕ JAMES VILA BLAKE

475

We, the Peoples of the
United Nations

We, the peoples of the United Nations,

Determined to save succeeding generations from the scourge of war,

To reaffirm faith in fundamental human rights, in the dignity and worth of the human person, in the equal rights of men and women, and of nations large and small,

To promote social progress and better standards of life in larger freedom,

And for these ends to practice tolerance and to live together in peace as good neighbors,

To unite our strength to maintain international peace and security,

To insure that armed force shall not be used, save in the common interest,

To employ international machinery in the promotion of the economic and social advancement of all people,

Have resolved to combine our efforts to accomplish these aims.

CHARTER OF THE UNITED NATIONS

Confessions

476

Before the wonders of life we acknowledge our failures to see and to revere;

Before the sanctities of life we are ashamed of our disrespects and indignities;

Before the gifts of life we own that we have made choices of lesser goods, and here today seek the gifts of the spirit;

Before the heroisms of life we would be enlarged to new devotion.

⊕ VON OGDEN VOGT

477

Forgive us that often we forgive ourselves so easily and others so hardly;

Forgive us that we expect perfection from those to whom we show none;

Forgive us for repelling people by the way we set a good example;

Forgive us the folly of trying to improve a friend;

Forbid that we should use our little idea of goodness as a spear to wound those who are different;

Forbid that we should feel superior to others when we are only more shielded;

And may we encourage the secret struggle of every person.

⊕ VIVIAN POMEROY

478

A PRAYER OF SORROW

We have forgotten who we are. We have alienated ourselves from the unfolding of the cosmos.

We have become estranged from the movements of the earth. We have turned our backs on the cycles of life.

We have sought only our own security, we have exploited simply for our own ends, we have distorted our knowledge, we have abused our power.

Now the land is barren, and the waters are poisoned, and the air is polluted.

Now the forests are dying, and the creatures are disappearing, and the humans are despairing.

We ask forgiveness.
We ask for the gift of remembering.
We ask for the strength to change.
U.N. Environmental Sabbath Program

Meditations and Prayers

Meditations

479

An awe so quiet I don't know
    when it began.

A gratitude had begun to sing
    in me.

Was there some moment dividing
    song from no song?

When does dewfall begin?

When does night fold its arms
    over our hearts to cherish them?

When is daybreak?

Denise Levertov

480

Let us open our minds and hearts to the place of quiet, to the silent prayer for the healing of pain, and the soft, gentle coming of love.

Composite

481

It is our quiet time.
We do not speak, because the
    voices are within us.
It is our quiet time.
We do not walk, because the earth
    is all within us.
It is our quiet time.
We do not dance, because the
    music has lifted us to a place
    where the spirit is.
It is our quiet time.
We rest with all of nature. We
    wake when the seven sisters
    wake.
We greet them in the sky over the
    opening of the kiva.

Nancy Wood

482

If it is language that makes us human, one half of language is to listen.

Silence can exist without speech, but speech cannot live without silence.

Listen to the speech of others. Listen even more to their silence.

To pray is to listen to the revelations of nature, to the meaning of events.

To listen to music is to listen also to silence, and to find the stillness deepened and enriched.

⊕ Jacob Trapp

483

When despair for the world grows in me and I wake in the night at the least sound in fear of what my life and my children's lives may be, I go and lie down where the wood drake rests in his beauty on the water, and the great heron feeds.

I come into the peace of wild things who do not tax their lives with forethought of grief. I come into the presence of still water. And I feel above me the day-blind stars waiting with their light. For a time I rest in the grace of the world, and am free.

Wendell Berry

484

To live content with small means;

To seek elegance rather than luxury, and refinement rather than fashion;

To be worthy, not respectable, and wealthy, not rich;

To study hard, think quietly, talk gently, act frankly;

To listen to stars and birds, to babes and sages, with open heart;

To bear all cheerfully, do all bravely, await occasions, hurry never.

To let the spiritual, unbidden and unconscious, grow up through the common.

This is to be my symphony.

⊕ William Henry Channing

485

Turn scarlet, leaves!
Spin earth!
Tumble the shadows into dawn,
The morning out of night;
Spill stars across these skies
And hide them with the suns.

Teach me to turn
My sullen sense toward marvel.

Let green and red
And dark and day
Concur with the returning life
I am.

⊕ Raymond J. Baughan

486

I am being driven forward
Into an unknown land.

The pass grows steeper
The air colder and sharper
A wind from my unknown goal
Stirs the strings of expectation.

Still the question
Shall I ever get there?
There where life resounds
A clear pure note in the silence.

DAG HAMMARSKJÖLD

487

The bell is full of wind
though it does not ring.

The bird is full of flight
though it is still.

The sky is full of clouds
though it is alone.

The word is full of voice
though no one speaks it.

Everything is full of fleeing
though there are no roads.

Everything is fleeing
toward its presence.

ROBERTO JUARROZ

488

Hold fast to dreams
for if dreams die
life is a broken-winged bird
that cannot fly.

Hold fast to dreams
for when dreams go
life is a barren field
frozen with snow.

LANGSTON HUGHES

489

When love is felt or fear is known,

*When holidays and holy days
and such times come,*

When anniversaries arrive by calen-
dar or consciousness,

*When seasons come, as seasons
do, old and known, but somehow
new,*

When lives are born or people die,

*When something sacred's sensed
in soil or sky,*

Mark the time.

*Respond with thought or prayer
or smile or grief,*

Let nothing living slip between the
fingers of the mind,

*For all of these are holy things we
will not, cannot, find again.*

⊕ MAX A. COOTS

490

WILD GEESE

You do not have to be good.

*You do not have to walk on your
knees for a hundred miles
through the desert, repenting.*

You only have to let the soft animal
of your body love what it loves.

*Tell me about despair, yours, and
I will tell you mine.*

Meanwhile the world goes on.

*Meanwhile the sun and the clear
pebbles of the rain are moving
across the landscapes, over the
prairies and the deep trees, the
mountains and the rivers.*

Meanwhile the wild geese, high in
the clean blue air, are heading home
again.

*Whoever you are, no matter how
lonely, the world offers itself to
your imagination, calls to you
like the wild geese, harsh and ex-
citing—over and over announc-
ing your place in the family of
things.*

MARY OLIVER

491

THE APHORISMS OF JESUS

The Reign of God is not coming as
you hope to catch sight of it. No one
will say "Here it is" or "There it
is," for the Reign of God is now in
your midst . . .

Look how the lilies neither spin nor
weave, and yet I tell you Solomon
in all his grandeur was never robed
like one of them . . .

Where your treasure lies, your heart
will lie there too . . .

No one lights a lamp to put it under
a bowl, but on a stand, so that those
who come in can see the light . . .

Wisdom is vindicated by all her
children . . .

Figs are not gathered from thorns,
and grapes are not picked from a
bramble bush . . .

Judge not, and you will not be
judged yourselves . . .

Do to others as you would have
them do to you.

LUKE

492

FRAGILE AND ROOTED

See a blossom in your mind's eye.
Allow it to fill the interior of your
   imagination.

Greater perfection of form in
   nature cannot be imagined.
With inward gaze absorb each
   wondrous fluted petal.

Slide down its humid surface
   until you drop as the dew into
   its velvety core.

Immerse your senses in this safe
   chamber.

Such fragile beauty gives impulse
   to weep.

Slowly reverse the journey;
as you ascend the shaft toward
   wider light, turn your
   imagination around and around
   to see its many facets.
Stored within is the memory of
   all flowers.

Marvel that this creation, while
   utterly fragile—yet undaunted,
   boldly buds forth turning
   resolutely toward the sun.

We, too, shimmer with
expectation, exuding our own
illumination, color, pulse, and
scent.

Vulnerable, still we venture our
lives courageously toward hope
and light, at once fragile and
rooted.

✛ CAROLYN S. OWEN-TOWLE

Prayers

493

Fire of the Spirit,
life of the lives of creatures,
spiral of sanctity,
bond of all natures,
glow of charity,
lights of clarity,
taste of sweetness to the fallen,
be with us and hear us.
Composer of all things,
joy in the glory,
strong honor,
be with us and hear us.

HILDEGARD OF BINGEN
(ADAPTED)

494

The prayer of our souls is a petition
for persistence; not for the one good
deed, or single thought, but deed on
deed, and thought on thought, until
day calling unto day shall make a
life worth living.

W. E. B. DU BOIS

495

Hear me, four quarters of the
world.
A relative I am!

Give me the strength to walk the
soft earth. Give me the eyes to
see and the strength to
understand.

Look upon these faces of children
without number,
That they may face the winds and
walk the good road to the day of
quiet.

This is my prayer; hear me.

BLACK ELK

496

From arrogance, pompousness, and
from thinking ourselves more important than we are, may some sav-
ing sense of humor liberate us. For
allowing ourselves to ridicule the
faith of others, may we be forgiven.

From making war and calling it
peace, special privilege and calling
it justice, indifference and calling it
tolerance, pollution and calling it
progress, may we be cured.

For telling ourselves and others that
evil is inevitable while good is im-
possible, may we stand corrected.

God of our mixed up, tragic, aspir-
ing, doubting, and insurgent lives,
help us to be as good as in our hearts
we have always wanted to be.
Amen.

✛ HARRY MESERVE

497

Prayer invites God to be present in our spirits and in our lives. Prayer cannot bring water to parched land, nor mend a broken bridge, nor rebuild a ruined city, but prayer can water an arid soul, mend a broken heart, and rebuild a weakened will.

ABRAHAM J. HESCHEL

498

In the quietness of this place, surrounded by the all-pervading presence of the Holy, my heart whispers:

Keep fresh before me the moments of my High Resolve, that in good times or in tempests,

I may not forget that to which my life is committed.

Keep fresh before me the moments of my high resolve.

HOWARD THURMAN

499

And I have felt a presence that
    disturbs me with the joy of
    elevated thoughts;
A sense sublime of something far
    more deeply interfused,
Whose dwelling is the light of
    setting suns,
And the round ocean and the
    living air,
A motion and a spirit, that impels

All thinking things, all objects of
    all thought,
And rolls through all things.

WILLIAM WORDSWORTH

500

Marvelous Truth, confront us at every turn, in every guise, iron ball, egg, dark horse, shadow, cloud of breath on the air,

Dwell in our crowded hearts, our steaming bathrooms, kitchens full of things to be done, the ordinary streets.

Thrust close your smile that we know you, terrible joy.

DENISE LEVERTOV

501

Spirit of Community, in which we share and find strength and common purpose, we turn our minds and hearts toward one another seeking to bring into our circle of concern all who need our love and support: those who are ill, those who are in pain, either in body or in spirit, those who are lonely, those who have been wronged.

(Here people may say the names of those to be remembered.)

We are part of a web of life that makes us one with all humanity, one with all the universe.

We are grateful for the miracle of consciousness that we share, the consciousness that gives us the power to remember, to love, to care.

☩ Frederick E. Gillis

502

Now is the accepted time, not to-morrow, not some more convenient season.

It is today that our best work can be done and not some future day or future year.

It is today that we fit ourselves for the greater usefulness of tomorrow.

Today is the seed time, now are the hours of work, and tomorrow comes the harvest and the play-time.

W. E. B. Du Bois

503

Bless Adonai
who spins day into dusk.

With wisdom watch
the dawn gates open;

With understanding let
time and seasons
come and go;

With awe perceive
the stars in lawful orbit.

Morning dawns,
evening darkens;

Darkness and light yielding
one to the other,

Yet each distinguished
and unique.

Marvel at Life!
Strive to know its ways!

Seek Wisdom and Truth,
the gateways
to Life's mysteries!

Wondrous indeed
is the evening twilight.

Rami M. Shapiro

504

i thank You God for most this amazing
day: for the leaping greenly spirits of trees
and a blue true dream of sky; and for everything
which is natural which is infinite which is yes

(i who have died am alive again today,
and this is the sun's birthday; this is the birth
day of life and of love and wings: and of the gay
great happening illimitably earth)

how should tasting touching hearing seeing
breathing any—lifted from the no
of all nothing—human merely being
doubt unimaginable You?

(now the ears of my ears awake and
now the eyes of my eyes are opened)

☩ E. E. Cummings

505

Let us be at peace with our bodies and our minds. Let us return to ourselves and become wholly ourselves.

Let us be aware of the source of being, common to us all and to all living things.

Evoking the presence of the Great Compassion, let us fill our hearts with our own compassion—towards ourselves and towards all living beings.

Let us pray that we ourselves cease to be the cause of suffering to each other.

With humility, with awareness of the existence of life, and of the sufferings that are going on around us, let us practice the establishment of peace in our hearts and on earth. Amen.

THICH N'HAT HANH

506

May the glory of the passing away
   of autumn
lie about us
fresh gold
for a time.
And when the dark comes, and
   the cold
may we remember how today we
   stand in glory,
how we walk in bounty
heaped upon earth's dark carpet,
how we move knee deep in
   abundance

flung against night's winter
   curtain.
We are thankful for its coming
and for its passing.

Let it be.

☩ BARBARA J. PESCAN

507

Grant us the ability to find joy
   and strength
not in the strident call to arms,
but in stretching out our arms
to grasp our fellow creatures
in the striving for justice and
   truth.

JEWISH PRAYER

508

Save us from weak resignation to
   violence,
teach us that restraint is the
   highest expression of power,
that thoughtfulness and
   tenderness are the mark of the
   strong;
Help us to love our enemies,
not by countenancing their sins,
but remembering our own.

CHRISTIAN PRAYER

509

Save us, our compassionate Lord,
from our folly, by your wisdom,
from our arrogance, by your
   forgiving love,

from our greed by your infinite
bounty,
and from our insecurity by your
healing power.

MUSLIM PRAYER

510

O Spirit of Life and Renewal,

We have wintered enough,
mourned enough, oppressed ourselves enough.

Our souls are too long cold and bur-
ied, our dreams all but forgotten,
our hopes unheard.

We are waiting to rise from the
dead.

In this, the season of steady rebirth,
we awaken to the power so abundant, so holy, that returns each year
through earth and sky.

We will find our hearts again, and
our good spirits. We will love, and
believe, and give and wonder, and
feel again the eternal powers.

The flow of life moves ever onward
through one faithful spring, and another, and now another.

May we be forever grateful.

Alleluia.

Amen.

✠ JANE RZEPKA

511

Let there be peace in the sky and in
the atmosphere, peace in the plant
world and in the forests;

Let the cosmic powers be peaceful;
let Brahma be peaceful;

Let there be undiluted and fulfilling
peace everywhere.

ATHARVA VEDA

512

WE GIVE THANKS THIS DAY

For the expanding grandeur of Creation, worlds known and unknown,
galaxies beyond galaxies, filling us
with awe and challenging our
imaginations:

We give thanks this day.

For this fragile planet earth, its
times and tides, its sunsets and seasons:

We give thanks this day.

For the joy of human life, its won-
ders and surprises, its hopes and
achievements:

We give thanks this day.

For our human community, our
common past and future hope, our
oneness transcending all separation,
our capacity to work for peace and
justice in the midst of hostility and
oppression:

We give thanks this day.

For high hopes and noble causes, for faith without fanaticism, for understanding of views not shared:

We give thanks this day.

For all who have labored and suffered for a fairer world, who have lived so that others might live in dignity and freedom:

We give thanks this day.

For human liberty and sacred rites; for opportunities to change and grow, to affirm and choose:

We give thanks this day. We pray that we may live not by our fears but by our hopes, not by our words but by our deeds.

⊕ O. Eugene Pickett

513

Our Father in heaven,
hallowed be your name.
Your kingdom come,
Your will be done
on earth, as it is in heaven.
Give us this day our daily bread.
And forgive us our debts,
as we also have forgiven our
  debtors.
And do not bring us to the time of
  trial,
but rescue us from evil.

Matthew 6

514

God, lover of us all,
most holy one,
help us to respond to you

to create what you want for us
  here on earth.
Give us today enough for our
  needs;
forgive our weak and deliberate
  offenses,
just as we must forgive others
when they hurt us.
Help us to resist evil
and to do what is good;
for we are yours,
endowed with your power
to make our world whole.

Lala Winkley

515

We Lift Up Our Hearts
in Thanks

For the sun and the dawn
Which we did not create;

*For the moon and the evening
Which we did not make;*

For food which we plant
But cannot grow;

*For friends and loved ones
We have not earned and cannot
  buy;*

For this gathered company
Which welcomes us as we are,
from wherever we have come;

*For all our free churches
That keep us human and
  encourage us in our quest for
  beauty, truth, and love;*

For all things which come to us
As gifts of being from sources
  beyond ourselves;

Gifts of life and love and
friendship
We lift up our hearts in thanks
this day.

☩ RICHARD M. FEWKES

516

O God, root and source of body and soul, we ask for boldness in confronting evil. When you are within us, we have the power to counter all that is untrue. O Father and Mother of all humankind, may we redeem our failings by the good work that we do. In the name of the one, the only God.

☩ KHASI UNITARIAN PRAYER

517

I who am the beauty of the green earth and the white moon among the stars and the mysteries of the waters,

I call upon your soul to arise and
come unto Me.

For I am the soul of nature that gives life to the universe.

From Me all things proceed and
unto Me they must return.

Let My worship be in the heart that rejoices, for behold—all acts of love and pleasure are My rituals.

Let there be beauty and strength,
power and compassion, honor

and humility, mirth and rever-
ence within you.

And you who seek to know Me, know that your seeking and yearning will avail you not, unless you know the Mystery:

For if that which you seek, you
find not within yourself, you will
never find it without.

For behold, I have been with you from the beginning,

And I am that which is attained
at the end of desire.

STARHAWK

518

Grandfather,
Look at our brokenness.

We know that in all creation
Only the human family
Has strayed from the Sacred
Way.

We know that we are the ones
Who are divided,

And we are the ones
Who must come back together
To walk in the Sacred Way.

Grandfather,
Sacred One,
Teach us love, compassion, and
honor

That we may heal the earth
And heal each other.

FROM THE OJIBWAY INDIANS
OF NORTH AMERICA

519

Let me not pray to be sheltered
from dangers,

> *But to be fearless in facing
> them.*

Let me not beg for the stilling of
my pain,

> *But for the heart to conquer it.*

Let me not look for allies in life's
battle-field,

> *But to my own strength.*

Let me not crave in anxious fear
to be saved,

> *But hope for the patience to
> win my freedom.*

Grant me that I may not be a
coward, feeling your mercy in
my success alone;

> *But let me find the grasp of
> your hand in my failure.*
>
> RABINDRANATH TAGORE

520

O our Mother the Earth,
O our Father the Sky,

> *Your children are we, and with
> tired backs we bring you the
> gifts you love.*

Then weave for us a garment of
brightness;

> *May the warp be the white
> light of morning,
> May the weft be the red light of
> evening,*

May the fringes be the falling rain,

> *May the border be the standing
> rainbow.*

Thus weave for us a garment of
brightness,

> *That we may walk fittingly
> where birds sing,*

That we may walk fittingly where
grass is green,

> *O our Mother the Earth,
> O our Father the Sky.*
>
> FROM THE TEWA INDIANS
> OF NORTH AMERICA

521

May I be no one's enemy and may I
be the friend of that which is eternal and abides.

> *May I wish for every person's
> happiness and envy none.*

May I never rejoice in the ill fortune
of one who has wronged me.

> *May I, to the extent of my power,
> give needful help to all who are
> in want.*

May I never fail a friend.

> *May I respect myself.*

May I always keep tame that which
rages within me.

> *May I accustom myself to be gentle and never be angry with others because of circumstances.*

May I know good people and follow
in their footsteps.

> EUSEBIUS

522

Can any of you by worrying add a single hour to your span of life?

You know how to interpret the appearance of earth and sky, but why do you not know how to interpret the present time?

Why do you see the speck in your neighbor's eye, but do not notice the log in your own eye?

What does it profit them if they gain the whole world, but lose or forfeit themselves?

LUKE

523

Thou art the path
and the goal that paths never
reach.
Thou feedest and sustainest
all that one sees, or seems.
Thou art the trembling grass
and the tiger that creeps under it.
Thou art the light in sun and
moon,
the sounds fading into silence,
and the sanctity of sacred books.
Thou art the good that destroys
evil.

PRAYER FROM INDIA

524

Earth mother, star mother,
You who are called by
a thousand names,
May all remember
we are cells in your body
and dance together.
You are the grain and the loaf
that sustains us each day,
And as you are patient
with our struggles to learn
So shall we be patient
with ourselves and each other.
We are radiant light
and sacred dark—the balance—
You are the embrace that heartens
And the freedom beyond fear.
Within you we are born,
we grow, live, and die—
You bring us around the circle to
rebirth,
Within us you dance
Forever.

STARHAWK

525

WEB

Intricate and untraceable
weaving and interweaving,
dark strand with light:

Designed, beyond
All spiderly contrivance,
To link, not to entrap:

Elation, grief, joy, contrition,
  entwined;
shaking, changing, forever
  forming, transforming:

All praise, all praise to the great
  web.

DENISE LEVERTOV

526

TREMBLING WITH JOY

The great sea has set me in
  motion,
set me adrift,
moving me like a weed in a river

The sky and the strong wind
have moved the spirit inside me
till I am carried away
trembling with joy.

INUIT SHAMAN UVAVNUK

527

IMMORTALITY

It is eternity now.
I am in the midst of it.

It is about me, in the sunshine;
I am in it, as the butterfly in the
  light-laden air.

Nothing has to come,
It is now.

Now is eternity,
Now is the immortal life.

RICHARD JEFFRIES

528

I'VE KNOWN RIVERS

I've known rivers:
I've known rivers ancient as the
  world and older than the flow of
  human blood in human veins.

My soul has grown deep like the
  rivers.

I bathed in the Euphrates when
  dawns were young.

I built my hut near the Congo and
  it lulled me to sleep.

I looked upon the Nile and raised
  the pyramids above it.
I heard the singing of the
  Mississippi when Abe Lincoln
  went down to New Orleans and
  I've seen its muddy bosom turn
  all golden in the sunset.

I've known rivers:
Ancient, dusky rivers.

My soul has grown deep like the
rivers.

LANGSTON HUGHES

529

THE STREAM OF LIFE

The same stream of life that runs
through my veins night and day
runs through the world and dances
in rhythmic measures.

It is the same life that shoots in joy
through the dust of the earth in
numberless blades of grass and
breaks into tumultuous waves of
leaves and flowers.

It is the same life that is rocked in
the ocean-cradle of birth and death,
in ebb and in flow.

I feel my limbs are made glorious by
the touch of this world of life. And
my pride is from the life-throb of
ages dancing in my blood this moment.

RABINDRANATH TAGORE

530

OUT OF THE STARS

Out of the stars in their flight, out
  of the dust of eternity, here
  have we come,
Stardust and sunlight, mingling
  through time and through space.

*Out of the stars have we come,
  up from time;*

Out of the stars have we come.

Time out of time before time in
  the vastness of space, earth
  spun to orbit the sun,
Earth with the thunder of
  mountains newborn, the boiling
  of seas.

*Earth warmed by sun, lit by
  sunlight:*
This is our home;
Out of the stars have we come.

Mystery hidden in mystery, back
  through all time;
Mystery rising from rocks in the
  storm and the sea.

*Out of the stars, rising from
  rocks and the sea,
kindled by sunlight on earth,
  arose life.*

Ponder this thing in your heart;
  ponder with awe:
Out of the sea to the land, out of
  the shallows came ferns.

*Out of the sea to the land, up
  from darkness to light,
Rising to walk and to fly,
  out of the sea trembled life.*

Ponder this thing in your heart,
  life up from sea:
Eyes to behold, throats to sing,
  mates to love.

*Life from the sea, warmed by
  sun, washed by rain,
life from within, giving birth,
  rose to love.*

This is the wonder of time; this is
  the marvel of space; out of the

stars swung the earth; life upon earth rose to love.

This is the marvel of life, rising
to see and to know;
Out of your heart, cry wonder:
sing that we live.

⊕ Robert T. Weston

Praise and Transcendence

531

The Oversoul

Let us learn the revelation of all nature and thought; that the Highest dwells within us, that the sources of nature are in our own minds.

As there is no screen or ceiling
between our heads and the
infinite heavens, so there is no
bar or wall in the soul where we,
the effect, cease, and God, the
cause, begins.

I am constrained every moment to acknowledge a higher origin for events than the will I call mine.

There is deep power in which we
exist and whose beatitude is ac-
cessible to us.

Every moment when the individual feels invaded by it is memorable.

It comes to the lowly and simple;
it comes to whosoever will put
off what is foreign and proud; it
comes as insight; it comes as se-
renity and grandeur.

The soul's health consists in the fullness of its reception.

For ever and ever the influx of
this better and more universal
self is new and unsearchable.

Within us is the soul of the whole; the wise silence, the universal beauty, to which every part and particle is equally related; the eternal One.

When it breaks through our intel-
lect, it is genius; when it breathes
through our will, it is virtue;
when it flows through our affec-
tions, it is love.

⊕ Ralph Waldo Emerson

532

The Music of the Spheres

The music of the spheres.

A harmonious universe—
like a harp.

Its rhythms are the equal,
repeated seasons.
The beating of the heart.

Day/night. The going and
returning of migratory birds.

The cycles of stars and corn.

The mimosa that unfolds by
day and folds up again by
night.

Rhythms of moon and tide. One single rhythm in planets, atoms, sea,

And apples that ripen and fall,
and in the mind of Newton.

Melody, accord, arpeggios
The harp of the universe.
Unity behind apparent
multiplicity.

That is the music.

Ernesto Cardenal

533

Comfort My People

Comfort, O comfort my people,
says your God.
Speak tenderly to Jerusalem,
and cry to her that she has served
her term.

A voice cries out: "In the
wilderness prepare the way of
the Lord, make straight in the
desert a highway for our God.

"Every valley shall be lifted up,
and every mountain and hill be
made low;
the uneven ground shall become
level, and the rough places a
plain."

A voice says, "Cry out!"
And I said, "What shall I cry?"
"All people are grass, their
constancy is like the flower of
the field.
The grass withers, the flower
fades.
But the word of our God will
stand forever."

Isaiah 40

534

Gloria!

Gloria

*The tenacity of Earth and its
creatures.*

Kyrie eleison

*These children who will go on
to save what we cannot*

Baruch ata Adonai

*The ordinary tenacity of plants
and of people.*

Om

*The center of the universe
which is everywhere, not the
least place in the human
heart.*

Alleluia

*Love that survives anger, and
winter, and despair, and
sorrow, and even death.*

Shalom

Love that persists.

Nam myo-ho renge kyo

*Calm that is the seed in the
dark.*

Amen

*For endings that are beginnings,
for beginnings that are
endings.*

Alleluia

*For the circle, the spiral, the
web, the egg, the orbit, the
center, the seed, the flower,*

the fruit, the opening, the
death, the release, the seed.

Amen

We are going on.

Amen

It is going on.

Amen

Blessed be.

⊕ Barbara J. Pescan

535

Deep Calls to Deep

As a deer longs for flowing
  streams,
so my soul longs for you, O God.

My soul thirsts for the living
  God.

My tears have been my food,
day and night, while people say to
  me, continually,
"Where is your God?"

These things I remember, as I
  pour out my soul:
how I went with the throng
and led them in procession
  with glad shouts and
songs of thanksgiving, a
  multitude keeping festival.

My soul is cast down within me;
therefore I remember you.
Deep calls to deep at the thunder
  of your cataracts;
all your waves and your billows
  have gone over me.

Why are you cast down, O my
  soul?
Hope in God.

Psalm 42
(abbreviated)

Morning

536

Morning Poem

Every morning the world is
  created.

Under the orange sticks of the
  sun the heaped ashes of the
  night turn into leaves again

And fasten themselves to the high
  branches—and the ponds appear
  like black cloth on which are
  painted islands of summer lilies.

If it is your nature to be happy
  you will swim away along
  the soft trails for hours, your
  imagination alighting
  everywhere.

And if your spirit carries within it
  the thorn that is heavier than
  lead—if it's all you can do to
  keep on trudging—

There is still somewhere deep
  within you a beast shouting
  that the earth is exactly what
  it wanted—

Each pond with its blazing lilies is
  a prayer heard and answered
  lavishly, every morning,

Whether or not you have ever
 dared to be happy,
whether or not you have ever
 dared to pray.

MARY OLIVER

Seasons and Cycles

537

OUR WHOLE SYSTEM

Small as is our whole system compared with the infinitude of creation,

Brief as is our life compared with
the cycles of time,

We are so tethered to all by the
beautiful dependencies of law,

That not only the sparrow's fall is
felt to the uttermost bound but the
vibrations set in motion by the
words that we utter reach through
all space and the tremor is felt
through all time.

⊕ MARIA MITCHELL

538

HARBINGERS OF FROST

Autumn, we know,
Is life en route to death.
The asters are but harbingers of
 frost.

The trees, flaunting their colors at
 the sky,

In other times will follow where
 the leaves have fallen,
And so shall we.

Yet other lives will come.
So may we know, accept, embrace,
The mystery of life we hold a
 while

Nor mourn that it outgrows each
 separate self, but still rejoice
 that we may have our day.

Lift high our colors to the sky!
 and give,
In our time, fresh glory to the
 earth.

⊕ ROBERT T. WESTON

539

LATE OCTOBER

Carefully
the leaves of autumn
sprinkle down the tinny
sound of little dyings

And skies sated
of ruddy sunsets
of roseate dawns

roil ceaselessly in
cobweb greys and turn
to black
for comfort.

Only lovers
see the fall
a signal end to endings

a gruffish gesture alerting
those who will not be alarmed

that we begin to stop
in order simply
to begin
again.

MAYA ANGELOU

540

THE PEACE OF AUTUMN

Today the peace of autumn pervades the world.

In the radiant noon, silent and motionless, the wide stillness rests like a tired bird

Spreading over the deserted fields to all horizons its wings of golden green.

Today the thin thread of the river flows without song, leaving no mark on its sandy banks.

The many distant villages bask in the sun with eyes closed in idle and languid slumber.

In the stillness I hear in every blade of grass,

In every speck of dust, in every part of my own body, in the visible and invisible worlds,

In the planets, the sun, and the stars, the joyous dance of the atoms through endless time.

RABINDRANATH TAGORE

541

WINTER MEDITATION

The bare trees have made up their seed bundles.

They are ready now. The warm brown light pauses briefly, shrugs and moves on.

They are ready now to play dead for a while. I, human, have not as yet devised how to obtain such privilege.

Their spring will find them rested. I and my kind battle a wakeful way to ours.

DENISE LEVERTOV

542

SOLSTICE

Again did the earth shift
Again did the nights grow short,
And the days long.

And the people
of the earth were glad
and celebrated
each in their own ways.

DIANE LEE MOOMEY

543

WINTER

Let us not wish away the winter. It is a season to itself, not simply the way to spring.

When trees rest, growing no leaves, gathering no light, they

*let in sky and trace themselves
delicately against dawns and
sunsets.*

The clarity and brilliance of the
winter sky delight. The loom of fog
softens edges, lulls the eyes and ears
of the quiet, awakens by risk the
unquiet. A low dark sky can snow,
emblem of individuality, liberality,
and aggregate power. Snow invites
to contemplation and to sport.

*Winter is a table set with ice and
starlight.*

Winter dark tends to warm light:
fire and candle; winter cold to hugs
and huddles; winter want to gifts
and sharing; winter danger to vi-
sions, plans, and common endeav-
oring—and the zest of narrow es-
capes; winter tedium to merry-
making.

*Let us therefore praise winter,
rich in beauty, challenge, and
pregnant negativities.*
⊕ GRETA CROSBY

544

NEW YEAR'S DAY

The first of January is another day
dawning, the sun rising as the sun
always rises, the earth moving in its
rhythms,

*With or without our calendars to
name a certain day as the day of
new beginning, separating the
old from the new.*

So it is: everything is the same,
bound into its history as we ourselves are bound.

*Yet also we stand at a threshold,
the new year something truly
new, still unformed, leaving a
stunning power in our hands:*

What shall we do with this great gift
of Time, this year?

*Let us begin by remembering
that whatever justice, whatever
peace and wholeness might
bloom in our world this year,*

We are the hearts and minds, the
hands and feet, the embodiment of
all the best visions of our people.

*The new year can be new ground
for the seeds of our dreams.*

Let us take the step forward together, onto new ground,

*Planting our dreams well, faith-
fully, and in joy.*
⊕ KATHLEEN MCTIGUE

545

IN TIME OF SILVER RAIN

In time of silver rain
The earth puts forth new life
    again,

Green grasses grow
And flowers lift their heads,

And over all the plain
The wonder spreads

Of life, Of life, Of life.

In time of silver rain

The butterflies lift silken wings
To catch a rainbow cry

And trees put forth
New leaves to sing
In joy beneath the sky.

When spring

And life
Are new.

Langston Hughes

546

To Free the Heart

Through dreary sodden days
The field sponged up
The greying skies.

And now the sun
Lies soft as birth again
As if the earth had just begun.

And blossoms on the vines
Designed in spring
Come out to sing again.

And everywhere the ripening
Pushes falling leaves apart
To free the heart
For freshening.

As through the seasons
Of our years

Becoming
Often waits the nourishment
Of tears.

⊕ Francis C. Anderson, Jr.

547

Summer Meditation

Now blows the wind with soft, re-
laxing warmth.

The sun beats down.
The schools are out.

Children swarm in the playgrounds
and the streets, and eager city folk,
vacation-bound, crowd the broad
highways.

The lakes and seashores lose
their solitude
And all the world seems turned
to carnival.

What of ourselves? There could be,
now, deep peace, a time for soul-
searching.

We might turn to examine our
own lives, to sort and probe our
tendencies of thought,

To sift the true from false in the
things of doubt,

The beautiful from ugliness un-
marked.

The sun beats down; it is a time for
pause.

Even the trees seem resting for a
time as if to meditate and gather
strength for the more strenuous
times that lie ahead.

And shall not we? Here's the un-
finished clay, half-moulded, that
still waits on us

*To think what we have been and
as we are
Still yet have to become.*

⊕ ROBERT T. WESTON

548

SUMMER WARMTH

We stand at the edge of summer.

*The sun has at last warmed us
enough that we begin to trust in
its presence.*

The last burst of spring blossoms,
lavender and white and deep pink
banks of rhododendron, are giving
way to summer peonies and roses.

O source of the turning seasons,

Of earth, of life, of promise gradually becoming fulfillment,

*May your people find a lightening
of the burdens with the brighten-
ing of the sky.*

⊕ HELEN COHEN

The World of Nature

549

HYMN TO MATTER

Blessed be you, harsh matter, barren
soil, stubborn rock: you who yield
only to violence;

*You who force us to work if we
would eat.*

Blessed be you, perilous matter, vio-
lent sea, untameable passion;

*You who unless we fetter you will
devour us.*

Blessed be you, mighty matter, irre-
sistible march of evolution, reality
ever new-born;

*You who, by constantly shatter-
ing our mental categories, force
us to go ever further and further
in our pursuit of the truth.*

Blessed be you, universal matter,
unmeasurable time, boundless
ether, triple abyss of stars and atoms and generations;

*You who by overflowing and dis-
solving our narrow standards of
measurement reveal to us the di-
mensions of God.*

TEILHARD DE CHARDIN

550

WE BELONG TO THE EARTH

This we know. The earth does not
belong to us; we belong to the earth.

*This we know. All things are con-
nected like the blood which
unites one family.*

All things are connected.

*Whatever befalls the earth be-
falls the sons and daughters of
the earth.*

We did not weave the web of life;
We are merely a strand in it.

Whatever we do to the web,
we do to ourselves.

ATTRIBUTED TO
CHIEF NOAH SEALTH

551

EARTH TEACH ME

Earth teach me stillness
as the grasses are stilled with light.

Earth teach me suffering
as old stones suffer with
memory.

Earth teach me caring
as parents who secure their young.

Earth teach me courage
as the tree which stands all
alone.

Earth teach me limitation
as the ant which crawls on the
ground.

Earth teach me freedom
as the eagle which soars in the
sky

Earth teach me resignation
as the leaves which die in the fall.

Earth teach me regeneration
as the seed which rises in the
spring.

Earth teach me to forget myself
as melted snow forgets its life.

Earth teach me to remember
kindness as dry fields weep
with rain.

FROM THE UTE INDIANS
OF NORTH AMERICA

552

MY HELP IS IN THE MOUNTAIN

My help is in the mountain
Where I take myself to heal
The earthly wounds
That people give to me.

I find a rock with sun on it
And a stream where the water
runs gentle
And the trees which one by one
give me company.

So I must stay for a long time
Until I have grown from the rock.

And the stream is running
through me
And I cannot tell myself from
one tall tree.

Then I know that nothing touches
me
Nor makes me run away.

My help is in the mountain
That I take away with me.

NANCY WOOD

553

Earth cure me.
Earth receive my woe.

Rock strengthen me.
Rock receive my weakness.

Rain wash my sadness away.
Rain receive my doubt.

Sun make sweet my song.
Sun receive the anger from my
heart.

NANCY WOOD

554

Water flows from high in the
    mountains.
Water runs deep in the Earth.
Miraculously, water comes to us,
    and sustains all life.

Water and sun
green these plants.
When the rain of compassion falls,
even a desert becomes an
    immense, green ocean.

THICH N'HAT HANH

Transience

555

SOME THINGS WILL
NEVER CHANGE

Some things will never change.

*Some things will always be the
same.*

The voice of forest water in the
night, a woman's laughter in the
dark, the clean, hard rattle of raked
gravel, the cricketing stitch of mid-
day in hot meadows, the delicate
web of children's voices in bright
air—

These things will never change.

The glitter of sunlight on roughened
water, the glory of the stars, the in-
nocence of morning, the smell of
the sea in harbors—

*These things will always be the
same.*

The feathery blur and smoky bud-
dings of young boughs, and some-
thing there that comes and goes and
never can be captured, the thorn of
spring, the sharp and tongueless
cry—

These things will never change.

The leaf, the blade, the flower, the
wind that cries and sleeps and
wakes again, the trees, whose stiff
arms clash and tremble in the dark,
and the dust of lovers long since
buried in the earth—

*All things belonging to the earth
will never change.*

All things proceeding from the
earth to seasons, all things that
lapse and change and come again
upon the earth, these come up from
the earth that never changes, they
go back into the earth that lasts forever.

*Only the earth endures, but it en-
dures forever.*

The tarantula, the adder, and the
asp will also never change.

*Pain and death will always be
the same.*

But under the pavements trembling
like a pulse, under the buildings
trembling like a cry, under the
waste of time, under the hoof of the
beast above the broken bones of cities, there will be something growing like a flower—

Something bursting from the earth again, forever deathless, faithful, coming into life again like April.

THOMAS WOLFE

556

THESE ROSES

These roses under my window make no reference to former roses or to better ones; they are for what they are; they exist with God today.

There is no time to them. There is simply the rose; it is perfect in every moment of its existence.

Before a leaf-bud has burst, its whole life acts; in the full-blown flower there is no more, in the leafless root there is no less.

Its nature is satisfied and it satisfies nature in all moments alike.

But we postpone or remember. We do not live in the present, but with reverted eye lament the past, or, heedless of the riches that surround us, stand on tiptoe to foresee the future.

We cannot be happy or strong until we too live with nature in the present, above time.

⊕ RALPH WALDO EMERSON
(ADAPTED)

557

A COMMON DESTINY

All living substance, all substance
  of energy, being, and purpose,
are united and share the same
  destiny.

All people,
those we love and those we
  know not of, are united and
  share the same destiny.

Birth-to-death
we share this unity with
the sun,
earth,

  our brothers and sisters,
  strangers,

flowers of the field,
snow flakes,
volcanoes and moon beams.

  Birth—Life—Death
  Unknown—Known—Unknown

Our destiny: from unknown to
unknown.

  May we have the faith to
  accept this mystery and build
  upon its everlasting truth.
  ⊕ DAVID H. EATON

558

FOR EVERYTHING A SEASON

For everything there is a season,
  and a time for every matter
  under heaven:

  A time to be born, and a time
  to die;

A time to plant, and a time to pluck up what is planted;

A time to kill, and a time to heal;

A time to break down, and a time to build up;

A time to weep, and a time to laugh;

A time to mourn, and a time to dance;

A time to throw away stones, and a time to gather stones together;

A time to embrace, and a time to refrain from embracing;

A time to seek, and a time to lose;

A time to keep, and a time to throw away;

A time to tear, and a time to sew;

A time to keep silence, and a time to speak;

A time to love, and a time to hate;

A time for war,

And a time for peace.

ECCLESIASTES 3

Words and Deeds
of Prophetic Women and Men

Commitment and Action

560

559

COMMITMENT

Some day, men and women will rise, they will reach the mountain peak, they will meet big and strong and free, ready to receive, to partake, and to bask in the golden rays of love. What fancy, what imagination, what poetic genius can foresee the potentialities of such a force in the life of men and women.

EMMA GOLDMAN

People say, what is the sense of our small effort.

They cannot see that we must lay one brick at a time, take one step at a time.

A pebble cast into a pond causes ripples that spread in all directions. Each one of our thoughts, words and deeds is like that.

No one has a right to sit down and feel hopeless.

There's too much work to do.

DOROTHY DAY

561

Never doubt that a small group of thoughtful, committed citizens can change the world; indeed it's the only thing that ever has.

MARGARET MEAD

562

A LIFELONG SHARING

Love cannot remain by itself—it has no meaning.

Love has to be put into action and that action is service.

Whatever form we are,
able or disabled,
rich or poor,
it is not how much we do,
but how much love we put in the doing;
a lifelong sharing of love with others.

MOTHER TERESA

563

A PERSON WILL WORSHIP SOMETHING

A person will worship something—have no doubt about that.

We may think our tribute is paid in secret in the dark recesses of our hearts—but it will out.

That which dominates our imaginations and our thoughts will determine our lives, and character.

Therefore, it behooves us to be careful what we worship, for what we are worshipping we are becoming.

⊕ RALPH WALDO EMERSON

564

LOVE IS NOT CONCERNED

Love is not concerned
with whom you pray
or where you slept
the night you ran away
from home.
Love is concerned
that the beating of your heart
should kill no one.

ALICE WALKER

565

PROPHETS

Always it is easier to pay homage to prophets than to heed the direction of their vision.

It is easier blindly to venerate the saints than to learn the human quality of their sainthood.

It is easier to glorify the heroes of the race than

To give weight to their examples.

To worship the wise is much easier than to profit by their wisdom.

Great leaders are honored, not by adulation, but by sharing their insights and values.

Grandchildren of those who stoned the prophet sometimes gather up the stones to build the prophet's monument.

Always it is easier to pay homage to prophets than to heed the direction of their vision.

⊕ CLINTON LEE SCOTT

566

GOD IS ONE

In this world there have always been many opinions about faith and salvation.

You need not think alike to love alike.

There must be knowledge in faith also.

Sanctified reason is the lantern of faith.

Religious reform can never be all at once, but gradually, step by step.

If they offer something better, I will gladly learn.

The most important spiritual function is conscience, the source of all spiritual joy and happiness.

Conscience will not be quieted by anything less than truth and justice.

We must accept God's truth in this lifetime. Salvation must be accomplished here on earth.

God is indivisible.

Egy Az Isten*

God is one.

*(Hungarian, pronounced: Edge Oz Eeshten)

⊕ FRANCIS DAVID
ADAPTED BY
⊕ RICHARD FEWKES

567

TO BE OF USE

I want to be with people who submerge in the task,

Who go into the fields to harvest and work in a row and pass the bags along,

Who stand in the line and haul in their places,

Who are not parlor generals and field deserters but move in a common rhythm when the food must come in or the fire be put out.

The work of the world is common as mud. Botched, it smears the hands, crumbles to dust.

But the thing worth doing well done has a shape that satisfies, clean and evident.

Greek amphoras for wine or oil, Hopi vases that held corn, are put in museums but you know they were made to be used.

The pitcher cries for water to carry and a person for work that is real.

MARGE PIERCY

568

Connections Are Made Slowly
(The Seven of Pentacles)

Connections are made slowly,
sometimes they grow underground.

*You cannot tell always by look-
ing what is happening.*

More than half a tree is spread out
in the soil under your feet.

*Penetrate quietly as the earth-
worm that blows no trumpet.*

Fight persistently as the creeper
that brings down the tree.

*Spread like the squash plant that
overruns the garden.*

Gnaw in the dark and use the sun
to make sugar.

*Weave real connections, create
real nodes, build real houses.*

Live a life you can endure: make
love that is loving.

*Keep tangling and interweaving
and taking more in, a thicket and
bramble wilderness to the out-
side but to us interconnected
with rabbit runs and burrows
and lairs.*

Live as if you like yourself, and it
may happen:

*Reach out, keep reaching out,
keep bringing in.*

This is how we are going to live for
a long time: not always,

*For every gardener knows that af-
ter the digging, after the planting,*

*after the long season of tending
and growth, the harvest comes.*

MARGE PIERCY

569

Stand by This Faith

Stand by this faith. Work for it and
sacrifice for it.

*There is nothing in all the world
so important as to be loyal to this
faith which has placed before us
the loftiest ideals,*

Which has comforted us in sorrow,
strengthened us for noble duty and
made the world beautiful.

*Do not demand immediate re-
sults but rejoice that we are worthy to be entrusted with this
great message,*

That you are strong enough to work
for a great true principle without
counting the cost.

*Go on finding ever new applica-
tions of these truths and new en-
joyments in their contemplation,
always trusting in the one God
which ever lives and loves.*

⊕ FROM OLYMPIA BROWN

570

Prayer for the Earth

Spirit of love
That flows against our flesh
Sets it trembling
Moves across it as across grass

Erasing every boundary that we
accept
And swings the doors of our lives
wide—

This is a prayer I sing:
Save our perishing earth!

Spirit that hears each one of us,
Hears all that is—
Listens, listens, hears us out—

Inspire us now!

Our own pulse beats in every
stranger's throat, and also there
within the flowered ground
beneath our feet,

And—teach us to listen!—

We can hear it in water, in wood,
and even in stone.
We are earth of this earth, and we
are bone of its bone.

This is a prayer I sing, for we
have forgotten this and so the
earth is perishing.

BARBARA DEMING

571

UNIVERSAL MINISTRY

The spirit of God has sent me
to bring good news to the
oppressed,

To bind up the brokenhearted,

To proclaim liberty to the captives
and release to the prisoners,

To comfort all who mourn,

To give them a garland instead of
ashes,

The oil of gladness instead of
mourning,

The mantle of praise instead of a
faint spirit.

They shall build up the ancient
ruins, they shall raise up the
former devastations, the
devastations of many
generations.

You shall be named ministers of
our God.

ISAIAH 61

572

WHAT IS REQUIRED?

How shall I enter the Eternal's presence?

Shall I come with sacrifices, with
yearling calves to offer?

Would the Eternal care for rams in
thousands, or for oil flowing in myr-
iad streams?

What does the Eternal ask from
you

But to be just and kind

And live in quiet fellowship with
your God?

MICAH

573

Arise, then, women of this day!

Arise all women who have hearts, whether your baptism be that of water or of fears!

Say firmly: "We will not have great questions decided by irrelevant agencies,

"Our husbands shall not come to us, reeking with carnage, for caresses and applause.

"Our sons shall not be taken from us to unlearn all that we have been able to teach them of charity, mercy, and patience.

"We women of one country will be too tender of those of another country to allow our sons to be trained to injure theirs."

From the bosom of the devastated earth a voice goes up with our own. It says, "Disarm, Disarm!"

The sword of murder is not the balance of justice! Blood does not wipe out dishonor nor violence indicate possession.

As men have often forsaken the plow and the anvil at the summons of war, let women now leave all that may be left of home for a great and earnest day of counsel.

Let them meet first, as women, to bewail and commemorate the dead.

Let them then solemnly take counsel with each other as the means whereby the great human family can live in peace,

And each bearing after her own time the sacred impress, not of Caesar, but of God.

⊕ Julia Ward Howe

Peace, Justice, and Equity

574

The Glories of Peace

They shall beat their swords into
  plowshares,
and their spears into pruning-
  hooks;
nation shall not lift up sword
  against nation,
neither shall they learn war any
  more;

But they shall all sit under their
  own vines and fig trees,
and no one shall make them
  afraid.

Micah 4:3

575

A New Manifestation

A new manifestation is at hand, a new hour is come.

When Man and Woman may regard one another as brother and sister, able both to appreciate and to prophesy to one another.

A new manifestation is at hand, a new hour is come.

What Woman needs is not as a woman to act or rule, but as a nature to grow, as an intelligence to discern, as a soul to live freely and unimpeded, to unfold such powers as were given her.

A new manifestation is at hand, a new hour is come.

Man does not have his fair share either; his energies are repressed and distorted by the interposition of artificial obstacles.

A new manifestation is at hand, a new hour is come.

We would have every arbitrary barrier thrown down. We would have every path laid open to Woman as freely as to Man.

Were this done, we believe a divine energy would pervade nature to a degree unknown in the history of former ages.

A new manifestation is at hand, a new hour is come.

⊕ Margaret Fuller

576

A Litany of Restoration

If, recognizing the interdependence of all life, we strive to build community, the strength we gather will be our salvation. If you are black and I am white,

It will not matter.

If you are female and I am male,

It will not matter.

If you are older and I am younger,

It will not matter.

If you are progressive and I am conservative,

It will not matter.

If you are straight and I am gay,

It will not matter.

If you are Christian and I am Jewish,

It will not matter.

If we join spirits as brothers and sisters, the pain of our aloneness will be lessened, and that does matter.

In this spirit, we build community and move toward restoration.

⊕ Marjorie Bowens-Wheatley

577

It Is Possible to Live in Peace

If someone with courage and vision can rise to lead in nonviolent action, the winter of despair can, in the twinkling of an eye, be turned into the summer of hope.

It is possible to live in peace.

Nonviolence is not a garment to put on and off at will. Its seat is in the heart, and it must be an inseparable part of our being.

It is possible to live in peace.

Nonviolence, which is a quality of the heart, cannot come by an appeal to the brain. It is a plant of slow growth, growing imperceptibly, but surely.

It is possible to live in peace.

If a single person achieves the highest kind of love it will be sufficient to neutralize the hate of millions.

It is possible to live in peace.

If we are to reach real peace in this world, and if we are to carry on a real war against war, we shall have to begin with the children.

It is possible to live in peace.

The future depends on what we do in the present.

It is possible to live in peace.
MOHANDAS K. GANDHI

578

THIS GREAT LESSON

We can never make the world safe by fighting.

Every nation must learn that the people of all nations are children of God, and must share the wealth of the world.

You may say this is impracticable, far away, can never be accomplished, but it is the work we are appointed to do.

Sometime, somehow, somewhere, we must ever teach this great lesson.

⊕ OLYMPIA BROWN

579

THE LIMITS OF TYRANTS

Those who profess to favor freedom, and yet deprecate agitation, are people who want crops without plowing up the ground.

They want rain without thunder and lightning; they want the ocean without the awful roar of its waters.

This struggle may be a moral one; or it may be both moral and physical; but it must be a struggle.

Power concedes nothing without a demand; it never did and it never will.

Find out what people will submit to, and you have found out the exact amount of injustice which will be imposed upon them.

The limits of tyrants are prescribed by the endurance of those whom they oppress.
FREDERICK DOUGLASS

580

THE TASK OF THE RELIGIOUS COMMUNITY

The central task of the religious community is to unveil the bonds that bind each to all. There is a connectedness, a relationship discovered amid the particulars of our own lives and the lives of others. Once felt, it inspires us to act for justice.

It is the church that assures us that we are not struggling for justice on our own, but as members of a larger community. The religious community is essential, for alone our vision is too narrow to see all that must be seen, and our strength too limited to do all that must be done. Together, our vision widens and our strength is renewed.

☩ Mark Morrison-Reed

581

PRAYER FOR HIROSHIMA DAY

Grey, out of pale nothingness
their agony appears.

*Like ash they are blown and
blasted in the wind's
vermilion breathlessness,*

Like shapeless smoke
Their shapes are torn across the
paper sky.

*They are not beautiful, yet
beauty is in the truth.*

There is no easy music in their
silent screams, no ordered
dancing in their grief's
distracted limbs.

*Their shame is ours. We, too,
are haunted by their fate.*

Their voices call to us, in pain
and indignation: "This is what
you have done to us!"

*Their accusation is our final
hope. Be comforted.*

Yes, we have heard you, Ghosts
of our indifference, we hear

your cry, we understand
your warnings.

*We, too, shall refuse to accept
our fate!*

Haunt us with the truth of our
betrayal
Until the earth's united voices
shout refusal, sing your peace!

*Forgive us, that we had to see
your passion to remember
what we must never again
deny: Love one another.*

James Kirkup

582

THE DIVINE JUSTICE

I hate, I despise your festivals,
and I take no delight in your
solemn assemblies.

*Even though you offer me your
burnt offerings,
I will not accept them;*

And the offerings of well-being of
your fatted animals
I will not look upon.

*Take away from me the noise of
your songs;
I will not listen to the melody
of your harps.*

But let justice roll down like
waters,

*and righteousness like an
ever-flowing stream.*

Amos 5

THE YOUNG DEAD SOLDIERS

The young dead soldiers do not speak.

Nevertheless, they are heard in the still houses: who has not heard them?

They have a silence that speaks for them at night and when the clock counts.

They say: We were young. We have died. Remember us.

They say: We have done what we could but until it is finished it is not done.

They say: We have given our lives but until it is finished no one can know what our lives gave.

They say: Our deaths are not ours; they are yours; they will mean what you make them.

They say: Whether our lives and our deaths were for peace and a new hope or for nothing we cannot say; it is you who must say this.

They say: We leave you our deaths. Give them their meaning.

We were young, they say. We have died. Remember us.

ARCHIBALD MACLEISH

A NETWORK OF MUTUALITY

We are caught in an inescapable network of mutuality, tied in a single garment of destiny.

Injustice anywhere is a threat to justice everywhere.

There are some things in our social system to which all of us ought to be maladjusted.

Hatred and bitterness can never cure the disease of fear, only love can do that.

We must evolve for all human conflict a method which rejects revenge, aggression, and retaliation.

The foundation of such a method is love.

Before it is too late, we must narrow the gaping chasm between our proclamations of peace and our lowly deeds which precipitate and perpetuate war.

One day we must come to see that peace is not merely a distant goal that we seek but a means by which we arrive at that goal.

We must pursue peaceful ends through peaceful means.

We shall hew out of the mountain of despair, a stone of hope.

MARTIN LUTHER KING, JR.

PEACE, JUSTICE, AND EQUITY

585

Councils

We must sit down
and reason together.

*Perhaps we should sit in the
   dark.
In the dark we could utter our
   feelings.*

In the dark we could propose
and describe and suggest.

*In the dark we could not see
   who speaks
and only the words
would say what they say.*

No one would speak more than
   twice.
No one would speak less than
   once.

*Thus saying what we feel and
   what we want,
what we fear for ourselves and
   each other into the dark,*

Perhaps we could begin
to begin to listen.

*The women must learn to dare
   to speak,
The men must learn to bother
   to listen.*

The women must learn to say I
   think this is so.

*The men must learn to stop
   dancing solos on the ceiling.*

After each speaks, she or he
will say a ritual phrase:

*It is not I who speaks but the
   wind.*

*Wind blows through me.
Long after me, is the wind.*
Marge Piercy

586

The Idea of Democracy

As labor is the common burden of
our race, so the effort of some to
shift their share of the burden onto
the shoulders of others is the great,
durable, curse of the race.

*As I would not be a slave, so I
would not be a master.*

This expresses my idea of democracy. Whatever differs from this, to
the extent of the difference, is no
democracy.

*Our reliance is in our love for lib-
erty; our defense is in the spirit
which prizes liberty as the heritage of all people in all lands
everywhere.*

Destroy this spirit, and we have
planted the seeds of despotism at
our own doors.

*Those who deny freedom to oth-
ers deserve it not for themselves,
and cannot long retain it.*

Why should there not be a patient
confidence in the ultimate justice of
the people? Is there any better or
equal hope in the world?

*Let us have faith that right
makes might, and in that faith,
let us, to the end, dare to do our
duty as we understand it.*
Abraham Lincoln

587

A Litany for Survival

For those of us who live at the
  shoreline
standing upon the constant edges
  of decision
crucial and alone

  For those of us who cannot
    indulge
  the passing dreams of choice

For those of us who were
  imprinted with fear like a faint
  line in the center of our
  foreheads learning to be afraid
  with our mother's milk

  For by this weapon,
  this illusion of some safety to
    be found—
  the heavy-footed hoped to
    silence us.

For all of us
this instant and this triumph—
we were never meant to survive.

  And when the sun rises we are
    afraid
  it might not remain
  When the sun sets we are afraid
  it might not rise in the morning

And when we speak we are afraid
our words will not be heard
nor welcomed

  But when we are silent
  we are still afraid.

So it is better to
speak remembering

We were never
meant to survive.

AUDRE LORDE
(ADAPTED)

588

To Loose the Fetters of
Injustice

Is not this the fast that I choose:

To loose the bonds of injustice,
to undo the thongs of the yoke,
to let the oppressed go free,
and to break every yoke?

Is it not to share your bread with
  the hungry,
and bring the homeless poor into
  your house;
when you see them naked, to
  cover them,
and not to hide yourself from your
  own kin?

  Then shall your light break
    forth like the dawn,
  and your healing shall spring
    up quickly;

If you remove the yoke from
  among you,
the pointing of the finger, the
  speaking of evil,
if you offer your food to the
  hungry
and satisfy the needs of the
  afflicted,

  You shall be like a watered
    garden,
  like a spring whose waters
    never fail.

ISAIAH 58

589

PEACE

Peace means the beginning of a
new world.

> It means that nations are
> friends;
> It means joy to the world.

Peace is quiet and calm; it is rest;
It is silence after a storm.

> It is love and friendship;
> It is the world's dream of
> dreams.

Peace brings comfort and
happiness;
It brings bread to the hungry;
It brings prosperity to the nations.

> It means the strong respect the
> weak,
> the great respect the small,
> the many respect the few.

It is like spring after winter;

> It brings sunshine into the
> world;
> It is like sweet music after
> harsh sounds.

PUPILS OF THE LINCOLN SCHOOL
(ADAPTED)

Freedom

590

PSALM 126

When the Spirit struck us free
we could scarcely believe it
for very joy.

> Were we free
> were we wrapt
> in a dream of freedom?

Our mouths were filled with
laughter
our tongues with pure joy.

> The oppressors were awestruck;

What marvels the Lord works for
them!

> Like a torrent in flood
> our people streamed out.

Locks, bars, gulags, ghettoes,
cages, cuffs,
a nightmare scattered.

> We trod the long furrow
> slaves, sowing in tears.

A lightning bolt loosed us.

> We tread the long furrow
> half drunk with joy
> staggering,

The golden
sheaves in our arms.

DANIEL BERRIGAN

591

I CALL THAT CHURCH FREE

I call that church free which enters
into covenant with the ultimate
source of existence,

> That sustaining and transform-
> ing power not made with human
> hands.

It binds together families and generations, protecting against the

idolatry of any human claim to absolute truth or authority.

This covenant is the charter and responsibility and joy of worship in the face of death as well as life.

I call that church free which brings individuals into a caring, trusting fellowship,

That protects and nourishes their integrity and spiritual freedom; that yearns to belong to the church universal;

It is open to insight and conscience from every source; it bursts through rigid tradition, giving rise to new and living language, to new and broader fellowship.

It is a pilgrim church, a servant church, on an adventure of the spirit.

The goal is the prophethood and priesthood of all believers, the one for the liberty of prophesying, the other for the ministry of healing.

It aims to find unity in diversity under the promptings of the spirit "that bloweth where it listeth . . . and maketh all things new."

⊕ JAMES LUTHER ADAMS

592

THE FREE MIND

I call that mind free which masters the senses, and which recognizes its own reality and greatness:

Which passes life, not in asking what it shall eat or drink, but in hungering, thirsting, and seeking after righteousness.

I call that mind free which jealously guards its intellectual rights and powers, which does not content itself with a passive or hereditary faith:

Which opens itself to light whencesoever it may come; which receives new truth as an angel from heaven.

I call that mind free which is not passively framed by outward circumstances, and is not the creature of accidental impulse:

Which discovers everywhere the radiant signatures of the infinite spirit, and in them finds help to its own spiritual enlargement.

I call that mind free which protects itself against the usurpations of society, and which does not cower to human opinion:

Which refuses to be the slave or tool of the many or of the few, and guards its empire over itself as nobler than the empire of the world.

I call that mind free which resists the bondage of habit, which does not mechanically copy the past, nor live on its old virtues:

But which listens for new and higher monitions of conscience, and rejoices to pour itself forth in fresh and higher exertions.

I call that mind free which sets no bounds to its love, which, wherever they are seen, delights in virtue and sympathizes with suffering:

Which recognizes in all human beings the image of God and the rights of God's children, and offers itself up a willing sacrifice to the cause of humankind.

I call that mind free which has cast off all fear but that of wrongdoing, and which no menace or peril can enthrall:

Which is calm in the midst of tumults, and possesses itself, though all else be lost.

⊕ William Ellery Channing

593

Liberation Is Costly

Liberation is costly.
Even after the Lord had delivered the Israelites from Egypt, they had to travel through the desert.

They had to bear the responsibilities and difficulties of freedom.

There was starvation and thirst and they kept complaining.

They complained that their diet was monotonous.

Many of them preferred the days of bondage and the fleshpots of Egypt.

We must remember that liberation is costly. It needs unity.

We must hold hands and refuse to be divided. We must be ready.

Some of us will not see the day of our liberation physically.

But those people will have contributed to the struggle.

Let us be united, let us be filled with hope, let us be those who respect one another.

Desmond Tutu

594

Principles and Purposes for All of Us

We affirm and promote the inherent worth and dignity of every person.

We believe that each and every person is important.

We affirm and promote justice, equity, and compassion in human relations.

We believe that all people should be treated fairly.

We affirm and promote acceptance of one another and encouragement to spiritual growth.

We believe that our churches are places where all people are accepted, and where we keep on learning together.

We affirm and promote a free and responsible search for truth and meaning.

We believe that each person must be free to search for what is true and right in life.

We affirm and promote the right of conscience and the use of the democratic process.

We believe that all people should have a voice and a vote about the things which concern them.

We affirm and promote the goal of world community with peace, liberty, and justice for all.

We believe that we should work for a peaceful, fair, and free world.

We affirm and promote respect for the interdependent web of all existence of which we are a part.

We believe that we should care for our planet earth.

ADAPTED FROM THE

⊕ UNITARIAN UNIVERSALIST ASSOCIATION PRINCIPLES AND PURPOSES

Wisdom from the World's Religions

Buddhism

595

FREE FROM SUFFERING

May all sentient beings be well
  and enjoy the root of happiness:
Free from suffering and the root of
  suffering.
May they not be separated from
  the joy beyond sorrow.
May they dwell in spacious
  equanimity
Free from craving, fear, and
  ignorance.

BODHISATTVA VOWS
(ADAPTED)

596

BOUNDLESS GOODWILL

Let us cultivate boundless goodwill.

Let none deceive another, or despise any being in any state.

Let none in anger or ill-will wish another harm.

Even as a mother watches over her child, so with boundless mind should one cherish all living beings,

Radiating friendliness over the whole world,

Above, below, and all around, without limit.

METTA SUTTA

597

Love Versus Hate

Never does hatred cease by hating in return;

Only through love can hatred come to an end.

Victory breeds hatred;

The conquered dwell in sorrow and resentment.

They who give up all thought of victory or defeat,

May be calm and live happily at peace.

Let us overcome violence by gentleness;

Let us overcome evil by good;

Let us overcome the miserly by liberality;

Let us overcome the liar by truth.

DHAMMAPADA

598

Without Hate

May every creature abound in well-being and peace.

May every living being, weak or strong, the long and the small, the short and the medium-sized, the mean and the great,

May every living being, seen or unseen, those dwelling far off, those living near by, those already born, those waiting to be born,

May all attain inward peace.

Let no one deceive another. Let no one despise another in any situation.

Let no one, from antipathy or hatred, wish evil to anyone at all.

Just as a mother, with her own life, protects her only child from hurt, so within yourself foster a limitless concern for every living creature.

Display a heart of boundless love for all the world in all its height and depth and broad extent,

Love unrestrained, without hate or enmity.

Then as you stand or walk, sit or lie, until overcome by drowsiness, devote your mind entirely to this: It is known as living the life divine.

BUDDHIST

Sikh

599

Why do you go to the forest in search of the Divine? God lives in all, and abides with you too. As fragrance dwells in a flower, or reflection in a mirror, so the Divine dwells inside everything; seek therefore in your own heart.

TEGH BAHADUR

600

THE SPACE WITHIN

Thirty spokes share the wheel's
  hub;
It is the center hole that makes it
  useful.
Shape clay into a vessel;
It is the space within that makes
  it useful.
Cut doors and windows for a
  room;
It is the holes that make it useful.
Therefore profit comes from what
  is there;
Usefulness from what is not there.

LAO-TSE

601

WHEN ALL THE PEOPLE

When all the people of the world
  love,
Then the strong will not
  overpower the weak.
The many will not oppress the
  few.
The wealthy will not mock the
  poor.
The honored will not disdain the
  humble.
The cunning will not deceive the
  simple.

MO-TSE

602

IF THERE IS TO BE PEACE

If there is to be peace in the world,

*There must be peace in the
  nations.*

If there is to be peace in the
  nations,

*There must be peace in the
  cities.*

If there is to be peace in the cities,

*There must be peace between
  neighbors.*

If there is to be peace between
  neighbors,

*There must be peace in the
  home.*

If there is to be peace in the home,

*There must be peace in the
  heart.*

LAO-TSE

603

BEYOND WORDS

Existence is beyond the power of
words to define:

*Terms may be used but are none
of them absolute.*

In the beginning of heaven and
earth there were no words,

*Words come out of the womb of
matter;*

And whether we dispassionately see to the core of life or passionately see the surface, the core and the surface are essentially the same,

Words making them seem different only to express appearance.

If name be needed, wonder names them both: from wonder into wonder existence opens.

LAO-TSE

604

A Vessel So Sacred

Those who would take over the earth
And shape it to their will never, I notice, succeed.

The earth is like a vessel so sacred that at the mere approach of the profane it is marred,

And when they reach out their fingers it is gone.

For a time in the world some force themselves ahead and some are left behind.

For a time in the world some make a great noise and some are held silent.

For a time in the world some are puffed fat and some are kept hungry.

For a time in the world some push aboard and some are tipped out.

At no time in the world will one who is sane
Over-reach,
Over-spend,
Over-rate.

LAO-TSE

605

Oh, how great is the divine moral law in humanity. Vast and illimitable, it gives birth and life to all created things. It towers high up to the very heavens. How wonderful and great it is! All the institutions of human society and civilization—laws, customs, and usages—have their origin there.

CHUNG YUNG

606

The Tao

Before creation a presence existed,
Self-contained, complete,
    formless, voiceless, mateless,
    changeless,
Which yet pervaded itself with
    unending motherhood.

Though there can be no name
    for it,
I have called it the "way of
    life."

Perhaps I should have called it
    "the fullness of life,"
Since fullness implies widening
    into space,
Implies still further widening,
Implies widening until the circle
    is whole.

In this sense
The way of life is fulfilled,
Heaven is fulfilled,
Earth is fulfilled,
And a fit person also is fulfilled.

There are the four amplitudes of
the universe
And a fit person is one of them:

People rounding the way of
earth,
Earth rounding the way of
heaven,
Heaven rounding the way of life
Till the circle is full.

LAO-TSE

Oh, Beloved Presence, more
beautiful than
all the stars together,

I trace your face in ivy that
climbs,
in clusters of grapes,
in morning flaming the
mountains,
in the clear arch of sky.

You gladden the whole earth and
make every heart great.

You are the breathing of the
world.

FROM SHAMS UD-DUN
MOHAMMAD HAFIZ

Islam

607

BELOVED PRESENCE

Cloak yourself in a thousand ways;
still shall I know you, my Beloved.

Veil yourself with every
enchantment
and yet I shall feel you,
Presence
most dear, close and intimate.

I shall salute you in the springing
of cypresses
and in the sheen of lakes, the
laughter of fountains.

I shall surely see you in
tumbling clouds,
in brightly embroidered
meadows.

608

THIS CLAY JUG

Inside this clay jug there are canyons and pine mountains, and the
maker of canyons and pine mountains!

All seven oceans are inside, and
hundreds of millions of stars.

The acid that tests gold is there, and
the one who judges jewels.

And the music from the strings
no one touches, and the source of
all water.

If you want the truth, I will tell you
the truth:

Friend, listen:
the God whom I love is inside.

KABIR

609

TO SERVE THE PEOPLE

To worship God is nothing other than to serve the people.

It does not need rosaries, prayer carpets, or robes.

All peoples are members of the same body, created from one essence.

If fate brings suffering to one member

The others cannot stay at rest.

SAADI

610

THE JOURNEY OF LOVE

Where in our hearts is
That burning of desire?

*It is true that we are made of dust
And the world is also made of dust,
But the dust has motes rising.*

Whence comes that drive in us?

*We look to the starry sky
And love storms in our hearts.*

Whence comes that storm?

The journey of love is a very long journey,

But sometimes with a sigh you can cross that vast desert.

Search and search again without losing hope;

You may find sometime a treasure on your way.

My heart and my eyes are all devoted to the vision.

MOHAMMED IQBAL

Hinduism

611

BRAHMAN

I am the Self that dwells in the heart of every mortal creature:
I am the beginning, the life span, and the end of all.

*I am the radiant sun among the light-givers:
I am the mind:
I am consciousness in the living.*

I am death that snatches all;
I, also, am the source of all that shall be born.

*I am time without end:
I am the sustainer: my face is everywhere.*

I am the beginning, the middle, and the end in creation:
I am the knowledge of things spiritual.

I am glory, prosperity, beautiful speech, memory, intelligence, steadfastness, and forgiveness.

I am the divine seed of all lives.
In this world nothing animate or inanimate exists without me.

I am the strength of the strong;
I am the purity of the good.

I am the knowledge of the knower.
There is no limit to my divine
manifestations.

Whatever in this world is
powerful, beautiful, or
glorious, that you may know
to have come forth from a
fraction of my power and
glory.

Bhagavad-Gita

612

Fearful Joy

Is it beyond thee to be glad with the
gladness of this rhythm? To be
tossed and lost and broken in the
whirl of this fearful joy?

All things rush on, they stop not,
they look not behind, no power
can hold them back, they rush
on.

Keeping step with that restless,
rapid music, seasons come dancing
and pass away.

Colors, tunes, and perfumes pour
in endless cascades in the
abounding joy that scatters and
gives up and dies every moment.

Rabindranath Tagore

613

You could have golden treasure bur-
ied beneath your feet, and walk over
it again and again, yet never find it
because you don't realize it is there.
Just so, all beings live every moment in the city of the Divine, but
never find the Divine because it is
hidden by the veil of illusion.

Chandogya Upanishad

Native American

614

The Sacred Hoop

Then I was standing
on the highest mountain
of them all,

And round beneath me
was the whole hoop
of the world.

And while I stood there
I saw more than I can tell

And I understood
more than I saw.

For I was seeing
in the sacred manner
the shape of all things
of the spirit

And the shapes
as they must live
together like one being.

And I saw that the sacred hoop
of my people

was one of many hoops
that make one circle,
wide as daylight and starlight,

And in the center grew one
mighty flowering tree

To shelter all the children
of one mother
and one father.

And I saw that it was holy.

BLACK ELK

Jewish and Christian Teachings

Christmas

615

THE WORK OF CHRISTMAS

When the song of angels is stilled,
When the star in the sky is gone,
When the kings and princes are
    home,
When the shepherds are back with
    their flock,
The work of Christmas begins:
    to find the lost,
    to heal the broken,
    to feed the hungry,
    to release the prisoner,
    to rebuild the nations,
    to bring peace among the brothers,
    to make music in the heart.

HOWARD THURMAN

616

FOR SO THE CHILDREN COME

For so the children come
And so they have been coming.

Always in the same way they
come

born of the seed of man and
    woman.

No angels herald their beginnings.
No prophets predict their future
    courses.

No wisemen see a star to show
where to find the babe that
will save humankind.

Yet each night a child is born is a
holy night,

Fathers and mothers—
sitting beside their children's
cribs
feel glory in the sight of a new
life beginning.

They ask, "Where and how will
this new life end?
Or will it ever end?"

Each night a child is born is a
holy night—
A time for singing,
A time for wondering,
A time for worshipping.

⊕ SOPHIA LYON FAHS

617

AND IT CAME TO PASS

And it came to pass in those days
that there went out a decree from
Caesar Augustus that all the world
should be taxed.

*And Joseph also went up from
Galilee unto the city of David,
which is called Bethlehem, to be
taxed with Mary, his espoused
wife, being great with child.*

And so it was, that, while they were
there, the days were accomplished
that she should be delivered.

*And she brought forth her first-
born son and wrapped him in
swaddling clothes, and laid him
in a manger because there was no
room for them in the inn.*

LUKE 2

618

IN THIS NIGHT

In this night
the stars left their habitual places

*And kindled wildfire tidings
that spread faster than sound.*

In this night
the shepherds left their posts

*To shout the new slogans
into each other's clogged ears.*

In this night
the foxes left their warm burrows

*And the lion spoke with
deliberation,*

*"This is the end
revolution."*

In this night
roses fooled the earth

*And began to bloom
in the snow.*

DOROTHEE SÖLLE

619

MAGNIFICAT

My soul magnifies God
We are enlarged.

*And my spirit breaks out,
rejoicing in the face of
freedom,*

That God (something now within,
yet not mine) has glanced at
this daughter of hope.

*And behold, henceforth, time
will know and regard me.*

For that great mystery is a beam
Drawn through this lens,

*Comforting me and all people,
The shadows now dispersed.*

There is strength here
Like the sinew of a mother's arm.

*It shatters the brittle pride of
wealth;*

It levels the clay-foot thrones of
tyrants;

*It upholds the forgotten, the
scarred.*

Hunger, both body and soul, will
be filled.

*Riches will no more be
rewarded.*

The holy one cleaves to those
who keep faith; it will endure in
those who serve mercy.

*And the promise made to
legend ancestors will be kept.*
⊕ W. FREDERICK WOODEN

620

TO JESUS ON HIS BIRTHDAY

For this your mother sweated in
the cold,

*For this you bled upon the
bitter tree:*

A yard of tinsel ribbon bought and
sold;

*A paper wreath; a day at home
for me.*

The merry bells ring out, the
people kneel;

*Up goes the preacher before the
crowd;*

With voice of honey and with
eyes of steel

*Droning your humble gospel to
the proud.*

Nobody listens. Less than the
wind that blows are all your
words to us you died to save.

*O Prince of Peace! O Sharon's
dewy Rose!
How mute you lie within your
vaulted grave.*

The stone the angel rolled away
with tears

*Is back upon your mouth these
thousand years.*
EDNA ST. VINCENT MILLAY

621

WHY NOT A STAR

They told me that when Jesus was
born a star appeared in the heavens
above the place where the young
child lay.

*When I was very young I had
no trouble believing wondrous
things; I believed in the star.*

It was a wonderful miracle, part of
a long ago story, foretelling an uncommon life.

*They told me a super nova ap-
peared in the heavens in its dying
burst of fire.*

When I was older and believed in
science and reason I believed the
story of the star explained.

*But I found I was unwilling to
give up the star, fitting symbol for
the birth of one whose uncommon life has been long remembered.*

The star explained became the star
understood, for Jesus, for Buddha,
for Zarathustra.

*Why not a star? Some bright star
shines somewhere in the heavens
each time a child is born.*

Who knows what it may foretell?

Who knows what uncommon life
may yet again unfold, if we but
give it a chance?

⊕ Margaret Gooding

Lent and Easter

622

Good Friday

They brought Jesus to the Place of a Skull.

They offered him wine mixed
with myrrh but he would not
take it.

They crucified him and divided his clothes among them, casting lots to decide what each should take. It was nine o'clock in the morning when they crucified him.

Those who passed by derided
him, saying, "Save yourself."

Those who were crucified with him also taunted him.

When it was noon, darkness
came over the whole land.

At three o'clock Jesus cried, "My God, my God, why have you forsaken me?"

Then Jesus gave a loud cry and
breathed his last.

Mark 15

623

Easter Morning

On the first day of the week, at early dawn they came to the tomb, saying:

Who will roll away the stone
from the entrance to the tomb?

They looked up and saw that the stone had already been rolled back, and on the right they saw a young man. They were alarmed. But the man said to them:

Why do you seek the living
among the dead?

So they went out and fled from the tomb, for terror and amazement had seized them. And they said nothing, for they were afraid.

Mark 16

624

Hope Again

God of Easter and infrequent
  Spring:
announce the large covenant to
  deceitful lands,
Drive the sweet liquor through
  our parched veins,
Lure us to fresh schemes of life.
Rouse us from tiredness, self-pity,
Whet us for use,
Fire us with good passion.
Restore in us the love of living,
Bind us to fear and hope again.

⊕ Clarke Dewey Wells

625

An Eye for Miracles

You who have an eye for miracles
regard the bud now appearing on
the bare branch of the fragile young
tree.

It's a mere dot, a nothing.

But already it's a flower, already a
fruit, already its own death and res-
urrection.

DIEGO VALERI

626

Life Again

Out of the dusk a shadow,
Then, a spark.

Out of the cloud a silence,
Then, a lark.

Out of the heart a rapture,
Then, a pain.

Out of the dead, cold ashes,
Life again.

JOHN BANISTER TABB

627

Seasons of the Self

We need a celebration that speaks
the Spring-inspired word about life
and death,

About us as we live and die,

Through all the cycling seasons,
days, and years.

*We need the sense of deity to
crack our own hard, brown De-
cember husks*

And push life out of inner tombs
and outer pain.

*Unless we move the seasons of
the self, and Spring can come for
us,*

The Winter will go on and on.

*And Easter will remain a myth,
and life will never come again,
despite the fact of Spring.*

⊕ MAX A. COOTS

628

Rolling Away the Stone

In the tomb of the soul, we carry
secret yearnings, pains, frustrations,
loneliness, fears, regrets, worries.

*In the tomb of the soul, we take
refuge from the world and its
heaviness.*

In the tomb of the soul, we wrap
ourselves in the security of dark-
ness.

*Sometimes this is a comfort.
Sometimes it is an escape.*

Sometimes it prepares us for experience. Sometimes it insulates us
from life.

*Sometimes this tomb-life gives
us time to feel the pain of the
world and reach out to heal others. Sometimes it numbs us and
locks us up with our own concerns.*

In this season where light and dark balance the day, we seek balance for ourselves.

Grateful for the darkness that has nourished us, we push away the stone and invite the light to awaken us to the possibilities within us and among us—possibilities for new life in ourselves and in our world.

⊕ Sara Moores Campbell

Hanukkah

629

Hanukkah Lights

We gather in the chill of winter solstice, finding warmth from each other, nourishing hope where reason fails.

Grateful for small miracles, we rejoice in the wonder of light and darkness and the daring of hope.

Holy One of Blessing
Your Presence
fills creation.

You made us holy with Your commandments and called us to kindle the Hanukkah lights.

Holy One of Blessing
Your Presence
fills creation.

You performed miracles for our ancestors in days of old at this season.

Holy One of Blessing
Your Presence
fills creation.

*You have kept us alive
You have sustained us
You have brought us
to this moment.*

Congregation Beth El,
Sudbury, MA

630

The Feast of Lights

Kindle the taper like the steadfast star

Ablaze on evening's forehead o'er the earth,

And add each night a lustre till afar

An eightfold splendor shine above thy hearth.

Clash, Israel, the cymbals, touch the lyre,

Blow the brass trumpet and the harsh-tongued horn;

Chant psalms of victory till the heart take fire,

The Maccabean spirit leap new-born.

Emma Lazarus

Passover

631

PASSOVER

What sacrifices would we make for freedom today?

What would we leave?

How far would we go? How deeply would we look within ourselves?

Our ancestors had no time to await the rising of the bread.

Yet we, who have that time, what do we do to be worthy of our precious inheritance?

We were slaves in Egypt . . . but now we are free.

How easy it is for us to relive the days of our bondage as we sit in the warmth and comfort of our seder.

How much harder to relieve the pain of those who live in the bitterness of slavery today.

CONGREGATION BETH EL, SUDBURY, MA

632

PASSOVER REMEMBERED
(A Reading for Individual Voices)

Pack nothing. Bring only your determination to serve and your willingness to be free. Don't wait for the bread to rise. Take nourishment for the journey, but eat standing, be ready to move at a moment's notice.

Do not hesitate to leave your old ways behind—fear, silence, submission. Only surrender to the need of the time—to love justice and walk humbly with your God. . . .

Begin quickly, before you have time to sink back into old slavery. Set out in the dark. I will send fire to warm and encourage you. I will be with you in the fire and I will be with you in the cloud. . . .

I will give you dreams in the desert to guide you safely home to that place you have not yet seen. . . . I am sending you into the wilderness to make a new way and to learn my ways more deeply. . . .

Some of you will be so changed by weathers and wanderings that even your closest friends will have to learn your features as though for the first time. Some of you will not change at all.

Some will be abandoned by your dearest loves and misunderstood by those who have known you since birth and feel abandoned by you. Some will find new friendship in unlikely faces, and old friends as faithful and true as the pillar of God's flame. . . .

Sing songs as you go, and hold close together. You may at times grow confused and lose your way. . . . Touch each other and keep telling the stories. . . . Make maps as you go, remembering the way back from before you were born. . . .

(continued)

So you will be only the first of many waves of deliverance on these desert seas.

It is the first of many beginnings—your Paschaltide.

Remain true to this mystery.

Pass on the whole story. . . . Do not go back. I am with you now and I am waiting for you.

ALLA RENÉE BOZARTH

Rosh Hashanah and Yom Kippur

633

ATONEMENT DAY

Once more Atonement Day has come.

All pretense gone, naked heart revealed to the hiding self,

We stand on holy ground, between the day that was and the one that must be.

We tremble.
At what did we aim?

How did we stumble?
What did we take?

What did we give?
To what were we blind?

Last year's confession came easily to the lips.

Will this year's come from deeper than the skin?

Say then: Why are our paths strewn with promises like fallen leaves?

Say then: When shall our lust be for wisdom?

Say now:

Love and truth shall meet;
justice and peace shall embrace.

CHAIM STERN

634

ON TURNING

Now is the time for turning.

The leaves are beginning to turn from green to red and orange.

The birds are beginning to turn and are heading once more toward the South.

The animals are beginning to turn to storing their food for the winter.

For leaves, birds, and animals turning comes instinctively.

But for us turning does not come so easily.

It takes an act of will for us to make a turn. It means breaking with old habits.

It means admitting that we have been wrong; and this is never easy.

It means losing face; it means starting all over again; and this is always painful.

It means saying: I am sorry.

It means recognizing that we have the ability to change. These things are hard to do.

But unless we turn, we will be trapped forever in yesterday's ways.

God, help us to turn—from callousness to sensitivity, from hostility to love, from pettiness to purpose, from envy to contentment, from carelessness to discipline, from fear to faith.

Turn us around, O God, and bring us back toward You.

Revive our lives, as at the beginning.

And turn us toward each other, God, for in isolation there is no life.

JACK RIEMER

635

A New Heart

Who can say: I have purified my heart, and I am free from sin?

There are none on earth so righteous that they never sin.

Cast away all the evil you have done, and get yourselves a new heart and a new spirit.

A new heart will I give you, a new spirit put within you. I will remove the heart of stone from your flesh, and give you a heart that feels.

For thus says the Eternal God: I, Myself, will search for My sheep, and seek them out.

As a shepherd seeks them out when any of the flock go astray, so will I seek out My sheep.

I will put My spirit within you, and teach you to live by My laws.

For I desire love and not sacrifices, the knowledge of God rather than burnt offerings.

CHAIM STERN

636

Bless Us with Peace

O Source of peace, lead us to peace, a peace profound and true; lead us to a healing, to mastery of all that drives us to war within ourselves and with others.

May our deeds inscribe us in the Book of life and blessing, righteousness and peace!

O Source of peace, bless us with peace.

GATES OF REPENTANCE

637

A Litany of Atonement

For remaining silent when a single voice would have made a difference

We forgive ourselves and each other; we begin again in love.

For each time that our fears have made us rigid and inaccessible

We forgive ourselves and each other; we begin again in love.

For each time that we have struck out in anger without just cause

We forgive ourselves and each other; we begin again in love.

For each time that our greed has blinded us to the needs of others

We forgive ourselves and each other; we begin again in love.

For the selfishness which sets us apart and alone

We forgive ourselves and each other; we begin again in love.

For falling short of the admonitions of the spirit

We forgive ourselves and each other; we begin again in love.

For losing sight of our unity

We forgive ourselves and each other; we begin again in love.

For those and for so many acts both evident and subtle which have fueled the illusion of separateness

We forgive ourselves and each other; we begin again in love.
⊕ ROBERT ELLER-ISAACS

638

LOVE

If I speak in the tongues of mortals and angels but do not have love, I am a noisy gong or clanging cymbal.

And if I have prophetic powers, and understand all mysteries and knowledge, and if I have faith so as to remove mountains but do not have love, I am nothing.

If I give away all my possessions, and if I hand over my body to be burned, but do not have love, I gain nothing.

Love is patient; love is kind; love is not envious or boastful or arrogant or rude. It does not insist on its own way; it is not irritable or resentful, it does not rejoice in wrong doing, but rejoices in the truth.

It bears all things, believes all things, hopes all things, endures all things. Love never ends. Prophecies will come to an end. Tongues will cease. Knowledge will come to an end. We know in part, we prophesy in part. But when the complete comes, the partial will come to an end.

When I was a child, I spoke like a child, I thought like a child, I reasoned like a child;

When I became an adult, I put an end to childish ways. Now, we see in a mirror, in a riddle.

Then we will see face to face.
Now I know in part.
Then I will know fully.

Now faith, hope, and love abide, these three, and the greatest of these is love.

I CORINTHIANS 13

639

LOVE ONE ANOTHER

Let us love one another, because love is from God.

Whoever does not love God does not know God, for God is love.

No one has ever seen God; if we love one another, God lives in us.

God is love, and those who abide in love, abide in God, and God abides in them.

There is no fear in love, for perfect love casts out fear.

Those who say "I love God" and hate their brothers and sisters are liars, for those who do not love a brother or sister, whom they have seen, cannot love God, whom they have not seen.

No one has ever seen God; if we love one another, God lives in us.

I JOHN 4

640

THE BEATITUDES

Blessed are you poor. The realm of God is yours.

Blessed are you who hunger to-
day. You shall be satisfied.

Blessed are you who weep today. You shall laugh.

Blessed are the humble. They will inherit the earth.

Blessed are the merciful. They will find mercy.

Blessed are the peacemakers. They will be ranked as children of God.

You are the salt of the earth. And if salt become tasteless, how is its saltiness to be restored? It is good for nothing.

You are the light of world. When a lamp is lit, it is not put under a bushel, but on the lampstand, where it gives light to everyone in the house.

MATTHEW AND LUKE

641

THE HEART OF THE TORAH

Heed not unreal Gods:

*You shall be holy, for I your God
am holy.*

When you reap the harvest of your land, you shall not reap to the very edges of your field nor gather the gleanings of your harvest. You shall not strip your vineyard bare, nor gather the fallen grapes of your vineyard; you shall leave them for the poor and the alien.

*You shall be holy, for I your God
am holy.*

You shall not steal, cheat, or lie to one another. You must not take a false oath in my name.

*You shall be holy, for I your God
am holy.*

You shall not defraud nor rob; and you shall not keep for yourself the wages of a laborer until the morning.

*You shall be holy, for I your God
am holy.*

You must not curse a deaf person, nor put obstacles in the way of a blind person.

*You shall be holy, for I your God
am holy.*

You shall not be guilty of any injustice, neither showing partiality to the poor, nor deferring to the powerful, but judging fairly.

*You shall be holy, for I your God
am holy.*

You shall not play the part of a talebearer against your people. You shall not avenge yourself nor bear a grudge, but you must love your neighbor as you love yourself.

I am the Eternal.

LEVITICUS 19

642

PSALM 23

You are my shepherd.
I shall not want.

*You cradle me in green pastures.
You lead me beside the still
    waters.
You restore my soul.*

You guide me in paths of
righteousness for You are
righteous.

*Though I walk through the
    valley of the shadow of
    death, I fear no evil, for You
    are with me;
Your rod and Your staff comfort
    me.*

You spread a table before me in
the presence of my enemies.
You soothe my head with oil;
my cup runs over.

*Surely goodness and mercy will
follow me all the days of my
life
and I will dwell in Your house
forever.*

CONGREGATION BETH EL,
SUDBURY, MA

643

SHOUT FOR JOY

You make the outgoings of the
morning and the evening to
shout for joy.

*You visit the earth, watering it,
making it very rich.*

The great river swells with water,
filling the ridges, blessing the
growth of grain.

*You crown the year with your
abundance,*

The pastures are perfumed with
dew.

*The hills deck themselves with
joy.*

The meadows adorn themselves
with flocks,

*The valleys gown themselves
with grain.*

They shout for joy;

They join in song.

PSALM 65

644

AN UNFAILING TREASURE

I called on God, and the spirit of
wisdom came to me.

I preferred her to scepters and
thrones,
and I accounted wealth as nothing
in comparison with her.

Neither did I liken to her any
priceless gem,
because all gold is but a little sand
in her sight,
and silver will be accounted as
clay before her.

I loved her more than health and
beauty,
and I chose to have her rather
than light,
because her radiance never ceases.

All good things came to me along
with her,
and in her hands uncounted
wealth.

I rejoiced in them all, because
wisdom leads them;
but I did not know that she was
their mother.

I learned without guile and I
impart without grudging;

I do not hide her wealth,
for it is an unfailing treasure for
mortals.

WISDOM OF SOLOMON

Humanist Teachings

Humanity: Women and Men

645

Song of the Open Road

Afoot and light-hearted, I take to
the open road,
healthy, free, the world before me.

*Henceforth I ask not good
fortune—*
I myself am good-fortune;
strong and content,
I travel the open road.

I inhale great draughts of space;
the east and the west are mine,
and the north and the south are
mine.

All seems beautiful to me;
*I can repeat over to men and
women,*
You have done such good to me,
I would do the same to you.

Whoever you are, come travel
with me!
However sweet these laid-up
stores—however convenient
this dwelling, we cannot remain
here;

However sheltered this port,
*and however calm these
waters, we must not anchor
here;*

Together! the inducements shall
be greater;
We will sail pathless and wild seas;

We will go where winds blow,
*waves dash, and the Yankee
clipper speeds by under full
sail.*

Forward! after the great
Companions!
and to belong to them!
They too are on the road!

*Onward! to that which is
endless,*
as it was beginningless,
*to undergo much, tramps of
days, rests of nights,*

To see nothing anywhere but
what you may reach it and
pass it.
To look up or down no road but it
stretches and waits for you—

*To know the universe itself as a
road—*
as many roads—
as roads for traveling souls.
                              Walt Whitman

646

The Larger Circle

We clasp the hands of those that
go before us,

*And the hands of those who
come after us.*

We enter the little circle of each
other's arms

And the larger circle of lovers,

whose hands are joined in a
dance,

And the larger circle of all
creatures,

Passing in and out of life,
who move also in a dance,

To a music so subtle and vast that
no ear hears it

Except in fragments.

WENDELL BERRY

647

AN ETERNAL VERITY

Ancient as the home is the temple;
ancient as the workbench is the altar.

Ancient as the sword is the sac-
rificial fire; ancient as the soldier
is the priest.

Older than written language is spo-
ken prayer; older than painting is
the thought of a nameless one.

Religion is the first and last—the
universal language of the human
heart.

Differing words describe the outward appearance of things; diverse
symbols represent that which
stands beyond and within.

Yet every person's hunger is the
same, and heart communicates
with heart.

Ever the vision leads on with many
gods or with one, with a holy land
washed by ocean waters, or a holy
land within the heart.

In temperament we differ, yet we
are dedicated to one august des-
tiny; creeds divide us, but we
share a common quest.

Because we are human, we shall
ever build our altars; because each
has a holy yearning, we offer everywhere our prayers and anthems.

For an eternal verity abides be-
neath diversities; we are children
of one great love, united in our
one eternal family.

⊕ W. WALDEMAR W. ARGOW

648

BEGINNERS

But we have only begun to love the
earth. We have only begun to imagine the fullness of life

How could we tire of hope?—so
much is in bud.

How can desire fail?—we have only
begun to imagine justice and mercy,

Only begun to envision how it
might be to live as siblings with
beast and flower, not as oppres-
sors.

Surely our river cannot already be
hastening into the sea of nonbeing?

Surely it cannot drag, in the silt,
all that is innocent?

Not yet, not yet—there is too much
broken that must be mended,

Too much hurt that we have done
to each other that cannot yet be
forgiven.

We have only begun to know the power that is in us if we would join our solitudes in the communion of struggle.

So much is unfolding that must complete its gesture, so much is in bud.

DENISE LEVERTOV

The Eternal Now

649

FROM GENERATION TO GENERATION

In a house which becomes a home, one hands down and another takes up the heritage of mind and heart, laughter and tears, musings and deeds.

Love, like a carefully loaded ship, crosses the gulf between the generations.

Therefore we do not neglect the ceremonies of our passage: when we wed, when we die, and when we are blessed with a child;

When we depart and when we return; when we plant and when we harvest.

Let us bring up our children. It is not the place of some official to hand to them their heritage.

If others impart to our children our knowledge and ideals, they will lose all of us that is wordless and full of wonder.

Let us build memories in our children, lest they drag out joyless lives, lest they allow treasures to be lost because they have not been given the keys.

We live, not by things, but by the meanings of things. It is needful to transmit the passwords from generation to generation.

ANTOINE DE ST.-EXUPÉRY

650

CHERISH YOUR DOUBTS

Cherish your doubts, for doubt is the attendant of truth.

Doubt is the key to the door of knowledge; it is the servant of discovery.

A belief which may not be questioned binds us to error, for there is incompleteness and imperfection in every belief.

Doubt is the touchstone of truth; it is an acid which eats away the false.

Let no one fear for the truth, that doubt may consume it; for doubt is a testing of belief.

The truth stands boldly and unafraid; it is not shaken by the testing:

For truth, if it be truth, arises from each testing stronger, more secure.

Those that would silence doubt are filled with fear; their houses are built on shifting sands.

But those who fear not doubt, and know its use, are founded on rock.

They shall walk in the light of growing knowledge; the work of their hands shall endure.

Therefore let us not fear doubt, but let us rejoice in its help:

It is to the wise as a staff to the blind; doubt is the attendant of truth.

⊕ Robert T. Weston

651

The Body Is Humankind

I am a single cell in a body of four billion cells. The body is humankind.

I am a single cell. My needs are individual but they are not unique.

I am interlocked with other human beings in the consequences of our actions, thoughts, and feelings.

I will work for human unity and human peace; for a moral order in harmony with the order of the universe.

Together we share the quest for a society of the whole equal to our needs,

A society in which we need not live beneath our moral capacity, and in which justice has a life of its own.

We are single cells in a body of four billion cells. The body is humankind.

Norman Cousins

652

The Great End in Religious Instruction

The great end in religious instruction is not to stamp our minds upon the young, but to stir up their own;

Not to make them see with our eyes, but to look inquiringly and steadily with their own;

Not to give them a definite amount of knowledge, but to inspire a fervent love of truth;

Not to form an outward regularity, but to touch inward springs;

Not to bind them by ineradicable prejudices to our particular sect or peculiar notions,

But to prepare them for impartial, conscientious judging of whatever subjects may be offered to their decision;

Not to burden the memory, but to quicken and strengthen the power of thought;

Not to impose religion upon them in the form of arbitrary rules, but to awaken the conscience, the moral discernment.

In a word, the great end is to awaken the soul, to excite and cherish spiritual life.

⊕ WILLIAM ELLERY CHANNING

653

REFLECTIONS ON THE
RESURGENCE OF JOY

How short the daylight hours have now become. How gray the skies, how barren seem the trees.

A damp and chilling wind has gripped my mind and made me gloomy, too.

But there is that in me which reaches up toward light and laughter, bells, and carolers,

And knows that my religious myth and dream of reborn joy and goodness must be true,

Because it speaks the truths of older myths;

That light returns to balance darkness, life surges in the evergreen—and us,

And babes are hope, and saviours of the world, as miracles abound in common things.

Rejoice!
And join in the gladness of Christmas.

⊕ DORI JEANINE SOMERS

654

IMPASSIONED CLAY

Deep in ourselves resides the religious impulse.

Out of the passions of our clay it rises.

We have religion when we stop deluding ourselves that we are self-sufficient, self-sustaining, or self-derived.

We have religion when we hold some hope beyond the present, some self-respect beyond our failures.

We have religion when our hearts are capable of leaping up at beauty, when our nerves are edged by some dream in the heart.

We have religion when we have an abiding gratitude for all that we have received.

We have religion when we look upon people with all their failings and still find in them good; when we look beyond people to the grandeur in nature and to the purpose in our own heart.

We have religion when we have done all that we can, and then in confidence entrust ourselves to the life that is larger than ourselves.

⊕ RALPH N. HELVERSON

Integrity

655

Change Alone Is Unchanging

Whosoever wishes to know about the world must learn about it in its particular details.

Knowledge is not intelligence.

In searching for the truth be ready for the unexpected,

Change alone is unchanging.

The same road goes both up and down.

The beginning of a circle is also its end.

Not I, but the world says it: all is one.

And yet everything comes in season.
> Heraklietos of Ephesos

656

A Harvest of Gratitude

Once more the fields have ripened to harvest, and the fruitful earth has fulfilled the promise of spring.

The work of those who labor has been rewarded: They have sown and reaped, planted and gathered.

How rich and beautiful is the bounty gathered: The golden grain and clustered corn, the grapes of purple and green,

The crimson apples and yellow pears, and all the colors of orchard and garden, vineyard and field.

Season follows after season, after winter the spring, after summer the harvest-laden autumn.

From bud to blossom, from flower to fruit, from seed to bud again, the beauty of earth unfolds.

From the harvest of the soil we are given occasion to garner a harvest of the heart and mind:

A harvest of resolve to be careful stewards of all life's gifts and opportunities.

A harvest of reverence for the wondrous power and life at work in things that grow, and in the soul.

A harvest of gratitude for every good which we enjoy, and of fellowship for all who are sustained by earth's beauty.
> Percival Chubb

657

It Matters What We Believe

Some beliefs are like walled gardens. They encourage exclusiveness, and the feeling of being especially privileged.

Other beliefs are expansive and lead the way into wider and deeper sympathies.

Some beliefs are like shadows, clouding children's days with fears of unknown calamities.

Other beliefs are like sunshine, blessing children with the warmth of happiness.

Some beliefs are divisive, separating the saved from the unsaved, friends from enemies.

Other beliefs are bonds in a world community, where sincere differences beautify the pattern.

Some beliefs are like blinders, shutting off the power to choose one's own direction.

Other beliefs are like gateways opening wide vistas for exploration.

Some beliefs weaken a person's selfhood. They blight the growth of resourcefulness.

Other beliefs nurture self-confidence and enrich the feeling of personal worth.

Some beliefs are rigid, like the body of death, impotent in a changing world.

Other beliefs are pliable, like the young sapling, ever growing with the upward thrust of life.

⊕ Sophia Lyon Fahs

658

To Risk

To laugh is to risk appearing the fool.

To weep is to risk appearing sentimental.

To reach out for another is to risk exposing our true self.

To place our ideas—our dreams—before the crowd is to risk loss.

To love is to risk not being loved in return.

To hope is to risk despair.

To try is to risk failure.

To live is to risk dying.

Anonymous

659

For You

The sum of all known reverence I add up in you, whoever you are;

Those who govern are there for you, it is not you who are there for them;

All architecture is what you do to it when you look upon it;

All music is what awakes from you when you are reminded by the instruments;

The sun and stars that float in the open air; the apple-shaped earth and we upon it;

The endless pride and outstretching of people; unspeakable joys and sorrows;

The wonder everyone sees in everyone else they see, and the wonders that fill each minute of time forever;

It is for you whoever you are—it is no farther from you than your hearing and sight are from you; it is hinted by nearest, commonest, readiest.

We consider bibles and religions divine—I do not say they are not divine; I say they have all grown out of you, and may grow out of you still;

It is not they who give the life—it is you who give the life.

Will you seek afar off? You surely come back at last, in things best known to you, finding the best, or as good as the best—

Happiness, knowledge, not in another place, but this place—not for another hour, but this hour.

WALT WHITMAN

Wisdom and Understanding

660

TO LIVE DELIBERATELY

Why should we live in such a hurry and waste of life?

We are determined to be starved before we are hungry.

I wish to live deliberately, to front only the essential facts of life.

I wish to learn what life has to teach, and not, when I come to die, discover that I have not lived.

I do not wish to live what is not life, living is so dear,

Nor do I wish to practice resignation, unless it is quite necessary.

I wish to live deep and suck out all the marrow of life,

I want to cut a broad swath, to drive life into a corner, and reduce it to its lowest terms.

If it proves to be mean, then to get the whole and genuine meanness of it, and publish its meanness to the world;

Or if it is sublime, to know it by experience, and to be able to give a true account of it.

⊕ HENRY DAVID THOREAU

661

The Heart Knoweth

We have a great deal more kindness than is ever spoken.

The whole human family is bathed with an element of love like a fine ether.

How many persons we meet in houses, whom we scarcely speak to, whom yet we honor and who honor us!

How many we see in the street, or sit with in church, whom though silently, we warmly rejoice to be with!

Read the language of these wandering eye-beams.

The heart knoweth.

⊕ Ralph Waldo Emerson

662

Strange and Foolish Walls

The years of all of us are short, our lives precarious.

Our days and nights go hurrying on and there is scarcely time to do the little that we might.

Yet we find time for bitterness, for petty treason and evasion.

What can we do to stretch our hearts enough to lose their littleness?

Here we are—all of us—all upon this planet, bound together in a common destiny,

Living our lives between the briefness of the daylight and the dark.

Kindred in this, each lighted by the same precarious, flickering flame of life, how does it happen that we are not kindred in all things else?

How strange and foolish are these walls of separation that divide us!

⊕ A. Powell Davies

663

One Small Face

With mounds of greenery, the brightest ornaments, we bring high summer to our rooms, as if to spite the somberness of winter come.

In time of want, when life is boarding up against the next uncertain spring, we celebrate and give of what we have away.

All creatures bend to rules, even the stars constrained.

There is a blessed madness in the human need to go against the grain of cold and scarcity.

We make a holiday, the rituals varied as the hopes of humanity,

The reasons as obscure as ancient solar festivals, as clear as joy on one small face.

Margaret Starkey

664

Give us the spirit of the child.
Give us the child who lives within:

*The child who trusts, the child
who imagines, the child who
sings,*

The child who receives without res-
ervation, the child who gives without judgment.

*Give us a child's eyes, that we
may receive the beauty and
freshness of this day like a sunrise;*

Give us a child's ears, that we may
hear the music of mythical times;

*Give us a child's heart, that we
may be filled with wonder and
delight;*

Give us a child's faith, that we may
be cured of our cynicism;

*Give us the spirit of the child,
who is not afraid to need; who is
not afraid to love.*

⊕ Sara Moores Campbell

665

Transcendental Etude

No one ever told us we had to study
our lives,

*Make of our lives a study, as if
learning natural history or music,*

That we should begin with the sim-
ple exercises first and slowly go on
trying the hard ones,

*Practicing till strength and accu-
racy become one with the daring
to leap into transcendence.*

And in fact we can't live like that:
we take on everything at once before we've even begun to read or
mark time, we're forced to begin in
the midst of the hardest movement,

*The one already sounding as we
are born.*

Adrienne Rich

666

The Legacy of Caring

Despair is my private pain
Born from what I have failed to say
failed to do, failed to overcome.

*Be still my inner self
let me rise to you, let me reach
down into your pain
and soothe you.*

I turn to you to renew my life
I turn to the world, the streets of
the city, the worn tapestries of
brokerage firms,

*drug dealers, private estates
personal things in the bag
lady's cart*

rage and pain in the faces that
turn from me
afraid of their own inner worlds.

*This common world I love anew,
as the life blood of generations*

who refused to surrender their
   humanity
in an inhumane world,
courses through my veins.

From within this world
my despair is transformed to hope

   and I begin anew
   the legacy of caring.

                              ✝ THANDEKA

667

THE CRY OF THE REALIST

Vanity of vanities, says the Teacher,
vanity of vanities. All is vanity.

   What do people gain from all the
   toil at which they toil under the
   sun?

A generation goes and a generation
comes, but the earth remains forever.

   The sun still rises, and the sun
   goes down, and hurries to the
   place where it rises.

The wind blows to the south, and
goes around to the north; round and
round goes the wind, and on its cir-
cuits the wind returns.

   All streams run to the sea, but
   the sea is not full; to the place
   where the streams flow, there
   they continue to flow.

All things are wearisome; more
than one can express;

   The eye is not satisfied with see-
   ing, or the ear filled with hearing.

What has been is what will be, and
what has been done is what will be
done. There is nothing new under
the sun.

   Go, eat your bread with enjoy-
   ment, and drink your wine with
   a merry heart; for God has long
   ago approved what you do.

Light is sweet and it is pleasant for
the eyes to see the sun.

   Even those who live many years
   should rejoice in them all.

                              ECCLESIASTES

668

FAITH CANNOT SAVE

What good is it my brothers and sis-
ters, if you say you have faith but do
not have works? Can faith save
you?

   If a brother or sister is naked and
   lacks daily food, and one of you
   says to them:

"Go in peace. Keep warm and eat
your fill,"

   And yet you do not supply their
   bodily needs, what is the good of
   that?

So faith by itself, if it has no works,
is dead.

   Show me your faith apart from
   your works, and I by my works
   will show you my faith.

                              JAMES 2

669

Psalm 1

Blessed are the man and the
woman
who have grown beyond their
greed

*and have put an end to their
hatred
and no longer nourish illusions.*

But they delight in the way
things are
and keep their hearts open, day
and night.

*They are like trees planted near
flowing rivers,
which bear fruit when they are
ready.*

Their leaves will not fall or wither.

Everything they do will succeed.
STEPHEN MITCHELL

670

The Way

Friend, I have lost the way.

The way leads on.

Is there another way?

The way is one.

I must retrace the track.

It's lost and gone.

Back, I must travel back!

None goes there, none.

Then I'll make here my place—

The road runs on—

Stand still and set my face—

The road leaps on.

Stay here, forever stay.

None stays here, none.

I cannot find the way.

The way leads on.

Oh, places I have passed!

That journey's done.

And what will come at last?

The way leads on.

EDWIN MUIR

671

Freedom

Our faith and knowledge thrive by
exercise, as well as our limbs and
complexion.

*If the waters of truth flow not in
a perpetual progression, they
sicken into a muddy pool of con-
formity and tradition.*

The light which we have gained
was given us not to be ever staring
on, but by it to discover onward
things more remote from our
knowledge.

*Where there is much desire to
learn, there of necessity will be
much arguing, much writing,
many opinions.*

Give me liberty to know, to utter,
and to argue freely according to conscience, above all liberties.

And though all the winds of doctrine were let loose to play upon the earth, so truth be in the field, we do injuriously to misdoubt her strength.

For who knows not that truth is strong, next to the Almighty; she needs no policies, no stratagems, to make her victorious.

Let her and falsehood grapple; whoever knew truth put to the worse in a free and open encounter.

JOHN MILTON

Offertory Words

672

Anne Sexton wrote:
*"Look to your heart
    that flutters in and out like a moth,
God is not indifferent to your
    need.
You have a thousand prayers
    but God has one."*

Dear God, we give thanks for
    those moments when we can
    feel that we live in a world that
    is not indifferent to our need.

We all have so many needs—
a thousand prayers—a thousand
    needs—
that really only need one answer:
let the world not be indifferent.

And may we live and be with
    each other in the way that
    shows this truth whatever the
    day brings:
that neither are we indifferent to
    each other.

⊕ JUDITH MEYER

673

Freely have we received of gifts that minister to our needs of body and spirit. Gladly we bring to our church and its wide concerns a portion of this bounty.

⊕ ARTHUR FOOTE II

674

Let there be an offering to sustain and strengthen this place which is sacred to so many of us, a community of memory and of hope, for we are now the keepers of the dream.

⊕ BRANDOCH L. LOVELY

675

The offering is a sacrament of the free Church. It is supported by the voluntary generosity of all who join with us.

The offering will now be given and received in grateful appreciation of our shared hopes and values.

⊕ ELLEN JOHNSON-FAY

676

So when you are offering your gift at the altar, if you remember that your brother or sister has something against you, leave your gift there before the altar and go; first be reconciled to your brother or sister, and then come and offer your gift.

MATTHEW 5:23–24

Benedictions and Closing Words

677

The peace which passeth
  understanding,
the peace of God,
which the world can neither give
  nor take away,
be among us, and abide in our
  hearts.

COMPOSITE

678

The courage of the early
  morning's dawning,
and the strength of the eternal
  hills,
and the peace of the evening's
  ending,
and the love of God,
be in our hearts.

ANONYMOUS

679

Be ye lamps unto yourselves; be
  your own confidence.
Hold to the truth within
  yourselves as to the only lamp.

BUDDHIST

680

Because of those who came before,
we are;
in spite of their failings, we
  believe;
because of, and in spite of the
  horizons of their vision,
we, too, dream.

✝ BARBARA PESCAN

681

Deep peace of the running wave
  to you.
Deep peace of the flowing air
  to you.
Deep peace of the quiet earth
  to you.
Deep peace of the shining stars
  to you.
Deep peace of the infinite peace
  to you.

ADAPTED FROM GAELIC RUNES

682

Beauty is before me, and
Beauty behind me,
above me and below me
hovers the beautiful.
I am surrounded by it,
I am immersed in it.
In my youth, I am aware of it,
and, in old age,
I shall walk quietly the beautiful
  trail.
In beauty it is begun.
In beauty, it is ended.

FROM THE NAVAJO INDIANS
OF NORTH AMERICA

683

Be ours a religion which, like
  sunshine, goes everywhere;
its temple, all space;
its shrine, the good heart;
its creed, all truth;
its ritual, works of love;
its profession of faith, divine
  living.

⊕ THEODORE PARKER

684

The blessing of truth be upon us,
the power of love direct us and
  sustain us,
and may the peace of this
  community preserve our going
  out and our coming in,
from this time forth, until we
  meet again.

⊕ DUKE T. GRAY

685

I.

What we call a beginning is often
  the end
and to make an end is to make a
  beginning.
The end is where we start from.

II.

We shall not cease from
  exploration
and the end of all our exploring
will be to arrive where we started
and know the place for the first
  time.

T. S. ELIOT

686

Go in peace. Live simply, gently,
  at home in yourselves.
Act justly.
Speak justly.
Remember the depth of your own
  compassion.
Forget not your power in the days
  of your powerlessness.

Do not desire to be wealthier than
  your peers
and stint not your hand of charity.
Practice forebearance.
Speak the truth, or speak not.
Take care of yourselves as bodies,
  for you are a good gift.

Crave peace for all people in the
  world,
beginning with yourselves,
and go as you go with the dream
  of that peace alive in your heart.

⊕ MARK L. BELLETINI

687

Go your ways,
knowing not the answers to all
    things,
yet seeking always the answer
to one more thing than you know.

⊕ JOHN W. BRIGHAM

688

Hold on to what is good
even if it is
a handful of earth.

Hold on to what you believe
even if it is
a tree which stands by itself.

Hold on to what you must do
even if it is
a long way from here.

Hold on to my hand even when
I have gone away from you.

NANCY WOOD

689

Sorrow will one day turn to joy. All
that breaks the heart and oppresses
the soul will one day give place to
peace and understanding and everyone will be free.

PAUL ROBESON

690

You shall know the truth, and the
truth will set you free.

JOHN 8

691

Help us to be the always hopeful
gardeners of the spirit
who know that without darkness
nothing comes to birth
as without light
nothing flowers.

⊕ MAY SARTON

692

If, here, you have found freedom,
take it with you into the world.

If you have found comfort,
go and share it with others.

If you have dreamed dreams,
help one another,
that they may come true!

If you have known love,
give some back
to a bruised and hurting world.

Go in peace.

⊕ LAURALYN BELLAMY

693

And now, may we have faith in life
to do wise planting that the generations to come may reap even more
abundantly than we. May we be
bold in bringing to fruition the
golden dreams of human kinship
and justice. This we ask that the
fields of promise become fields of
reality.

⊕ V. EMIL GUDMUNDSON

694

May the Love which overcomes
  all differences,
which heals all wounds,
which puts to flight all fears,
which reconciles all who are
  separated,
be in us and among us
now and always.

⊕ FREDERICK E. GILLIS

695

Lead me from death to life,
from falsehood to truth.
Lead me from despair to hope,
from fear to trust.
Lead me from hate to love,
from war to peace.
Let peace fill our hearts,
our world, our universe.

PROJECT PLOUGHSHARES

696

To live in this world
you must be able
to do three things:

To love what is mortal;
to hold it
against your bones knowing
your own life depends on it;

And, when the time comes to let
  it go,
to let it go.

MARY OLIVER

697

The love and the work of friends
  and lovers
belong to the task and are its
  health.
Rest and rejoicing belong to the
  task,
and are its grace.
Let tomorrow come tomorrow.
Not by your will is the house
  carried through the night.

WENDELL BERRY

698

Take courage friends.
The way is often hard, the path is
  never clear,
and the stakes are very high.
Take courage.
For deep down, there is another
  truth:
you are not alone.

⊕ WAYNE B. ARNASON

699

Whatsoever things are true,
whatsoever things are honorable,
whatsoever things are just,
whatsoever things are pure,
whatsoever things are lovely,
whatsoever things are of good
  report;
if there be any virtue,
and if there be any praise,
think on these things.

PHILIPPIANS 4

700

For all who see God,
may God go with you.

For all who embrace life,
may life return your affection.
For all who seek a right path,
may a way be found . . .

And the courage to take it,
step by step.

⊕ ROBERT MABRY DOSS

701

We receive fragments of holiness,
glimpses of eternity, brief moments
of insight. Let us gather them up for
the precious gifts that they are and,
renewed by their grace, move boldly
into the unknown.

⊕ SARA MOORES CAMPBELL

702

Where hate rules, let us bring love;
where sorrow, joy.

Let us strive more to comfort
others than to be comforted,
to understand others,
than to be understood,
to love others more than to be
    loved.

For it is in giving that we receive,
and in pardoning that we are
    pardoned.

ATTRIBUTED TO
ST. FRANCIS OF ASSISI

703

Spirit of the East, be with us
    always.
Spirit of the South, be with us
    always.
Spirit of the West, be with us
    always.
Spirit of the North, be with us
    always.
Blessed be.

ANONYMOUS

704

Go out into the highways and
    by-ways.
Give the people something of
    your new vision.

You may possess a small light,
but uncover it, let it shine,
use it in order to bring more light
    and understanding
to the hearts and minds of men
    and women.

Give them not hell, but hope and
    courage;
preach the kindness and
everlasting love of God.

⊕ JOHN MURRAY

705

If we agree in love, there is no dis-
agreement that can do us any in-
jury, but if we do not, no other
agreement can do us any good.

Let us endeavor to keep the unity of
the spirit in the bonds of peace.

⊕ HOSEA BALLOU

706

May the light around us guide our
  footsteps,
and hold us fast to the best and
  most righteous that we seek.

May the darkness around us
  nurture our dreams,
and give us rest so that we may
  give ourselves to the work of
  our world.

Let us seek to remember the
  wholeness of our lives,
the weaving of light and shadow
  in this great and astonishing
  dance in which we move.

⊕ Kathleen McTigue

707

It is written in the Torah:

"I call heaven and earth to
  witness today that I have set
  before you life and death,
  blessings and curses.
Choose life so that you and your
  descendants may live."

Deuteronomy 30

708

For you shall go out in joy, and be
  led back in peace;
the mountains and the hills before
  you shall burst into song,
and all the trees of the field shall
  clap their hands.

Isaiah 55

709

Be doers of the word, and not
  merely hearers.
Those who look into the perfect
  law,
the law of liberty, and persevere,
being not hearers who forget
but doers who act—they will be
  blessed in their doing.

James 1

710

I lift my eyes to the mountains.
Ah, where is help to come from?
Help comes from the Eternal,
who made heaven and earth.
The Eternal guards you, sheltering
  you.
The Eternal will protect you as
  you come and go,
now and forever.

Psalm 121

711

May the Eternal bless you and
  protect you!
May the Eternal smile on you and
  favor you!
May the Eternal befriend you and
  prosper you!

Numbers 6

712

Do not be conformed to this world, but be transformed by the renewing of your minds.

ROMANS 12

713

Keep alert, stand firm in your faith; be courageous, be strong. Let all that you do be done in love.

1 CORINTHIANS 16

Readings for Ceremonial Occasions

Namings and Child Dedications

714

CONGREGATIONAL BLESSING
FOR CHILD DEDICATION

It is our faith that each child born is one more redeemer.

By this Service of Dedication, we commit ourselves to the nurture of this child.

Are you ready to dedicate your-selves to (name)?

We are prepared. We dedicate our minds and hearts to this child and to (her/his) parents.

Will you strive to love and cherish them in times of struggle as well as gladness?

We will love and cherish them al-ways.

We acknowledge the divine spark within each child.

May we be worthy guardians of this young life. May we build a community in which (she/he)

will grow old surrounded by beauty, embraced by love, and cradled in the arms of peace.

⊕ ROBERT ELLER-ISAACS

715

YOUR CHILDREN

Your children are not your children.
They are the sons and daughters of life's longing for itself.

*They come through you but not from you,
and though they are with you yet they belong not to you.*

You may give them your love but not your thoughts,
for they have their own thoughts.

*You may house their bodies but not their souls,
for their souls dwell in the house of tomorrow,
which you cannot visit,
not even in your dreams.*

You may strive to be like them, but seek not to make them like you.

For life goes not backward nor
tarries with yesterday.

You are the bows from which
your children as living arrows
are sent forth.

The Archer sees the mark upon
the path of the infinite, and
bends you with might that the
arrows may go swift and far.

Let your bending in the
Archer's hand be for gladness.

KAHLIL GIBRAN

716

Hail the day on which this child,
(*name*), was born. Rejoice! Let us all
sing and praise her that gave birth
to a (*son/daughter*) for whom she
longed. Greet this day with joy. Our
hearts are glad.

THE MASAI PEOPLE

717

NEW LIFE COMES TO US

New life comes to us as a gift.

Each new life makes its demand,
exacts our attentiveness, enlists
and organizes our energies, and
blesses us. May we be worthy of
the gift, and glad receivers of the
blessing.

New life appeals to us.

Each new life is helpless and so
calls forth our help, is weak and
so calls forth our strength, is in-
nocent and so calls forth our wis-

dom. *May we be wise in our*
strength, and ever-strong in our
help.

New life grows.

Each new life ventures first
words, first steps, first essays in
the art of living. Each grows, ever
surpassing the life that was for
the life that shall be. May we pa-
tiently wait, and watch in won-
der.

New life bears untold promise.

Each new life has a story to tell,
and we shall listen. Each new life
goes forth from us, laying the
child's sovereign claim on whole
realms of being we had called our
own.

All: God of grace, may they be
blessed, whatever the pathways
they follow, whatever the life they
claim as their own.

⊕ GEORGE KIMMICH BEACH

Funerals and Memorials

718

ALL SOULS

Did someone say that there would
be an end,

An end, Oh, an end, to love
and mourning?

What has been once so interwoven
cannot be raveled, nor the gift
ungiven.

*Now the dead move through all
  of us
still glowing,*

Mother and child, lover and lover
  mated,
are wound and bound together
  and enflowing.

*What has been plaited cannot
  be unplaited—
only the strands grow richer
  with each loss*

And memory makes kings and
  queens
of us.

*Dark into light, light into
  darkness, spin.
When all the birds have flown
  to some real haven,*

We who find shelter in the
  warmth within,
Listen, and feel new-cherished,
  new-forgiven,

*As the lost human voices speak
  through us and blend our
  complex love,
our mourning without end.*

⊕ MAY SARTON

719

THOSE WHO LIVE AGAIN

O, may I join the choir invisible of
those immortal dead who live again
in minds made better by their presence:

*Live in pulses stirred to generos-
ity, in deeds of daring rectitude,
in scorn of miserable aims that
end with self;*

In thoughts sublime that pierce the
night like stars, and with their mild
persistence urge our search to
vaster issues.

*So to live is heaven, to make un-
dying music in the world, breath-
ing a beauteous order that con-
trols with growing sway the
growing life of humanity.*

That better self shall live till human
time fold its eyelids, and the human
sky be gathered like a scroll within
the tomb.

*This is life to come, which mar-
tyred souls have made more glo-
rious for us, who strive to follow.*

May I reach that purest heaven —be
to other souls the cup of strength in
some great agony;

*Enkindle generous ardor, feed
pure love, beget the smiles that
have no cruelty;*

Be the sweet presence of a good dif-
fused, and in diffusion ever more in-
tense.

*So shall I join the choir invisible,
whose music is the gladness of
the world.*

GEORGE ELIOT
(MARY ANN EVANS)

720

WE REMEMBER THEM

In the rising of the sun and in its
going down, we remember them.

*In the blowing of the wind and in
the chill of winter, we remember
them.*

In the opening of buds and in the
rebirth of spring, we remember
them.

*In the blueness of the sky and in
the warmth of summer, we remember them.*

In the rustling of leaves and in the
beauty of autumn, we remember
them.

*In the beginning of the year and
when it ends, we remember
them.*

When we are weary and in need of
strength, we remember them.

*When we are lost and sick at
heart, we remember them.*

When we have joys we yearn to
share, we remember them.

*So long as we live, they too shall
live, for they are now a part of us,
as we remember them.*

FROM ROLAND B. GITTELSOHN
(ADAPTED)

721

THEY ARE WITH US STILL

In the struggles we choose for ourselves, in the ways we move for-
ward in our lives and bring our
world forward with us,

*It is right to remember the names
of those who gave us strength in
this choice of living. It is right to*

name the power of hard lives
well-lived.

We share a history with those lives.
We belong to the same motion.

*They too were strengthened by
what had gone before. They too
were drawn on by the vision of
what might come to be.*

Those who lived before us, who
struggled for justice and suffered injustice before us, have not melted
into the dust, and have not disap-
peared.

*They are with us still.
The lives they lived hold us
steady.*

Their words remind us and call us
back to ourselves. Their courage
and love evoke our own.

We, the living, carry them with us:
we are their voices, their hands and
their hearts.

*We take them with us, and with
them choose the deeper path of
living.*

(*Let us name those who lend
strength in our lives.*)

⊕ KATHLEEN MCTIGUE

722

I THINK CONTINUALLY OF THOSE

I think continually of those who
    were truly great.

*Who, from the womb,
    remembered the soul's history*

*through corridors of light where
the hours are suns,*
endless and singing.

Whose lovely ambition
was that their lips, still touched
with fire,
should tell of the spirit clothed
from head to foot in song.

*And who hoarded from the
spring branches
the desires falling across their
bodies like blossoms.*

What is precious is never to forget
the essential delight of the blood
drawn from ageless springs
breaking through rocks in worlds
before our earth;

*Never to deny its pleasure in
the simple morning light,
nor its grave evening demand
for love;*

Never to allow gradually the
traffic to smother
with noise and fog the flowering
of the spirit.

*Near the snow, near the sun, in
the highest fields
See how these names are feted
by the waving grass
and by the streamers of white
cloud
and whispers of wind in the
listening sky:*

The names of those who in their
lives fought for life,
who wore at their hearts the fire's
center.

*Born of the sun they traveled a
short while towards the sun
and left the vivid air signed
with their honor.*

STEPHEN SPENDER

Flower Communion

723

FLOWER COMMUNION PRAYER

In the name of Providence, which
implants in the seed the future of
the flower and in our hearts the
longing for people to live in harmony;

In the name of the highest, in whom
we move and who makes the
mother and father, the brother and
sister, lover and loner what they
are;

In the name of sages and great religious leaders, who sacrificed their
lives to hasten the coming of the
age of mutual respect—

Let us renew our resolution—sin-
cerely to be real brothers and sisters
regardless of any kind of bar which
estranges us from each other.

In this holy resolve may we be
strengthened knowing that we are
God's family; that one spirit, the
spirit of love, unites us; and endeavor for a more perfect and more
joyful life. Amen.

⊕ NORBERT F. CÁPEK
(REVISED)

724

Infinite Spirit of Life, we ask thy blessing on these thy messengers of fellowship and love.

May they remind us, amid diversities of knowledge and of gifts, to be one in desire and affection and devotion to thy holy will.

May they also remind us of the value of comradeship, of doing and sharing alike.

May we cherish friendship as one of thy most precious gifts.

May we not let awareness of another's talents discourage us, or sully our relationship, but may we realize that whatever we can do, great or small, the efforts of all of us are needed to do thy work in this world.

⊕ Norbert F. Čápek

Communion

725

The Simplest of Sacraments

Simply to be, and to let things be as they speak wordlessly from the mystery of what they are.

Simply to say a silent yes to the hillside flowers, to the trees we walk under.

To pass from one person to another a morsel of bread, an answering yes, this is the simplest, the quietest, of sacraments.

⊕ Jacob Trapp

726

Food for the Spirit

I was hungry and you gave me food,
I was thirsty and you gave me drink,

I was a stranger and you welcomed me,
I was naked and you clothed me,

I was sick and you visited me,
I was in prison and you came to me.

Here is the bread of life, food for the spirit.
Let all who hunger come and eat.

Here is the fruit of the vine, pressed and poured out for us.
Let all who thirst now come and drink.

We come to break bread.
We come to drink of the fruit of the vine.
We come to make peace.

May we never praise God with our mouths while denying in our hearts or by our acts the love that is our common speech.

I come to be restored in the love of God.

*I come to be made new as an
instrument of that love.*

I know that I am worthy. I know
that I am welcome.
All are worthy.

All are welcome.

Come into the embrace and
remembrance of this
communion.

⊕ Robert Eller-Isaacs,
based on Matthew 25

727

The Bread We Share

The bread we share this day is sacred.

Grain, gift of the earth gives life.

The friendship we share this day is
sacred.

*All gatherings when people meet
and touch, celebrate life.*

The laughter we share this day is
sacred.

*Joy and sorrow that rise from
love are springs of life.*

The stillness we share this day is
sacred.

*In this peace is a haven for the
spirit which nurtures life.*

For bread, for friends, for joy and
sorrow, for the comfort of quietness: let us ever be grateful and caring.

⊕ Rudolph Nemser

Membership
and Recognition

728

Blessed Are Those

Blessed are those who yearn for
deepening more than escape; who
are not afraid to grow in spirit.

*Blessed are those who take seriously the bonds of community;
who regularly join in celebration
and learning; who come as much
to minister as to be ministered
unto.*

Blessed are those who bring their
children; who invite their friends to
come along, to join in fellowship,
service, learning, and growth.

*Blessed are those who support
the church and its work by their
regular, sustained, and generous
giving; and who give of themselves no less than their money.*

Blessed are those who know that
the church is often imperfect, yet
rather than harbor feelings of anger
or disappointment, bring their concerns and needs to the attention of
the church leaders.

*Blessed are those who when
asked to serve, do it gladly; who
realize that change is brought
about through human meeting,
who do the work of committees,
and stay till the end.*

Blessed are those who speak their
minds in meetings, who can take

and give criticism; who keep alive their sense of humor.

Blessed are those who know that the work of the church is the transformation of society; who have a vision of Beloved Community transcending the present, and who do not shrink from controversy, sacrifice, or change.

All: Blessed are they indeed.

⊕ John Buehrens

Ingathering

729

The Winds of Summer

You and I and all of us blew about with the winds of summer,

Following the sun in different ways of freedom and play,

Finding rest in the cool stillness of shadows, and moving to the slow heatstruck rhythms which turned the long hours of summer light.

Now it is time for gathering in. We come together at this time and in this place on the bridge of autumn.

Summer is fading backward into memory, and winter waits in snowy brilliance.

We meet with eagerness and delight, needing one another for sharing.

We have joys and sorrows and hopes to share, questions, things we care about and want to help make better,

Things that we would like to understand, ideas waiting to be heard.

Today, we are together in gladness, once more the special community that we call our church,

A community of all ages that sings its songs, tells its thoughts, asks its questions, and searches together with courage and with love.

⊕ Patricia Shuttee

Weddings and Services of Union

730

Make Not a Bond of Love

Love one another, but make not a
  bond of love:
let it rather be a moving sea
  between the shores of your
  souls.

Fill each other's cup but drink
  not from one cup.
Give one another of your bread
  but eat not from the same
  loaf.

Sing and dance together and be
  joyous, but let each one of you
  be alone, even as the strings of
  a lute are alone though they
  quiver with the same music.

*Give your hearts, but not into
each other's keeping.
For only the hand of Life can
contain your hearts.*

And stand together yet not too
near together:

*For the pillars of the temple
stand apart,
And the oak tree and the
cypress grow not in each
other's shadow.*

But let there be spaces in your
togetherness,
And let the winds of the heavens
dance between you.

*Love one another, but make not
a bond of love.*

KAHLIL GIBRAN

731

Entreat me not to leave you,
and to turn back from following
you.
Wherever you go, there I will go.
Wherever you stay, there I will
stay.
Your people shall be my people
and your God shall be my God.

RUTH 1:16

*Martin Luther King, Jr.
Sunday*

732

FOR MARTIN LUTHER KING, JR.

Great Spirit of light and of darkness;

*We gather once again to remem-
ber a fallen friend, and nourish
ourselves from the fountain of
reflections.*

Open our hearts to the anguish of
our pain, to the tired taste of swal-
lowed tears, and to our unrealized
vision.

*In this place we bring our scat-
tered lives together, groping for
meaning and looking for truth.*

Be with us as we continue our
search for understanding of the
mystery of the temporal.

*Stay with us as we wander
through our memories, seeking
pathways to the future.*

Move with us as we unravel the im-
plied imperatives of hopes un-
fulfilled.

*Justice makes tireless demands,
and we grow weary.*

As we touch one another in common cause, and with the great Spirit
in our midst,

*Let us find the way and the cour-
age to realize the dream which
still lives within us. Amen.*

⊕ TONI VINCENT

733

A Place of Meeting

Out of wood and stone,
out of dreams and sacrifice,
the People build a home.
Out of the work of
their hands and hearts and minds
the People fashion a symbol
and a reality.

May this house be truly
a place of Meeting—
meeting one with another
in warmth and joy and
* openness;*
meeting one with another
in courage and love and trust.

May all who enter here
trust one another so surely
that they dare to share the deep
  fires
that burst into anger
as much as the sweet springwaters
that swell into laughter;
the slow erosion of wounded tears
as much as the soaring song.

May these walls know silence
as a hundred hearts search
* inward*
each for its own small spark of
* hope*
that might otherwise
be snuffed out in the noise.

May these rafters hear the voice of
the child
as surely as that of the orator,
and the sound of the lute,
the clack of the typewriter,
the swish of the broom,
and know that all are as holy
as the shout of a million stars.

May the rain fall lightly on this
* house,*
the sun shine warmly,
the winds blow softly,
and bless it
as a place of joy and peace.

⊕ Eileen B. Karpeles

Acknowledgments

We gratefully acknowledge our indebtedness to those individuals and publishers who have granted permission for use of their copyrighted material. Every effort has been made to trace the owner(s) and/or administrator(s) of each copyright. We regret any omission and will, upon written notice, make the necessary correction(s) in subsequent printings.

1   Words: Harcourt Brace Jovanovich, Inc.
2   Words: John Andrew Storey. Music: Unitarian Universalist Association.
3   Music: Unitarian Universalist Association.
4   Music: Alec Wyton.
5   Music: Beacon Press.
6   Words: Alicia S. Carpenter. Harm.: Unitarian Universalist Association.
7   Words: Don Cohen. Music: John Corrado.
8   Words: Unitarian Universalist Association. Harm.: David Dawson.
11 Words: Doris Holmes Eyges.
13 Music: Unitarian Universalist Association.
14 Words: Sydney Henry Knight. Music: Unitarian Universalist Association.
18 New words: Unitarian Universalist Association. Alt. harm.: Abingdon Press.
19 Words: Vs. 2–3, John Andrew Storey. Music: David Dawson.
20 Harm.: Abingdon Press.
22 Words: Unitarian Universalist Association.
23 Words, Music: Hope Publishing Co.
24 Music: I-to Loh.
28 Words, Harm.: Unitarian Universalist Association.
30 Arr.: Unitarian Universalist Association.
31 Words: Hope Publishing Co. Music: Unitarian Universalist Association.
33 Music: Unitarian Universalist Association.
34 Words, Music adapt.: Hope Publishing Co.
36 Words: Hope Publishing Co.
37 Words, Harm.: Unitarian Universalist Association.
38 Words: David Higham Associates, Ltd. Music: Oxford University Press. From *Enlarged Songs of Praise.*
43 Music: Henmar Press, Inc. (C. F. Peters Corp.)
44 Words: American Ethical Union, Library Catalog number 54:11625.
45 Music: Unitarian Universalist Association.
49 Music: Oxford University Press.
50 Words: Philip A. Porter. Music: David Hurd.

51 Words: Unitarian Universalist Association. Music: G.I.A. Publications, Inc.
52 Words: Hodgin Press. Music: Oxford University Press. From *Enlarged Songs of Praise.*
54 Words: "Slow Season" from *The Collected Poems of Theodore Roethke* by Theodore Roethke. 1939 by Theodore Roethke. Used by permission of Doubleday, a division of Bantam Doubleday Dell Publishing Group, Inc. Music: Church of the Ascension, Atlantic City, NJ.
55 Words, Music: Shelley Jackson Denham.
56 Words, Music: Unitarian Universalist Association.
57 Music: Oxford University Press.
58 Music: Oxford University Press.
60 Words: From *Selected Poems of Langston Hughes* by Langston Hughes. Copyright © 1974 by Langston Hughes. Used by permission of Alfred A. Knopf, Inc. Music: George Walker.
62 Words: Unitarian Universalist Association.
63 Music: Unitarian Universalist Association.
64 Music: Hope Publishing Co.
65 Music: Oxford University Press.
66 Words: Sydney Henry Knight. Acc.: Margaret W. Mealy.
67 Words: Katherine Buehrer Baxter and Marilyn Buehrer Saveson.
70 Music, Harm.: J. Fischer and Brothers Co.
71 Words: John Andrew Storey. Music: David Dawson.
72 Engl. trans.: Jeanne C. Maki.
73 Words, Harm.: Unitarian Universalist Association.
75 Music: Jane Marshall.
77 Music: Hope Publishing Co.
78 Words: Unitarian Universalist Association.
79 Harm.: Dale Grotenhuis.
80 Words: Sydney Henry Knight. Music: Unitarian Universalist Association.
81 Words: Philip A. Porter.
82 Music: G.I.A. Publications, Inc.

83 Words: Tirik Productions, Falmouth, ME.
84 Words, Music: Carl Fischer, Inc.
85 Music: Faber Music, Ltd.
86 Words, Music: Shelley Jackson Denham.
90 Music: Hope Publishing Co.
91 Words: Vs. 2–4, Unitarian Universalist Association.
96 Music: Unitarian Universalist Association.
98 Harm.: The United Methodist Publishing House.
100 Words, Music: Marvin V. Frey.
102 Words: John Andrew Storey. Music: The United Methodist Publishing House.
103 Music: Oxford University Press.
104 Music: 1947, 1974 Simon & Schuster, Inc. and Artists and Writers, Inc., renewed 1981 by Simon & Schuster, Inc. Reprinted by permission of Simon & Schuster, Inc.
105 Music: Unitarian Universalist Association.
106 Music: Oxford University Press.
109 Words, Music: Hodgin Press. Harm.: Unitarian Universalist Association.
112 Words: Unitarian Universalist Association. Music: Eugene Hancock.
113 Words: Unitarian Universalist Association.
116 Arr.: Unitarian Universalist Association.
117 Words, Music: Unitarian Universalist Association.
120 Words: The Peters Fraser & Dunlop Group, Ltd.
121 Words, Music: Surtsey Publishing Co. Arr.: Unitarian Universalist Association.
123 Words, Music: Carolyn McDade. Harm.: Unitarian Universalist Association.
124 Words, Music: Unitarian Universalist Association.
125 Words: Unitarian Universalist Association. Music: Hope Publishing Co.
126 Words: Vs. 2–3, Eugene B. Navias.
128 Music: Unitarian Universalist Association.
129 Words: Berkley L. Moore. Music: John Ireland Trust.
130 Words: Unitarian Universalist Association. Music: Larry Phillips.
131 Words: Thrushwood Press Publishing. Arr.: Unitarian Universalist Association.
133 Words: American Ethical Union, Library Catalog number 54:11625. Music: Unitarian Universalist Association.
134 Words, Music: Galaxy Music Corp., Boston.
136 Words: Hodgin Press. Harm.: Unitarian Universalist Association.
137 Words, Music: Hope Publishing Co.
139 Words: Jacob Trapp.
147 Music: Unitarian Universalist Association.
148 Words: Jacob Trapp.
149 Words, Music: Edward B. Marks Music Co.
155 Words, Music: Linda Hirschhorn.

156 Arr.: Unitarian Universalist Association.
157 Music adapt. and arr.: Waldemar Hille.
158 Words: Thomas H. Troeger. Music: Henmar Press, Inc. (C. F. Peters Corp.).
159 Words: Lorenz Publishing Co. Arr.: Presbyterian Board of Christian Education.
160 Words: John Andrew Storey.
161 Arr.: The Church Pension Fund.
162 Arr.: Unitarian Universalist Association.
163 Words, Music: Boosey & Hawkes, Inc.
164 Music: Church of the Ascension, Atlantic City, NJ.
165 Words: Hutchinson, one of the publishers in the Random Century Group. Music: Oxford University Press. From Enlarged Songs of Praise.
167 Words, Music: Jim Scott.
168 Words, Music: Joyce Poley. Harm.: Unitarian Universalist Association.
169 Music adapt.: The United Methodist Publishing House.
170 Words, Music: Hereford Music (ASCAP). All rights reserved. Harm.: Unitarian Universalist Association.
172 Words, Music: Utryck. Used by permission of Walton Music Corp.
173 Words: Hodgin Press.
174 Words: John Andrew Storey.
175 Words: Alicia S. Carpenter.
176 Arr.: Sanjeev Ramabhadran.
177 Words (alt. text): Mrs. William Wolff.
180 Words, Music: W. Allaudin Mathieu.
186 Words: John Andrew Storey.
188 Music: Lynn Adair Ungar.
191 Music: Church of the Ascension, Atlantic City, NJ.
192 Music: Unitarian Universalist Association.
193 Words: John Andrew Storey.
194 Words: Unitarian Universalist Association. Music: I-to Loh.
195 Harm.: The United Methodist Publishing House.
196 Music: G.I.A. Publications, Inc.
197 Harm.: Unitarian Universalist Association.
198 Words, Music: Hope Publishing Co.
199 Words, Music: Unichappell Music, Inc.
201 Harm.: Unitarian Universalist Association.
202 Words, Music: G. Schirmer, Inc.
203 Music: Oxford University Press.
205 Harm.: Abingdon Press.
206 Arr.: J. Jefferson Cleveland.
207 Words: Roberta Bard Ruby.
208 Music adapt. and arr.: The United Methodist Publishing House.
209 Music: Oxford University Press.
210 Arr.: Unitarian Universalist Association.
212 Words: Carole A. Etzler.
214 Arr.: Mills Music, Inc. Used by permission of Belwyn-Mills.
218 Music: Max Janowski; © Friends of Jewish Music, Inc.

220 Words: Unitarian Universalist Association.
221 Words, Music: Silver Dawn Music. Arr.: Unitarian Universalist Association.
224 Words: John Hanly Morgan. Music: Oxford University Press. From *Enlarged Songs of Praise.*
225 Harm.: John Weaver.
226 Words: David Higham Associates Ltd. Harm.: Oxford University Press.
227 Words, Music: Unitarian Universalist Association.
228 Music: Novello & Co., Ltd.
229 Words, Music: Heather Lynn Hanson.
232 Words: Augsburg Fortress.
234 Words: Unitarian Universalist Association.
238 Music: Unitarian Universalist Association.
239 Harm.: Walton Music Corp.
240 Music: Oxford University Press.
243 Harm.: The United Methodist Publishing House.
247 Music: Oxford University Press.
248 Words: American Ethical Union, Library Catalog number 54:11625.
250 Words: From *XAIPE* by E. E. Cummings, edited by George James Firmage. Used by permission of Liveright Publishing Corp. © 1950 by E. E. Cummings. © 1979, 1978, 1973 by Nancy T. Andrews. © 1979, 1973 by George James Firmage. Music: Elkan-Vogel, Inc.
254 Harm.: Alphonse Leduc, Paris.
256 Words, Music: Shelley Jackson Denham.
257 Engl. text: The Frederick Harris Music Co., Ltd., Oakville, Ont. Arr.: H. Barrie Cabena.
263 Words: Unitarian Universalist Association. Music: Westminster Press.
264 Words: Devin-Adair Publishers, Inc. Music: Unitarian Universalist Association.
266 Words: Oxford University Press. Harm.: Alphonse Leduc, Paris.
275 Words: Hope Publishing Co. Music: Carlton R. Young.
277 Music, Harm.: J. Fischer & Brothers Co.
284 Music: Beacon Press.
286 Words, Music: Jim Reilly.
288 Music: Unitarian Universalist Association.
289 Words adapt.: Beth Ide. Harm.: Oxford University Press.
291 Words: American Ethical Union, Library Catalog number 54:11625.
292 Music: Leo Smit.
294 Music: Oxford University Press.
295 Words: Unitarian Universalist Association.
297 Words: John Andrew Storey. Music: Unitarian Universalist Association.
298 Harm.: Abingdon Press.
299 Music, Harm.: J. Fischer & Brothers Co.
300 Words: Alicia S. Carpenter.
301 Words, Music: Grace Lewis-McLaren.
302 Words: John Andrew Storey. Music: Unitarian Universalist Association.
303 Words: Kenneth L. Patton.
305 Words: Hodgin Press. Arr.: Unitarian Universalist Association.
306 Words: Thomas J. S. Mikelson. Music: Unitarian Universalist Association.
307 Words: John Andrew Storey. Music: Theodore Presser Co.
308 Words: Kenneth L. Patton.
309 Words: Unitarian Universalist Association. Music adapt.: Fred Bock Music Co.
310 Words: Kenneth L. Patton. Music: Elkan-Vogel, Inc.
311 Words, Music: Mastenville Music (BMI). Arr.: Unitarian Universalist Association.
313 Words: Schroder Music Co. Harm.: The United Methodist Publishing House.
314 Words: Alicia S. Carpenter.
316 Words, Music: Jim Scott.
317 Words: Hope Publishing Co. Music: David Hurd.
318 Arr.: Presbyterian Board of Christian Education.
319 Music: Unitarian Universalist Association.
320 Words: John Andrew Storey. Music: David Dawson.
321 Music: Unitarian Universalist Association.
322 Words: Unitarian Universalist Association.
323 Words: Hope Publishing Co. Music: Unitarian Universalist Association.
324 Words: Alicia S. Carpenter. Music: Oxford University Press.
325 Words: Hope Publishing Co. Music: Gerald Wheeler.
326 Words: Deborah W. Greeley. Music: Oxford University Press. From *Enlarged Songs of Praise.*
328 Music: Hope Publishing Co.
329 Music: Leo W. Collins.
330 Words: Unitarian Universalist Association.
331 Words: Hodgin Press. Harm.: David Dawson.
332 Words: George Kimmich Beach. Music: Boosey & Hawkes, Inc.
334 Words: From *W. H. Auden: Collected Poems* by W. H. Auden, ed. by Edward Mendelson. © 1943, renewed 1971 by W. H. Auden. Reprinted by permission of Random House, Inc. Music: Carl Flentge Schalk.
337 Words: "The Mystic" from *The Best of Don Marquis* by Don Marquis. © 1946 by Doubleday, a division of Bantam Doubleday Dell Publishing Group, Inc. Used by permission.
338 Words: Unitarian Universalist Association. Music: Oxford University Press.
339 Music: Hope Publishing Co.
340 Words: Christine Doreian Michaels.

629   ACKNOWLEDGMENTS

Music: Unitarian Universalist
Association.

341 Music: Oxford University Press.
342 Words: North Point Press. Excerpted
from *Sabbaths.* Reprinted by permission.
344 Words: Alicia S. Carpenter.
346 Words, Music: Surtsey Publishing Co.
347 Words, Music: Jim Scott.
349 Words: Unitarian Universalist
Association.
350 Words: John Andrew Storey.
352 Words, Harm.: Unitarian Universalist
Association.
353 Words: V. 2, John Andrew Storey. Harm.:
David Dawson.
354 Words, Music: Shelley Jackson Denham.
Harm.: Unitarian Universalist
Association.
355 Words: American Ethical Union, Library
Catalog number 54:11625.
356 Words, Arr.: Walton Music Corp.
357 Arr.: Plymouth Music. Used by
permission of Walton Music Corp.
358 New words: Unitarian Universalist
Association. Music: Oxford University
Press for the Trustees of the Walford
Davies Estate.
359 Words: Unitarian Universalist
Association.
360 Words: Alicia S. Carpenter.
361 Arr.: Unitarian Universalist Association.
363 Words, Music: Unitarian Universalist
Association.
364 Music: G.I.A. Publications, Inc.
365 Music: Unitarian Universalist
Association.
366 Music transcription: The United
Methodist Publishing House.
370 Words: Alicia S. Carpenter.
378 Kenneth L. Patton.
379 Kenneth L. Patton.
380 American Ethical Union, Library Catalog
number 54:11625.
385 Music: G.I.A. Publications, Inc.
389 Words, Music: Philip A. Porter.
390 Music: Carl Fischer, Inc.
391 Words, Music: John Corrado.
396 Words, Music: Mary E. Grigolia.
401 Harm.: The United Methodist Publishing
House.
402 Words, Music: Nathan Segal (Joseph and
Nathan).
404 Words, Music: Hope Publishing Co.
405 Music: Oxford University Press.
407 Arr.: Unitarian Universalist Association.
408 Words: Hope Publishing Co. Music:
Unitarian Universalist Association.
409 Words: Alicia S. Carpenter.
410 Words: Hope Publishing Co. Harm.: John
Weaver.
411 Harm.: The Church Pension Fund.
412 Words: Hope Publishing Co.
413 Words, Music: Hinshaw Music, Inc.
417 Barbara J. Pescan.
421 From *The Holy Bible,* James Moffat (ed.).
Copyright © 1935 by Harper & Row

Publishers, Inc. Reprinted by permission
of HarperCollins Publishers.

422 From *The New Revised Standard
Version of the Bible.* Copyright © 1989
by Division of Christian Education of the
National Council of the Churches of
Christ in the United States of America.
423 From *The Holy Bible,* James Moffat (ed.).
Copyright © 1935 by Harper & Row
Publishers, Inc. Reprinted by permission
of HarperCollins Publishers.
424 From *The New Revised Standard
Version of the Bible.* Copyright © 1989
by Division of Christian Education of the
National Council of the Churches of
Christ in the United States of America.
425 From *Psalms Anew: In Inclusive
Language,* compiled by Nancy Schreck
and Maureen Leach. Copyright © 1986
by St. Mary's Press, Winona, MN.
426 From *The New Revised Standard
Version of the Bible.* Copyright © 1989
by Division of Christian Education of the
National Council of the Churches of
Christ in the United States of America.
427 From *The New Revised Standard
Version of the Bible.* Copyright © 1989
by Division of Christian Education of the
National Council of the Churches of
Christ in the United States of America.
428 From *A Grain of Mustard Seed* by May
Sarton. Copyright © 1971 by May Sarton.
Reprinted by permission of W. W. Norton
& Co, Inc.
429 William F. Schulz.
430 From *The New Revised Standard
Version of the Bible.* Copyright © 1989
by Division of Christian Education of the
National Council of the Churches of
Christ in the United States of America.
431 Barbara Wells.
433 From *The Holy Bible,* James Moffat (ed.).
Copyright © 1935 by Harper & Row
Publishers, Inc. Reprinted by permission
of HarperCollins Publishers.
435 Kathleen McTigue.
436 David C. Pohl.
437 Kenneth L. Patton.
438 Unitarian Universalist Association.
440 Phillip Hewett.
441 Jacob Trapp.
442 Richad Seward Gilbert.
443 Kenneth L. Patton.
444 Kenneth L. Patton.
445 Joy Atkinson.
446 Joan Goodwin.
448 Christine Robinson.
449 Albert Thelander.
450 From *Gates of the House.* Copyright ©
1976 by Central Conference of American
Rabbis and Union of Liberal and
Progressive Synagogues (London).
451 Leslie Pohl-Kosbau.
452 Marjorie Montgomery.
454 Christine Robinson.
456 Elizabeth Selle Jones.

458 Walter Royal Jones, Jr.

459 William F. Schulz.

460 Schlesinger Library, Radcliffe College, Cambridge, MA.

462 From *The Whole World in His Hand: A Pictorial Biography of Paul Robeson* by Susan Robeson. Copyright © 1981 by Susan Robeson. Used by permission of Carol Publishing Group/Citadel Press.

463 From *Dream of A Common Language* by Adrienne Rich. Copyright © 1978 by W. W. Norton & Co., Inc.

464 Copyright © 1979 by Judy Chicago.

465 From *Clearing* by Wendell Berry. Copyright © 1977 by Wendell Berrry. Reprinted by permission of Harcourt Brace Jovanovich, Inc.

466 Elizabeth P. Silliman.

467 From *The Holy Bible,* James Moffat (ed.). Copyright © 1935 by Harper & Row Publishers, Inc. Reprinted by permission of HarperCollins Publishers.

468 From *Gates of Repentance.* Copyright © 1979 by Central Conference of American Rabbis and Union of Liberal and Progressive Synagogues.

469 From *The New Revised Standard Version of the Bible.* Copyright © 1989 by Division of Christian Education of the National Council of the Churches of Christ in the United States of America.

470 Leonard Mason.

479 From *Oblique Prayers* by Denise Levertov. Copyright © 1989 by Denise Levertov. Reprinted by permission of New Directions Publishing Corporation.

481 From *Hollering Sun* by Nancy Wood. Copyright © 1972 by Nancy Wood. All rights reserved.

482 Jacob Trapp.

483 From *Openings* by Wendell Berry. Copyright © 1968 by Wendell Berry. Reprinted by permission of Harcourt Brace Jovanovich, Inc.

485 Raymond J. Baughan.

487 From *Vertical Poetry,* ed. by W. S. Merwin. © 1976. Used by permission of North Point Press.

488 From *Selected Poems of Langston Hughes* by Langston Hughes. Copyright © 1974 by Langston Hughes. Used by permission of Alfred A. Knopf, Inc.

489 Max A. Coots.

490 From *Dream Work* by Mary Oliver. Copyright © 1986 by Mary Oliver. Used by permission of the Atlantic Monthly Press.

492 Carolyn S. Owen-Towle.

493 From *The Oxford Book of Prayer.* Oxford University Press.

494 From *Prayers for Dark People* by W. E. B. Du Bois, ed. by Herbert Aptheker (Amherst: University of Massachusetts Press, 1980). Copyright © 1980 by The University of Massachusetts Press.

497 Adapted from *Gates of Prayer.* Copyright

© 1975 by Central Conference of American Rabbis and Union of Liberal and Progressive Synagogues (London).

498 The Howard Thurman Educational Trust.

500 From *Poems 1960–1967* by Denise Levertov. Copyright © 1961 by Denise Levertov Goodman. Reprinted by permission of New Directions Publishing Corporation.

501 Frederick E. Gillis.

502 From *Prayers for Dark People* by W. E. B. Du Bois, ed. by Herbert Aptheker (Amherst: University of Massachusetts Press, 1980). Copyright © 1980 by The University of Massachusetts Press.

504 Reprinted from *XAIPE* by E. E. Cummings, edited by George James Firmage. Used by permission of Liveright Publishing Corporation. Copyright © 1950 by E. E. Cummings. 1979, 1978, 1973 by Nancy T. Andrews. 1979, 1973 by George James Firmage.

505 From *Being Peace* by Thich N'hat Hanh. Copyright © 1987 by Parallax Press, Berkeley, CA.

506 Barbara J. Pescan.

507 U.S. Interreligious Committee for Peace in the Middle East.

508 U.S. Interreligious Committee for Peace in the Middle East.

509 U.S. Interreligious Committee for Peace in the Middle East.

510 Jane Rzepka.

512 O. Eugene Pickett.

513 From *The New Revised Standard Version of the Bible.* Copyright © 1989 by Division of Christian Education of the National Council of the Churches of Christ in the United States of America.

515 Richard M. Fewkes.

517 From *The Spiral Dance* by Starhawk. Copyright © 1979 by Miriam Simos. Reprinted by permission of HarperCollins Publishers.

522 From *The New Revised Standard Version of the Bible.* Copyright © 1989 by Division of Christian Education of the National Council of the Churches of Christ in the United States of America.

524 From *The Spiral Dance* by Starhawk. Copyright © 1979 by Miriam Simos. Reprinted by permission of HarperCollins Publishers.

525 From *A Door in the Hive* by Denise Levertov. Copyright © 1989 by Denise Levertov. Reprinted by permission of New Directions Publishing Corporation.

526 From *The Enlightened Heart* by Stephen Mitchell. Copyright © 1989 by Stephen Mitchell. Reprinted by permission of HarperCollins Publishers.

528 From *Selected Poems of Langston Hughes* by Langston Hughes. Copyright © 1974 by Langston Hughes. Used by permission of Alfred A. Knopf, Inc.

532 From *Cosmic Canticle* by Ernesto

631

Cardenal, translated by John Lyons, published in 1993 by Curbstone Press, a nonprofit arts organization.

533 From *The New Revised Standard Version of the Bible.* Copyright © 1989 by Division of Christian Education of the National Council of the Churches of Christ in the United States of America.

534 Barbara J. Pescan.

535 From *The New Revised Standard Version of the Bible.* Copyright © 1989 by Division of Christian Education of the National Council of the Churches of Christ in the United States of America.

536 From *Dream Work* by Mary Oliver. Copyright © 1986 Mary Oliver. Used by permission of the Atlantic Monthly Press.

539 From *Just Give Me a Cool Drink of Water 'Fore I Diiie* by Maya Angelou. Copyright © 1981 by Maya Angelou. Reprinted by permission of Random House, Inc.

541 From *A Door in the Hive* by Denise Levertov. Copyright © 1989 by Denise Levertov. Reprinted by permission of New Directions Publishing Corporation.

543 Greta Crosby.

544 Kathleen McTigue.

545 From *Selected Poems of Langston Hughes* by Langston Hughes. Copyright © 1974 by Langston Hughes. Used by permission of Alfred A. Knopf, Inc.

546 Francis C. Anderson, Jr.

548 Helen Cohen.

549 From *Hymn of the Universe* by Pierre Teilhard de Chardin. Copyright © 1961 by Editions de Deuil. English translation 1965 William Collins and Harper & Row Publishers, Inc. Reprinted by permission of HarperCollins Publishers.

552 From *Hollering Sun* by Nancy Wood. Copyright © 1972 by Nancy Wood. All rights reserved.

553 From *Hollering Sun* by Nancy Wood. Copyright © 1972 by Nancy Wood. All rights reserved.

554 From *Present Moment, Wonderful Moment* by Thich N'hat Hanh. Copyright © 1990 Parallax Press, Berkeley, CA.

555 From *The Web and The Rock* by Thomas Wolfe. Copyright © 1937, 1939 Maxwell Perkins as Executor of the Estate of Thomas Wolfe. Renewed 1965 by Paul Gitlin, CTA/Administrator of the Estate of Thomas Wolfe. Reprinted by permission of HarperCollins Publishers.

557 David H. Eaton.

558 From *The New Revised Standard Version of the Bible.* Copyright © 1989 by Division of Christian Education of the National Council of the Churches of Christ in the United States of America.

562 From *Words to Love By* by Mother Teresa. Copyright © 1983 by Ave Maria Press. All rights reserved.

564 From *Horses Make a Landscape More Beautiful: Poems* by Alice Walker. Copyright © 1984 by Alice Walker. Reprinted by permission of Harcourt Brace Jovanovich, Inc.

565 Unitarian Universalist Association.

566 Richard M. Fewkes.

567 From *Circles on the Water: Selected Poems of Marge Piercy* by Marge Piercy. Copyright © 1982 by Marge Piercy. Reprinted by permission of Alfred A. Knopf, Inc.

568 From *Circles on the Water: Selected Poems of Marge Piercy* by Marge Piercy. Copyright © 1982 by Marge Piercy. Reprinted by permission of Alfred A. Knopf, Inc.

570 From *Thinking Like A Mountain,* ed. by John Seed, Joanna Macy et al., New Society Publishers, 4527 Springfield Avenue, Philadelphia, PA. © 1988.

571 From *The New Revised Standard Version of the Bible.* Copyright © 1989 by Division of Christian Education of the National Council of the Churches of Christ in the United States of America.

572 From *The Holy Bible,* James Moffat (ed.). Copyright © 1935 by Harper & Row Publishers, Inc. Reprinted by permission of HarperCollins Publishers.

574 From *The New Revised Standard Version of the Bible.* Copyright © 1989 by Division of Christian Education of the National Council of the Churches of Christ in the United States of America.

576 Marjorie Bowens-Wheatley.

580 Mark Morrison-Reed.

582 From *The New Revised Standard Version of the Bible.* Copyright © 1989 by Division of Christian Education of the National Council of the Churches of Christ in the United States of America.

583 From *Actfive and Other Poems* by Archibald MacLeish. Copyright © 1948. Reprinted by permission of Random House, Inc.

585 From *Circles on the Water: Selected Poems of Marge Piercy* by Marge Piercy. Copyright © 1982 by Marge Piercy. Reprinted by permission of Alfred A. Knopf, Inc.

587 Adapted from *The Black Unicorn* by Audre Lorde. Copyright © 1978 by Audre Lorde. Reprinted by permission of W. W. Norton & Co., Inc.

588 From *The New Revised Standard Version of the Bible.* Copyright © 1989 by Division of Christian Education of the National Council of the Churches of Christ in the United States of America.

590 From *Uncommon Prayers* by Daniel Berrigan. Copyright © 1978 by Seabury Press.

591 James Luther Adams.

593 From *Hope and Suffering* by Desmond Tutu. Copyright © 1983 by Desmond Tutu, Skotaville Publishers, South Africa, William B. Eerdmans Publishing Co., USA. Reprinted by permission of William B. Eerdmans Publishing Co.

608 From *The Kabir Book* by Robert Bly. Copyright © 1992 by Beacon Press.

615 The Howard Thurman Educational Trust.

616 Unitarian Universalist Association.

618 From *Revolutionary Patience* by Dorothee Sölle. Copyright © 1977 by Orbis Books, Maryknoll, NY.

619 W. Frederick Wooden.

620 From *The Buck in Snow and Other Poems.* Copyright © 1928, renewed 1956 by Edna St.Vincent Millay.

621 Margaret Gooding.

622 From *The New Revised Standard Version of the Bible.* Copyright © 1989 by Division of Christian Education of the National Council of the Churches of Christ in the United States of America.

624 Clarke Dewey Wells.

625 From *My Name on the Wind: Selected Poems of Diego Valeri.* M. Palma, trans. Copyright © 1989 by Princeton University Press.

627 Max A. Coots.

628 Sara Moores Campbell.

629 Congregation Beth El, Sudbury, MA.

631 Congregation Beth El, Sudbury, MA.

632 Copyright © 1984 by Alla Renée Bozarth. Abridged from *Womanpriest: A Personal Odyssey* by Alla Renée Bozarth, revised edition, LuraMedia 1988; and *Stars in Your Bones: Emerging Signposts on Our Spiritual Journeys*, Bozarth, Barkley, and Hawthorne, North Star Press of St. Cloud, Inc., 1990.

637 Robert Eller-Isaacs.

638 From *The New Revised Standard Version of the Bible.* Copyright © 1989 by Division of Christian Education of the National Council of the Churches of Christ in the United States of America.

639 From *The New Revised Standard Version of the Bible.* Copyright © 1989 by Division of Christian Education of the National Council of the Churches of Christ in the United States of America.

642 Congregation Beth El, Sudbury, MA.

644 From *The New Revised Standard Version of the Bible.* Copyright © 1989 by Division of Christian Education of the National Council of the Churches of Christ in the United States of America.

646 From "Healing" from *What Are People For?* Copyright © 1990 by Wendell Berry. Published by North Point Press and reprinted by permission.

647 W. Waldemar W. Argow.

648 From *Candles in Babylon* by Denise Levertov. Copyright © 1982 by Denise Levertov. Reprinted by permission of New Directions Publishing Corporation.

649 From *Wisdom of the Sands* by Antoine De St.-Exupéry. Copyright © 1950, 1978 by Harcourt Brace Jovanovich, Inc. Reprinted by permission of Harcourt Brace Jovanovich, Inc.

651 From *Human Options: An Autobiographical Notebook* by Norman Cousins. Copyright © 1981 by Norman Cousins. Reprinted by permission of W. W. Norton & Co., Inc.

653 Dori Jeanine Somers.

654 Ralph N. Helverson.

656 The American Ethical Union.

664 Sara Moores Campbell.

665 From *The Dream of A Common Language* by Adrienne Rich. Copyright © 1978 by W. W. Norton & Co., Inc.

666 Thandeka.

667 From *The New Revised Standard Version of the Bible.* Copyright © 1989 by Division of Christian Education of the National Council of the Churches of Christ in the United States of America.

668 From *The New Revised Standard Version of the Bible.* Copyright © 1989 by Division of Christian Education of the National Council of the Churches of Christ in the United States of America.

669 From *The Enlightened Heart* by Stephen Mitchell. Copyright © 1989 by Stephen Mitchell. Reprinted by permission of HarperCollins Publishers.

670 From *Collected Poems, 1921–1951* by Edwin Muir, copyright 1957, renewed 1985 by perm. of Grove Press.

672 Judith Meyer and from *The Awful Rowing Toward God* by Anne Sexton. Copyright © 1975 by Loring Conant, Jr., Executor of the Estate of Anne Sexton. Reprinted by permission of Houghton Mifflin Co.

673 Arthur Foote II.

674 Brandoch L. Lovely.

675 Ellen Johnson-Fay.

676 From *The New Revised Standard Version of the Bible.* Copyright © 1989 by of Division Christian Education of the National Council of the Churches of Christ in the United States of America.

680 Barbara J. Pescan.

684 Duke T. Gray.

685 From *Four Quartets* by T. S. Eliot. Copyright © 1968 by T. S. Eliot. Reprinted by permission of Harcourt Brace Jovanovich, Inc.

686 Mark L. Belletini.

687 John W. Brigham.

688 From *Many Winters* by Nancy Wood. Copyright © 1974 by Nancy Wood. All rights reserved.

689 From *The Whole World in His Hands: A Pictorial Biography of Paul Robeson* by Susan Robeson. Copyright © 1981 by Susan Robeson. Reprinted by permission of Carol Publishing Group/Citadel Press.

691 From *A Grain of Mustard Seed* by May

Sarton. Copyright © 1971 by May Sarton. Reprinted by permission of W. W. Norton & Co., Inc.

692   Lauralyn Bellamy.

694   Frederick E. Gillis.

696   From *American Primitive* by Mary Oliver. Copyright © 1983 by Mary Oliver. Reprinted by permission of Little, Brown & Co.

697   From "Healing" from *What Are People For?* Copyright © 1990 by Wendell Berry. Published by North Point Press and reprinted by permission.

698   Wayne B. Arnason.

700   Robert Mabry Doss.

701   Sara Moores Campbell.

706   Kathleen McTigue.

707   From *The New Revised Standard Version of the Bible.* Copyright © 1989 by Division of Christian Education of the National Council of the Churches of Christ in the United States of America.

708   From *The New Revised Standard Version of the Bible.* Copyright © 1989 by Division of Christian Education of the National Council of the Churches of Christ in the United States of America.

709   From *The New Revised Standard Version of the Bible.* Copyright © 1989 by Division of Christian Education of the National Council of the Churches of Christ in the United States of America.

710   From *The Holy Bible*, James Moffat (ed.). Copyright © 1935 by Harper & Row Publishers, Inc. Reprinted by permission of HarperCollins Publishers.

711   From *The Holy Bible*, James Moffat (ed.). Copyright © 1935 by Harper & Row Publishers, Inc. Reprinted by permission of HarperCollins Publishers.

713   From *The New Revised Standard Version of the Bible.* Copyright © 1989 by Division of Christian Education of the National Council of the Churches of Christ in the United States of America.

714   Robert Eller-Isaacs.

715   From *The Prophet* by Kahlil Gibran. Copyright © 1923 by Kahlil Gibran, renewed 1951 by Administrators/CTA of Kahlil Gibran Estate and Mary G. Gibran. Reprinted by permission of Alfred A. Knopf, Inc.

716   From *The Masai, Herders of East Africa* by Sonia Bleeker. Copyright © 1963 by Sonia Bleeker. Reprinted by permission of Morrow Junior Books.

717   George Kimmich Beach.

718   From *Selected Poems of May Sarton*, edited by May Sarton and Serena S. Hilsinger. Copyright © 1978 by May Sarton. Reprinted by permission of W. W. Norton & Co., Inc.

720   From *Gates of Prayer.* Copyright © 1975 by Central Conference of American Rabbis and Union of Liberal and Progressive Synagogues (London).

721   Kathleen McTigue.

722   From *Selected Poems* by Stephen Spender. Copyright © 1934, renewed 1962 by Stephen Spender. Reprinted by permission of Random House.

725   Jacob Trapp.

726   Robert Eller-Isaacs.

727   Rudolph Nemser.

728   John Buehrens.

729   Patricia Shuttee.

730   From *The Prophet* by Kahlil Gibran. Copyright © 1923 by Kahlil Gibran, renewed 1951 by Administrators/CTA of Kahlil Gibran Estate and Mary G. Gibran. Reprinted by permission of Alfred A. Knopf, Inc.

731   From *The Holy Bible*, James Moffat (ed.). Copyright © 1935 by Harper & Row Publishers, Inc. Reprinted by permission of HarperCollins Publishers.

732   Toni Vincent.

733   Eileen B. Karpeles.

Index of First Lines and Titles of Readings

When they differ, a selection's title, as well as its first phrase, is listed. Titles are in capital letters.

INDEX OF FIRST LINES AND TITLES OF READINGS

Topical Index of Readings

THE ETERNAL NOW *(cont.)*

TOPICAL INDEX OF READINGS

MOTHERS (*See* PARENTS)

NAMINGS AND CHILD DEDICATIONS
664 Give us the spirit of the child
716 Hail the day on which this child
     was born
469 I am mortal, like everyone else
649 In a house which becomes a home
714 It is our faith that each child born
     is one more redeemer
715 Your children are not your children

NATIONS (*See also* PEACE AND WAR;
     WORDS AND DEEDS OF
     PROPHETIC WOMEN AND MEN;
     WORLD COMMUNITY)
535 As a deer longs for flowing streams
602 If there is to be peace in the world
574 They shall beat their swords into
     plowshares

NATIVE AMERICAN SPIRITUALITY
682 Beauty is before me
551 Earth teach me stillness
518 Grandfather, look at our
     brokenness
526 great sea has set me in motion, The
495 Hear me, four quarters of the world
481 It is our quiet time
520 O our Mother the Earth
614 Then I was standing on the highest
     mountain
550 This we know. The earth does not
     belong to us

NATURE AND THE COUNTRYSIDE
549 Blessed be you, harsh matter
551 Earth teach me stillness
504 I thank You God for most this
     amazing day
465 If we will have the wisdom to
     survive
552 My help is in the mountain
520 O our Mother the Earth
492 See a blossom in your mind's eye
555 Some things will never change
490 You do not have to be good
643 You make the outgoings of the
     morning

THE NEW YEAR
542 Again did the earth shift
544 first of January is another day
     dawning, The

NON-VIOLENCE
462 I shall take my voice
577 If someone with courage and
     vision can rise

564 Love is not concerned with whom
     you pray
598 May every creature abound in
     well-being and peace
597 Never does hatred cease by hating
     in return
508 Save us from weak resignation to
     violence
584 We are caught in an inescapable
     network of mutuality
578 We can never make the world safe
     by fighting

ORDINATION AND INSTALLATION
591 I call that church free
571 spirit of God has sent me to bring
     good news, The

PAGAN
524 Earth mother, star mother
451 Flame of fire, spark of the universe
517 I who am the beauty of the green
     earth
703 Spirit of the East, be with us always
446 Spirit of the East, spirit of air
663 With mounds of greenery, the
     brightest ornaments

PARADOX AND AMBIGUITY
487 bell is full of wind though it does
     not ring, The
608 Inside this clay jug there are
     canyons and pine mountains
588 Is not this the fast that I choose
626 Out of the dusk a shadow
667 Vanity of vanities, says the Teacher
685 What we call a beginning is often
     the end

PARENTS
616 For so the children come
596 Let us cultivate boundless goodwill
715 Your children are not your children

PASSOVER
593 Liberation is costly
453 May the light we now kindle
632 Pack nothing. Bring only your
     determination
631 What sacrifices would we make for
     freedom today?
590 When the Spirit struck us free

PEACE AND WAR
573 Arise, then, women of this day!
640 Blessed are you poor
681 Deep peace of the running wave to
     you
686 Go in peace. Live simply, gently

Index of Composers, Arrangers, Authors, Translators, and Sources

Buehrer, Edwin, 67
Bunyan, John, 106
Burleigh, Harry T., 148, 350
Byrne, Mary, 20

Cabena, H. Barrie, 257
Calvisius, Seth, 127
Campbell, Sara Moores, 628, 664, 701
Caniadau y Cyssegr, 122, 273
Čápek, Norbert F., 8, 28, 78, 723, 724
Cardenal, Ernesto, 532
Carpenter, Alicia S., 6, 175, 300, 314,
    324, 344, 356, 360, 370, 409
Carruth, William Herbert, 343
Cassels-Brown, Alastair, 161, 411
Cather, Willa, 328
Chandogya Upanishad, 613
Channing, William Ellery, 592, 652
Channing, William Henry, 484
Chao, T. C., 353
Chapin, Amzi, 48
Chesterton, Gilbert Keith, 5
Chicago, Judy, 464
Christian prayer, 508
Christmas Carols Ancient and Modern,
    237
Chubb, Percival, 248, 355, 656
Chung Yung, 605
Cleveland, J. Jefferson, 206
Cohen, Don, 7
Cohen, Helen, 548
Coleridge, Mary, 267
Collins, Leo W., 329
Collyer, Robert, 35
Colum, Padraic, 264
Columbian Harmony, 205, 206
Compleat Melody, 272
Compleat Psalmodist, 61, 268
Composite, 381, 480, 677
Confucius, 186
Congregation Beth El, Sudbury, MA, 629,
    631, 642
Coots, Max A., 489, 627
1 Corinthians 13, 638
1 Corinthians 16, 713
Corrado, John, 7, 391
Cotter, Joseph, 74
Cousins, Norman, 651
Croft, William, 281
Crosby, Greta W., 543
Crotch, William, 113
Crüger, Johann, 32
Crum, John MacLeod Campbell, 266
cummings, e. e., 250, 504
Cutts, Peter, 125, 137

Dallas, Dick, 151
Daniel ben Judah Dayyan, 215
David, Francis, 566

Davies, A. Powell, 662
Davies, Henry Walford, 358
Davies, William Henry, 94
Davis, Frances W., 142
Dawson, Albert M. P., 107
Dawson, David, 8, 19, 71, 320, 331, 353
Day, Dorothy, 560
Decius, Nikolaus, 412
Deming, Barbara, 570
Denham, Shelley Jackson, 55, 86, 194,
    256, 354
Desprez, Josquin, 27
Deuteronomy 6, 467
Deuteronomy 30, 707
DeWolfe, Mark, 295
Dhammapada, 597
Dickinson, Emily, 292
Dillard, Annie, 420
Dorian, Nancy Currier, 22
Dorsey, Thomas A., 199
Doss, Robert, 700
Douglass, Frederick, 579
Du Bois, W. E. B., 494, 502
*Dulcimer, or New York Collection of
    Sacred Music*, 283
Dupré, Marcel, 254, 266
Duson, Dede, 133, 297, 319
Dykes, John Bacchus, 26, 39, 290

Eaton, David, 557
Ebeling, Johann G., 6
Ecclesiastes, 667
Ecclesiastes 3, 558
Eliot, George, 719
Eliot, T. S., 685
Eller-Isaacs, Robert, 637, 714, 726
Ellington, Duke, 202
Elvey, George Job, 68, 282
Emerson, Ralph Waldo, 44, 79, 531, 556,
    563, 661
English folk melody, 9
Erfurt, Enchiridion, 127
Erneuertes Gesangbuch II, 278
Etzler, Carole, 212
European Magazine and Review, 236
Eusebius, 521
Evans, David, 38, 293
Evans, Mary Ann (*See* Eliot, George)

Faber, Frederick William, 213
Fahs, Sophia Lyon, 439, 616, 657
Fariña, Richard, 136
Farjeon, Eleanor, 38, 226
Fewkes, Richard M., 515, 566
Filitz, Friedrich, 46, 74
Findlow, Bruce, 128
Fleming, Robert J. B., 142
Foote, Arthur, II, 673
Fosdick, Harry, 115

INDEX OF COMPOSERS, AUTHORS, AND SOURCES

Mo-Tse, 601
Mohr, Joseph, 251, 252
Monk, William Henry, 101, 107
Montgomery, Marjorie Sams, 452
Moomey, Diane Lee, 542
Moore, Berkley L., 129
Morgan, John Hanly, 224
Morrison-Reed, Mark, 580
Mozart, Wolfgang Amadeus, 384
Muir, Edwin, 670
Munk, Anita, 8, 78
Munk, Paul, 8, 78
Murray, John, 704
Musicalisches Handbuch, 145, 345
Muslim prayer, 509

Nachman, Rabbi, 219
Naidu, Sarojini, 183, 192
Native American sources, 196, 366, 518,
    520, 551, 682
Navias, Eugene B., 126
Neale, John Mason, 225
Neander, Joachim, 278
Near, Holly, 170
Nederlandtsch Gedenckclanck, 67, 349
Nemser, Rudolph, 727
New England folk melody, 343
Newton, John, 205, 206
N'hat Hanh, Thich, 505, 554
Niebuhr, Reinhold, 461
Niles, Daniel, 353
Noble, T. Tertius, 42
Noyes, Alfred, 339
Numbers 6, 711

Oakeley, Frederick, 253
Odell, George E., 468
Oler, Kim, 163
Oliver, Mary, 490, 536, 696
Oliver, William E., 331
Oppenheim, James, 109
*Oude en niewe Hollantse Boernlities en
    Contradanseu*, 139, 189
Owen-Towle, Carolyn S., 492

Pachelbel, Johann, 386
Page, Nick, 163
Palestrina, Giovanni Pierluigi da, 107
Parker, Theodore, 683
Parry, Charles Hubert Hastings, 337, 359
Parry, Joseph, 174
Passover Haggadah, 453
Patton, Kenneth L., 303, 308, 310, 378,
    379, 437, 443, 444
Persichetti, Vincent, 250
Pescan, Barbara, 417, 506, 534, 680
Petti, Anthony, 27
Philippians 4, 699
Phillips, Larry, 37, 130, 352

Piae Cantiones, 63, 249
Pickett, Helen R., 309
Pickett, O. Eugene, 512
Piercy, Marge, 567, 568, 585
Pierpoint, Folliott Sandford, 21
Plenn, Doris, 108
Pohl, David C., 436
Pohl-Kosbau, Leslie, 451
Poley, Joyce, 168
Pomeroy, Vivian, 477
Pope, Alexander, 91
Porter, Philip A., 50, 81, 389
Praetorius, Christoph, 362
Praetorius, Hieronymus, 412
Praetorius, Michael, 393
Price, Frank W., 353
Prichard, Rowland Hugh, 140, 166, 207
Project Ploughshares, 695
Proulx, Richard, 196
Psalms, 217, 277, 279, 392, 421, 423,
    425, 433, 535, 642, 643, 710
Psalmodia Evangelica, 12, 138
Purcell, Henry, 295

Quaile, Robert N., 1
Quaker song, 108
Quang, Nguyen-Duc, 59, 314
Quimada, Bishop Toribio, 182

Ramabhadran, Samjeev, 176
Ravenscroft, Thomas, 185
Redhead, Richard, 132
Redner, Lewis H., 246
Reilly, Jim, 286
Repository of Sacred Music, Part II, 53,
    126
Revivalist, The, 248
Reynolds, Malvina, 313
Rice, Joyce Painter, 295
Rich, Adrienne, 463, 665
Rickey, Patrick L., 128, 170, 363, 365
Riemer, Jack, 634
Rinkart, Martin, 32
Ripley, Sarah Alden, 460
Robb, John Donald, 230
Robeson, Paul, 462, 689
Robinson, Christine, 448, 454
Robinson, Robert, 126
Robinson, Wayne Bradley, 405
Roethke, Theodore, 54
Rogers, Sally, 131
Romans 12, 712
Rossetti, Christina Georgina, 241, 296
Routley, Eric, 410
Rowan, William P., 198
Ruby, Roberta Bard, 207
Rumi, Jalal al-Din, 188
Ruspini, Louise, 361
Russian melody, 47

Ruth 1, 731
Rzepka, Jane R., 510

Saadi, 609
Sacred Melodies, 285
St.-Exupéry, Antoine de, 649
Sanders, Robert L., 5, 284, 322
Santayana, George, 341
Sarton, May, 428, 691, 718
Sarum Antiphonal, 184
Savage, Minot Judson, 77, 293
Schalk, Carl Flentge, 334
Schein, Johann Hermann, 183, 300, 308
Scherf, Royce J., 232
Schleische Volkslieder, 42
Schulz, Willam F., 429, 459
Schweitzer, Albert, 447
Scott, Clinton Lee, 438, 565
Scott, Jim, 163, 167, 316, 347
Scottish psalter, 185
Seaburg, Carl G., 37, 62, 124, 228, 234, 338, 352, 358
Sealth, Noah, 550
Sears, Edmund, 244
Secunda, S., 214
Segal, Joseph, 402
Segal, Nathan, 402
Sen, Keshab Chandra, 474
Senesh, Hannah, 450
Senghas, Dorothy, 349
Senghas, Robert, 349
Sexton, Anne, 672
Shaker tune, 16
Shams ud-dun Mohammad Hafiz, 607
Shapiro, Rami M., 503
Shaw, Martin, 226
Shepard, Odell, 161
Shuttee, Patricia, 729
Sibelius, Jean, 159, 318
Silliman, Vincent B., 42, 133, 287, 414, 466
Sjolund, Paul, 239
Skrine, John Huntley, 358
Slater, Gordon, 405
Sleeth, Natalie, 390, 413
Slegers, Mark, 280
Smart, Henry T., 270
Smit, Leo, 292
Smith, Alfred Morton, 54, 164, 191
Smith, Walter Chalmers, 273
Smith, William Farley, 169, 208
Solesmes, 242, 336
Sölle, Dorothee, 618
Somers, Dori Jeanine, 653
Somerville, Thomas, 232
Song of Solomon, 430
Sontongo, Enoch, 171
Southern Harmony, 15, 18, 44, 66, 161, 193, 232, 312, 313, 315, 351, 411

Spender, Stephen, 722
Stainer, John, 237
Stanford, Charles Villiers, 36
Starhawk, 517, 524
Starkey, Margaret, 663
Stein, Leopold, 223
Stern, Chaim, 633, 635
Stevenson, J. A., 47
Stevenson, Robert Louis, 195
Stone, Lloyd, 159
Storey, John Andrew, 2, 19, 71, 102, 160, 174, 186, 241, 297, 302, 307, 320, 350, 353
Sullivan, Arthur Seymour, 114
Sutta Nopata, 181
Swiss tune, 342
Symonds, John, 138
Synagogue melody, 215

Tabb, John, 335, 626
Tagore, Rabindranath, 185, 191, 197, 519, 529, 540, 612
Tallis, Thomas, 88, 330
Taylor, Billy, 151
Taylor, Cecily, 134
Taylor, Cyril V., 64, 77, 90, 339
Teasdale, Sara, 329
Tegh Bahadur, 599
Teilhard de Chardin, Pierre, 549
Tennyson, Alfred Lord, 58, 143
Teresa, Mother, 562
Texcoco Nahjuatal poem, 196
Thandeka, 666
Thelander, Albert Hill, 449
Thoreau, Henry David, 660
Thorn, Emily, 112
Thurman, Howard, 498, 615
Torrence, Ridgely, 284
Traditional texts and tunes: African (Yoruba), 179; Alsatian, 291; Asian, 136; Chinese, 194; Czech, 73; English, 34, 209, 224, 237, 240, 247, 289; Finnish, 72, 293; French, 98, 132, 226, 243, 296; Gaelic, 38; German carol, 49; Hebrew, 214, 216, 260, 280, 392, 394, 400, 415; Hindu, 176, 178; Hispanic, 230; Hungarian, 56, 227; Indian, 181; Irish, 10, 20, 91, 157, 298; Japanese, 177; Latin, 225, 388, 393; Provençal, 233; Rounds, 397, 395; South African, 172; Spanish, 305; Taiwanese, 195; United States, 18, 70, 112, 357; Visayan (Philippines), 182; Welsh, 122, 235, 273, 409
Transylvanian hymns, 37, 352
Trapp, Jacob, 139, 148, 441, 482, 725
Trench, Richard, 299
Troeger, Thomas, 158
Tutu, Desmond, 593

INDEX OF COMPOSERS, AUTHORS, AND SOURCES

Ulp, Grace L., 78
Ungar, Lynn, 188
Union Harmony, 69, 112
Unitarian Universalist Association, 594
United Nations, 475, 478
U.S. Sacred Harmony, The, 213
Untermeyer, Louis, 1, 85
Uvavnuk, 526

Valley Harmonist, 79
Valeri, Diego, 625
Van Dyke, Henry, 29
Vaughan Williams, Ralph, 17, 49, 52, 57,
    65, 89, 103, 106, 165, 203, 209, 224,
    240, 247, 271, 289, 324, 326, 338, 341
Vincent, Toni, 732
Vogt, Von Ogden, 476
Volständige Sammlung, 262
von Schiller, Friedrich, 327
Vulpius, Melchior, 175

Wade, John Francis, 253
Waggoner, A., 344
Walden, Mary Allen, 116, 151, 162, 201,
    210, 407
Walker, Alice, 564
Walker, George Theophilus, 60
Watts, Isaac, 245, 281, 381, 382
Weaver, John, 225, 410
Webb, Charles H., 70, 299, 313
Webb, George James, 144
Wells, Barbara, 431
Wells, Clarke Dewey, 624
Wesley, Charles, 268
Wesley, Samuel S., 83
Weston, Robert Terry, 369, 530, 538, 547,
    650
Westwood, Horace, 403
Wetzel, Richard D., 263
Whalum, Wendell, 141, 348
Wheeler, Gerald, 325

Whitman, Walt, 356, 645, 659
Whittier, John Greenleaf, 9, 10, 70, 75,
    122, 274
Whitmarsh, Frances Wile, 57
Williams, L. Griswold, 471
Williams, Robert, 269
Williams, Theodore Chickering, 242
Williams, Thomas John, 119
Willis, Richard Storrs, 244
Wilson, Edwin Henry, 113
Wilson, John, 272
Winkley, Lala, 514
Winkworth, Catherine, 32, 278
Wisdom of Solomon, 469, 644
Wolfe, Thomas, 555
Wolff, William, 177
Wollständige Sammlung, 262
Wood, Nancy, 481, 552, 553, 688
Wooden, W. Frederick, 3, 31, 96, 306,
    340, 619
Wordsworth, William, 333, 499
Wotton, Henry, 135
Wren, Brian, 23, 31, 198, 275, 317, 325,
    408, 412
Wright, Samuel Anthony, 318
Wurtemberg Gesangbuch, 11
Wyatt, Janet, 337
Wyeth, John, 126
Wylder, Betty A., 109, 131, 221, 305, 311,
    361
Wyton, Alec, 4

Yarrow, Peter, 221
Young, Carlton R., 18, 20, 23, 98, 243,
    275, 298, 401
Young, Michael, 91

Zangwill, Israel, 418
Zanotti, Barbara, 121
Zimmerman, Heinz Werner, 84

Alphabetical Index of Tunes

Metrical Index of Tunes

6.5.6.5. Triple
ST. GERTRUDE, 114

6.5.6.5.6.6.6.5.
MONK'S GATE, 106

6.6.6.6.
COLUM, 264

6.6.6.6. with refrain
GILU HAGALILIM, 220

6.6.6.6.D.
FOUNDATION, 112

6.6.6.6.6.6. with refrain
PERSONENT HODIE, 249

6.6.6.6.6.6.
SHERMAN ISLAND, 128

6.6.6.6.6.6.5.6.
DIE GEDANKEN SIND FREI,
291

6.6.6.6.8.8.
LOVE UNKNOWN, 129

6.6.6.6.8.8.8.
INITIALS, 130

6.6.8.4.D.
LEONI, 215

6.6.9.6.
BIKO, 95

6.6.9.6.6.8.
SCHÖNSTER HERR JESU, 42

6.6.11.D.
DOWN AMPNEY, 271

6.7.6.7.6.6.6.6.
NUN DANKET ALLE GOTT,
32

6.7.7.7.7.6.6.
SAKURA, 177

6.7.8.7. with refrain
WINTER LULLABY, 256

6.7.9.D. with refrain
BASHANAH, 146

6.7.9.8.
TOUCH THE EARTH, 301

6.8.8.
ZIMMERMANN, 84

6.8.10.10.6.
LANGSTON, 60

7.5.7.5.D.
ADORO TE DEVOTE, 336
CON X'OM LANG, 59, 314

7.6.7.6.D.
ADLER, 248
BLACKBURN, 63
COMPLAINER, 44
ELLACOMBE, 262
FAR OFF LANDS, 187
LANCASHIRE, 270
MEIRIONYDD, 40, 276
MERLE'S TUNE, 328
MUNICH, 11
NEW ENGLAND, 343
NYLAND, 293
PASSION CHORALE, 265
SOLIDARITY, 157
WEBB, 144

7.6.7.6.6.6.3.3.6.
MOOZ TSUR, 223

7.6.8.6.D.
ANDUJAR, 82

7.6.8.6.8.6.
CHRISTMAS DAWN, 72

7.7.6.6.7.
FRANCIS DAVID, 37

7.7.7.6.8.9.7.6.
WINTER MEDITATION, 55

7.7.7.7.
CALL, THE, 17, 89
CHORALE, 332
HASIDIM, 62, 234
MANTON, 33
NUN KOMM, DER HEIDEN
HEILAND, 127
ORIENTIS PARTIBUS, 132
SEGNE UNS, 414
TOA-SIA, 195
VIENNA, 111
WOODLAND, 2, 124, 288

**7.7.7.7. with
Alleluias**
EASTER HYMN, 61, 268
LLANFAIR, 269

7.7.7.7. with refrain
GLORIA, 231
SABBATH, 204

7.7.7.7.D.
ST. GEORGE'S WINDSOR,
68, 282
SALZBURG, 150
SERVETUS, 13, 302

7.7.7.7.7.6.9.7.7.
PRAYER, 86

7.7.7.7.7.7.
DIX, 21
NICHT SO TRAURIG, 6

7.7.7.8.
BRIGHT MORNING STARS,
357

8.8.8.8. with refrain
INDIAN PRAYER, 176

8.8.8.8.6.
META, 117

8.8.8.8.7.
WAS GOTT THUT, 76

8.8.8.8.8.
WAS GOTT THUT, 267, 344

8.8.8.8.8.8.
BARNFIELD, 19
FILLMORE, 312
MACH'S MIT MIR, GOTT,
183, 300, 308
VENI EMMANUEL, 225

8.8.8.8.8.9.
SUSSEX CAROL, 338

8.8.11.
DOVER KNIGHT, 50

8.9.8.5.
NEXUS, 317

8.9.8.7.D.
MOUNTAIN ALONE, 173

8.12.8.12.8.10
SPIRIT OF LIFE, 123

9.5.5.D.
SINGING FOR OUR LIVES,
170

9.7.7.9.
NOTHING BUT PEACE, 167

9.8.9.8.
ALBRIGHT, 310

9.8.9.8.D.
LEE, 45

9.8.11.8.
DEN STORE HVIDE FLOK,
398

9.9.6.5.6.5.
D'OÙ VIENS TU, BERGÈRE,
258

9.9.9.9. with refrain
EKO A BA KO, 179

9.9.9.10. with refrain
GATHER THE SPIRIT, 347

9.10.6.5.5.4.
WESTCHASE, 23

10.8.10.8.
TRUE RELIGION, 286

10.10. with refrain
LET US BREAK BREAD, 406

10.10.8.8.
DOXOLOGY, 365

10.10.9.10.
SLANE, 20

10.10.10. with
Alleluia
ENGELBERG, 36

10.10.10. with
Alleluias
SINE NOMINE, 103

10.10.10.4.
ALL LIFE IS ONE, 7

10.10.10.5.5.
WHEATLEY, 97

10.10.10.10.
COOLINGE, 64, 77, 90
DOXOLOGY, 363
EVENTIDE, 101
FLENTGE, 334
INDIA, 181
SHELDONIAN, 339
SLANE, 298
SURSUM CORDA, 54, 164,
191

10.10.10.10.10.
ADAM'S SONG, 284
OLD 124TH, 120, 360

10.10.10.10.10.10.
SONG I, 341

10.10.11.10.
LINDNER, 275

10.10.11.11.
LYONS, 285
UPPSALA, 137

10.11.10.11.
YADDO, 323

11.10.10.11.
NOEL NOUVELET, 266

11.10.11.10.
DONNE SECOURS, 369
KEITH, 5
NAIDU, 192

11.10.11.10. with
refrain
CREATION OF PEACE, 121

11.10.11.10.11.10.
FINLANDIA, 159, 318

11.11.8.6.8.9.
SYMPHONY, 309

11.11.9.10.
CIRCLE OF SPIRIT, 316

11.11.10.11.
NOEL NOUVELET, 254

11.11.11.5.
KRISZTUS URUNKNAK, 56

11.11.11.6.6.6.6.
MANDELA, 151

11.11.11.11.
ANNIVERSARY SONG, 404
ST. DENIO, 122, 273

11.11.12.12.
FOUNDATION, 69

12.9.12.12.9.
WONDROUS LOVE, 18

12.11.13.12.
KREMSER, 67, 349

12.12.12.10. Irregular
NICAEA, 26

12.12.12.12.
CRADLE SONG, 52

12.13.12.10.
NICAEA, 39, 290

14.14.4.7.8.
LOBE DEN HERREN, 278

Irregular

ADESTE FIDELES, 253
AFRIKA, 171
ALLELU, 367
ALLELUIA AMEN, 383
AMADEUS, 384
AUCTION BLOCK, 154
BERTHIER, 364
BREAD AND ROSES, 109
BRING A TORCH, 233
CIRCLE CHANT, 155
CREDO, 354
DESMOND, 401
DONA NOBIS PACEM, 388
DOUGLASS, 255
DOWN BY THE RIVERSIDE,
    162
ELEMENTS, 387
ELLINGTON, 202
ETHELRED, 116
GATHERING CHANT, 389
GAUDEAMUS HODIE, 390
GO IN PEACE, 413
GUIDE MY FEET, 348
HALELUHU, 280
HASHIVEINU, 216
HAVA NASHIRAH, 394
HELELUYAN, 366
HEVENU, 260, 415
JACQUES, 385
JUBILATE DEO, 393
KINGS OF ORIENT, 259
LACQUIPARLE, 196
LATTIMER, 118
LEAD ME LORD, 83
LIFT EVERY VOICE, 149
LUMINA, 184
MACCABEE, 221
MCCREE, 210
MARTIN, 169
MASTEN, 311
MATHIEU, 180
MI Y'MALEL, 222
MO-LI-HUA, 194
MOORE, 395
NEW NAME, 141
ONE MORE STEP, 168

ORIENTIS PARTIBUS, 243
PACHELBEL'S CANON, 386
PENTECOST, 208
PILGRIMAGE, 188
PRAHA, 73
PRECIOUS LORD, 199
PSALM 133, 392
QUIMADA, 182
RABBI, 402
RAM, 178
REEB, 30
ROBESON, 368
ROSA, 156
ROSE IN WINTER, A, 346
SAMUEL, 31
SHABBAT SHALOM, 214
SHALOM, 400
SMIT, 292
SOJOURNER, 201
SONG SPRINGS, 321
STAR, 250
STILLE NACHT, 251, 252
TAGORE, 197
UNKNOWN, 279
VINE AND FIG TREE, 399
VOICE STILL AND SMALL,
    391
WATKINS HARPER, 153
WELCOME TABLE, 407
YIH'YU L'RATZON, 218
YULE, 235

Irregular with refrain

A LA RU, 230
AVINU MALKEINU, 217
DE COLORES, 305
DRINKING GOURD, 152
DUBOIS, 99
FIRST NOWELL, THE, 237
GO TELL IT ON THE
    MOUNTAIN, 239
SIMPLE GIFTS, 16

Topical Index of Hymns

BUDDHISM

184 Be ye lamps unto yourselves
181 No matter if you live now far or near
183 wind of change forever blown, The

CELEBRATION AND PRAISE

180 Alhamdulillah
203 All creatures of the earth and sky
384 Alleluia
383 Alleluia. Amen
386 Alleluia Chaconne
39 Bring, O morn, thy music!
309 Earth is our homeland
128 For all that is our life
76 For flowers that bloom about our feet
21 For the beauty of the earth
163 For the earth forever turning
347 Gather the spirit
390 Gaudeamus hodie
385 Gloria
201 Glory, glory, hallelujah!
280 Haleluhu
75 harp at Nature's advent strung, The
394 Hava nashirah
26 Holy, holy, holy, author of creation!
60 In time of silver rain
29 Joyful, joyful, we adore thee
393 Jubilate Deo
7 leaf unfurling, The
326 Let all the beauty we have known
311 Let it be a dance we do
282 Let the whole creation cry
149 Lift every voice and sing
38 Morning has broken
47 Now on land and sea descending
107 Now sing we of the brave of old
217 O sing hallelujah
296 O ye who taste that love is sweet
278 Praise be to God, the Almighty
158 Praise the source of faith and learning
215 Praise to the living God!
214 Shabbat Shalom
395 Sing and rejoice
19 sun that shines across the sea, The
322 Thanks be for these
354 We laugh, we cry
44 We sing of golden mornings
285 We worship thee, God
36 When in our music God is glorified
The Celebration of Life (1–19)
Praise and Transcendence (20–37)
Praise Songs and Doxologies (363–381)

CHALICE LIGHTING

362 Rise up, O flame

CHANGE

56 Bells in the high tower
192 Nay, do not grieve
191 Now I recall my childhood
281 O God, our help in ages past
196 Singer of Life, all flowers are songs
359 When we are gathered
183 wind of change forever blown, The
Transience (96–101)

CHANTS AND RESPONSES

364 Alleluia, Alleluia

CHILDREN

110 Come, children of tomorrow, come!
338 I seek the spirit of a child
329 Life has loveliness to sell
191 Now I recall my childhood
117 O light of life that lives in us
409 Sleep, my child
97 Sometimes I feel like a motherless child
146 Soon the day will arrive
301 Touch the earth, reach the sky!

CHRISTMAS, ADVENT, AND EPIPHANY

Advent (224–226)
Christmas 227–258)
Epiphany (259)

THE CITY

85 Although this life is but a wraith
88 Calm soul of all things
140 Hail the glorious golden city

CLOSINGS

367 Allelu, allelu
384 Alleluia
383 Alleluia. Amen
386 Alleluia Chaconne
184 Be ye lamps unto yourselves
394 Hava nashirah
393 Jubilate Deo
378 Let those who live in every land
365 Praise God
380 Rejoice in love we know and share
214 Shabbat Shalom
400 Shalom, havayreem!
376 Sing loudly till the stars have heard
49 Stillness reigns
316 Tradition held fast
Recessionals (413–415)

COMMITMENT

124 Be that guide whom love sustains
194 Faith is a forest
343 firemist and a planet, A
125 From the crush of wealth and power

84 How far can reach a smile
116 I'm on my way
6 Just as long as I have breath
107 Now sing we of the brave of old
153 Oh, I woke up this morning
168 One more step
157 Step by step the longest march
211 We are climbing Jacob's ladder
212 We are dancing Sarah's circle
169 We shall overcome
318 We would be one
106 Who would true valor see
Commitment and Action (108–122)

COMMUNION
323 Break not the circle
220 Bring out the festal bread
89 Come, my way, my truth, my life
385 Gloria
26 Holy, holy, holy, author of creation!
393 Jubilate Deo
209 O come, you longing thirsty souls
236 O thou joyful day
276 O young and fearless Prophet
34 Though I may speak with bravest fire
121 We'll build a land
Communion (405–407)

COMPASSION
86 Blessed Spirit of my life
127 Can I see another's woe
125 From the crush of wealth and power
84 How far can reach a smile
151 I wish I knew how it would feel to be free
148 Let freedom span both east and west
332 Perfect Singer, songs of earth
213 There's a wideness in your mercy
93 To Mercy, Pity, Peace, and Love

COURAGE
85 Although this life is but a wraith
115 God of grace and God of glory
396 I know this rose will open
119 Once to every soul and nation
172 Siph' amandla Nkosi
297 star of truth but dimly shines, The
28 View the starry realm of heaven
137 We utter our cry
106 Who would true valor see

DEATH AND LIFE
101 Abide with me
337 Have I not known the sky and sea
96 I cannot think of them as dead
52 In sweet fields of autumn

87 Nearer, my God, to thee
306 Sing of living, sing of dying
324 Where my free spirit onward leads
183 wind of change forever blown, The

DEDICATION OF BUILDING
288 All are architects of fate
308 blessings of the earth and sky, The
1 May nothing evil cross this door

DEDICATION OF ORGAN
75 harp at Nature's advent strung, The
332 Perfect Singer, songs of earth
13 Songs of spirit, like a prayer
322 Thanks be for these
36 When in our music God is glorified

EARTH
203 All creatures of the earth and sky
155 Circle 'round for freedom
310 earth is home, The
309 Earth is our homeland
207 Earth was given as a garden
21 For the beauty of the earth
163 For the earth forever turning
75 harp at Nature's advent strung, The
43 morning, noiseless, flings its gold, The
91 Mother of all, in every age
74 On the dusty earth drum
82 This land of bursting sunrise
301 Touch the earth, reach the sky!
317 We are not our own
175 We celebrate the web of life
44 We sing of golden mornings
81 wordless mountains bravely still, The
3 world stands out on either side, The

EASTER
275 Joyful is the dark
61 Lo, the earth awakes again
98 Loveliest of trees
265 O sacred head, now wounded
344 promise through the ages rings, A
250 purer than purest
369 This is the truth that passes understanding
62 When the daffodils arrive
Easter (266–270)

ECOLOGY
91 Mother of all, in every age
117 O light of life that lives in us
137 We utter our cry
Stewardship of the Earth (173–175)

ELDERS

191 Now I recall my childhood
306 Sing of living, sing of dying
314 We are children of the earth
324 Where my free spirit onward leads

THE ELEMENTS

203 All creatures of the earth and sky
309 Earth is our homeland
387 earth, the water, the fire, the air,
    The
25 God of the earth, the sky, the sea
175 We celebrate the web of life
81 wordless mountains bravely still,
   The

THE ETERNAL NOW

289 Creative love, our thanks we give
321 Here in the flesh is all that we can
    know
312 Here on the paths of every day
9 No longer forward nor behind
12 O Life that maketh all things new
335 Once when my heart was passion
    free
398 To see the world in a grain of sand
    Here and Now (350–356)

EVENING

101 Abide with me
204 Come, O Sabbath day
55 Dark of winter, soft and still
54 Now light is less
409 Sleep, my child
165 When windows that are black and
    cold
    Evening (45–50)

EVOLUTION

304 fierce unrest seethes at the core, A
343 firemist and a planet, A
174 O earth, you are surpassing fair

FAILINGS AND FRAILTIES

205 Amazing grace! How sweet the
    sound
206 Amazing grace!
    (alt. accompaniment)
289 Creative love, our thanks we give
186 Grieve not your heart
120 Turn back
102 We the heirs of many ages

FAITH

85 Although this life is but a wraith
20 Be thou my vision
202 Come Sunday
274 Dear Mother-Father of us all
194 Faith is a forest

287 Faith of the larger liberty
304 fierce unrest seethes at the core, A
396 I know this rose will open
351 long, long way the sea-winds
    blow, A
40 morning hangs a signal, The
42 Morning, so fair to see
108 My life flows on in endless song
281 O God, our help in ages past
341 O world, thou choosest not
193 Our faith is but a single gem
344 promise through the ages rings, A
297 star of truth but dimly shines, The
303 We are the earth upright and proud

FAMILIES (*See also* PARENTS)

21 For the beauty of the earth
360 Here we have gathered
7 leaf unfurling, The
19 sun that shines across the sea, The
314 We are children of the earth
317 We are not our own
324 Where my free spirit onward leads

FATHERS (*See* PARENTS)

FLOWER COMMUNION

177 Cherry blooms
78 Color and fragrance
305 De colores
352 Find a stillness
76 For flowers that bloom about our
   feet
8 Mother Spirit, Father Spirit
64 Oh, give us pleasure in the flowers
   today
196 Singer of Life, all flowers are songs
63 Spring has now unwrapped the
   flowers
62 When the daffodils arrive

FORGIVENESS AND RECONCILIATION

323 Break not the circle
178 Raghupati, Raghava, Raja Ram
213 There's a wideness in your mercy
315 This old world is full of sorrow
179 Words that we hold tight

FREE AND RESPONSIBLE SEARCH FOR
TRUTH AND MEANING

85 Although this life is but a wraith
145 As tranquil streams that meet and
    merge
286 core of silence, A
2 Down the ages we have trod
90 From all the fret and fever of the
   day
190 Light of ages and of nations
    (Austria)

TOPICAL INDEX OF HYMNS

TOPICAL INDEX OF HYMNS

LOVE *(cont.)*
95   There is more love somewhere
82   This land of bursting sunrise
315 This old world is full of sorrow
34   Though I may speak with bravest fire
18   What wondrous love is this
334 When shall we learn
324 Where my free spirit onward leads
     Love and Compassion (123–137)

MARRIAGE AND SERVICES OF UNION
325 Love makes a bridge
     Weddings and Services of Union (410)

MARTIN LUTHER KING, JR. DAY
149 Lift every voice and sing
156 Oh, freedom
199 Precious Lord, take my hand
169 We shall overcome

MAUNDY THURSDAY
(See COMMUNION)

MEMBERSHIP AND RECOGNITION
360 Here we have gathered
296 O ye who taste that love is sweet

MEMORIAL AND FUNERAL SERVICES
101 Abide with me
336 All my memories of love
27   I am that great and fiery force
96   I cannot think of them as dead
396 I know this rose will open
412 Let hope and sorrow now unite
87   Nearer, my God, to thee
411 Part in peace!

MEMORIALS AND FUNERALS
101 Abide with me
336 All my memories of love
357 Bright morning stars are rising
27   I am that great and fiery force
96   I cannot think of them as dead
396 I know this rose will open
87   Nearer, my God, to thee
     Memorials and Funerals (411–412)

MEN AND WOMEN (See WOMEN AND MEN)

MINISTRY
145 As tranquil streams that meet and merge
124 Be that guide whom love sustains
103 For all the saints
114 Forward through the ages
96   I cannot think of them as dead

298 Wake, now, my senses
36   When in our music God is glorified

MORNING
357 Bright morning stars are rising
24   Far rolling voices of the sea
353 Golden breaks the dawn
75   harp at Nature's advent strung, The
397 Morning has come
9   No longer forward nor behind
395 Sing and rejoice
82   This land of bursting sunrise
     Morning (38–44)

MOTHERS (See PARENTS)

NAMINGS AND CHILD DEDICATIONS
396 I know this rose will open
338 I seek the spirit of a child
256 Winter night, clear and bright
238 Within the shining of a star
     Namings, Dedications, and Christenings (408–409)

NATIONS
160 Far too long, by fear divided
142 Let there be light
190 Light of ages and of nations (Austria)
189 Light of ages and of nations (In Babilone)
119 Once to every soul and nation
122 Sound over all waters
138 These things shall be
159 This is my song
399 Vine and fig tree

NATIVE AMERICAN SPIRITUALITY
366 Heleluyan

NATURE AND THE COUNTRYSIDE
203 All creatures of the earth and sky
59   Almond trees, renewed in bloom
39   Bring, O morn, thy music!
177 Cherry blooms
21   For the beauty of the earth
163 For the earth forever turning
353 Golden breaks the dawn
27   I am that great and fiery force
328 I sought the wood in summer
53   I walk the unfrequented road
52   In sweet fields of autumn
173 In the branches of the forest
71   In the spring, with plow and harrow
60   In time of silver rain
29   Joyful, joyful, we adore thee
282 Let the whole creation cry
15   lone, wild bird in lofty flight, The

TOPICAL INDEX OF HYMNS

133 One world this, for all its sorrow
134 Our world is one world
146 Soon the day will arrive
138 These things shall be
159 This is my song
314 We are children of the earth
67 We sing now together

WORLD RELIGIONS (*See* 176–197)

YOM HA-SHO'AH
8 Mother Spirit, Father Spirit
28 View the starry realm of heaven
165 When windows that are black and cold

YOM KIPPUR
336 All my memories of love
280 Haleluhu
216 Hashiveinu
219 O hear, my people, hear me well
217 O sing hallelujah
215 Praise to the living God!
218 Who can say, "I am free . . ."

Index of First Lines and Titles of Hymns

When they differ, a hymn's title, as well as its first line, is listed. Titles are in capital letters.